An Open Secret

Bolivia. Courtesy Janet S. Cohen.

An Open Secret

*The History of Unwanted Pregnancy
and Abortion in Modern Bolivia*

Natalie L. Kimball

RUTGERS UNIVERSITY PRESS
NEW BRUNSWICK, CAMDEN, AND NEWARK,
NEW JERSEY, AND LONDON

Library of Congress Cataloging-in-Publication Data
Names: Kimball, Natalie L., author.
Title: An open secret: the history of unwanted pregnancy and abortion
   in modern Bolivia / Natalie L. Kimball.
Description: New Brunswick: Rutgers University Press, [2020] | Includes
   bibliographical references and index.
Identifiers: LCCN 2019035745 | ISBN 9780813590738 (paperback) |
   ISBN 9780813590745 (hardback) | ISBN 9780813590752 (epub) |
   ISBN 9780813590769 (mobi) | ISBN 9780813590776 (pdf)
Subjects: LCSH: Abortion—Bolivia—History. | Unwanted pregnancy—
   Bolivia—History. | Reproductive rights—Bolivia—History.
Classification: LCC HQ767.5.B5 K56 2020 | DDC 362.1988/800984—dc23
LC record available at https://lccn.loc.gov/2019035745

A British Cataloging-in-Publication record for this book is available from
the British Library.

All photos by the author.

⊚ The paper used in this publication meets the requirements of the American
National Standard for Information Sciences—Permanence of Paper for Printed
Library Materials, ANSI Z39.48-1992.

www.rutgersuniversitypress.org

Manufactured in the United States of America

*To my father and mother, and to each of the women
I interviewed in La Paz and El Alto.*

Contents

Illustrations

Abbreviations

ALP	Archivo Histórico La Paz (La Paz Historical Archive)
AMEU	Aspiración manual endo-uterina (manual vacuum aspiration method and device)
CEB	Conferencia Episcopal Boliviana (Episcopal Conference of Bolivia)
CENAFA	Centro Nacional de Familia (National Family Center)
CEPROSI	Centro de Promoción y Salud Integral (Center for Promotion and Integral Health)
CIDEM	Centro de Información y Desarrollo de la Mujer (Center for Information and Development of Women)
CIDOB	Confederación de Pueblos Indígenas de Bolivia (Confederation of Indigenous Peoples of Bolivia)
CIES	Centro de Investigación, Educación y Servicios en Salud Sexual y Reproductiva (Center for Investigation, Education, and Services in Sexual and Reproductive Health)

CNMCIOB-BS Confederación Nacional de Mujeres Campesinas Indígenas Originarias de Bolivia "Bartolina Sisa" (Bartolina Sisa National Confederation of Campesino, Indigenous, and Native Women of Bolivia)

CNS/CNSS Caja Nacional de Salud, previously the Caja Nacional de Seguro Social (National Health Fund)

CSUTCB Confederación Sindical Unica de Trabajadores Campesinos de Bolivia (Unified Syndical Confederation of Rural Workers of Bolivia)

ENDSA Encuesta Nacional de Demografía y Salud (National Demographic and Health Survey)

FELCC Fuerza Especial de Lucha Contra el Crimen (Special Force of the Fight Against Crime)

FOF Federación Obrera Femenina (Federation of Female Workers)

HM Hospital de la Mujer (Women's Hospital)

HMBH Hospital Municipal Boliviano-Holandés (Bolivian-Dutch Municipal Hospital)

HPME Programa por el Tratamiento de Hemorragias en la Primera Mitad del Embarazo (Program for the Treatment of Hemorrhages in the First Half of Pregnancy)

INA Instituto de Maternidad "Natalio A. Aramayo" ("Natalio A. Aramayo" Maternity Institute)

INBOMETRAKA Instituto Boliviano de Medicina Tradicional Kallawaya (Bolivian Institute of Kallawaya Traditional Medicine)

INE	Instituto Nacional de Estadística (National Statistics Institute)
IUD	Intrauterine device
MAS	Movimiento al Socialismo (Movement for Socialism)
MNR	Movimiento Nacionalista Revolucionario (Nationalist Revolutionary Movement)
MSD/MPSSP	Ministerio de Salud y Deportes, previously the Ministerio de Previsión Social y Salud Pública (Ministry of Health)
NEP	Nueva Política Económica (New Economic Policy)
NGO	Nongovernmental organization
PAHO	Pan-American Health Organization
REBOHUPAN	Red Boliviana para la Humanización del Parto y Nacimiento (Bolivian Network for the Humanization of Delivery and Birth)
SAFCI	Salud Familiar Comunitaria e Intercultural (Intercultural Community and Family Health System)
SBS	Seguro Básico de Salud (Basic Health Insurance)
SCISP	Servicio Cooperativo Interamericano de Salud Pública (Inter-American Cooperative Public Health Service)
SEDES	Servicios Departamentales de Salud (Departmental Health Services)
SIS	Servicios Integrales de Salud (Integral Health Services)
SOBOMETRA	Sociedad Boliviana de Medicina Tradicional (Bolivian Society of Traditional Medicine)

SUMI   Seguro Universal Materno Infantil (Universal
              Maternal and Child Insurance)

TAHIPAMU   Taller de Historia y Participación de la Mujer
              (Workshop for the History and Participation of
              Women)

TCP   Tribunal Constitucional Plurinacional (Plurina-
              tional Constitutional Tribunal)

THOA   Taller de Historia Oral Andina (Andean Oral
              History Workshop)

UMSA   Universidad Mayor de San Andrés

UN   United Nations

UNESCO   United Nations Educational, Scientific, and
              Cultural Organization

UNFPA   United Nations Population Fund

USAID   United States Agency for International
              Development

WHO   World Health Organization

WRA   Women of reproductive age

An Open Secret

Introduction

It was a chilly, crystal-clear morning when I met with Maura Choque, a thirty-six-year-old Aymara woman from the town of Viacha, to interview her about her experiences with pregnancy. Squinting against the bright sun pouring through the window, Maura told me that she felt differently about the birth of her third and fifth children than she did about the others. "I always thought I'd have just two children," she recalled. Maura and I were seated in the office of a community group situated in a busy neighborhood of El Alto, a city about 22 kilometers from Viacha. The organization was helping Maura in a custody dispute against her husband, from whom she was separated. "When I found out I was pregnant a third time, I cried a lot; I didn't want to have my baby because my husband didn't have work. My third son was an unwanted child." When, six years later, she became pregnant yet again, Maura said to herself, "'That's all right, so I'll have four—this will be my last.' But then, when my daughter was just six months old, I found out I was pregnant a fifth time." By that time, in 2007, Maura and her husband were not getting along well. "I'd thought about ending my life," recalled Maura. "I didn't want to suffer anymore—all the insults, the cheating. . . . I didn't want my child. I even threw myself down the stairs twice to try to lose it—but nothing happened." When I asked Maura if she ever considered getting help from a midwife, herbalist, or doctor to terminate the pregnancy, she said she once asked a doctor at a hospital in El Alto if she would perform an abortion, but the doctor refused. "She chided me. She said, 'You're too thin, your body won't be able to handle it. And besides, that isn't done.' So, I had all five of my children."[1]

Many women in Bolivia traverse the difficult experience of becoming pregnant when they do not want or expect to. National data, most based on surveys of women in urban centers, suggest that over a third of the pregnancies that occurred annually during the last few decades were unwanted.[2] Women facing unwanted pregnancy navigate complex emotions and life circumstances in deciding, first, how they feel about being pregnant, and second, how to confront these events. Despite laws prohibiting abortion in Bolivia and social stigma surrounding the procedure in urban areas of the country, many women terminate their unwanted pregnancies, visiting providers or resorting to any number of strategies to abort on their own. Since abortion is prohibited in most circumstances, its provision is largely unregulated. As a result, some women, especially those who are poor, suffer complications like hemorrhage and infection after their abortions; other women die.[3] Most women facing unwanted pregnancy, however, end up carrying their pregnancies to term, as Maura did— often because they fear undergoing abortion, or suffering the judgment of individuals who might discover their abortion. Despite the frequency of unwanted pregnancy and abortion in Bolivia, there is little written about women's personal experiences with these phenomena, or their feelings and attitudes toward these events.[4]

This book examines women's personal experiences with unwanted pregnancy and abortion in Bolivia's highland cities of La Paz and El Alto between 1952 and 2010. Some of these experiences took place in public or private hospitals, doctor's offices (*consultorios*), or clinics. Others took place in individuals' homes, in hotel rooms, or, after a woman had ingested an herbal or pharmaceutical abortifacient, in the street. I draw on approximately three thousand personal medical records from three public hospitals, two in La Paz and one in El Alto, to learn about the experiences of women who sought clinical follow-up care after an abortion or miscarriage across these years. Open-ended interviews with fifty-eight women and informal conversations with many more provide insight into women's experiences with pregnancy, abortion, miscarriage, and childbirth. I examine women's testimonies alongside those of sixty-three additional individuals—including activists, medical personnel, and officials from the government, police, and religious sectors—to trace changes in social attitudes toward unwanted pregnancy and abortion, and toward women's and men's places in society more broadly. To allow the reader to place women's experiences with pregnancy and abortion in appropriate political, economic, and sociocultural context, this book also traces shifts in reproductive health policies in Bolivia and the changing methods of fertility regulation available to, and used by, women in La Paz and El Alto. I use demographic and medical reports, government documents, and secondary sources to outline changes in state policies on abortion and contraception, as well as the various strategies women used to negotiate their reproductive lives, with and without the approval of the state.

The book argues that women's personal experiences with unwanted pregnancy and abortion in Bolivia matter, for three reasons. First, these experiences shape the evolution of polices on and services in reproductive health care. Second, the contours of women's reproductive experiences reveal deeply ambivalent attitudes about women, and about sexuality more broadly, held by a variety of sectors of urban Andean society—attitudes that have a significant bearing on the ways in which women experience sex and pregnancy. Third, women's experiences matter simply because they occur. Most women worldwide experience pregnancy, yet few historical studies directly explore their experiences. Unwanted pregnancy and abortion are often matters of life and death. Furthermore, recentering the discussion of unwanted pregnancy and abortion on women and their personal experiences with these phenomena challenge common assumptions, often generated in top-down narratives, about the ways that women make decisions about their reproductive lives.

Although the research for this project was carried out in La Paz and El Alto, I intend for the insights it provides to transcend national, or even regional, boundaries. At a most basic level, women around the world and across every historical period have traversed the experience of becoming pregnant when they did not want or expect to, and of having to decide how to confront this reality. If a woman needs to interrupt a pregnancy in a place where the procedure is prohibited (or where abortion is difficult to access, regardless of its legal status), she must locate a provider who is willing to assist her or determine means to do so on her own. When faced with complications following abortion or miscarriage, women are often forced to navigate underdeveloped health systems, as well as societal judgment, in order to seek treatment. At a broader, geopolitical level, women's experiences with unwanted pregnancy in La Paz and El Alto—cities where the majority of the population is poor and indigenous—share further commonalities with women's experiences in other world contexts with similar demographic profiles. Women living in places where domestic and foreign states and institutions implemented eugenic, and often imperialist, policies to combat the perceived overpopulation of poor people of color may face still greater challenges in navigating their unwanted pregnancies.[5] In these places, women may feel deeply fearful of utilizing western-derived contraceptive methods or of visiting western health providers, from whom they may have suffered discrimination or abuse. In other words, as noted by Katrina Ackerman et al., "Colonialism and imperialism have ensured that the histories of reproductive injustice transgress contemporary national boundaries."[6] Finally, broader social structures such as patriarchy and racism also shaped women's experiences with unwanted pregnancy across diverse geographical and historical contexts.

There are four principal features of the history of unwanted pregnancy as it unfolded in La Paz and El Alto since the mid-twentieth century that have generated debate among scholars and activists working in other contexts, and toward which this book gestures at contributing: (1) The sexual and reproductive practices of individuals of indigenous and African descent (particularly women) have often been targeted by national and international states, institutions, and medical authorities across distinct historical periods for a number of political and economic objectives that were directly related to broader national and global processes.[7] The specific shape, tenor, and overall efficacy of these interventions varied according to place and time, yet each was typically undergirded by projects of, as Laura Briggs notes in the case of Puerto Rico, "difference making," in which local populations and their practices were pathologized in order to justify their "improvement" by local and foreign elites.[8] (2) The methods that women used to regulate their fertility and to terminate pregnancies were derived from multiple, and often overlapping, medical systems. These systems, which are sometimes dichotomized as "traditional" and "western," were each undergirded by specific, often competing, understandings of health, illness, and the body that were integral to shaping women's reproductive experiences. Providers of traditional medicine, like individuals' sexual and reproductive practices, were also often targeted for reform, or in some cases annihilation, by dominant medical and policy-making sectors.[9] (3) Despite this, most women's experiences with pregnancy and fertility regulation occurred outside the bounds of the state, in that most policies were unsuccessful in preventing abortions or other forms of fertility regulation from occurring, or alternative medical traditions from being practiced.[10] (4) The ongoing oppression of mostly poor individuals of color and of their political movements often coincided with competing discourses around rights in ways that sometimes pit nationalist or ethnically based interests against those of women, often from those same ethnic groups, who were seeking greater control over their reproductive lives.[11]

ON REPRODUCTIVE EXPERIENCES AND THEIR HISTORY

It has now been so thoroughly demonstrated that intimate phenomena such as sex and pregnancy are inextricably connected to public life as to be a truism. A large and diverse body of work has shown how debates about gender, sexuality, and reproduction across a range of geographical and historical contexts played key roles in state-building projects, religious movements, the construction and maintenance of labor systems, and the formation of political and social alliances.[12] In Bolivia, as in so many other contexts, women's experiences with sex and pregnancy were intimately related to larger social, political, and economic processes at the national and international levels. The fifty years that followed the country's national revolution in 1952 witnessed significant changes in women's status and in attitudes toward western-derived contraceptive methods and reproduction. In 1952, women were granted full political rights, while the decades following the revolution saw improvements in public health, leading to a decrease in infant death that added urgency to some women's need to limit pregnancies. At the same time, the 1960s and 1970s saw a backlash against western-derived contraceptive methods by several sectors of Bolivian society.[13] This criticism stemmed in part from fears that international organizations were either forcing or coercing women to use birth control in order to limit Bolivia's indigenous populations for eugenic reasons.[14] As a result, some national government administrations and societal sectors adopted pronatalist positions, casting official disapproval on women who sought to prevent pregnancy and shrouding in secrecy women's strategies for confronting unwanted pregnancy.[15]

The political and social history of reproduction in Bolivia, comprising changes in legal codes, health policies, and methods of fertility regulation, cannot be adequately understood without considering women's personal experiences with reproduction. Far from constituting private events with little bearing on the public sphere, women's experiences with unwanted pregnancy helped spur changes in public policies and services concerning abortion and postabortion care. These changes were further related to Bolivia's 1982 democratic opening and the subsequent implementation of neoliberal policies in the country, and to growing international concern with abortion-related death worldwide in the 1980s and 1990s. The changes in reproductive policies and methods of fertility regulation that took place during these years ultimately made the experience of terminating a pregnancy safer for women, even for those who were poor. At the same time, abortion's continuing prohibition means that, for most women, terminating a pregnancy remains a dangerous and sometimes life-threatening undertaking.

Just as important is what the book reveals about women's personal experiences with reproduction—irrespective of the impact of these experiences on state policy.[16] Women's feelings and reactions toward their pregnancies were shaped by a range of factors, including women's assessments of their relationships with male partners and families of origin, and their economic circumstances, spiritual beliefs, and life goals and aspirations. These personal factors were inseparable from the broader sociocultural, political, and economic contexts within which women lived their lives. Periods of economic boom or bust, shifting employment possibilities, and changing racial, cultural, and gender dynamics invariably shaped women's perceptions of what future was desired or possible. Changes in the reproductive technologies available in La Paz and El Alto over these years also impacted women's experiences with miscarriage, abortion, and childbirth. These changes often meant the difference between surviving a pregnancy loss and suffering severe medical complications, even death, in its wake. It is widely demonstrated that policies prohibiting abortion do not stop abortions from occurring[17]—just as laws regulating sexual practices do not prevent people from seeking sex or companionship. This book reveals that, rather than responding to state policies, women's experiences with unwanted pregnancy and abortion tended to be more directly impacted by personal factors and by broader structural patterns. In this respect, like Carrie Hamilton's study of sexuality in Cuba, this book demonstrates that "changes in popular sexual values and behavior . . . were as much in response to wider social and economic transformation as to legal reform."[18]

PERSONAL EXPERIENCES, PUBLIC FRAMEWORKS

Women's personal reproductive experiences are embedded in a number of structural realities that operate in the public sphere and organize relations within both society and the home. Chief among these are ideologies and practices concerning race, gender, and class. As do perhaps most social historians and theorists working today, I understand race and gender to be socially constructed and historically contingent categories, divorced from biological fixedness. Their creation and operation are best understood by examining them from the ground up as they manifest in specific settings and situations, rather than assuming that they contain any inherent or a priori meaning. Race and gender, furthermore, are embedded in and constitutive of broader structures of power and domination, come into being and are re-created in articulation with one another in everyday interactions, and are implicated in lived experiences of inequality.[19] In other words, as Mary Weismantel has argued of race and sex in the Andes, while fictions, these categories also have very real implications for individuals' lives.[20]

Over the last few decades, a growing number of scholars and activists of feminism and critical race theory have drawn on the concepts of intersectionality, introduced by Kimberlé Crenshaw in 1989, and stratified reproduction, developed by Shellee Colen in 1995, to explain how these multiple and intersecting, hierarchically ordered categories of difference shape women's lives in general, and their reproductive experiences in particular.[21] In Bolivia, women's experiences with pregnancy, abortion, and childbirth were marked by a range of intersecting hierarchies of difference and of access to resources (such as health care and the ability to speak Spanish) that shaped the ways that women understood and navigated these experiences. In La Paz and El Alto, women's reproductive experiences were stratified according to age, relationship status, race and ethnicity, class and occupational category, migratory status, and geographical location. Patriarchy and its effects, such as intimate partner violence, were particularly powerful forces shaping women's personal experiences. Machismo, patri- archy's perhaps most visible Latin American variant, was often cited by interviewees as a factor shaping attitudes toward contraceptives, sex, and pregnancy in society at large, and the circumstances surrounding and tenor of women's reproductive experiences in particular. Throughout the book, I highlight how these evolving structural inequalities may have shaped the reproductive experiences of the women I interviewed and of those whose experiences are represented in medical records.

Hierarchies such as race, gender, and class also shape the design and implementation of policies on gender, reproduction, and health care, which themselves have a bearing on women's reproductive experiences[22]— particularly in urban areas such as those featured in this book. Recently, Lynn M. Morgan and Elizabeth F. S. Roberts developed the concept of reproductive governance to explain the changes in policies on population and reproduction that have taken place over the last few decades in a vari- ety of Latin American countries. Write the authors, "Reproductive gov- ernance refers to the mechanisms through which different historical con- figurations of actors—such as state institutions, churches, donor agencies, and non-governmental organizations (NGOs)—use legislative controls, economic inducements, moral injunctions, direct coercion, and ethical incitements to produce, monitor and control reproductive behaviours and practices."[23] Morgan and Roberts demonstrate how public debates over reproduction in Latin America "are increasingly framed through moral- ity and contestations over 'rights,' where rights-bearing citizens are pit- ted against each other in claiming reproductive, sexual, indigenous, and natural rights, as well as the 'right to life' of the unborn."[24] The rise of rights-based discourses on reproduction in Latin America (and their cod- ification via juridical processes) dates to the late 1980s and early 1990s, when declining fertility rates led to the abandonment of Cold War–era jus- tifications for curtailing perceived overpopulation.[25] While the recent emphasis on rights might initially appear to have an emancipatory effect on individuals' sexual and reproductive lives, it suffers serious limitations "because it increasingly allows the claims of rights-bearing citizens to be pitted against one another. . . . Part of the genius of rights is that anyone can use them to make claims on behalf of any individuals as separate from the state."[26] David Murray, examining the decriminalization of homosexuality in Barbados, further emphasizes the poor fit that universalizing discourses of rights may find in territories that were colonized by western powers—regions from which these discourses typically originated. Writes Murray, "We cannot assume that sexual rights have a universal value, and, in fact, in post-colonial societies like Barbados certain rights discourses can be interpreted as hostile and/or connected to the political interests of former colonizing powers."[27]

This book contributes to some conversations and debates about the processes through which policies on gender and reproduction change, while leaving aside an in-depth treatment of others. First, *An Open Secret* sheds light on the operation of competing rights-related discourses on reproduction on the ground in urban Bolivia. I trace shifts in reproductive policies at a national level over the last sixty years, showing how the debates about rights articulated at the Cairo International Conference on Population and Development in 1994 and the Fourth World Conference on Women in Beijing in 1995 shaped the nature of advocacy pursued by (mostly white and mestiza, middle-class) women's organizations for the decriminalization of abortion in La Paz and El Alto. I also explore the evolution of social attitudes on a variety of sexual and reproductive phenomena in society at large. In La Paz and El Alto, debates about abortion and contraception often pit notions of women's and sexual and reproductive rights that are associated with European Enlightenment ideas of individual autonomy, western culture, and imperialism against understandings of indigenous rights that are rooted in notions of collective rights and ethnic justice.[28] I show how these conversations play out among competing, yet often intersecting, groups of individuals and activists, many of whom claim identities and rights both as indigenous citizens of Bolivia's Plurinational State and as women.

Second, *An Open Secret* contributes to understandings of reproductive governance by providing a microhistorical view of how individual women and men in La Paz and El Alto contributed to shaping policies on unwanted pregnancy and abortion through specific, sometimes calculated, yet often uncoordinated, actions and inactions. Chief among these were the actions of women in, on the one hand, making decisions regarding their pregnancies, and on the other, participating in gender-based movements for change, both as middle-class activists and as (generally) poor constituents. Collectively, women's persistence in terminating pregnancies drew local, national, and international attention to unsafe abortion and its impact on maternal mortality. This increased attention ultimately spurred changes in policies regulating the treatment of complications after pregnancy loss; it also contributed to the emergence of new forms of abortion provisioning in La Paz and El Alto.

These developments also reveal women's resilience in the face of the state's refusal to decriminalize abortion, as well as some of the perhaps unintended consequences of changes in policies concerning abortion care. For instance, policies expanding treatment options for women experiencing complications after pregnancy loss unwittingly provided women who had intentionally interrupted pregnancies access to low-cost medical care—albeit with possible, even if limited, risks of legal repercussions. I further illustrate the role of activists and constituents of a range of organizations in facilitating greater public dialogue on unwanted pregnancy, abortion, and gender-based violence in the context of a broader resurgence in activism following Bolivia's democratic opening. In the course of conversations generated as part of the initiatives pursued by these organizations and their constituents—which included classes on gender-related issues, services for reproductive and psychological health, legal advocacy, and street protests—individual women (and some men) referred other women to abortion providers, facilitating greater access to abortion and to methods of fertility regulation.

As I will address in greater detail here, a concerted commitment to protect my oral history narrators has led me to eschew an in-depth examination of the role of individuals and groups engaged in the direct provisioning of abortion care, as well as of some of the institutional and political mechanisms and economic processes that make this care possible—and, indeed, necessary. At the same time, *An Open Secret* does trace, in a general way, the contours of reproductive health care provisioning, including abortion, in the cities of La Paz and El Alto. I describe the work of western medical personnel and of Andean midwives and herbalists, some of whom provided abortions and facilitated women's access to methods of fertility regulation during years when their distribution was prohibited, in shaping the landscape of reproductive health options available to women in these cities. The book also examines, in general terms, the roles of the legal, political, and medical systems in making it possible for some women to terminate pregnancies without suffering legal persecution. I describe how some police officers and medical providers (some empathetic to the plight of women facing unwanted pregnancy, others cognizant of the challenges such cases entail), decided not to report or to arrest women or providers in connection with abortion, respectively, despite legal stipulations requiring them to do so. An examination of these individual and collective, often calculated but generally uncoordinated, actions (i.e., pregnancy termination and health provisioning despite legal prohibitions) and inactions (i.e., reporting and arrests) can contribute to an understanding of not only the processes through which policies are enacted but also the contours and consequences of varied degrees of distance between policy enactment and implementation.

Attention to the social and economic hierarchies shaping women's experiences with reproduction, as well as to the varied relationships between personal experiences and state power, transforms another notion common in the public sphere—that of "choice," which is often applied to political debates over abortion. Since at least the 1980s, scholars who have examined women's reproductive experiences, as well as activists of reproductive justice movements, have questioned the idea that a woman makes an autonomous or individual choice regarding her pregnancy. Instead, these authors urge attention to the intersecting web of oppressions, such as poverty, patriarchy, racism, and societal and familial pressure, which constrain women's reproductive choices—in addition to other choices that women ostensibly wield over their intimate lives, such as that of sexual partner.[29]

This book lends credence to the notion that processes of reproductive decision making are constrained by a range of factors. It further suggests that models to explain women's experiences with unwanted pregnancy and abortion—and to expand women's reproductive autonomy—are most fruitful when embedded in local historical and cultural context.[30] The interviews I carried out in La Paz and El Alto affirm that western, Enlightenment-era concepts of individual choice and rights to bodily autonomy were inadequate to capture women's personal experiences with pregnancy. Yet Andean notions of reproductive decision making emphasizing a woman's responsibility to consider the wishes of the indigenous community when deciding the outcome of her pregnancy were similarly peripheral to most urban-dwelling women's reproductive decisions— including women who self-identified as Aymara or Quechua. Despite the prevalence of the rhetoric of choice in debates surrounding abortion (including among some activists in the urban Andes), the women I interviewed in La Paz and El Alto rarely claimed that they had "decided" or "chosen" to continue or to terminate their pregnancies; instead, they argued that they were "obligated" or even "forced" to keep or to abort them. This was the case due to personal and structural factors, such as local gender and racial hierarchies; Andean, Catholic, and Protestant spiritual beliefs; sexual and familial relationships; and shifting economic circumstances. That said, although women's choices were constrained by a range of circumstances, they were never entirely absent. What emerges from women's testimonies is the persistence of women's efforts to shape their sexual and reproductive lives, despite the structural factors shaping the conditions in which women's choices were made.

The Women and Men of La Paz and El Alto

On the eve of Bolivia's 1952 revolution, the majority of the country's population resided in rural areas and spoke indigenous languages (mostly Quechua or Aymara) to the exclusion of Spanish. While in 1950 La Paz represented Bolivia's largest city with some 321,000 residents, it contained less than 11 percent of the nation's inhabitants. Most Bolivians lived in the countryside, where indigenous peasants labored on haciendas (large plantations typically owned by Bolivians of European descent) and lacked access to land, education, or citizenship rights.[31] In both cities and rural areas, Bolivians faced high birth and death rates, with average life expectancy in 1950 reaching only thirty-eight years for men and forty-two years for women.[32] It is difficult to overestimate the changes that took place in Bolivian society between the early 1950s and 1976, the year of the country's next census. While reforms instituted by the revolutionary government enfranchised indigenous women and men, redistributed land to rural-dwelling Bolivians, and led to significant advances in education, the same years witnessed vast improvements in public health. These changes resulted in significant shifts in the country's social structure (particularly an increase in the number of urban-dwelling indigenous Bolivians) and considerable population growth. By 1976, the population of La Paz exceeded 635,000, and Spanish for the first time represented the country's dominant language, although most paceños (La Paz residents) also spoke an indigenous language, principally Aymara.[33]

As in other Latin American contexts,[34] women in La Paz and El Alto during these years suffered sociocultural, legal, economic, and political disadvantages with respect to men. Women were legally subordinated to their husbands and male family members across much of the twentieth century, facing limits to their political participation, educational opportunities, and property and parenting rights.[35] Until the passage of national legislation in the mid-1940s, women in common-law marriages in Bolivia lacked most formal rights and protections, as did children born out of wedlock.[36] In urban areas, notions of honor and morality, carried over from Spanish colonization, often rendered a woman's sexual conduct key to her family's social status.[37] Women frequently undermined the legal and cultural norms shaping their status, working, engaging in political mobilization, raising children, and otherwise living their lives. At the same time, structural differences in the status of women and men in these cities were palpable and continue to persist; thus the country's 1976 census found that roughly five times as many *paceña* women as men were illiterate.[38] More recent studies highlight the challenges facing women in Bolivia as a whole; while sexual and physical violence affect nearly a quarter of partnered women in the country, measures of women's inequality in the areas of health and education remain significant.[39] Since 2014, women have held unprecedented representation in national and municipal politics, due in part to the efforts of President Evo Morales and the Movimiento al Socialismo (Movement for Socialism, or MAS) Party to introduce Andean principles of gender equality and complementarity into the political system; however, some women politicians in the country report suffering harassment and violence as a result of their work.[40]

Socioracial hierarchies also bore a strong influence on the lives of residents of La Paz and El Alto. At the same time, ethnic and cultural definitions were considerably fluid, and individuals might shift ethnic identification as they moved among social circles, altered their styles of dress, or migrated from one place to another. During the years of this study, individuals of indigenous descent were usually referred to by nonindigenous people as *indígena* (indigenous), the somewhat more derogatory word *indio* (Indian), or, after the revolutionary years, campesino (peasant). While "campesino" was typically used to refer to an indigenous person living in the rural countryside, "cholo" usually connoted an urban-dwelling indigenous person. Indígena and indio could refer to both urban and rural residents. Individuals of European descent, for their part, might be referred to as *blanco* (white) or *criollo* (creole or locally born European). While the term "mestizo" usually connoted an individual of mixed indigenous and

European descent, it was also sometimes used to refer to indigenous Bolivians who resided in urban areas, spoke Spanish, and adopted urban forms of dress.[41] The usage of these terms varied at different historical moments and was often linked to broader political or social trends. For instance, during the national revolution of 1952–1964, authorities of the ruling Movimiento Nacionalista Revolucionario (Nationalist Revolutionary Movement, or MNR) party substituted the term "campesino" for indígena as part of a larger attempt to "incorporate" (and to culturally assimilate) indigenous Bolivians into a new, revolutionary nation.[42]

During the years of this study, Bolivian women were referred to by the ethnic and cultural labels just outlined, but additional factors, such as forms of dress and hairstyle, also often signaled divisions between women. Rural indigenous women and their urban counterparts (known as cholas) often wear a multilayered skirt or *pollera*, along with a matching hat and shawl, while arranging their hair in two long braids. The specific style of this outfit varies from one region to another as well as from one year to the next, as fashions change. However, wearing the pollera typically connotes a stronger adherence to indigenous identity and cultural norms than does dressing *de vestido*, or in more modern skirts, dresses, or pants.[43] Scholars have examined the range of cultural and symbolic meanings associated with the chola identity. Some argue, for instance, that the use of the pollera represents a form of resistance to assimilationist projects or an expression of pride in indigenous heritage. Like the adoption of indigenous or mestizo identity, the significance of the pollera varied at different historical moments—and according to whom one asks.[44]

Ethnic identity is complex in La Paz and El Alto and encompasses not only language and geographical location but also cultural, social, and sometimes political factors. According to Herbert S. Klein, the past few decades have witnessed significant changes in Bolivia's social structure and the ways in which categories of difference operate in the country— changes that are especially visible in the urban Andes. Since the early 1980s, argues Klein, Andean society has traversed a process of *mestizaje* (racial and cultural "mixing") characterized by a decrease in monolingualism, the persistent survival of indigenous languages, and an increase in the political power and social mobility of the urban mestizo class.[45] The growing power of the mestizo class in recent years (and what might be called the indigenization of these mestizos) has had a profound effect upon La Paz; however, it has found particular expression in the city of El Alto.[46] The city's relatively lower cost of living, as well as elevated demand for workers to fill the government posts created when El Alto became a self-governing city in 1988, helped spur the social mobility of mestizos in the region. At the same time, El Alto possesses "a distinctive identity as an indigenous city," particularly when considering the long-standing political importance of the mobilization of indigenous Bolivians that has taken place there.[47]

At the beginning of the twentieth century, settlements began to appear in what was then the mostly rural territory located some 500 meters above La Paz, where El Alto now sits.[48] The development of El Alto accelerated particularly after the 1952 revolution, in the wake of MNR policies outlawing unpaid labor (*pongueaje*) and disintegrating many of the large haciendas. As the MNR's land redistribution failed to transform indigenous peasants into the modern, capitalist-oriented farmers the party desired, many sought work in urban areas.[49] Thus the 1950s and 1960s witnessed the steady growth of urban settlements in El Alto, as rural migrants unable to survive on subsistence agriculture in the altiplano sought wage labor in La Paz or its higher-altitude neighbor. Migration to El Alto grew even more spectacularly in the decades of the 1970s and 1980s. Home to some 95,000 inhabitants in 1976, El Alto was at that time just a fraction of the size of La Paz.[50] After a series of crippling droughts in the countryside in 1982–1983 and the closing of the state-owned tin mines a few years later, waves of migration swelled the city, which grew to encompass 405,000 residents by 1992.[51] By 2005, the population of El Alto had surpassed that of La Paz, transforming El Alto into Bolivia's second-largest city, after Santa Cruz.[52] Comprising primarily indigenous migrants from rural areas, El

Alto presents forms of social and spatial organization and community mobilization different from those in cities of Spanish colonial heritage, such as La Paz.[53] In other respects, however, La Paz and El Alto are inextricably linked. While El Alto consistently scores more poorly than its neighbor in social indicators such as poverty and unemployment, many Bolivians live their lives in, and contribute to the social fabric of, both of these Andean cities.[54]

The links between La Paz and El Alto were palpable in the lives of the individuals I interviewed for this project, most of whom spent some portion of their days in both of the two cities. In El Alto, where thirty-eight of the women I interviewed resided, the relatively middle-class community of Ciudad Satélite figures prominently, as do the neighborhoods to its immediate north, west, and south, including Villa Tejada Triangular, Santa Rosa, and Villa Exaltación.[55] In La Paz, home to the remaining twenty women I interviewed, the neighborhoods most represented in the book are located in Macrodistrict II, Max Paredes, in the northeast section of the city. The majority of the women I interviewed resided in Max Paredes, an important commercial zone. Many of the medical clinics are also located in this area, the practices of which I refer to in the text.[56] While I endeavor to situate women's experiences with reproductive health care and family life in specific geographical locations, some aspects of the history of unwanted pregnancy and abortion in La Paz and El Alto will appear more unified than divided. At times, this unity is owed to the fact that women's experiences with unwanted pregnancy and abortion were indeed similar across the two locations, while at others the challenges of accurately gathering data on these phenomena make it difficult to discern if geographical differences exist. When addressing how reproductive health policy and provisioning changed over time, however, geography was more salient. Thus abortion became widely available in the two cities at distinct moments, with clinics emerging in significant numbers in La Paz in the 1970s, and in El Alto in the late 1980s.

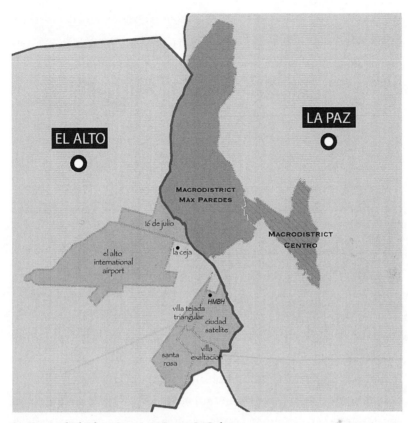

La Paz and El Alto. Courtesy Janet S. Cohen.

REPRODUCTION IN RURAL AND URBAN BOLIVIA

The experience of a woman facing an unwanted or unintended pregnancy in La Paz or El Alto during these years was likely quite different from that of a woman confronting this circumstance in one of the predominantly rural provinces of the western highlands. This book is fundamentally about urban Bolivia; that is, the individuals discussed herein who drafted public policy, as well as most of the other women and men interviewed for the project, are from the cities and thus come from a sociocultural background that differs considerably from that of most rural-dwelling Bolivians. At the same time, the reader will notice that many of the testimonies

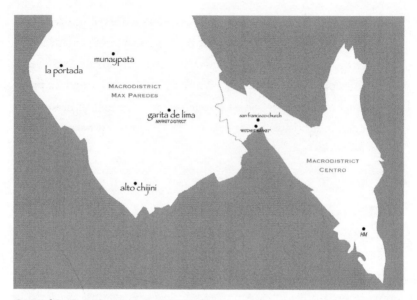

Central La Paz. Courtesy Janet S. Cohen.

included in the book—some of which were delivered by individuals who migrated to La Paz or El Alto from rural areas—refer to ideas and practices of reproduction prevalent in the countryside. These overlaps are, at times, significant. The differences (and, often, conflicts) between western and Andean conceptualizations and practices of reproduction have had a considerable bearing on the trajectory of public policies on health, debates about contraception and abortion, and women's personal experiences with these phenomena. While a complete treatment of these differences is beyond the scope of this book, an outline of some of the most significant helps to place in context the experiences of the women whose stories are featured herein.

A wealth of scholarship makes clear that ideas about and practices of sexuality and reproduction, as well as modes of health care concerning these phenomena, are markedly different in rural and urban areas of Bolivia (as is true in other parts of the Andes).[57] Cities like La Paz and El Alto are characterized by the prevalence (though far from hegemony) of

western-derived, biomedical conceptions and practices of health. Western ideas of health tend to conceive of the body as a biological, bounded
organism divorced from the spiritual or supernatural realms. This results
in processes of diagnosis and treatment designed to locate and fix problems rooted in the body. The Andean conceptualizations of health that
predominate in rural areas are quite distinct, viewing bodily health as intimately linked with social and communal life, the natural world, and the
spiritual realm.[58] In line with these notions, rural-dwelling Bolivians
ensure health and diagnose and treat illness not only by intervening into
the physical body but by engaging with the broader social, natural, and
supernatural worlds. The latter is achieved through activities such as performing rituals for or making offerings to the Pachamama (earth mother)
or other deities (some of whom are conceived of as ancestors), and by
engaging in conviviality within the household or community, during
which food and alcohol are consumed and coca leaves chewed.[59]

Practices concerning reproduction in the urban and rural spheres are
shaped by these distinct notions of health. While in urban areas many
women seek prenatal care and deliver children at hospitals and in other
clinical facilities, in rural areas, women typically receive prenatal checks
and give birth at home with the assistance of midwives or family members.
Write Denise Y. Arnold and Juan de Dios Yapita of the rural community
of Qaqachaka, "The process of child birth is experienced as a gradual
'heating' (junt'uptayaña) of the woman's body, an Andean cultural feature that practitioners of biomedicine disregard."[60] Practices followed by
rural-dwelling Bolivians to facilitate a healthy delivery for mother and
child therefore include heating the body by ingesting warm liquids, among
other means; women also give birth in a squatting position (rather than
lying down) and consume warm, hearty foods during and after labor.[61]
These (and other) practices preferred by women in childbirth are often
inaccessible, or outright denied, to them in clinical facilities.

To prevent pregnancy, women in urban areas are more likely than those
in rural ones to use methods of contraception to which I refer in this book

as "western derived," such as birth control pills or the intrauterine device. Most, but certainly not all, abortions performed in La Paz and El Alto are surgical (involving the insertion of instruments into the body) or medical (provoked by pharmaceuticals).[62] In rural areas, women prevent pregnancy by practicing periodic abstinence, or, less commonly, through withdrawal or by using a western-derived birth control method.[63] Although their cost makes them inaccessible for many rural-dwelling Bolivians, couples may also use condoms, which they sometimes wash and reuse.[64] Abortion in rural areas is achieved primarily through herbal remedies, which are taken as teas (mates) or as vaginal suppositories. Women may also terminate pregnancies by inflicting physical trauma on themselves (these methods are also used in urban areas).[65]

Moral frameworks surrounding and practices concerning sex and partnership are similarly distinct in urban and rural areas. Cities like La Paz and El Alto tend to be heavily influenced by Catholic values and colonial-era notions of morality, and many individuals speak of the powerful effects of stigma against women who engage in premarital sex or experience out-of-wedlock pregnancy. Women in these cities who cohabitate with their partners outside the confines of marriage—a relationship described as concubinato—may also face social stigma; this was particularly true prior to the last few decades. Stigma against abortion, for its part, is fierce—at least in public discourse. There is also a degree of stigma against women who use western-derived contraceptive methods, whose partners and even neighbors may contend use of birth control to have sex with other men without fearing pregnancy (a pattern interviewees attribute to patriarchy and machismo).[66]

Many rural areas of the Andes, in contrast, show very little, if any, penetration of these Catholic notions linking a woman's sexual chastity to honor (either her own or that of her family). As Olivia Harris writes of the Laymi people of Northern Potosí, Bolivia, "There is no value attached to virginity and most people have a variety of [sexual] experiences before they eventually get married."[67] It is also customary for women in rural areas to have children prior to marriage, a practice against which there is no stigma whatsoever.[68] In some regions it is widely accepted, and in others even encouraged, for women to take measures to prevent pregnancy.[69] Gender relations in rural areas are undergirded by markedly different understandings of the sexes than in the western world,[70] which also shapes attitudes toward pregnancy prevention. As Andrew Canessa notes of the Aymara-speaking community of Wila Kjarka, "I [did not] find any suggestion that men thought that contraception would lead to promiscuity on the part of their wives. . . . The kind of sexual jealousy that is iconic of machismo in much of Latin America, including indigenous Latin America, appears largely absent in Wila Kjarka."[71] Abortion, for its part, is not widely stigmatized in the countryside; any prohibitions attached to it (or, indeed, to infanticide) are generally derived from improper burial of the fetus according to broader, supernatural understandings of the deities that govern, or in some cases ancestral souls that reside within, the earth.[72]

Differing ideas about abortion in urban and rural areas are linked in part to divergent notions of personhood (fetal and otherwise) in the two settings. As Canessa writes, "In Western discourse one is simply born human, and there are many parts of the Western world where people extend the recognition of human nature to the fetus and embryo."[73] In most rural areas of the Andes, individuals acquire personhood gradually; important steps toward its achievement, depending on the region, may include a naming ceremony or Christian baptism, civil registry, and the acquisition of language.[74] In many places of the rural Andes, infants who have not yet been named are "totally unsocialized and in a sense non-human," and, upon death, are typically not mourned in the same way as adults.[75] The acquisition of personhood in rural areas is, therefore, a process—one further related to an individual's growing ability to perform productive tasks, as "accorded by the community and the earth spirits."[76] While some argue that this process is not achieved completely until death, most individuals in the rural Andes are not considered full social beings until marriage.[77] Like personhood, gender differences in the rural Andes are made over time and are understood largely in terms of the tasks women and men most commonly perform.[78] Thus understandings of personhood and of gender—and, indeed, of relations *between* the sexes, addressed later in the book—are markedly distinct in rural and urban areas.

Where ideas and practices of reproduction characteristic of rural Bolivia emerge in the primary data, I draw on secondary literature to place the analysis of women's testimonies in the context of the range of ideas about health and illness, in general, and about sex and reproduction, in particular, among people in rural and urban areas. In line with the approach developed by critical medical anthropologists, I also examine women's experiences with different forms of medical care through a lens that considers personal experiences of racial, ethnic, and gender discrimination in western medical centers alongside larger political and institutional factors, such as the evolution of insurance coverage, flaws in the biomedical system, and the shifting relationship between western and Andean medical traditions.[79] Throughout the book, I employ the term "biomedicine" (as theorized by scholars such as Carmen Beatriz Loza) to refer to the institutionally backed and western-derived medical tradition, rather than labels such as "modern" or "scientific," which may be strategically employed to articulate western medicine's ostensible "superiority over other medicines in Bolivian society."[80] For the sake of variety, I use the term "biomedicine" interchangeably with "western medicine," the latter written in lowercase to illustrate its lack of hegemony in the contexts I examine.

The "promise and dilemma" of oral history (and other methodological questions)

Any project that relies heavily on oral sources wrestles with the unique possibilities and challenges of conducting interviews and crafting written work with the testimonies that these produce.[81] Among the most fruitful gifts offered by oral sources is, most obviously, the opportunity to learn about a given phenomenon directly from those who have experienced it. Oral history can also challenge conventional periodization, since "interviewees tend to measure historical change less with reference to concrete dates and more through a movement back-and-forth in time with reference to generations."[82] Foregrounding women's feelings about unwanted pregnancy and their experiences with reproduction, for instance, tends to highlight patterns of continuity, rather than change, across otherwise meaningful junctures in Bolivia's political history. This project owes any successes it achieves to the individuals whose testimonies appear here. The process of gathering and interpreting these testimonies, however, was not an uncomplicated one and comprised both scholarly and personal challenges—particularly with regard to ethics, the politics of knowledge production, and the overall role of the historian. My approach to these issues is informed by the considerable work of scholars and activists in the fields of oral history, feminist ethnography, Latin American *testimonio*, and subaltern studies.[83]

During the course of my fieldwork, I conducted a total of 113 interviews with 121 individuals. While all of these conversations bore on the scope and content of this project, the book directly cites seventy-one of these interviews.[84] In general, the interviews were broken into two groups; that is, I interviewed women to learn about their experiences with pregnancy, and both women and men about their work as activists, medical personnel, or government officials. Despite these groupings, information gleaned from the interviews sometimes overlapped—in four cases, for instance, women I approached to learn about their work shared with me their personal experiences with abortion. Each of my narrators' stories are unique and important, yet examining all of them would result in a truncated and dizzying treatment that would ultimately obscure the complexity of women's reproductive experiences (and of their lives more broadly). For this reason, I examine the testimonies of a smaller group of women in each chapter so that I may delve more deeply into their lives than I otherwise could. I also reference the stories of a few other women in a more limited way when their experiences are especially illustrative of a particular pattern that I am examining.

There are complex dynamics of power at work in interviewing, and these dynamics shape both the relationship between the interviewer and the narrator and the written work resulting from it. The historian, after all—not her narrators—selects individuals to interview, shapes the testimony through the design and delivery of her questions, transcribes the oral text into written form, and edits and analyzes the resulting testimony.[85] Unequal power relations in oral interviewing are exacerbated when the interviewer is an individual wielding a degree of social and economic capital—such as a western education and the interpretive authority this ostensibly grants—and the interviewee originates from an underdeveloped region and possesses fewer economic resources and less formal education.[86] At the same time, the oral history source does not exist without its narrator, who exercises a degree of control over both the interaction and the narrative source resulting from it.[87]

There were several lines of difference between myself, a white, U.S.-born, aspiring historian with a graduate degree, and the individuals with whom I spoke in La Paz and El Alto—most of whom were indigenous or mestiza and poor and had limited access to education. As Italian oral historian Alessandro Portelli remarked of his experiences conducting research in Kentucky, any successes I achieved in interviewing people in these cities lay primarily in our mutual efforts to acknowledge and engage, rather than eschew conscious treatment of, the differences between us and the inequalities that these engendered.[88] In conducting interviews, I was guided by a concern with balancing my own desire to learn about the history of unwanted pregnancy in Bolivia with the interests of the women and men who chose to participate in the project, and in so doing, achieving at least some degree of "shared authority" with these individuals over the process.[89] Although I was primarily interested in how women navigated pregnancies they described as unwanted, I sought interviewees by explaining that I was investigating women's experiences with pregnancy in general. In order to establish a more holistic view of women's lives, I began by asking each woman about her experiences early in life, including her upbringing and childhood. Then, following a chronological and thematic order of interviewing,[90] I asked women about their romantic liaisons and about each of their pregnancies. Although I sometimes asked women directly if they had wanted a pregnancy or not, I began by asking each woman in an open-ended manner how she felt when she discovered she was pregnant and whether these feelings changed over time. I did this in an effort to allow women's comments to guide the interview and to avoid imposing categories such as "wanted" and "unwanted" onto women's feelings about their pregnancies.[91] Although the prevalence of "unwanted pregnancy" in national statistical data suggested that many of the women I interviewed would have experienced this phenomenon, I was more interested in hearing women describe their feelings toward pregnancies on their own terms. While most of the questions I posed focused on women's reproductive experiences, women typically discussed these in the context of relaying broader stories about their lives. In the course of our conversations, women told me about migrating to and from the countryside, of the strategies they used to provide for their families through periods of economic crisis, and of their educational and professional aspirations. Thus, in asking about their reproductive experiences, I came to learn about a variety of aspects of women's personal histories and everyday lives.

When working with testimonies collected in contexts like Bolivia that possess their own rich traditions of oral history and folklore—as well as conceptualizations of health and illness—conflicts often emerge between local and dominant (i.e., western) modes of understanding the world and the experiences taking place within it.[92] Those of us seeking to learn about the lives of subaltern groups, in particular, are often met with explanations of phenomena that defy those of a so-called modern or rational nature. This pattern arises frequently when one is examining ideas about pregnancy.[93] Take, for instance, the pregnant woman I interviewed who avoids knitting in order to prevent the umbilical cord from wrapping tightly around the neck of her unborn child. When turning to the page, we then seem called upon to make individuals' testimonies intelligible to readers in western academe—which sometimes flies in the face of a commitment to stay as true as possible to narrators' own interpretations of their experiences. While striking this balance (between fidelity to the sources and intelligibility to western audiences) typically involves linguistic translation and editing, it also comprises translation—or at the very least thoughtful analysis—of a cultural nature. In editing, interpreting, and analyzing oral testimonies, as well as inserting them into a broader narrative, scholars are engaged in a contentious process of meaning making with serious ramifications for both academic and political struggles. In other words, those of us writing about the experiences of marginalized populations necessarily confront broader epistemological questions about the politics of knowledge production, to whom it falls to write historical narratives— and to whom, precisely, history belongs.[94]

As the preceding passage suggests, I frequently encountered cultural and linguistic challenges while conducting research in La Paz and El Alto, despite my fluency in Spanish and previous experience living in highland Bolivia. All of the women I interviewed spoke Spanish (or, more precisely, what narrators called Castellano), and I conducted these interviews without the assistance of an interpreter. The local variant of Castellano spoken by many of my interviewees is heavily influenced by Aymara (and occasionally Quechua) words and syntax. My ability to grasp the cultural and linguistic subtleties of interviewees' testimonies would have been very difficult without the assistance of Sayuri Loza, a paceña historian fluent in Aymara, who not only transcribed all of my interviews—an unbelievably arduous task—but carefully answered my every query regarding linguistic and cultural references. While my translations of the interviews were both clarified and enriched by consultation with Sayuri and other colleagues, I bear sole responsibility for any errors therein.

When I began this project, my approach to the ethical dilemmas I expected to confront in undertaking research on unwanted pregnancy and abortion was relatively simplistic, encompassed by "the medical injunction: do no harm."[95] I was also motivated by a commitment to social and economic justice—that is, to conduct research to support efforts to decriminalize, or at the very least destigmatize, the exceedingly common experience of abortion. Some of my concerns about the project centered on the possible emotional impact to women of sharing their intimate stories of unwanted pregnancy and abortion. In some respects, I was surprised by the degree to which women shared with me details of these personal experiences. On the one hand, it is a relatively universal part of the human experience to want to share with others the trials and victories of our lives. Women may have felt at ease speaking with me because of the anonymity and confidentiality of the interview setting, or because they had grown to know me as we sat together at one of a number of weekly workshops and classes I attended in commercial- and working-class neighborhoods of La Paz and El Alto. With a few exceptions, the women I interviewed were constituents of one of three organizations that offered classes in crafts; led workshops about health, pregnancy, or gender relations; or provided legal or mental health services. After I interviewed a woman privately, she would usually return to the group and chat about the encounter with other attendees, which probably put some of these women at ease and encouraged them to volunteer. Although these were rarely easy conversations, my own comfort in speaking with women about pregnancy and abortion was likely facilitated by the fact that I had done it before. Prior to my fieldwork in Bolivia, I spoke with hundreds of women about their decisions to terminate their pregnancies while working at clinics providing abortions in the states of Washington and Pennsylvania.

Together with their personnel, I have opted not to identify the organizations at which I met interviewees in order to shield them from any potential negative repercussions of association with this book or the topics it addresses. Protecting the anonymity of these organizations also prevents me from fleshing out with precision the geographical locations of these groups and, concomitantly, part of the cultural contexts in which their work took place. Instead, I attempt, wherever possible, to situate in specific geographical, cultural, and historical context the lives of the women I met and interviewed at these organizations. I also include information regarding the circumstances surrounding individuals' participation in the project—for instance, whether I met a narrator at a knitting workshop or during the course of her search for help with a custody dispute or divorce. These varying dynamics, which could have a bearing on a woman's emotional state or economic circumstances, may have shaped both the topics discussed in the interview and the tone of a woman's testimony. I also describe the situational context in which the interviews took place, since such information "helps to give a 'feel' for the interview and to recognize the importance of elements such as physical environment, body language, and the subtle (or not so subtle) interaction between interviewers, narrators, and other people present."[96] Finally, I often include in the text the questions I asked along with interviewee responses and point to moments in which my comments and queries—unwittingly, at the time, yet more clearly in retrospect—may have shaped a narrator's testimony.[97]

Although it would be reasonable to assume that women would feel reticent to discuss deeply personal subjects such as sex and abortion, many women expressed the opposite sentiment, remarking that they were glad to have the chance to speak about these themes. Women often said that they had lacked the opportunity to talk about their experiences previously or had not felt comfortable doing so with friends or family members. Several women I spoke with remarked that the interview had been cathartic, or even emotionally healing, which partially eased my concerns and lent credibility to scholars' contentions that oral history narrators may experience psychological benefits from participating in the interview.[98] Still, I have remained troubled by the fear that, for other women, these conversations may have been painful or damaging.

As Victoria Sanford notes in her study of Guatemala, the process of conducting interviews not only teaches the interviewer about the subjects discussed but also may "mark [her] life" in irrevocable ways.[99] Drawing on the work of Dominick LaCapra, who conducted oral histories with survivors of the Holocaust, Sanford describes the process in which an interviewer is impacted by an interviewee as one of transference in which one "'[opens] oneself to empathetic unsettlement.'"[100] It is important to note the thematic distance between discussions of violence and trauma, explored earlier, and those of abortion and unwanted pregnancy—phenomena that, while unpleasant, I would hesitate to cast as necessarily "traumatic." At the same time, interviewing women in La Paz and El Alto about their pregnancies undoubtedly made a deep impression on my life.[101] When, during the course of an interview, a woman wept about her experience with pregnancy or the loss of the loved one, I responded as a human being rather than a historian, abandoning my prepared questions to express empathy and to ask if she had individuals to whom she could turn for support. Rather than perceiving these deviations from the script as drawbacks, I view them as inevitable expressions of our humanity and individuality as researchers—as well as further evidence of the impossibility of achieving "objectivity" in social science research. Try as we might to approach our narrators as historians, we are first humans—and not only the interview, but also our scholarship, is likely the better for it.

An obvious challenge of my research that raised not only ethical but also logistical issues is the stigmatized nature of abortion in La Paz and El Alto and the legal prohibition of most of the abortions that take place there. Dozens of the individuals I interviewed were implicated to some degree in the so-called crime of abortion. Several women I interviewed terminated pregnancies, an act that may result in between one and three years of imprisonment in the case of legal conviction.[102] Other interviewees referred women to abortion providers, performed abortions themselves, or worked as administrators, nurses, and educators at clinics that provided the procedure. Still others, such as doctors and police officers, did not report or arrest women or medical personnel in connection with abortion—which also constituted a breach of legal codes. With a few exceptions, the individuals I interviewed agreed to speak with me on the condition of anonymity. In the book, I refer to all narrators by pseudonyms as a measure to protect the identities of those who preferred to remain anonymous.[103] In designating pseudonyms, I endeavored to select names of a similar cultural background of interviewees' real first and last names, if I knew them. Since I did not know the last names of most of the women I interviewed about their experiences with pregnancy (unlike most of the medical personnel, police officers, and activists with whom I spoke), I assigned women pseudonymous surnames consistent with those of the ethnic or linguistic background with which they identified. Notwithstanding these measures, many interviewees requested additional assurances before they agreed to speak with me. Most individuals who performed abortions consented to the interview only after I explained in detail my own views on abortion and my experiences working in abortion care; many only agreed to meet in the first place because I had been referred by other trusted abortion providers or activists.

While I originally felt I had taken adequate precautions to ensure the anonymity of narrators who performed abortions, the serious limitations of my approach came to light a few years after I concluded research for the project. At that time, I returned to La Paz to share with my narrators and the broader community one of the project's central findings: namely, that women's persistent demand for abortion, and the ingenuity of the strategies that they employed to procure it, helped change policies and programs on abortion and unwanted pregnancy in La Paz and El Alto. Impressed by women's resilience and angered by the conditions that made such resilience necessary, and at the same time encouraged by some of the positive changes that had taken place to reduce the terrible impacts of unsafe abortion, I naively shared details, albeit anonymously, regarding innovative responses to unwanted pregnancy that emerged in these cities over the last few decades. I did so at a public conference organized by several local organizations and, subsequently, in two interviews that I granted to the press. The stories that resulted from these interviews mischaracterized my own interest in the subject matter, and furthermore,

made abundantly clear that the chief concern—if not of the specific journalists who authored the stories, than of other actors within the social climate into which these stories were released—was to facilitate the identification and prosecution of abortion providers, rather than raise awareness
about the public health and psychological impacts of abortion's penaliza-
tion and stigmatization for women in the country. While my research suggested that women and health care providers were rarely imprisoned in
connection with abortion, I failed to grasp that this relative lack of policing was not necessarily evidence of the lack of will to do so. In the aftermath of these stories, authorities brought increased scrutiny to abortion
in the country—although, as far as I am aware, this scrutiny did not result
in legal action.

This episode, highly unpleasant for me but potentially disastrous for
some of my closest oral history narrators, is a harsh reminder of the persistence of societal stigma against abortion—including the women who
get it and the individuals who perform it—in La Paz and El Alto. It also
crystallizes the importance of long-standing debates about the ethical
responsibilities of, and one might daresay the debts owed by, us as individuals conducting research in places we are not from and the local conditions of which we may remain inherently ignorant, despite our best
attempts at preparation. These events also shaped the design of this book.[104]
In addition to altering its scope (omitting details about how, precisely,
abortion is provided in these cities), conversations with narrators in the
months following this event led me to revise the language and terminol-
ogy employed in the project. Terms such as "clandestine" and "illegal," for
instance, have an insidious tendency to cast moralistic doubt on abortion
in a way that is neither objectively true nor an accurate reflection of my
own personal perspective on abortion. Referring to the decisions of some
medical personnel and police officers not to report women and providers
in connection with abortion as a "failure," despite any literal precision the
term may reflect, is similarly fraught. Its use, furthermore, may erroneously suggest to readers that I believe that more should be done to police

what constitutes one of the most commonly experienced, needed, and nonetheless vilified, reproductive events that a woman living anywhere in the world will have.

In writing this book, the aforementioned events led me to dive more deeply into the literature examining the ethics of research, in general, and to adopt some of the theories and practices developed by feminist oral history, in particular. I share the conviction, articulated by other scholars who work with oral testimonies, that the decisions we make with respect to interviewing, editing, and publication comprise questions of both personal morality and training—and may have real-life consequences.[105] In interviewing women and men in Bolivia, I have attempted to place "[individuals'] well-being at the center of decisions, not as a second consideration where searching for truth is first."[106] Some of the implications of my adoption of a feminist approach to ethics contradict oral history's "best practices" as defined by the Oral History Association—such as making testimonies available to other researchers in an archive or repository.[107] Instead, this project disallows for verification of specific oral testimonies by the reader—or, indeed, of specific medical records included in the book, since the citation of these might allow the discovery of patients' identities, many of whom may still be living.[108] Ultimately, my experience conducting research in Bolivia taught me that the dilemmas associated with the ethical production of history and ethnography are largely unresolvable; instead, it falls to the researcher to signal these challenges as they arise and navigate them as deftly as possible.[109]

Outline of Book

The first chapter of *An Open Secret* traces a broad history of reproductive policies in Bolivia, in general, and in the cities of La Paz and El Alto, in particular. It argues that ideas about women and their reproduction were central to nation-making processes, and that women's efforts to regulate their fertility and their participation in political organizing shaped the development of policies on these phenomena. The chapter, which comprises a traditional, sociopolitical and socioeconomic history of reproductive health policy, provides a contextual foundation for the largely ethnographic chapters that follow.

Chapter 2 examines societal attitudes toward sex, contraception, and abortion in urban Bolivia between the early 1950s and 2010. The chapter finds persistent stigma around abortion (and toward sexuality more broadly) in La Paz and El Alto, notwithstanding support for legal abortion among a smaller sector of middle- and upper-class activists and health care providers. At the same time, the chapter, echoing the work of Bonnie Shepard for Latin America as a whole, argues that there is a "double discourse" concerning abortion in these cities; that is, when discussing the phenomenon in private, or when an unwanted pregnancy affects a friend or family member, abortion is far more tolerated and even accepted.[110] The third chapter explores the feelings and reactions of women who confronted unwanted or unexpected pregnancies between the 1950s and 2010. The chapter reveals that women's feelings toward their pregnancies were complex, marked by ambivalence, and shaped by both personal and structural factors. This chapter, like scholarship exploring women's reproductive experiences in other geographical contexts, suggests that those legal and political frameworks for understanding reproductive decision making that center on a rhetoric of "choice" are too limited to capture women's personal experiences. Instead, the chapter shows that women making decisions about their pregnancies consider a range of personal and social factors that are best understood when explored in the specific cultural and historical context in which these decisions take place.

In chapters 4 and 5 I examine women's personal experiences with reproductive health care—specifically methods of fertility regulation, treatment for complications following pregnancy loss, and childbirth assistance—between the early 1950s and the early 1980s, and between 1982 and 2010, respectively. These chapters demonstrate the persistence of women's efforts to negotiate their reproductive lives, as well as their ongoing reliance on Andean childbirth practices and forms of fertility regulation. This was true despite the pronatalism of state regimes and the efforts of state and medical officials to subsume traditional reproductive health care to western forms. After the democratic opening, renewed political mobilization among the public, in combination with women's continued demand for abortion and other methods of fertility regulation, spurred a number of unprecedented developments in services for unwanted pregnancy and abortion between the late 1980s and 2010. While these services contributed to making abortion and treatment following pregnancy loss safer, even for poor women, they did not erase all health inequities. Instead, the prevalence of unregulated health services in the urban Andes contributed to the emergence of an unequal health system that leaves women of limited economic and social capital particularly vulnerable.

Chapter 6 examines the complexities of the relationship between abortion and the law in Bolivia, drawing comparisons to the legal context surrounding abortion in other Latin American countries. It also explores broader questions regarding the relationship between policies regulating reproductive behaviors, health services, and providers and their implementation (or lack thereof) on the ground. The conclusion draws together the book's central arguments, highlighting the ambivalence and contradiction that weave through the histories of policies and services on reproductive health care, societal attitudes toward women and sexuality, and women's own conceptualizations of and experiences with their pregnancies. The chapter further reflects on the consequences of these intersecting patterns of ambivalence for women seeking to regulate their fertility in contemporary Bolivia—as well as to navigate their lives more broadly.

CHAPTER 1

Legislating Unwanted Pregnancy and Abortion in Bolivia

Abortion is like an iceberg, where we only see the tip. . . . It is something that is done with or without laws and that is practiced in the entire country. When I ask women who come to medical consults, it is rare that they say they never had an abortion. . . . It's something so hidden, this mountain beneath the water. Whether or not permission is given by the state to do it, abortions will continue to be performed.
        —Dolores Ticahuanca, a physician who performed abortions
                                                in El Alto in 2009

When asked to describe abortion in Bolivia, individuals in La Paz and El Alto draw on a variety of metaphors. Whether characterizing abortion as an iceberg—a significant, and perhaps menacing, reality obscured by the waters of social convention—or as an open secret, rarely discussed but widely acknowledged, these metaphors about abortion point to the same truth. Abortion in Bolivia, although prohibited in most circumstances since 1973, occurs frequently and is spoken of sparingly. While abortion has remained illegal due to the strength of those political and religious forces that oppose it, recent government programs for the treatment of incomplete abortion and miscarriage belie an official recognition of the frequency with which women confront unwanted pregnancy and abortion in the country. This recognition does not mean that the state condones abortion, or even necessarily empathizes with the women who need it; however, it reveals an acknowledgment that women will terminate pregnancies regardless of its legal status—and a tacit acceptance of that fact. In leaving intact prohibitions against abortion, policy makers pass on to women the consequences of unsafe abortion and social stigma associated with the procedure in the urban Andes.

This chapter illuminates the conflictive history of reproductive policy in Bolivia, which is marked by significant rates of unwanted pregnancy and abortion alongside restrictive laws on these phenomena. Reproductive policies after the revolution were deeply embedded in longer-standing, elite anxieties concerning indigenous people and the place they occupied in the Bolivian nation. For this reason, the first section of the chapter considers the perspectives of politicians, medical doctors, and other professionals in regard to women and men of different sociocultural and racial groups in the late nineteenth and early twentieth centuries. The second section of the chapter draws on interviews, political documents, newspaper articles, and medical and demographic policy reports to explore how evolving historical attitudes about race and gender shaped the development of reproductive policies across the revolutionary, military, and democratic periods.

This chapter finds that shifts in public policies on reproduction were deeply intertwined with broader social, political, and economic trends at the local, national, and global levels. Issues surrounding women and their reproduction—and particularly that of indigenous women—were, in the minds of creole and mestizo elites, central to Bolivia's progress as a nation. Policy makers, intellectuals, and other dominant sectors measured the value of women and their health primarily in terms of their role as mothers. Through the 1950s, domestic elites were primarily concerned with what they perceived as Bolivia's underpopulation vis-à-vis other Latin American countries, and voiced concerns that indigenous women, who they saw as dirty and culturally backward, were ill-equipped to produce a healthy population of citizens and laborers. Reforms during the period attempted to solve this "problem" by improving public health and by westernizing indigenous women's mothering practices (and the indigenous family more broadly). In the 1960s and 1970s, in the context of the Cold War, international observers became concerned with the supposed *over*population of poor people of color in a variety of locations worldwide, including the indigenous residents of Bolivia. Foreign officials from organizations such as USAID alleged that high birth rates threatened Bolivia's economic and political progress and made the country susceptible to political unrest. Yet the efforts undertaken by foreign and domestic policy makers to implement family planning programs during the period were largely unsuccessful, partly because they were confronted by pushback from a variety of social sectors concerned with the projects' eugenicist and imperialist aims. Instead, it was women's persistent efforts to negotiate their reproductive lives, mobilization on the part of women's groups and health activists, and broader international trends that spurred the Bolivian state to implement programs in western-derived contraceptive methods and for the clinical treatment of incomplete abortion and miscarriage, largely after the mid-1990s.

The policy developments that took place during these years—changes that ultimately made abortion safer while ensuring that it remained both ubiquitous and illegal—suggest that most biomedical doctors and government officials conceived of abortion and unexplained miscarriage primarily as issues of public health, rather than of women's or human rights. At the same time, the persistence of legal restrictions against abortion reveal urban society's continuing ambivalence toward those aspects of women's lives that fell outside of their role as mothers, such as their engagement in sex for pleasure or companionship, and their efforts to limit pregnancies in order to pursue social or economic mobility. The stories of some of these women, most of whom are also mothers, are explored in the remainder of this book.

Reproduction and Indigenous "Difference" at the Turn of the Twentieth Century

Following independence, Bolivia's population was primarily rural, and the status of indigenous Bolivians within the political, economic, and social order hinged in large part on the varied nature of land tenure claimed by individuals, families, and kinship groups.[1] Up to 1880, *ayllus* (independent kin-based communities) held half of the land and comprised half of the country's total population; the rest of the rural indigenous either labored as *colonos* (servile tenants) on private haciendas or worked as freeholders. While, in theory, all indigenous people were required to pay a tax (or tribute) to the state, in practice the majority of tributaries were members of ayllus; landless peasants often succeeded in avoiding these obligations. While the relationship that Bolivia's peasantry shared with state bureaucracies varied according to land tenure, however, these differences did not necessarily determine variations in the perspectives of creole and mestizo elites toward individuals of indigenous ancestry.[2] While elites' perspectives on rural-dwelling indigenous people often emphasized their natural submissiveness and thus their suitability to agricultural labor, the upper classes tended to feel greater ambivalence toward the racially mixed, who were deemed more threatening to the socioracial order. At the same time, the contours of elite perspectives on indigenous women and men shifted in response to national political and economic patterns—and particularly, to the specter of political mobilization by indigenous populations.[3]

The last third of the nineteenth century saw a rising tide of economic and political liberalism that placed the political mobilization of indigenous women and men, and elite anxieties about it, at the center of the national stage.[4] The country's liberal reformers, as those elsewhere in the Andes and in Mexico in the nineteenth century, sought to dismantle the status of the rural indigenous community in order to consolidate land into large *latifundios* (privately owned estates) for the development of export-oriented agriculture and the construction of railroads.

The reforms were further designed to convert indigenous peasants into modern, yeoman farmers (and thus prevent their migration to the cities) and to force indigenous Bolivians to adopt western lifeways, which were seen as necessary for national progress.[5] Liberal policies were often thwarted by resistance and rebellion, which peasants unleashed via paper campaigns filed in bureaucratic offices and courts, as well as through direct action in the countryside.[6]

Undergirding the liberal reforms were discriminatory and racist attitudes toward both rural- and urban-dwelling indigenous people, which were widely expressed in the late nineteenth and early twentieth centuries in a range of literary, photographic, and artistic forms throughout the Andean region.[7] Among these was *indigenismo*, "a reformist movement led by mestizo and Creole intellectuals and artists who sought to defend a marginalized Indian population and vindicate its cultural past or future potential."[8] While not as consolidated in Bolivia as in other Andean contexts, Bolivian indigenismo, which seized upon the historical significance of the Aymara archaeological site at Tiwanaku, emphasized the latent value of the country's indigenous populations for the modernizing projects that would eventually be pursued during the 1952 revolution.[9] The rise of indigenismo in the Andes and of scientific racism in Latin America more broadly in the early twentieth century had particular implications for women and families. As nations in the region pursued modernization, "state policies . . . fastened onto gender as both a precept and a tool in their attempts to subordinate popular households to the interests of national development, social order and patriarchal power."[10] In Bolivia, this process was facilitated by an extraordinary rural education movement that swept through the countryside in the first decades of the twentieth century. As described by Brooke Larson, "Gender difference became the device through which rural schools might accomplish their dual ends: the stabilization of the rural peasant class (whose station in life would be narrowly confined to agriculture) and the incremental incorporation of normative values and hygienic routines into the peasant family. . . . To mold the *campesino* into Bolivia's modern (albeit still landless) farm producer was one aim; to fold the *campesina* into universal womanhood was its essential complement."[11]

Key to the rural education movement were broader concerns about the "inability" of indigenous families, and particularly women, to reproduce a robust and healthy population of future laborers. Ethnographic texts from the early twentieth century depicted the indigenous family as fragile, unhealthy, and unstable, haunting elites concerned with populating the Bolivian nation with strong and modern yeoman farmers.[12] Reformers seized upon indigenous women and their bodies as crucial sites in which "improvements" to the indigenous family might take place. Through educational courses in "home economics," modern campesinas would adopt the trappings of bourgeois femininity, including western nutritional habits, practices of infant care, and beauty products, and thus be converted into housewives safely subordinated to their husbands' (and the nation's) patriarchal authority.[13]

Dominant notions of womanhood such as those espoused as part of the rural educational reforms were also at work in cities, where they confronted pushback by both white and mestiza liberal feminist and Aymara anarchist groups of women in La Paz across the first half of the twentieth century.[14] Legal records from the period articulated socioeconomic and racial distinctions between upper-class creole *señoras*, pollera-clad indigenous *mujeres*, and rural-dwelling *indígenas*.[15] Each of these hierarchically ordered groups referenced a different relationship with the racialized female and maternal body, which in turn worked to "'[naturalize] social differences,'" particularly, the exclusion of women from the public realm— an exclusion that only upper-class women could readily accommodate.[16] Working-class cholas (urban-dwelling women of indigenous ancestry) who labored in La Paz as merchants, domestic servants, laundresses, and cooks, "profoundly unsettled the dominant ideology of womanhood by powerfully disrupting gendered categories of the 'natural.'"[17] They did so, in part, by organizing for labor rights, and thus thrusting into public debate the domestic spheres of the elite women for whom they labored, which until then had been safely protected from politics. In so doing, urban cholas refuted broader ideologies of womanhood that linked biological notions of the female body to an apolitical sphere centered in the home.[18]

By the 1930s, militant groups of working-class women organized unions representing cooks, flower sellers, and other professions, coming together under the Federación Obrera Femenina (Federation of Female Workers, or FOF), which itself formed part of a broader anarchist labor federation. Members of the unions, "raised issues related to their professions, but also made gender-based demands that later governments would be pleased to take credit for implementing, such as child care facilities for working mothers."[19] The upper-class, liberal wing of the early twentieth-century feminist movement was represented by cultural and artistic societies, such as the Ateneo Femenino, whose members agitated for educational and voting rights. The Ateneo's exclusion of working-class women of the FOF from a national convention the society organized in 1929 was, according to Marcia Stephenson, emblematic of the ways in which upper-class women during the period sought to maintain their racial and socioeconomic authority even as various groups of women agitated against patriarchal authority and for their rights.[20]

The activism of urban women in the 1930s took place in the context of Bolivia's Chaco War against Paraguay (1932–1935), a national debacle in which the country suffered devastating losses. The conflict, which resulted in the deaths of more than 50,000 Bolivians (mostly indigenous soldiers who died as a result of disease and thirst, rather than combat), placed in stark relief the profound racial and class inequalities plaguing Bolivian society. In its aftermath, large sectors of the middle classes for the first time became sympathetic to the plight of the country's indigenous peasants and workers; the war also lent weight to the demands of Bolivia's popular sectors that the state repay its constituents' sacrifice to the nation in concrete social and political rights.[21]

In the years during and after the war, upper- and working-class women mobilized for social reform in ways that continued to emphasize their distinct interests and identities. While both groups referenced their contributions to national life as Bolivians (despite their continued exclusion from citizenship rights), their struggles centered around different issues and highlighted divergent conceptualizations of womanhood. In 1938, for instance, chola market vendors demanding access to public streets where they could sell their wares, "justified their demands on the basis of their sacrifice to the nation as widows, mothers, daughters, or sisters of men killed in the front-line trenches of the Chaco War."[22] Upper-class women, for their part, emphasized their "natural" roles as mothers to agitate for greater access to the public sphere, where they could work to maintain national peace and provide moral (i.e., maternal) guidance to the underclasses. As part of these efforts, well-to-do women organized under the Legión Femenina de Educación Popular América to design initiatives providing assistance to poor women, children, and unwed mothers.[23] Working-class women continued to reject these dominant, naturalized connections between women, motherhood, and the home. Unable to access the privileges enjoyed by upper-class mothers, working-class women faced the burden of finding childcare for their own children in order to secure employment in the homes of the upper-class women in whose homes they worked as domestic employees or cooks. Those few women whose employers allowed them to bring their children to work were often forced to rely on their own children's labor in order to complete their many duties— labor that was uncompensated by upper-class bosses.[24] In their personal lives, too, working-class cholas rejected the submission to patriarchal authority inherent in hegemonic notions of modern womanhood; rather than engaging in formal marriage, seen as an institution of the state prone to abuses, working women preferred the practice of cohabitation, common in the Andes.[25]

Public health reforms following the Chaco War further reinscribed differences in perceptions of the mothering capacity and appropriate womanhood of elite creole and mestiza and working-class indigenous women in La Paz.[26] While the war unleashed an era of more progressive ideas concerning the rights of all women and indigenous people to public health, the La Paz Municipal Council sought to solve pressing health problems, such as infant and maternal mortality, largely by instituting coercive measures directed at working-class women. Initiatives included forced gynecological exams for women seeking to work as childcare providers or domestic employees and those designed, "to force parents to seek medical attention for sick children" at clinics, rather than from Andean healers.[27] Measures aimed at westernizing working-class and indigenous mothers were undergirded by ideas, relatively widespread among the upper classes, that cast indigenous parents, especially women, as ignorant, dirty, morally suspect, and responsible for high rates of child mortality.[28] Concerns in the city about the role of working-class prostitutes in spreading venereal disease also led to attempts to confine sex workers in hospitals, police the locations of establishments where sex-for-money exchanges took place, and save the city's young men from diseases that might threaten their ability to populate the Bolivian nation.[29]

Undergirding many of the public health measures undertaken by policy makers and doctors in La Paz during the first half of the twentieth century, as well as the charity and social welfare programs created by the city's elite women, were broader, racialized and gendered perceptions about indigenous women, in general, and about urban-dwelling cholas, in particular. Mary Weismantel has explored the profoundly ambivalent societal attitudes toward Andean cholas across the region's history. "An unsettled racial identity is one source of the chola's offensiveness," writes Weismantel; "Indians when visible in the city," urban-dwelling cholas are at the same time "whites among the Indians."[30] Cholas' liminal racial status, as well as their centuries-long presence in urban areas of the Andes, articulated broader elite fears of indigenous people "invading" the region's cities and disrupting the modernity budding there.[31] Attitudes of ambivalence toward the indigenous woman over the past several decades often centered on her body, which has been alternately sexualized and cast as monstrous by nonindigenous domestic elites. Members of the creole and mestizo upper classes lamented, on the one hand, the "vulgarity" of cholas in the marketplace, where they labored as vendors, while subjecting them to sexual harassment and rape in the homes of well-to-do urban families, where they worked as domestic employees.[32] Ambivalent perspectives toward cholas also emerged in elites' assessments of their pollera and braided hair. Thus upper-class señoras who employed indigenous women as domestic workers might force them to wear the pollera, "so that social distinctions are duplicated in the home," or forbid them from donning the garment, in order to project a more modern household image.[33] Elite concerns about cholas were further undergirded by fears of the economic and political power of these women. "Legendary figures of working-class political solidarity," cholas have been at the forefront of labor and political mobilization in La Paz and El Alto.[34] Some cholas who work as market vendors accumulate considerable wealth, which they display in and on their bodies through their distinctive (and expensive) clothing and jewelry, as well as in the rolls of cash they carry in the folds of their polleras and in the gold teeth adorning their mouths.[35] These varied notions of the threatening, yet enticing, "difference" of the indigenous female body contributed to national—and, in the second half of the twentieth century, international—efforts to control women's sexual and reproductive behavior (and their lives more broadly). Thus, by the time of Bolivia's national revolution, an elite project of cultural modernization of the native polity was well under way, with both racialized and gendered implications that would work to shape the landscape of reproductive health policy in the period after 1952.

POLICIES ON SEX AND REPRODUCTION
SINCE THE NATIONAL REVOLUTION

In April 1952 tin miners joined students and urban workers in La Paz to launch a popular uprising that culminated in a twelve-year-long nationalist revolution. "The revolution was led by a coalition that had formed after a radical indigenous movement in the countryside challenged the established neo-feudal order in the 1940s, demanding that the government abolish slave labor and regulate landowner-tenant farmer relationships."[36] Upon coming to power, the MNR party that assumed leadership of this coalition passed a number of progressive legislative measures. The measures included the nationalization of the country's mineral resources, an agrarian reform, and the extension of citizenship and voting rights to women and indigenous people—groups that, up to that time, had been formally excluded from national politics. The party also expanded educational programs and enacted measures to combat the country's most pressing public health challenges, such as infant and maternal mortality, and diseases like smallpox and malaria.[37] The MNR described its political ideology as one of "revolutionary nationalism" and owed its popular support to its embrace of two slogans, "land to the Indians" and "mines to the state," first launched by radical intellectual Tristan Marof in the 1920s.[38] The MNR asserted that its new legislative reforms would raise the social and economic status of urban workers and indigenous peasants, as well as facilitate the "incorporation" of the latter into national life. Since peasants had been denied political rights, and because most labored as indebted workers on latifundios, which limited their capacity to participate in the national market as consumers, the party considered rural-dwelling indigenous to reside "outside" of political and economic activity and thus intended to "incorporate" them into the revolutionary nation. In seeking for the first time to correct tremendous inequities in access to land, health care, education, and the political system, the national revolution was significant in ways that were both real and symbolic. While the revolutionary measures effectively restructured the country's political, economic, and social systems, they also expanded citizens' expectations of the state, bolstering progressive movements.[39]

While the MNR's policies improved to some degree the lives of both workers and peasants, including women, the party's attitudes toward Bolivia's indigenous majority had a darker dimension. Similar to the attitudes espoused by nineteenth-century liberal reformers, key to the MNR's plan to "incorporate" indigenous Bolivians was the assimilation of these groups into dominant mestizo culture, which would be accomplished by replacing "traditional" ways of life with more "modern" customs. Lifeways targeted for improvement included language, housing, forms of dress, nutritional habits, religious beliefs, agricultural and medicinal practices, and sexual and reproductive behaviors. Western cultural habits and beliefs were deemed more "hygienic" and, thus, compatible with a modern, revolutionary nation. (Hygiene was understood not only in terms of scientific notions of rationality and "cleanliness," but also in terms of eugenic ideas about racial, moral, and sexual purity.) The MNR also rebranded indigenous people "campesinos." Arguing that the terms "Indian" and "indigenous" were tainted by centuries of discrimination, this move effectively sought to erase indigenous Bolivians' ethnic identifications and, along with them, their cultural and political autonomy.[40]

The MNR's policies concerning reproduction formed part of a larger package of public health reforms related to the party's economic and political goals; the measures were also laced with similarly conflicted attitudes about Bolivia's indigenous majority. As a whole, the MNR's health reforms were pronatalist, designed to swell the country's population by decreasing disease, mortality, and malnutrition; improving health systems; and spurring birth rates. In so doing, the party hoped to foster a healthy body of revolutionary citizens who would participate in the labor force and contribute to the nation's economic and political development. On the one hand, the health reforms were decidedly revolutionary for the era and succeeded in building a national health "infrastructure that resembled a modern welfare state."[41] Thus, over the course of the 1950s, the MNR passed a comprehensive social security measure that included coverage for maternity care, as well as a new sanitary code that explicitly declared its intention to improve the health of all Bolivians, rural and urban.[42] The social security code required employers, including the state-owned mining corporation, COMIBOL, to provide health care to its workers and to their families.[43] The measures of the 1950s significantly expanded health care services into the countryside and increased training and oversight of Bolivia's health care personnel.[44]

At the same time, reformers during the revolutionary era deemed the indigenous population at least partially responsible for Bolivia's poor health record. Nicole Pacino shows how many rural health workers saw indigenous women as "unhygienic disease carriers" ill-equipped to fulfill their revolutionary duty of reproducing a nation of healthy, modern citizens.[45] Reformers also tied indigenous people's failure to spur agricultural production to Bolivian citizens' nutritional deficiencies, which, the MNR argued, contributed to the incidence of diseases like tuberculosis and to the country's high mortality rates.[46] Infant mortality particularly concerned health reformers during the revolutionary era. Reviewing statistics from the late 1940s, the director of the MNR's Department of Biostatistics Hubert Navarro estimated that Bolivia's infant mortality rate was 126 per 1,000 live births, the worst of all Latin American countries except Colombia and Chile.[47] Navarro placed some of the blame for high rates of infant mortality on the country's population of workers and peasants. "Stillbirths are frequently registered, especially among the working and campesino classes, due to the lack of prenatal care."[48] Since they held indigenous mothers at least partially responsible for infant mortality, reformers targeted the childbirth and mothering customs of indigenous women for reform.[49]

The primary body charged with carrying out the MNR's health policies was the Servicio Cooperativo Interamericano de Salud Pública (Inter-American Cooperative Public Health Service, or SCISP), an institution jointly funded by the Bolivian government and USAID. Active between 1942 and 1963, the SCISP undertook a variety of initiatives to reshape the practices of indigenous mothers, including, "mothers' clubs, healthy children contests, and educational [programs]" that brought women under the increased surveillance of state health officials.[50] MNR reformers also sought to replace Andean childbirth and parenting practices with western forms and to increase the ratio of hospital to home birth.[51] (Undergirding some of these reforms were ideas of "puericulture," the French science of childrearing influenced by Lamarckian ideas of eugenics.[52]) Replacing the practices of native mothers with those of "foreign" (probably western European) women, alleged MNR health reformers, would decrease rates of infant mortality and contribute to the natural growth of a healthy and robust population; it would further fulfill reformers' objective of bolstering Bolivia's professional medical establishment vis-à-vis Andean healers and midwives.[53] Finally, some of the MNR's policies aimed to spur population growth by providing direct incentives to families to reproduce rather than decreasing mortality. Men employed by the state-owned mining corporation in Potosí in the 1950s and 1960s were paid according to the numbers of children in their households.[54] Cultural notions of masculinity and virility in Bolivia, at least in many urban areas, were also tied to men's ability to father many children, further incentivizing some men's interest in having large families. Thus, as a whole, the MNR's policies linked questions of public health, agrarian production, and national political and economic development to ideas about race, gender, and citizenship.[55]

The MNR's pronatalist position, which "cast [women] as reproducers of the family and of family values," likely put women seeking to limit births during the revolutionary era in a difficult position.[56] I was unable to find evidence that government or health officials, or society more broadly, worried that abortion or birth control was directly contributing to high rates of mortality or low rates of population growth during these years. However, MNR officials did express general disapproval of contraception and abortion as Malthusian-inspired attempts to limit population growth in poor countries. Navarro explicitly condemned both birth control and abortion in his 1953 report, citing Bolivia's Catholic foundations. In his comments, Navarro compared contraceptive use and abortion with prostitution and other "immoral" behaviors. "Limiting births through induced abortion or through contraceptive practices as is being done in Japan, India, and other countries, is to move toward the generalized availability of prostitution, the unhinging [*desquiciamiento*] of sexual morality, an increase in divorce, the destruction of the . . . family, and the ever-growing use of 'birth control.'"[57] Undoubtedly referencing the involvement of foreign entities like USAID in the family planning initiatives implemented in Latin America during the 1950s, Navarro wrote the term "birth control" above in English. Drawing on both religious rhetoric and commonly held beliefs that progressive measures concerning sexuality cast society down a slippery slope of moral degradation, Navarro expressed the government's disapproval for any interventionist efforts to limit births.

Navarro and other MNR officials were probably unconcerned with contraceptive use or abortion during the revolutionary period because the incidence of these in Bolivia was either unknown or not especially high, or because neither form of fertility regulation had drawn the attention of international health reformers (or both). At the same time, women may not have felt a particular urgency to limit their pregnancies during the revolutionary years. On the one hand, it was customary for Bolivian families to have many children during these decades, which might have shaped women's (and men's) expectations for and attitudes toward their reproductive lives.[58] On the other hand, the MNR's social and economic reforms, as well as organizing on the part of women, indigenous people, and workers during these years, may have resulted in increased well-being for families in both rural and urban areas and thus assuaged women's need to limit their pregnancies. Despite legal restrictions on abortion, the lack of availability of contraceptive methods, and the MNR's pronatalist policies and rhetoric, Bolivia's population rate remained relatively stable during the revolutionary years, while mortality rates actually increased slightly during the early years of the party's rule.[59]

Women's organizing efforts during the revolutionary period also contributed to shaping policies on reproduction and maternal and infant health. During the 1950s and 1960s, women's organizations mobilized to offer financial, emotional, and logistical support to their members. Two of the most active women's groups in La Paz during these decades were the MNR women's faction, the Comando Femenino de La Paz (Female Command of La Paz) and the Legión María Barzola. While the Comando largely mobilized in support of the national MNR program and did not articulate separate, gender-specific concerns, the Legión engaged in direct action and service provision in defense of women and children (including the families of its own low-income members). The Legión, or Barzolas, as they were commonly called, was a somewhat more militant, pro-MNR group whose namesake was a female mineworker killed in an infamous massacre of tin workers in 1942.[60] Unlike the Comandos, which were largely made up of middle- and upper-class relatives of male MNR activists, the Barzolas consisted largely of working-class women, many of whom were single mothers. The group worked in a number of arenas, including health care, literacy, and political advocacy.[61] When Bolivia suffered food shortages in the wake of the agrarian reform and was forced to accept donations of grain and other products from abroad, the Barzolas organized supply centers to make basic foodstuffs available to women, even engaging in contraband in order to do so. During the years from 1956 to 1964, women's formal political participation—at least that of the pro-MNR sectors—became even more firmly consolidated. In 1956, the same year she was elected to the Chamber of Deputies, Command activist Lidia Gueiler Tejada (who would later serve as president from 1979 to 1980) advanced a proposal for the creation of a sub-secretary of social welfare dedicated to the defense of women; the measure passed the following year. In 1961, during the third and final administration of the revolutionary regime, the Female Commands held their first departmental conference, which was so well attended that a national conference was convened the following year. In the 1962 and 1964 elections, between two and three female MNR candidates were elected each year to local or national posts.[62]

It is unclear whether women's organizing during the revolutionary era directly contributed to the passage of the social reforms of the period, such as the 1956 social security law for disability or the 1958 Sanitary Code. However, other aspects of women's collective actions did shape the evolution of policies concerning gender, sexuality, and reproduction. On the one hand, the changes in women's social, economic, and political status over the period likely shifted women's expectations and understandings of their own lives, as well as public attitudes toward women more broadly. Over the 1950s and 1960s, Bolivia became more urbanized, increased its formal base of citizens by approximately three million, and brought education to women and indigenous people. These broad demographic shifts spurred public support for maternity coverage and other benefits for working mothers—if not necessarily for the rights of women as nonprocreative beings. Women's shifting forms of political and economic involvement during these years, along with greater cultural changes, also undoubtedly impacted women's expectations for their reproductive lives.

Ultimately, neither the support of women nor that of the MNR's traditional base of peasants, mine workers, and the middle class could prevent the disintegration of the revolutionary regime, the causes of which were both political and economic. The nationalization of Bolivia's most lucrative tin mines (with compensation to the former owners) and the destruction of the capitalist-oriented latifundios liquidated the country's main sources of income.[63] This situation compelled the MNR to increase its national currency, sparking inflation and discontent at home, and eventually forced the party to turn to the United States for financial assistance. In the context of the Cold War, the United States extended food aid and other forms of assistance—including USAID's sponsorship of the health programs administered through the SCISP—with the partial aim of fostering dependence and weakening the strength of Bolivia's revolutionary movement.[64] Ultimately, the nature of the MNR's relationship with the United States limited the party's ability to pursue the revolutionary nationalist agenda to which it owed its political support. Tensions between Bolivia's Ministry of Health and U.S. officials over questions of strategic planning and, implicitly, national sovereignty, eventually resulted in the termination of U.S. involvement in SCISP in 1960; the organization dissolved a few years later.[65]

The Military Era and the Specter of International
Population Control

Following the collapse of the revolutionary government, Bolivia was plunged into eighteen years of military rule, which curtailed progressive organizing in many sectors. Intellectuals, activists, and civilian political leaders were forced into exile during the period, as the government cracked down on leftist movements and on democratic participation in general.[66] Some women joined the ranks of those exiled; what would later become one of La Paz's most active women's organizations in the struggle for reproductive rights, the Centro de Información y Desarrollo de la Mujer (Center for Information and Development of Women, or CIDEM), was founded by sociologist Sonia Montaño while she was exiled in Holland.[67] Attorney, author, and women's rights activist Julieta Montaño was placed under house arrest during the dictatorship in retaliation for her leadership of a women's union;[68] a few years after the fall of the regime, Montaño would go on to found Cochabamba's Oficina Jurídica de la Mujer (Women's Juridical Office), one of the leading women's rights organizations in the country. Like military regimes elsewhere in Latin America during these decades, Bolivia's military leaders viewed the authoritarian system as a path to modernizing the country and approached political parties and organizing on the part of labor and other groups with hostility. At the same time, the ideology of Bolivia's military establishment was less coherent than those, say, of the southern cone countries, and tended to shift in accordance with the individual personality and interests of the leader in charge. Whereas Hugo Banzer Suárez (1971–1978) was a somewhat traditional antidemocratic and anticommunist dictator (particularly after the 1973 rise of Augusto Pinochet in Chile), General Juan José Torres (1970–1971) supported the left-wing labor movement and accepted funding from the Soviet Union.[69]

In Bolivia, military leaders also courted the country's native populations, forming what they called a "Military-Peasant Pact." The military's

support of the native population manifest in continuing the land distribution initiated in 1953, but stopped short of extending other rights
demanded by rural-dwellers, such as credit or price controls to bolster
their position in local markets.[70] At the same time, Andean medicinal
forms and practitioners gained a degree of official support during the
military period, as "new maternal-infant care programs" led by the Ministry of Health fostered collaboration between western obstetricians and
indigenous *parteras*, or midwives.[71] The contradictory dimensions of
the relationship between military rulers and the peasantry highlighted
the continuing ambivalence of creole and mestizo leaders toward
native people and their practices. Some elements of the Military-Peasant
Pact were paternalist; however, military officials also violently repressed
both the peasantry and mine workers. Native women and men persistently
negotiated the bounds of the repression, as well as the political, economic,
and social measures imposed by dictators, to assert their own rights and
authority.[72]

Military leaders' ambivalence toward the country's indigenous population was echoed by similarly conflicted attitudes on the part of U.S. officials toward native Bolivians. In the context of the Cold War, the United
States partnered with both democratic and authoritarian regimes in Latin
America, providing financial assistance designed to eradicate poverty, foster economic growth and political stability, and quash potential Communist agitation. Beginning in 1961 under President John F. Kennedy, the
"Alliance for Progress" program financed a variety of projects in the region,
from hospitals and schools to ports and bridges, to achieve these economic
and political aims (which also included extending U.S. influence in Latin
America). In practice, the program, which ran out of steam toward the end
of the 1960s, contributed to the growing wave of authoritarianism in the
region. In Bolivia, Alliance funds were funneled toward campesinos and
miners in an attempt to "strengthen [MNR president] Víctor Paz Esten-
sorro's and later military presidents' control over the most rebellious sectors of the population."[73] The U.S. policy makers who designed Alliance

for Progress and its successor aid programs were "modernization theorists" who fundamentally agreed with Bolivian military leaders' contention that indigenous populations were primarily to blame for the country's poverty and lack of development.[74]

The various USAID-sponsored initiatives that were implemented in Bolivia in the 1960s and 1970s targeted the indigenous family for reform. The "New Directions" approach to U.S. financial assistance in Latin America introduced in the 1970s defined "the family" as "a social unit they implicitly defined as a male-headed household with children."[75] Reformers implemented a wide range of programs to benefit the family, including maternal-infant care initiatives, vaccination and sanitation projects, and education in nutrition and hygiene.[76] In educating the indigenous family, reformers hoped to transform campesinos into modern, market-oriented farmers—not unlike the goals of the earlier, MNR-led programs. Military dictator Hugo Banzer Suárez, who assumed control of the state in 1971, shared the vision of USAID officials toward the Bolivian family. According to Kathryn Gallien, Banzer's solution to the country's "Indian problem" was to foster the development of a "New Bolivian Man" and his partner, the "New Bolivian Woman," a "self-abnegating mother and wife who dedicated herself to domestic life and raising healthy children to serve the nation."[77] Thus the range of initiatives jointly undertaken by Bolivian military leaders and USAID officials in the 1960s and 1970s aimed to develop a modern and passive citizenry consisting of healthy, culturally "whitened" native families.

Some initiatives pursued during these years aimed to intervene in women's reproductive lives for the purposes of national modernization and development. Beginning in 1968, the USAID's "Family Wellbeing" program funneled US$1.3 million into reproductive initiatives in Bolivia over a period of six years and included carrying out studies on contraception and abortion, building the infrastructure of maternal-infant health services and facilities, developing sexual education courses, and distributing (or attempting to distribute) contraceptives to rural-dwelling indigenous women.[78] The program also financed the establishment of two new institutions within Bolivia's Ministry of Health, a Maternal-Infant Health Division (División Materno-Infantil) and the National Family Center (Centro Nacional de Familia, or CENAFA).[79] The latter held sexual education courses in Bolivia's urban centers, provided assistance to preventive-medicine centers in the country, and published dozens of studies on the family, contraception, and abortion in the 1970s and 1980s.[80]

In the midst of the Family Wellbeing initiatives, an international scandal erupted that would make further discussions of fertility regulation, which were already somewhat sensitive in Bolivia, even more contentious. In 1969, Bolivian director Jorge Sanjinés released his film *Yawar Mallku*, or *Blood of the Condor*, which drew on allegations leveled by a local radio show that U.S. Peace Corps volunteers in the countryside were sterilizing indigenous women without their knowledge or consent. The film, which drew audiences both at home and abroad, sparked a serious controversy concerning U.S. contraceptive initiatives in Latin America. Within Bolivia, the movie fanned the fires of existing anti-U.S. sentiments—culminating in the 1971 expulsion of the Peace Corps from the country by then military president Juan José Torres—and provoked widespread opposition toward birth control. At the same time, the film drew worldwide criticism of U.S. population policies as eugenicist projects designed to derail the "demographic explosion" by limiting the reproduction of poor, nonwhite populations abroad.[81]

When the Peace Corps came to Bolivia in 1962, it did so to investigate the efficacy of existing health programs in the countryside in an effort to bolster the success of any future projects.[82] According to Erica Nelson, the Peace Corps's evaluation of health initiatives "reinforced a particular ideology of development in Bolivia: that the acculturation of indigenous groups must necessarily precede the modernization of health services, and the subsequent modernization of the nation."[83] The Peace Corps shared the perspective of other U.S. agencies that Latin America (and other regions of the global south) was overpopulated, and that limiting the birth

rates of the poorest sectors of the population would spur economic development.[84] Documents drafted by USAID and the U.S. State Department
during these years betrayed the interest of the United States in using its
aid programs in Latin America, including the Peace Corps, "as a funnel
for contraceptive supplies and technical expertise."[85] While there is no evidence to suggest that the Peace Corps implemented a large-scale population program in Bolivia, it is clear that at least a handful of its volunteers
distributed birth control to women in the country on an individual basis.
Written correspondence of Peace Corps representatives and investigations
by Bolivian authorities after the episode found that volunteers had inserted
IUDs into indigenous women in the countryside. Disturbingly, at least
some of these women neither knew about, nor consented to, using the
method.[86] There is no way of knowing for certain if volunteers acted in
line with a well-articulated Peace Corps policy or inserted the devices of
their own accord. In either case, however, the IUD insertions—at least
those to which women did not consent—clearly represented both a gross
violation of the women's rights and evidence of eugenicist interventionism in Bolivia. The *Yawar Mallku*-Peace Corps scandal shaped the development of reproductive initiatives in Bolivia for at least two decades. The
USAID-sponsored initiatives that were already in motion at the time of
the debacle received the support of Bolivian officials only after U.S. representatives succeeded in convincing local policy makers that "clinics associated with the program would not provide abortions, or carry out forced
sterilizations or contraception."[87] Supporters of the projects deemed the
contraceptive initiatives programs in "responsible parenthood" rather
than "family planning" or "birth control," in an attempt to avoid drawing the attention or opposition of local populations.[88] Yet, according to
Susanna Rance, these early family planning measures "were not based on
existing demand for family planning services, rather on concrete goals to
reduce fertility levels."[89]

These projects were still in operation when, in September 1976, Catholic officials got wind of one contraceptive initiative sponsored by USAID,

the United Nations Population Fund (UNFPA), and the Banzer Suárez regime. According to then director of the Maternal-Infant Health Division Luis Kushner López, Bolivia decided to launch the family planning program in 1974 after participating in a population conference in Chile, where member countries expressed growing concern over high rates of fertility and maternal mortality.[90] The program would supply IUDs and birth control pills to public health facilities for distribution to a small percentage of women, with an increase in coverage in subsequent years.[91] In response to the allegations, the Minister of Health initially denied that the government was distributing birth control. The following month, however, German-born Cardinal Clemente Maurer met with Banzer, presenting proof of the project's existence and denouncing the program on various grounds, including Bolivia's low population density and the imperialist-eugenicist aims of the project.[92] The meeting was followed by a flurry of press coverage accusing the government of pursuing population control in the country.[93] In the wake of the controversy, Banzer abandoned the family planning program and, in 1977, passed a formal resolution prohibiting any public institution from providing birth control. The same year, the dictator sent a letter to the United Nations (UN) clarifying the pronatalist stance of his administration.[94]

Thus contraceptive debates highlighted conflicting ideas about and agendas concerning race, gender, citizenship, and status at the local, national, and international levels. Bolivian and U.S. health officials were able to come to agreement on the implementation of family planning programs by, as Gallien describes, "reconcil[ing] the New Bolivian Woman with an international development discourse that identified high birth rates as a threat to economic and political stability."[95] The alliance between local and international health experts was further based on the hierarchical ordering of Bolivia's mestizo and white populations over the indigenous majority. Nelson details how health reformers divided Bolivian women into two categories, "traditional" and "modern": "In making 'unregulated' reproduction a characteristic of the 'traditional' women and conversely making modern contraceptive use and a pro-family planning attitude characteristics of 'modern' women, they divided the female population into two halves: those who required the intervention of the state and those who did not."[96] While the "traditional" woman was implicitly indigenous and resided in a high plains region such as La Paz or El Alto, the "modern" woman was likely a mestiza or white inhabitant of a lowland urban center like Santa Cruz.[97] At the same time, contraceptive initiatives granted greater cultural authority and geopolitical status to U.S. reformers—who already "possessed" modernity—than to their Bolivian counterparts, who were attempting to achieve it.

Many Bolivians outside the public health arena opposed the contraceptive initiatives born of this hierarchical ordering of reproductive expertise. From the late 1960s, a variety of sectors of the population—including some national government administrations and many leftist and indigenous organizations—adopted staunchly pronatalist positions.[98] Concerns about international population control in Bolivia became so severe during these years that other forms of aid from abroad, such as powdered milk and medical vaccinations, were rumored to contain sterilizing agents.[99] Meanwhile, the various efforts undertaken during these years to increase access to birth control achieved little success. Western-derived contraceptive methods were not widely available in Bolivia until the late 1980s, and even after they became available, they were neither commonly used nor even necessarily known of until more recently.[100] Although one study from 1976 alleged that there was an "important contraband industry in contraceptives" in the country, the author admitted that the amount of birth control in Bolivia could probably only provide about 2 percent of women of reproductive age with protection from pregnancy.[101]

While health officials would not again take up the issue of birth control until after the return to democratic governance, Banzer did reconsider policy on abortion during his rule. In 1973, the dictator modified Bolivia's penal code to, for the first time, allow abortion in cases of rape and incest and to protect a woman's life or health—as long as the woman in question was able to obtain a judicial order authorizing the procedure.[102] Since few judges were willing to face the public scrutiny that granting such orders might provoke, the penal code modification proved to have little impact on women's access to legal abortion in the country.[103] Between 1973 and 2014, when the requirement for judicial authorization was finally lifted, only six abortions were legally authorized and performed.[104] Mala Htun has noted that, in other Latin American contexts, socially progressive legislation concerning reproduction and the family was sometimes implemented under conservative dictatorships, rather than ostensibly more liberal democratic regimes. Citing the tendency for military regimes to engage in legislative processes requiring little or no public debate or transparency, Htun demonstrates that conservative regimes in Argentina, Uruguay, and Brazil passed relatively progressive policies concerning "abortion, divorce, and the family" in the 1970s and 1980s.[105] This was true even when regimes shared relatively cordial relations with the Catholic Church. (Since the two institutions shared similar values, the Church did not typically view the minor liberalization of family legislation by the military as evidence of greater change to come.[106]) With respect to abortion, these southern cone countries (in addition to Mexico and Cuba) actually represented the vanguard in abortion legislation, decriminalizing the procedure in cases of rape in the 1920s and 1930s, several decades before most European countries did so. In the Latin American countries, military dictators clarified the language of existing abortion laws in the 1970s and 1980s but did not further liberalize access to the procedure—while in Europe, elective abortion became widely available during the same years.[107] To date in Latin America, women can legally access some form of elective abortion only in Cuba, Uruguay, and Mexico City.[108]

In Bolivia, military president Banzer Suárez probably rewrote the country's abortion law in 1973 for similar reasons as did other Latin American military leaders during these years—as part of broader efforts to modernize the state by updating criminal codes and other legislation.[109] (It is also possible that the leader opted to alter the abortion bill after the *Roe v. Wade* decision in the United States that same year.) An additional reason President Banzer may have loosened abortion restrictions at this time was that, by the 1970s, abortion had begun to worry Bolivia's medical community. Two phenomena dating from the 1970s contributed to the growing interest of Bolivia's medical professionals in unsafe abortion. First, by the early part of the decade, abortion in Latin America seems to have represented a significant phenomenon—even if exact rates of the procedure were consistently unclear.[110] In Bolivia, the first studies on abortion were carried out by CENAFA, the entity created under USAID's Family Wellbeing program. Among these were several studies by Antonio Cisneros, then director of CENAFA's Department of Social Research, including a volume from 1976 entitled, *El aborto inducido: Un estudio exploratorio* (Induced Abortion: An Exploratory Study). The study alluded to the severe social stigma against abortion in urban Bolivia and lamented the difficulties of accurately measuring rates of the procedure.[111] Characterizing the "'contraceptive climate'" in 1976 as "still somewhat hostile" and noting the persistence of pronatalist beliefs in the country, Cisneros asserted that women in Bolivia "resort[ed] to abortion as a means to regulate fertility."[112] Secondly, in the 1960s and 1970s, population reformers in the United States intentionally worked to draw the attention of Latin American medical professionals and policy makers to abortion in an effort to promote countries' adoption of family planning programs. While these efforts did not always succeed in increasing the use of contraceptive methods in the region, they did place abortion in the national and international spotlight.[113]

The reproductive policies that were implemented during the military period had contradictory effects on the ongoing efforts of western medical providers to establish dominance over Andean health forms and practitioners. Beginning in 1970, Ministry of Health officials empowered Andean reproductive health practitioners through training programs for indigenous parteras, believing that this would help to build "a bridge . . . between the biomedical system and Quechua and Aymara conceptions of health."[114] Efforts on the part of Bolivian health officials to partner with indigenous midwives during these years reflected a recognition on the part of doctors and policy makers that "parteras and other indigenous healers possessed authority within their communities. If Bolivia's public health system were ever to reach firmly into indigenous cities like El Alto and the still remote rural areas, physicians would need parteras on their side."[115] These partnerships also brought Bolivia's health establishment in line with the recommendations of international bodies such as the World Health Organization (WHO), while further assisting the efforts of local officials to "incorporate" and pacify the country's indigenous populations. Thus training programs for Andean midwives implemented during the military years firmly asserted the authority of doctors over parteras, which helped further consolidate the western medical fields of obstetrics and gynecology. Despite this, Andean midwives trained by Ministry officials continued their traditional practices as well as their activist work, and several went on to occupy significant positions in the public health system.[116]

Finally, although organizing was repressed under the military regimes, resistance and negotiation by Bolivians continued. Protests among miners and peasants, female and male, were prolific during the military years. While these protests in part responded to the military's violent repression and jailing of workers and campesinos, they also reflected opposition to the social, political, and economic reforms passed during the era. A devaluation of Bolivia's currency and Banzer's failure to reach an agreement with Chile over an outlet to the sea, both in the 1970s, spurred considerable protest and revealed the public's growing distrust of the military. A hunger strike led by wives of mine workers in La Paz in 1977, which instantly gained the support of the Catholic Church and human rights organizations, further contributed to the disintegration of military rule.[117] With respect to responses to the military's reproductive policies, women were persistent in negotiating their reproductive lives, terminating pregnancies (and practicing forms of fertility regulation) despite legal restrictions on abortion and birth control; thus concerns over abortion and its impact on rates of maternal death increased dramatically in the 1970s compared to the two previous decades, both in Bolivia and abroad. Following the democratic opening, women's persistent demand for abortion, coupled with broader domestic and international trends, produced dramatic changes in policies on reproduction between the late 1980s and the early twenty-first century.

An Era of Change: Reproduction and the Return to Democracy

The return to democratic governance in 1982 ushered in a new era of popular participation in politics, including the birth of several organizations dedicated to women's equality and renewed activity in existing women's groups. What remain among the most influential groups concerning women emerged in the 1980s, including, in La Paz and El Alto, the Confederación Nacional de Mujeres Campesinas Indígenas Originarias de Bolivia "Bartolina Sisa" (CNMCIOB-BS, 1980); CIDEM (1982); the Centro de Promoción de la Mujer Gregoria Apaza (1983); the Coordinadora de la Mujer (1984); Mujeres Creando (1985); the Taller de Historia y Participación de la Mujer (TAHIPAMU, 1985); and the Centro de Promoción y Salud Integral (CEPROSI, 1988). Of national significance were also the Oficina Jurídica para la Mujer, formed in Cochabamba in 1984, and the Centro Juana Azurduy, founded in Sucre in 1989.[118] While the majority of these organizations did not work directly with reproductive health (at least at first), by drawing women together in public forums such as educational workshops, many ended up facilitating conversations on a range of issues concerning women. These conversations generated awareness of women's experiences with unwanted pregnancy and abortion among the activist community, spurring a few institutions to later take up the banner of women's sexual and reproductive health (if not explicitly abortion rights). Cati Molina, an activist of CIDEM, noted that, during the course of workshops on domestic violence that the organization provided in the 1980s, the mostly Aymara-speaking attendees began to request information on pregnancy prevention and abortion: "When you begin to generate this type of interest, they begin to demand things of you."[119]

In 1985, a now-elderly Víctor Paz Estenssoro—once hero of the national revolution's MNR party—retook the presidency and implemented a series of structural adjustment policies known as the New Economic Policy (NEP). While the NEP succeeded in halting rampant hyperinflation, it exacerbated economic insecurity by slashing public-sector wages and price controls and dismissing over three-quarters of workers in the mining sector. As unemployment ballooned, reaching over 20 percent, so too did the populations of El Alto and La Paz, as migrants from the old mining centers flooded the cities in search of work.[120] Between the mid-1980s and 1992, the population of El Alto grew over 9 percent each year, slowing only slightly to 5 percent per year between 1992 and 2001.[121] The influx of population to the Andean cities increased pressure on an already struggling social services sector.

It was in these years that some women's groups began to offer information or services on contraception, while new organizations emerged that dealt more centrally with reproductive and sexual health. In 1985, CIDEM opened a clinic providing birth control and sexually transmitted infection testing (among other services) to women in El Alto at minimal cost. These years also witnessed the establishment of what today remain some of the largest and most active organizations providing sexual and reproductive health care, including Prosalud (1985); the Centro de Investigación, Educación y Servicios en Salud Sexual y Reproductiva (CIES) (1987); Marie Stopes International (1994); and Ipas (1997).[122] Cognizant of the conflictive history surrounding contraception in Bolivia, these organizations were careful to describe the services they provided as "family planning," rather than "birth control."[123] Alongside the efforts of these organizations, the activities of which largely consisted of western-derived health services, the 1980s also witnessed the emergence of organizations dedicated to the protection of traditional medicine, including Andean childbirth practices.[124]

While during these years the work of organizations providing contraception was no longer prohibited, neither was it actively supported by the government. This was due, in part, to continuing concerns about international eugenicist efforts in Bolivia. In 1988, for instance, the World Bank came under fire after the discovery of a document in which the institution recommended the widespread distribution of birth control.[125] The first government-led health program that included an explicit family planning component was instituted in 1989, when President Jaime Paz Zamora signed into law the National Plan for Survival, Infant Development, and Maternal Health.[126] Within a few months of the program's passage, the Maternal-Infant Health Division of the Ministry of Social Welfare and Public Health, in cooperation with a number of other institutions at home and abroad, formed a committee to determine the future direction of reproductive health efforts in the country. Although it disbanded in 2000 amid conflicts over financing and other matters, the Committee for the Coordination of Reproductive Health nonetheless played a key role in the development of policy on reproduction during these years.[127]

During the 1990s, doctors, activists, and government officials in La Paz and El Alto undertook a variety of initiatives to further public discussion on unwanted pregnancy and abortion. These initiatives included the formation of working groups and conferences, training programs to improve the treatment of women suffering postabortion complications, and social marketing projects to promote contraceptive methods. While some of these initiatives were supported by the Ministry of Health (or at least by some individuals within it), others were organized and implemented by international and/or local civil society organizations. This period also saw the development of a new narrative and language concerning reproductive health and contraception, as reformers sought to distance themselves from the eugenicist history of population control in Bolivia.[128]

One of the first, and largest, initiatives undertaken by progressive reformers was the 1989 Working Seminar Against Abortion, convened by the Ministry of Social Welfare and Public Health, in partnership with several private institutions. Attended by Bolivia's leading family planning reformers, the conference, like earlier contraceptive initiatives, tied the prevention of abortion to the promotion of family planning and women's health. As if to distance the seminar from notions of choice or rights then employed by advocates for legal abortion, ministry official Aida Carvajal de Bustillo declared in her opening comments, "The fight against abortion is about the right to life."[129] Transcripts from the event suggest that Bustillo and her colleagues were especially concerned with the lives of women, which conference attendees acknowledged were being lost in significant numbers due to unsafe abortion. "The risks of abortion are great," wrote medical doctor César Peredo in a paper he delivered at the event, "and family planning methods are practically free of risks."[130] Thus reformers in the late 1980s generally conceptualized abortion as an issue of women's health—and contraceptive methods were seen as a way to assuage that threat.

While by the late 1980s and early 1990s initiatives concerning family planning in Bolivia did not draw as much opposition as they had in earlier decades, those dealing more squarely with abortion sometimes did.[131] The experience of medical doctor Emma Alvarez, who helped organize one conference in 1994, indicates that some sectors of the population opposed public discussions of the procedure. "We were working in Sucre training a number of doctors from the Society of Gynecology in the demystification of abortion. . . . For the first time we were talking to them about it. . . . And a group of women and doctors went to throw stones at us at the hotel because we were doing a 'pro-abortion' workshop. We had to leave through a basement."[132] Medical doctor Daisy Serrato encountered similar—albeit less violent—resistance to a program with which she was involved in the mid-1990s to decrease the mistreatment of women seeking care at public hospitals in La Paz after abortion complications. Serrato remarked that the doctors she trained as part of the Let's Talk Openly (Hablemos con Confianza) program at first appeared to be receptive to instructions that they treat patients with respect, but that later, patients would complain that they had been rebuked by hospital staff. "Just deal with it, if it hurts," Serrato mimicked hospital personnel, "Why do you open your legs if you . . . don't want to get pregnant?"[133]

During the same years that doctors like Serrato and Alvarez were working to destigmatize abortion in Bolivia, two key UN conferences highlighted the increase of international attention to unsafe abortion. The International Conference on Population and Development (Cairo, 1994) and the Fourth World Conference on Women (Beijing, 1995) built on earlier conferences to tackle a range of issues, including population policy, socioeconomic development, and women's rights. The documents that emerged from these conferences urged states to comply with principles of human rights and ethical standards in health care, including guaranteeing patients' right to information in sexual and reproductive health.[134] Since abortion was prohibited in many of the countries that participated in the conferences, UN recommendations were designed, in part, to increase women's access to contraception in an effort to prevent unsafe abortion. According to one representative of a reproductive health clinic in La Paz, "These conventions were extremely important in influencing nations to assume responsibilities with respect to their populations, such as incorporating sexual and reproductive rights among their policies."[135] Following the meetings, the Bolivian government "promise[d] to take action to prevent abortions in conditions of risk and to promote high quality health care services."[136] Five years later, the government formalized the promise by signing a UN-sponsored commitment to eliminate unsafe abortions.[137]

In the years following the international conferences, the Bolivian government passed two unprecedented policies to improve care for women suffering from postabortion complications. The Program for the Treatment of Hemorrhages in the First Half of Pregnancy (Programa para el

Tratamiento de las Hemorragias de la Primera Mitad del Embarazo, or HPME), instituted in 1999, trained medical professionals in a vacuum-aspiration technique to resolve cases of incomplete abortion and miscarriage while providing sensitivity training to improve the bedside manner of staff treating women with abortion-related complications.[138] (The vacuum-aspiration technique can also be used to induce abortion, in addition to resolving cases of miscarriage.) That same year, the government expanded the Basic Health Insurance (Seguro Básico de Salud, or SBS) to include the treatment of complications related to pregnancy loss—which made the aspiration procedure free of charge to all women. While these policies were designed to treat cases of pregnancy loss that began spontaneously, in practice any woman who succeeded in provoking vaginal bleeding during her pregnancy could have her symptoms resolved free of charge in public medical facilities. Thus Bolivian authorities utilized the policies to address growing domestic and international concerns with maternal mortality while leaving aside the question of abortion's legal status.

While for moderate policy makers in Bolivia the world conferences highlighted the global nature of the commitment to prevent unsafe abortion, for women's rights activists the meetings for the first time sparked a serious interest in legalizing the procedure. Remarked Cati Molina, "Abortion['s legal status] is an issue that we took onto our agenda very strongly after Beijing, in particular. . . . It was precisely in 1996 that the 28th of September Campaign came to Bolivia."[139] Born at an international feminist conference in Argentina in 1990, the 28th of September Campaign for the De-Criminalization of Abortion in Latin America and the Caribbean represents the most consolidated sector of the abortion rights movement in the region.[140] In the 1990s, the activities of the Campaign in Bolivia focused primarily on promoting research on abortion and fostering links between supportive organizations at the local and international levels. The most fruitful initiative to emerge during the decade was the Working Group on Unwanted Pregnancy and Abortion, an organization made up of scholars, medical personnel, and activists working on health and human rights. Supported by funding from local and international organizations, the Working Group (active between 1994 and 1998) held conferences and produced publications in an effort to "find multi-faceted solutions to problems associated with unwanted pregnancy and abortion in Bolivia."[141] The group's initiatives succeeded in raising awareness about the impact of unsafe abortion on maternal mortality and ultimately spurred additional organizations and individuals to join the 28th of September Campaign.[142]

In the first decade of the twenty-first century, the Campaign's Bolivian sector focused its attention on abortion law, pursuing legislative change in a few arenas. First, in the late 1990s, activists introduced a measure to Congress to outline specific guidelines to ensure the implementation of Article 266 of the penal code regulating "unpunished" abortion (aborto impune).[143] Although abortion was ostensibly legal in certain circumstances, in practice the procedure was very difficult to obtain. As one study from 2004 remarked, "Past experience has shown us that . . . access to legal abortion depends on the will and the beliefs of the medical and judicial personnel in each case—and on the economic situation of the victim."[144] Although the campaign's proposal to implement guidelines for Article 266 was rejected by Congress at that time, Cati Molina told me the initiative helped spur continuing discussion of abortion: "It gave abortion political visibility during those years."[145]

The Constituent Assembly of 2006–2007 provided activists of the 28th of September Campaign with another avenue to press for the liberalization of abortion law. The Constitution of 2009, approved under President Evo Morales, represented a momentous document in a number of respects, including its measures supporting the rights of women and indigenous people. Particularly significant for women was the document's formal recognition of common-law, heterosexual partnerships, which endowed couples in stable unions with the same rights held by those who were legally married.[146] Due in large part to the participation of women's groups in the Constituent Assembly, the constitution also established Bolivia as a secular (rather than Catholic) nation and explicitly recognized citizens' sexual and reproductive rights.[147] Remarked Cati, "Many of the organizations that participated in the Constituent Assembly advanced proposals for the recognition of sexual and reproductive rights, but not of abortion. The Campaign had three nonnegotiable principles: recognition of sexual and reproductive rights, of a secular state, and . . . that the right to life from the moment of conception not be incorporated."[148] Fanny Barrutia, an activist with the Campaign, concurred that most of the women's advocates who participated in the assembly did not support raising the issue of abortion in the constitution, which was seen as too polarizing, and instead favored less contentious rights.[149] In the end, the constitution reflected the more moderate position of most of the women's organizations in attendance, and it makes no mention of abortion.[150] At the same time, all three of the Campaign's nonnegotiable principles were met by the document. Furthermore, in leaving the definition of sexual and reproductive rights unspecified, the 2009 constitution provided a path for future legislative action on the abortion law. Within a year, the Campaign, supported by activists from over fifty organizations, introduced a measure to the legislature to include abortion as one of the sexual and reproductive rights recognized by the new constitution.[151] Citing a legislative agenda that was already crowded with issues to address, Morales's Movimiento al Socialismo (Movement for Socialism, MAS) party announced that it was temporarily shelving the abortion debate.[152]

The disagreements on abortion that emerged between some of the women's groups at the Constituent Assembly are indicative of broader conflicts in the platforms of groups representing indigenous women and those whose primary constituency and leadership are made up of white and mestiza women.[153] (It is important to note that there are also important differences *within* each of these camps.[154]) One of the largest organizations representing indigenous women of the highlands is the CNMCIOB-BS, more commonly known as "las Bartolinas." Like many groups representing indigenous women, the Bartolinas are committed to notions and practices of Andean communal organization and of gender complementarity (described in chapter 2) and reject the designation of "feminist," which is seen as linked to the urban, mestiza-led movements. At the same time, a central goal of the Bartolinas is gender equity, and at the Constituent Assembly, the organization forwarded proposals aimed at achieving this objective in a number of areas, including, "political participation, land rights, education, and domestic violence."[155] The Bartolinas also urged support for traditional medicine and midwifery but opposed abortion rights. The Confederación de Pueblos Indígenas de Bolivia (Confederation of Indigenous Peoples of Bolivia, or CIDOB), a group representing indigenous women from Bolivia's lowlands, drafted its own proposal that included "women's right to choose the number of children they have and their right to use contraceptives."[156] Ultimately, the largest organizations representing indigenous people (both women and men) came together under the Pacto de Unidad (United Pact). The Pact eventually forwarded a proposal that, in terms of sexual and reproductive issues, assumed language closer to that of the dominant women's organizations than that of the Bartolinas; however, like many of the more moderate mestiza groups, it opposed abortion rights.[157] Other, more radical feminist groups, such as Mujeres Creando (Women Creating), which mobilizes against structural racism, patriarchy, neocolonialism, and heteronormativity in Bolivian society, "acted as a strong critique of the constituent assembly process and . . . the MAS government in general, denouncing what it considered the instrumentalization of women by Evo Morales's government."[158]

More recently, activists favoring abortion's decriminalization followed a two-pronged approach, trying to modify the penal code while at the same time advancing proposals for abortion to be recognized as a reproductive right under the constitution.[159] These efforts gained congressional support in 2012, when MAS-party deputy and Aymara woman Patricia Mancilla introduced a measure challenging the constitutionality of several articles of the 1973 penal code, three of which concerned abortion. Part of the reason that Deputy Mancilla may have introduced her measure when she did was the January 2012 jailing of a Guaraní woman known as Helena for taking tablets of misoprostol in order to induce an abortion.[160] The woman became pregnant after a rape and, fearful of reporting the rape to police and unaware that she was eligible for a legal abortion, Helena recurred to taking misoprostol; she was eventually jailed for eight months. (While few women are jailed for abortion in Bolivia, many women have a legitimate reason to fear it; 775 cases of abortion were investigated by the district attorney's office between 2008 and 2012.[161]) Mancilla's challenge to the penal code, which was turned over for debate to the Plurinational Constitutional Tribunal (TCP), resulted in the abolition of the requirement that a woman seeking a legal abortion first obtain authorization from a judge in February 2014.[162] The scrapping of this requirement expanded access to legal abortion, though most women still recurred to the procedure through other channels. By December 2016, Ipas estimated that 120 legal abortions had been performed—up from the 6 that took place between 1973 and 2014.[163]

In December 2017, the Morales administration promulgated a new penal code that would have included broader stipulations for legal abortion than ever before—had the code not been fully repealed a few months later. Article 153 expanded the circumstances in which a woman might obtain a legal abortion, including up to eight weeks in pregnancy for any woman who already had dependents (a common situation for women who terminate pregnancies), or who was an adolescent or a student. A final measure that would have decriminalized abortion for women living in "extreme poverty" was debated, but ultimately not included.[164] While the measures concerning abortion did not draw significant public opposition, other stipulations of the law sparked widespread protests by diverse groups, including physicians, transport workers, journalists, and religious organizations. In the wake of these protests, the code was fully repealed on January 21, 2018, leaving abortion's legal status unchanged from 2014.[165]

The failure of the state to *reglamentar* (specify) the terms on which laws are put into practice is a central complaint of many women's rights advocates in Bolivia. Referring to the Constitution's recognition of sexual and reproductive rights, medical doctor Alessandra Muñecas remarked, "We [Bolivians] are actually pretty progressive people, but what we're lacking is implementation. . . . We have norms and laws that are even more progressive than those in many other Latin American countries but . . . when it's time to put them into practice, things do not go as they should."[166] Thus many activists and medical doctors in Bolivia worry that the new guarantee of citizens' sexual and reproductive rights will go the way of the 1973 law on legal abortion and remain, essentially, a piece of paper.

Reproductive health reformers and advocates of women's rights in Bolivia lament the limited nature of recent policy shifts on unwanted pregnancy and abortion and often attribute these limitations to the influence of the Catholic Church.[167] Although most individuals I interviewed believed that the power of the Catholic Church in Bolivia has declined over the last few decades, most also asserted that its authority continues to be important, since the institution administers countless schools, health care facilities, and civil society organizations in the country.[168] Most Church-run institutions in Bolivia refuse to provide information on (or to administer) western-derived contraceptive methods, and some even refuse to treat women seeking emergency care for postabortion complications.[169] (Instead, some Church programs offer workshops to the public on the use of "natural" forms of birth control.[170]) In terms of its political work, the Catholic Church does not administer a "pro-life" movement of any significance; for instance, Father Mariano Solana remarked that the work of the Church in promoting the pro-life cause is ongoing and part of its daily activities, rather than taking the form of a specific campaign. However, officials of the Catholic Church regularly weigh in on social and political issues, and its positions continue to have a significant impact on both public opinion and policy in the country.[171] The continuing influence of

Catholicism in Bolivia has been joined in recent decades by other religious sects, especially Christian denominations, who together grew to represent nearly 20 percent of the population by 2001.[172]

In its proposal to the Constituent Assembly, the Conferencia Episcopal Boliviana (Episcopal Conference of Bolivia, or CEB), the official representative of the Catholic Church, declared that "the majority of the Bolivian population is Christian and Catholic [and] the new constitution . . . cannot deny this spiritual reality."[173] As part of its proposal, the CEB pushed for the right to life to be recognized from the moment of conception.[174] Although the measure was not incorporated into the new constitution, the document's existing declaration of the right to life is often cited as a potential obstacle to further liberalization of abortion law.[175] Following the constitution's passage, Catholics and Protestants alike bemoaned the establishment of a lay state and the recognition of sexual and reproductive rights as attacks on religious values.[176] In response to more recent efforts by 28th of September activists to push for the recognition of abortion as one of the aforementioned rights, Catholic officials have instead suggested an emphasis on sex education—albeit, education limited to "natural" forms of contraception.[177]

It is unclear to what degree average Bolivians support the position of the country's religious institutions on questions of sexual and reproductive rights—although evidence suggests that public opinion is more flexible than that of the Catholic Church. In a 2003 survey of 1,500 Bolivian Catholics, 56 percent of respondents believed that abortion should be permitted in some circumstances, while 50 percent "believe[d] it is possible [for a woman] to be a good Catholic even after having an abortion."[178] Survey respondents were even more accepting of western-derived contraceptive methods, with 91 percent believing that public health facilities in the country should provide birth control pills and condoms to adults free of charge.[179] Despite these figures, most progressive sectors in Bolivia believe that the power of the Church and other conservative elements will prevent further liberalization of abortion laws, or even the effective implementation of those laws that do exist. "The Church is very strong in Bolivia," remarked medical doctor Daisy Serrato. "There are some people who are working in government that are like us, that believe in women's rights. But society won't let you. . . . Even the law of sexual and reproductive rights in the Constitution is still asleep."[180]

CHAPTER 2

Double Discourses

SOCIAL ATTITUDES ON SEXUALITY
AND REPRODUCTION

When you talk about abortion with people, it's a theme that is still very sensitive. People don't have very clear positions on abortion, they prefer not to talk about it or take a stand on it—they prefer to put themselves behind the subject and never face it directly.

—Julián Costa, employee of a clinical facility
in La Paz that provides abortions

The contradictions that a community, culture, or text can contain eluci-date its myths, its ideologies, its worldview. Things that appear opposed from one perspective can be consistent and coherent from another point of view, much as two objects can blend into one when the observer stands at an angle that aligns them precisely. *—Laura Briggs*

When I asked Daisy Serrato if her family knew that she performed abor-tions as part of her job as a medical doctor in La Paz, she remarked, "My parents have always known what I do, but my sisters don't. But maybe they just pretend not to, because they also send me their friends. I mean, they continue with this discourse of, 'Oh, what a barbarity! [abortion],' but then women come and tell me, 'Your sister sent me, I would like you to help my daughter.' . . . This is the double discourse that everyone has."[1] As the comments of Julián and Daisy suggest, abortion is not a topic of frequent discussion in the public sphere in La Paz and El Alto, and when it is addressed, the subject is fraught. While some avoid taking a firm position on abortion, others, like Daisy's sisters, adopt a "double discourse," publicly condemning the procedure while privately tolerating it—even assisting friends and loved ones to locate abortion providers. This phenomenon is not new, unique to Bolivia, nor limited to attitudes on abortion. Examining divorce law in Chile and abortion advocacy in both Chile and Colombia, Bonnie Shepard argues that double discourses in Latin America extend beyond individuals' behavior to constitute a "political and cultural system"[2] that allows for the maintenance of repressive policies alongside "expanding private sexual and reproductive choices behind the scenes."[3] The conflict between publicly declared attitudes concerning sex and reproduction and behaviors practiced in private appears to be particularly prevalent in urban areas of Latin America where the power of the Catholic Church is strong.

This chapter examines social attitudes toward sexuality and reproduction in urban Bolivia between the mid-twentieth century and 2010. It first examines the efforts of doctors, population specialists, and government officials to capture the incidence of abortion and western-derived contraceptive use beginning in the 1960s. While the studies that these professionals produced reveal little about actual rates of abortion in urban Bolivia during these years, they do highlight the concern of public officials and medical authorities with the practice. They also reveal policy makers' preoccupation with encouraging women to use western-derived contraceptive methods, rather than the nonclinical methods used by indigenous women. Doctors' and policy makers' efforts to capture the incidence of individuals' use of birth control were more successful. The studies they produced revealed considerable distrust of western-derived contraceptive methods and an atmosphere of silence and stigma around sexual and reproductive behavior. In the first decade of the twenty-first century, studies suggested that rates of western-derived contraceptive use increased among many women in urban Bolivia, yet significant distrust remained.

The second section of the chapter examines a broader swath of attitudes toward sexuality and reproduction, beyond the medical and policy spheres, and focuses particularly on La Paz and El Alto. Based on interviews with women who live in these cities, police and religious officials, personnel at private clinics and public hospitals, and activists on both sides of the debate over abortion's legal status, this section illuminates the connections between social attitudes on sex and reproduction and broader conceptualizations of women and their place in society. It finds that most individuals in La Paz and El Alto claimed to oppose abortion, condemning both the women who sought the procedure and the doctors who performed it. At the same time, the chapter finds that individuals' opinions about abortion were much more nuanced in certain settings. In private conversations, or when an unwanted or unintended pregnancy touched the life of an interviewee or of an interviewee's friend or relative, many paceños (La Paz residents) and alteños (El Alto residents) believed that abortion was acceptable. The contradictions between individuals' public and private positions on abortion suggest that in urban Bolivia, as in other world regions, not only abortion providers and their clients but also individuals who admit to supporting women's recurrence to abortion continue to confront social stigma. Faced with the fear of what Bolivians call the qué dirán (what others might say), most individuals roundly claim to oppose abortion, even if, in private settings, they tolerate or accept it.

THE COMPLEXITIES OF INCIDENCE: OFFICIAL ANXIETIES WITH UNWANTED PREGNANCY AND ABORTION

In his 1976 book Induced Abortion: An Exploratory Study, Antonio Cisneros lamented the near impossibility of "obtaining a solid and clear picture of the . . . incidence [of abortion] in the country."[4] Published just three years after a modification of Bolivia's penal code decriminalized abortion in cases of rape and incest or when a pregnancy threated a woman's life or health, the study represented one of the first attempts to capture the incidence of abortion in the country. Judging by the tone of Cisneros's comments, completing this task in a nation such as Bolivia—where the procedure was officially unreported and often morally condemned—posed a significant challenge. "Unfortunately, due to the sociocultural context [surrounding abortion], we lack the systematized and calibrated information that would allow us to obtain a solid and clear picture of its incidence."[5]

Studies from Latin America, where abortion is prohibited in most countries, note that data on the incidence of the procedure are inconsistent, with underreporting representing a substantial problem. Most studies on abortion incidence in the region have relied on either household or hospital surveys for which "accurate reporting is discouraged by the nature of the subject and the general illegality of [the procedure]," or on registration or discharge statistics collected by medical facilities.[6] While household surveys ask women to discuss their reproductive histories on their doorsteps or in their living rooms—something many women are understandably loath to do—hospital surveys ask patients at the bedside whether they intentionally provoked their bleeding—and thus to admit to an illegal act. Hospital statistics, for their part, record numbers of women hospitalized for any type of pregnancy loss, including abortion, spontaneous miscarriage, or the loss of a pregnancy whose cause is unclear (which I refer to hereafter as unexplained miscarriage). According to Chilean medical doctor Benjamín Viel, hospital statistics "can never be expected to show more than the tip of the iceberg," since most abortions probably do not require follow-up care and in many regions, particularly rural areas of Latin America, medical facilities are scant.[7] In addition, many women, fearing interrogation or mistreatment, may hesitate to visit medical facilities for complications following pregnancy loss.[8] In general, most scholars concur that actual abortion rates in Latin America are likely much higher than calculated estimates suggest.[9] Recent measures for the region estimate that the rate of unsafe abortion in South America alone is higher than that of any other world region except middle and eastern Africa.[10]

Prior to the twentieth century, it is unlikely that abortion rates in Latin America were high, since infant mortality probably limited family size. With improvements in public health across much of the region in the first four decades of the twentieth century, infant mortality declined and the population ballooned, growing at a rate of between 1 and 3 percent per year after the 1930s. It is in these first decades of the twentieth century that abortion rates are thought to have increased.[11] What is believed to be the earliest and most accurate data on abortion incidence hails from Chile.[12] In her study of maternity in the country, Jadwiga Pieper Mooney notes that, as early as the 1930s, medical personnel began to record numbers of women hospitalized each year for complications they believed to be caused by abortion.[13] Despite doctors' suspicions that considerable numbers of maternal deaths were caused by induced abortion, medical personnel were reluctant to address the "abortion epidemic" publicly, due to the "treatment of sexuality and contraception as private matters, coupled with the illegal nature of abortion."[14] By the 1960s, rising rates of hospitalization attributed to abortion prompted doctors to undertake additional studies in an attempt to more accurately measure the procedure's incidence. The studies, based on household surveys in a number of different areas of the country, found that "illegal induced abortion [in Chile] was . . . much more frequent than hospital statistics indicated."[15] Although the total number of abortions per year was believed to have declined between 1960 and 1987 due to the increased availability of birth control, by 1990, estimates of abortions in Chile remained quite high—somewhere between 100,000 and 190,000 per year.[16] The studies conducted in Chile served to draw attention to the frequency of abortion in Latin America as a whole.[17]

From the early twentieth century in Bolivia, both medical doctors and policy makers expressed concern over what they believed to be high rates of abortion. Ann Zulawski reviews a sampling of medical records from La Paz's public Hospital General (General Hospital) from 1942 to 1949 which suggests that abortion may have been widespread by that time.[18] By the time of Cisneros's 1976 study, abortion ostensibly constituted "a major social and public health concern" in Bolivia.[19] Drawing on data from surveys of over 2,500 women (1,455 of whom lived in La Paz), Cisneros estimated rates of contraceptive use and abortion in three Bolivian cities. The study found that just over 10 percent of respondents in La Paz had terminated at least one pregnancy.[20] Based on these data, Cisneros elaborated figures of a "very exploratory and tentative [nature]" suggesting that 12,178 abortions took place each year in La Paz, or thirty-three per day.[21] With a population of 117,100 women of reproductive age (WRA) in La Paz in 1976, this amounts to an abortion rate of almost 104 abortions per 1,000 WRA—more than twice the rate in Chile in 1975, and about three times the rate that Cisneros found for the Bolivian cities of Cochabamba and Santa Cruz.[22]

Ten years later, a group of Bolivian doctors conducted a study on abortion based on hospital statistics that—considering some scholars' contention that hospital data may underestimate abortion incidence—somewhat predictably placed rates of the procedure much lower than Cisneros's figures. The study drew on the assessments of medical staff at twelve hospitals in the country as to whether women hospitalized for complications related to abortion, miscarriage, or unexplained miscarriage during a year-long period had induced their symptoms. Authored by the former director of Bolivia's Maternal-Infant Health Division, Luis Kushner López, in addition to other colleagues, the study estimated that 77 percent of hospitalized patients had probably suffered spontaneous abortions, while 23 percent had likely provoked their bleeding.[23] (To further complicate matters, the authors indicate that the number of women arriving to hospital facilities during the year of the study—and thus the number of recorded cases of abortion and miscarriage—may have been lower than usual due to labor strikes taking place at the time in the transport and health care sectors.) Based on the numbers of cases recorded at hospitals in each city, the study estimated an abortion rate in La Paz of less than 5 per 1,000 WRA—about one-twentieth of the figure estimated by Cisneros—with rates in Cochabamba and Santa Cruz at approximately

14 and 7 abortions per 1,000 WRA, respectively.[24] In other words, the 1986 study found abortion rates throughout the country at only a fraction of those estimated in 1976, with the rate in La Paz *lower*—not higher—than that of other Bolivian cities.[25] The Cisneros and Kushner López studies also differed with respect to their findings on the demographic profile of the woman most likely to terminate her pregnancy. Whereas in 1976, Cisneros reported that the woman most likely to seek abortion in La Paz was married, in her twenties or thirties, and already had more than three children, Kushner López et al. found almost the reverse. Thus, in 1986, a teenage, childless paceña who was single or separated was more likely to have sought abortion than an older or partnered woman. (The study by Kushner López et al., which also considered educational level, found that women were equally likely to have induced their abortions regardless of how many years they had attended school.[26]) This means that either abortion rates declined dramatically between 1976 and 1986 and the procedure was sought by women in remarkably different stages of life or the methods used to assess abortion during these years yielded incomplete or erroneous results—or both.

In an attempt to improve the accuracy of hospital data in estimating abortion rates, in the 1980s, the World Health Organization (WHO) developed a method of measuring the likelihood that women hospitalized with complications from pregnancy loss had intentionally induced their abortions. The WHO method relies on the combination of a physical exam for cervical trauma and a conversation with the hospitalized woman regarding her feelings about the pregnancy and her contraceptive use.[27] (The Kushner López study determined the likelihood that hospitalized patients had induced their abortions "according to the opinion of the medical investigator at the moment of [the woman's] admission to the hospital [upon assessing] the medical profile and physical condition [of the woman]"; it is unclear, however, if these researchers employed the specific method developed by WHO.[28]) Susheela Singh and Deirdre Wulf utilized the WHO method in a 1993 study on women hospitalized following

pregnancy loss in four Latin American countries. The study's findings
for Bolivia, which were based on data from five hospitals throughout the
country, suggested that a far greater proportion of patients had induced
their abortions than did the Kushner López study of just a few years earlier:
"In Bolivia . . . seventy-one percent of all women in the study were hospitalized with . . . complications that might have resulted from induced abortion, compared with thirteen percent reported by Bolivian women."[29]
The profile of the woman most likely to have terminated her pregnancy,
according to Singh and Wulf (and based on data from all four countries),
represented a combination of the characteristics found by Cisneros and
Kushner López et al. Thus the 1993 study found that the hospital patient
most likely to have induced her abortion was single, over thirty years old,
and already had five children.[30]

   Measures from the first decade of the twenty-first century suggest that
abortion remained a significant phenomenon in Bolivia. According to hospital statistics, the total number of pregnancy losses seen in medical
facilities in La Paz and El Alto between 2000 and 2010 was considerable—
although it is sometimes unclear what proportion of all medical visits
these pregnancy losses represented. Comparing numbers of pregnancy
losses of twenty weeks' gestational age and under (including cases of abortion, miscarriage, and unexplained miscarriage) to numbers of births
and cesarean sections at La Paz's Women's Hospital (HM) suggests at the
very least that the treatment of pregnancy loss constituted a significant
portion of the hospital's activity. In 2007, the HM saw about 1,300 cases
of pregnancy loss, compared to about 3,390 births and cesarean sections,
while numbers for 2008 were approximately 1,265 pregnancy losses and
3,630 full-term pregnancies.[31] At the public Bolivian-Dutch Municipal
Hospital (HMBH) in the city of El Alto, numbers of pregnancy losses for
the same years were fewer—about 600 in 2006, 740 in 2007, and 675 in
2008—but these represented a considerable percentage of total gynecological visits for those years. In 2006, pregnancy losses represented
almost 78 percent of gynecological visits at the facility, with percentages

amounting to 63 percent and 51 percent for 2007 and 2008, respectively.[32] The largest, most recent study on abortion in Bolivia concurs with the hospital data cited here. Based on a combination of household and hospital surveys and in-depth interviews, Louise Bury and her colleagues spoke with nearly 1,400 women from the cities of Sucre, Santa Cruz, Cochabamba, La Paz, and El Alto.[33] Of the 1,175 women who had engaged in sexual intercourse, 48 percent said they had experienced at least one unwanted pregnancy and of these, 31 percent attempted to abort their last unwanted pregnancy. Overall, 13 percent of women surveyed had terminated a pregnancy—a number the authors believed was almost certainly low due to underreporting.[34]

In general, a review of the available data on the incidence of abortion in urban Bolivia over the last half-century suggests two broad patterns: first, that abortion has been ubiquitous in the country, and second, that it is persistently unclear just *how* ubiquitous it has been. As the inconsistencies in these studies make clear, a number of obstacles exist to accurately measuring abortion rates in Latin America. One consists of the variations in the methods used to measure it. Beyond the challenges of working with hospital data and hospital surveys, categories employed to estimate rates of reproductive events, such as "women of reproductive age," are defined in inconsistent ways.[35] Perhaps the most obvious obstacle to obtaining accurate data on abortion's incidence is the various complications created by its prohibition. Since abortion is unregulated, the facilities and individuals that perform the procedure do not report these to any government body.[36] Most public hospitals in the region did not track numbers of women admitted for pregnancy loss until the 1990s. Measures of abortion that rely on discussions with women, for their part, may be equally unreliable. A woman who is asked by a survey-taker or a medical provider whether or not she has had an abortion may face both social stigma and legal repercussions if she chooses to respond honestly. A woman may also feel that sex, or any reproductive event resulting therefrom, is too private to discuss with hospital staff. This may be particularly true if members of the personnel are men or if she feels she has been treated insensitively.[37] Thus women may deny having had an abortion, or claim that bleeding during pregnancy was caused by an accidental trauma. Furthermore, it is difficult to discern an induced abortion from a spontaneous miscarriage by physical exam alone.[38]

Measures of western-derived contraceptive use in Latin America over the last several decades tended to be more reliable than those for abortion. Evidence suggests that abortion rates in some countries may have decreased in the 1980s due to the increased availability of western-derived birth control methods.[39] Data for Bolivia, however, reveal that these methods were not widely available until the early 1990s, and even after they became available, these were neither commonly used nor even necessarily known until more recently.[40] One 1983 study revealed that only about 20 percent of the 5,000 women interviewed could name a western-derived method of birth control, while 9 percent were using such a method.[41] By the time of Bolivia's 1989 national demographic survey, the use of western-derived birth control methods had increased somewhat; thus, 30 percent of partnered women aged fifteen to forty-nine were using contraception at the time of the survey, with 12 percent using western-derived and 18 percent traditional methods.[42] Having inaugurated its first comprehensive family planning program in late 1989, Bolivia was several years behind the development of similar programs in other Latin American countries. State-sponsored family planning initiatives were inaugurated in the mid-1970s in Chile, Peru, Argentina, Mexico, and Brazil, although many of these programs were later canceled or significantly reduced under military regimes or in the face of local opposition.[43] While this may speak to the underdeveloped nature of Bolivia's public health establishment vis-à-vis other Latin American countries, it also belies the fear of population control initiatives that emerged in response to international interventionism (described in detail in chapter 1).

Partly in response to this imperialist history, the 1980s and 1990s witnessed a widespread distrust of birth control in Bolivia; this continues, to a certain extent, today.[44] In studies examining ideas about birth control during the period, women often reported fearing the potential negative health impacts of using contraceptive methods. One study carried out between 1986 and 1987 found the "[fear of] health problems" to be a significant deterrent to women's use of contraception.[45] A 1994 study of nearly 700 urban Aymara women found that "almost all of the women [surveyed] had heard alarming stories and rumors about the harmful side effects of contraceptive methods."[46] According to the study, participants feared "general . . . and specific illnesses," in addition to the "consequences of having foreign objects or substances introduced into the body," such as the IUD and hormonal birth control.[47] While the first decade of the twenty-first century saw an increase in women's familiarity with western-derived contraceptive methods, their distrust of these remained. Bolivia's 2003 National Demographic and Health Survey found that only 16 percent of women reported not using contraception due to lack of knowledge, while 21 percent cited a fear of side effects.[48] My own interview data support the notion that women in La Paz and El Alto feared the health impacts of birth control. "Everyone used to say, 'That's going to cause cancer,'" remarked Marcela Flores, a mestiza woman who began to use a western-derived method of birth control for the first time in 2005.[49] In addition, some Bolivians simply doubted that methods could be relied upon to prevent pregnancy. The 1987 study cited earlier, which surveyed women in three Bolivian cities, found that "fear of inefficacy" constituted another reason women did not use birth control[50]; some women I interviewed also opted to use traditional methods of fertility regulation because they had become pregnant while using a western-derived method.

The lack of confidence in western-derived contraceptive methods is linked to a broader distrust of western medical notions, treatments, and facilities by both women and men in Bolivia; this may be particularly true for individuals of indigenous descent but is also the case for many mestizos. The 1994 study cited earlier found that most women were loath to use contraception due to "a deep suspicion of modern medicine and medical

practitioners, who are not seen as reliable sources of information."[51]
According to the study, women's suspicion of western medicine was owed
in part to the discrimination they suffered when visiting health facilities.[52]
Interview data suggest that the mistreatment of women at health facilities—
including condescending, rude, and even violent language and behavior
by medical personnel—continues to be a significant problem.[53] Women's
distrust of western medical care may be further exacerbated by the inad-
equacy of public health facilities, which can be overcrowded and lack even
basic infrastructure.[54] Finally, and perhaps related to the question of inadequate infrastructure, many women I interviewed preferred not to visit
western health facilities because the practices at these facilities in attending childbirth, in particular, differed so markedly from those with which
women were familiar and preferred (these practices are addressed in chapters 4 and 5).

Contemporary distrust of western medicine in the Andes may also be
entwined, historically and culturally, with broader processes of capital
accumulation and technological development that occurred across the
nineteenth and twentieth centuries. Mary Weismantel explores stories of
white bogeymen in the Bolivian and Peruvian countryside who would
attack indigenous campesinos for a range of nefarious purposes, usually
related to economic gain. In the 1970s and 1980s, campesinos alleged that
these terrifying figures, known as ñakaqs, kharisiris, or pishtacos, stole fat
from the bodies of indigenous people, using it to repay foreign debt, make
high-quality soap for export, or power U.S. electric companies.[55] (Andean
healers consider fat, along with blood and air, to be essential bodily fluids, the balance and circulation of which are essential to overall health.[56])
According to Weismantel, ideas about ñakaqs are intimately related to the
health and bodily integrity of indigenous campesinos struggling to survive in a capitalist system. Thus the "invisible labor" of indigenous residents of the Andes, "creates the wealth that belongs to others. For the very
poor in peripheral economies, such labor eats up their bodily health and
strength, leaving them thin and broken. . . . [G]oods and capital accumu-

late around the white body, while the Indian sees her possessions devoured by ever-accumulating debt."[57] In a context in which selling one's labor or land to a white, western employer in the nineteenth or twentieth centuries left indigenous Andeans on the short end of an unfair arrangement, present-day Bolivians may hesitate to trust the recommendations of western medical practitioners. Concomitantly, widespread suspicion (and low rates of use) of birth control stem from a range of historical and cultural circumstances that cannot be adequately explained by professionals' assessments that women are simply "ignorant" about contraception.

It is further important to note that the "traditional" or nonclinical forms of birth control to which many women recur in Bolivia—including periodic abstinence and, less commonly, withdrawal—are nearly as effective in preventing pregnancy as some western-derived forms of birth control. (In other words, it may be unwise to attach a value judgment to western-derived methods as necessarily being "better" or more reliable than nonclinical methods.) In one study, withdrawal was found to be 96 percent effective with "perfect" use, compared to a 98 percent efficacy rate when condoms are used "perfectly."[58] Measures of the typical, rather than perfect, use of condoms and traditional methods further suggest that the two types of methods are at least roughly comparable in efficacy.[59] A major problem with the use of both western-derived and nonclinical methods of fertility regulation in Bolivia, however, is opposition on the part of many men. Women interviewed for the 1994 study, for instance, reported picking fights with their male partners or sharing beds with their children in an attempt to enforce periods of abstinence with which their partners might otherwise not comply.[60] Some men in Bolivia also oppose their partners' use of western-derived contraceptives because they believe women use birth control in order to engage in sex with other partners without fearing pregnancy.[61]

Evidence suggests that a distrust of western medicine and machismo continued to shape attitudes toward, and the use of, contraception in Bolivia in the early twenty-first century. (This is in addition to structural barriers to contraceptive use, such as lack of access, which remained present.) Thus a 2010 survey of 1,175 sexually active women nationwide reported that "mistrust of . . . safety or effectiveness," opposition on the part of male partners, and shame associated with the use of contraceptives represented the most important deterrents to women's use of birth control.[62] At the same time, the study reveals that more women were using western-derived methods than ever before—suggesting that there have been *some* changes in attitudes toward birth control in recent years.[63]

Contemporary Attitudes toward Sex, Pregnancy, and Abortion in La Paz and El Alto

When I asked him if people's attitudes toward unwanted pregnancy and abortion had changed over the twenty-five years he had been working in medicine in La Paz, medical doctor Miguel Ramírez—who provided abortions, in addition to a range of other services—remarked somewhat pessimistically, "Culture does not change, you know? Sometimes . . . people don't want to come here [to the clinic] for birth control because they think people are watching them. . . . It's like a feeling of shame. Women tell me, 'People are going to say that I am a bad person.' So, unfortunately, no. We try to do a lot with education, but social control exists—the neighborhood, the town, one's brother, one's relative, one's neighbor—all with these closed-minded ideas."[64]

When asked, most men and women of a variety of social sectors—in addition to many doctors, political officials, and other individuals— claimed to oppose abortion in most circumstances, if not necessarily birth control. Despite this, when pressed, most people admitted to tolerating abortion in particular circumstances or when a friend or loved one had procured the procedure. The disconnect between individuals' public and private attitudes toward abortion was indicative of a broader stigmatization of the procedure in early twenty-first-century La Paz and El Alto, which stemmed from three main factors: (1) the powerful workings of machismo and broader structures of patriarchy in urban Andean society; (2) Catholic, and to a lesser extent Protestant, beliefs and education, in addition to a context of closed-minded attitudes toward sexuality, which interviewees described with the adjective, *cerrado*; (3) pronatalism, as well as the larger implications of what Lynn M. Morgan and Elizabeth F. S. Roberts describe as "contestations over 'rights'" that often take place in debates over abortion and other reproductive phenomena in Latin America.[65] Many individuals I interviewed opposed abortion not only due to religious convictions or demographic concerns but also because they conceived of the procedure as an attack on traditional family values and gender roles. Thus abortion was often seen as a tool that allowed women to postpone or reject motherhood in lieu of professional aspirations.

Machista attitudes and behaviors had a significant impact on social perceptions toward abortion, sexuality, and contraception in La Paz and El Alto. Machismo was frequently cited by interviewees to explain a variety of attitudes and behaviors on the part of men, including their opposition to women's use of western-derived contraceptive methods and their refusal to participate in periodic abstinence; their violent and controlling behavior toward female family members; and their tendency toward sexual infidelity. A few interviewees asserted that women could also be machista, or that a culture of machismo shaped society at large. As such, machismo emerged in interview testimony as the most visible component of broader structures of patriarchy that permeated urban Andean society. Interviewees' characterizations of machismo were overwhelmingly negative—which may be unsurprising, since the majority of my interviewees were women who shared sexual and familial relationships with men. However, several male interviewees I interviewed, particularly doctors and religious officials, also lamented the impacts of machismo on life in La Paz and El Alto—specifically, men's attitudes and behaviors that they felt led to unwanted pregnancies, such as their refusal to participate in fertility regulation and their tendency to pressure their partners for sex. As Matthew C. Gutmann argues of the Mexican context, machismo in Bolivia is multivalent and complex, impacting many areas of life.[66] In addition—as has been argued by numerous scholars regarding the workings of not only gendered hierarchies but also racial and sexual ones—machismo operates not as a static phenomenon but is produced, reproduced, and contested in everyday interactions and institutions.[67] In Bolivia, scholars have argued that compulsory military service is one institutional structure that reinforces notions of masculinity that degrade women, while at the same time hierarchically ordering men along racial and class lines.[68]

Concepción Camacho, a white, twenty-six-year-old mother of two living in the Ciudad Satélite neighborhood of El Alto, said that after the birth of her second child, "[my partner and I] talked about family planning. We don't have prejudices in talking about this topic." When I asked if it was common for partners to discuss this, Concepción remarked, "No, because our society is machista. Men think that if you want to use birth control, it's because you want to be with other men while they are off at work. So, it's complicated. But I have a strong character, and I've made my husband understand!"[69] (Concepción punctuated this comment with the sound "*ya!*," an expression often used in La Paz and El Alto to give what has been said a humorous connotation.) Paula Rojas, a forty-year-old mestiza woman also living in Ciudad Satélite, said that she hid her use of the contraceptive pill from her husband. "It's better if he doesn't know, because if he knew, we might fight."[70] Marcela Flores, the forty-five-year-old mestiza woman cited earlier, complained that, prior to the availability of birth control pills, her husband's tendency to pressure her for sex in the past had led her to face two unwanted pregnancies, which she eventually terminated. Fortunately, not all women lacked their partners' support in planning their families. Elsa Canqui, a fifty-year-old Aymara woman who wore the pollera, told me that after she had her son at fifteen years old, her husband suggested the couple use periodic abstinence to space their remaining children.[71]

When I asked her if she had observed changes in unwanted pregnancy in La Paz or El Alto since she began working in reproductive health in the early 1980s, medical doctor Antonia Rocio told me that adolescent girls were becoming pregnant at younger and younger ages, due in part to machismo. Explaining that women who decided to use contraceptive methods were often seen as sexually promiscuous, Antonia insisted, "Women should negotiate their own protection [from pregnancy] and not wait for men to do so. There's a lot of work to do."[72] Idelia Parra, who worked in a home for pregnant adolescents, argued that machismo contributed to high rates of male abandonment of their pregnant partners, as well as men's sexual infidelity. "Unfortunately, [abandonment] appears to be very common, judging by the numbers of girls I see in this situation. Machismo continues to be a part of our culture—the man who thinks he can have more than one partner, that he should have his harem, practically. He has his wife, he has his lover, and he bears no responsibility for his child."[73] Medical doctor Dolores Ticahuanca, who performed abortions in El Alto, cited machismo to explain why women sought to terminate their pregnancies. "It always strikes me how poor many women's relationships are with their partners. They say that they're mistreated, they say, 'I don't want to have a child with a man who mistreats me.' This is what we call machismo. [Men] think they own women, their decisions, even their bodies—they beat them, they cheat on them, and they think that women have no right to protest."[74]

Religious beliefs and education, as well as a cultural atmosphere of closed-mindedness concerning sexuality, also contributed to the stigmatization of abortion (and in some cases contraception) in La Paz and El Alto. On the one hand, Catholic and Protestant beliefs and values, which tend to condemn abortion, influenced the types of messages about sex and reproduction transmitted at school and at home. Closed-mindedness, for its part, seems to consist of a broader set of attitudes toward sexuality, reproduction, and romantic partnership that are not necessarily religious in origin. While some interviewees used this expression to describe the infrequency with which families and peers discussed themes such as sex and pregnancy, others used the term to mean something similar to what might be referred to in western contexts as "socially conservative," as when explaining opposition to premarital sex. In practice, it was not always easy to discern when opposition to abortion or contraception was religious in nature or when it arose from closed-mindedness. At the same time, while some religious institutions or doctrines articulate clear positions condemning abortion or western-derived contraceptive methods, individuals' religious beliefs tended to be much more varied. Thus not all individuals who identified as Catholic or Protestant opposed abortion or birth control.

Several women I interviewed said that their parents did not teach them about sex and pregnancy, or felt the information that they did receive from their families was unhelpful in preparing them to become sexually active. Idalina Achuta was forty years old when I interviewed her in El Alto in 2010. While she then wore pants or skirts (a style of dress described as de vestido), Idalina said that she soon planned to go back to wearing the pollera, the adult version of the *falda* (skirt) that she had worn as a young girl. Born in the countryside, she moved to La Paz with her parents at age seven. Later, the family moved to El Alto, where Idalina's mother operated a market stand.

> I met my husband because he was a customer of my mom's. . . . First, he approached me as a friend, and I confided everything in him. . . . I told him that before, I'd gone out with a boy, but that nothing had happened—just holding hands and one time, he stole a kiss. That's because my mom would always say, "Daughter, never kiss because you're going to end up [*aparecer*] pregnant. . . . And when you're on your period, don't walk by where men have urinated." She always told me that, so I was scared, you know? And I involved myself a lot [with the new man], until one day I told him, crying, "I haven't gotten my period," and he said, "Look at that! [*Mira!*]" So, that's how I found out about that [that missing a period could mean that you are pregnant]: I made a total fool of myself [*yo hubiera hecho un papelón*]. I have to laugh at myself.

I just must have grown up so cerrada, arriving from the countryside was a lot for me—nowadays kids aren't really like that, right?[75]

Several women I interviewed said that they did not know that missing a menstrual period could indicate pregnancy. Some explained this fact by saying that they did not have close enough relationships with their parents (or, more specifically, their mothers) to ask them about sex. Others (including Idalina) reported having very close relationships with their mothers, and instead cited closed-mindedness—meaning in this case that sexuality was not a subject that was discussed within the family. For instance, Idalina said that when she first got her period, she thought the bleeding was the result of having traveled in a truck over bumpy roads and was terrified when the symptoms continued over several days. "I was ignorant of so many things that my mother did not explain to me. So, now I talk to my daughter frankly [sin pelos en la lengua]. . . . It's better to talk about these things up front—although, of course, it's embarrassing." Interviewees were somewhat more likely to talk about sex or pregnancy with friends, but several said that closed-mindedness toward sexuality permeated urban highland society and was not confined to family life.

Several interviewees who claimed to oppose abortion cited religious or moral objections to the procedure, protesting that abortion was a "sin," "against God's laws," or "murder." Beatriz Chasqui, a forty-nine-year-old Aymara woman who dressed de vestido, reported that, when her daughter returned from a trip to Cuba (where abortion is legal), the two argued over the ethical implications of the procedure. "My daughter says that in Cuba, it [abortion] is normal, but to me, it should not be legal because it's like killing a child. . . . It would be better to first take care of oneself [to not get pregnant]. Contraceptives are everywhere nowadays."[76] Some women, rather than describing abortion as "taking a life," explained their opposition to abortion by citing God's ostensible prohibition of the procedure. "Maybe it's the economy that leads people to do things that they shouldn't," reflected Sandra Laura, a thirty-eight-year-old Aymara woman who dressed de vestido. "Abortion is a sin that's against God's laws."[77] Beatriz was born on an estancia in the province of Pacajes but moved to the city when she was three, while Sandra was a native paceña. Both women identified as Catholic. Lorena Mercado, Aymara and de vestido, and Nina Rojas, mestiza, both had abortions in the 1990s. Both Catholic, Lorena and Nina worried that God had not forgiven them for terminating their pregnancies and remarked that, in general, they opposed abortion. Lorena, then thirty-eight, explained, "I spoke with a priest and he told me . . . that God will forgive me, but I'm not sure that he ever will."[78] As has been noted in literature on attitudes toward abortion in other geographical and social contexts,[79] Bolivian women's opinions of the acceptability of abortion did not correspond in any particular way with their own reproductive histories. Thus some interviewees who claimed to oppose abortion had considered terminating their own pregnancies—or had done so—while other women who found the procedure acceptable had never considered terminating a pregnancy of their own.

Discussions of sexuality and pregnancy that took place in schools— both secular schools and those affiliated with religious institutions—also contributed to the stigmatization of abortion and, to a lesser extent, western-derived contraceptive methods. On the one hand, interviewees reported that religious (mostly Catholic) schools and those unaffiliated with religious institutions provided sexual education to students, including some treatment of birth control and sexually transmitted infections, since the late 1990s. (Prior to the passage of the 2009 Constitution, Bolivia was designated a Catholic country, and religious scripture and values were often taught in public schools. Thus there were not always clear differences between the types of sexual education transmitted by state-run schools and those affiliated with religious institutions.) Some interviewees believed that this education contributed to a progressive opening of attitudes toward contraception in recent years, while others, like the medical personnel quoted earlier, felt that shame associated with the use of western-derived birth control methods remained significant. Most interviewees concurred, however, that characterizations of abortion in school curricula were markedly negative.

Activist Fanny Barrutia, then in her fifties, attended a Catholic school in La Paz in the mid-1970s. "In high school, we didn't get a lot of information," recalled Fanny. "Sex was a sin, so if you were pregnant it was the result of sin. . . . And there were a lot of myths, taboos, and erroneous information—including that you could get pregnant by getting kissed."[80] Ida Torralba, a twenty-eight-year-old woman who attended a Catholic high school in La Paz in the 1990s, received more information about sex and pregnancy than did Fanny, but characterized attitudes of school officials toward these themes as closed-minded. When she undertook a class project on western-derived contraceptive methods, school officials allowed Ida to present her work to the class but prevented her from talking about the methods in detail. "I wanted to explain how to use condoms, birth control pills, and the IUD, but they would only let me show pictures of them. . . . And the other students didn't ask any questions because the nuns didn't allow them to."[81] While most interviewees under about thirty years of age received some sexual education in school, not all did. Muriel Rodríguez, who was in her early twenties at the time of our interview, attended a Catholic high school in El Alto. "As far as I remember, they never spoke to us about this at all."[82]

While some individuals believed that western-derived contraceptive methods were more widely accepted in Bolivia in the early twenty-first century than they were a few decades earlier, others felt that social attitudes toward birth control remained unfavorable. When I asked social worker Stefania Montoya if perspectives toward contraception had changed in the fifteen years she had counseled men and women in El Alto about birth control, she remarked, "Yes, there have been very important changes. . . . We are even seeing changes in men. They are beginning to take greater responsibility for their own reproductive health and that of their families." After thinking for a moment, Stefania continued, "But of course, these changes have been quite slow." She then told me that, to calm

angry husbands who burst into the health service demanding to know if
their wives were using contraception, doctors at the clinic would sometimes lie, claiming not to know why a woman had been unable to become
pregnant. "All this is confidential [referring to women's medical informa-
tion], but some men are aggressive, and we have cases in which sometimes
we must find a solution at that moment because it's a woman's decision
[to use birth control]."[83] Fanny, quoted earlier, felt that many Bolivians
continued to oppose birth control. Recalling an episode that had occurred
a few years prior, Fanny explained, "In [the city of] Sucre during Carnival in 2006, the ministry planned to distribute condoms. . . . But the gov-
ernor at the time was an evangelical [Protestant] and he decided to burn
the entire supply of condoms in the plaza. . . . There you can see how these
fundamentalist positions have penetrated people's mentality."[84]

A number of interviewees lamented the closed-minded attitudes of
people in La Paz and El Alto toward women who give birth either out of
wedlock or in a cohabitating relationship. As in other Latin American
countries, in Bolivia, pre-1945 laws that limited the social and property
rights of children born out of wedlock reveal the historically discriminated
status of "illegitimate" children and their mothers.[85] While some interviewees believed that single motherhood was more accepted in the twenty-
first century than it was in previous decades, other interviewees protested
that judgment against women in this situation remained severe. Belén
Cuellar, a mestiza from La Paz, was fifty-five years old when I interviewed
her in 2009. "It was a huge disappointment to me," recalled Belén of her
first experiences with courtship and pregnancy in the late 1970s. Belén,
who was twenty-three years old when her child was born, remarked that
it was very *mal visto* (poorly seen), to be a single mother at that time. "At
least now, there are some who defend us, who believe that being a single
mother is not a crime—back then, it was a serious offense."[86] Idelia Parra,
the social worker cited earlier, who worked at a house of refuge for pregnant adolescents, believed that attitudes against single motherhood

remained harsh. When I asked her how the young women living at the home were perceived by other students at the high school they attended, Idelia remarked, "Our society is very harsh and judges people without knowing what their lives have been like. At the high school, the judgment is fierce—although maybe not by the other kids their age, rather, by the parents of those kids, who say to them, 'How could you talk to that girl??' . . . So we have to teach them [the young women] these things—that they should learn to live their lives with their children and not feel ashamed." Fearing discrimination, some adolescents who lived at the refuge attended night school instead, where the students were older and may also have had children or partners. Reflecting on the phenomenon of single motherhood in La Paz and El Alto, Idelia remarked, "This situation where men abandon their partners is very strong and frequent here. But I don't think that a woman should let this define her—it's just another experience in life. They have to move forward, and that's what we try to help them do."

Most interviewees believed that treatment of abortion in schools, for its part, had been consistently negative over the last several decades. A number of interviewees reported having seen videos or television shows or heard lectures denouncing abortion at high schools and universities in La Paz and El Alto. Natividad Colque, a twenty-three-year-old mother of two, saw a video condemning abortion in one of her classes at La Paz's public Universidad Mayor de San Andrés (UMSA). "It was during a course in early childhood development," she recalled. "The documentary showed a woman's womb during an abortion. . . . It was obviously a Catholic or Christian video that was made to discourage women from getting abortions."[87] Rigoberta Justiniano reported seeing a similar film at her public high school in the late 1990s, which was accompanied by a lecture condemning abortion. "In the video, the child asked for help, saying that he wanted to live, that he had a right to life. . . . But piece by piece, they took out the baby."[88] Based on their descriptions of the footage they viewed, the film that these women saw may have been the 1984 documentary *The Silent Scream*, which has drawn the criticism of pro-choice communities in the United States for its graphic and medically inaccurate portrayal of an abortion at eleven weeks' gestation.[89]

While religious values and closed-mindedness appeared to be the most important factors contributing to the stigmatization of abortion in La Paz and El Alto, pronatalist attitudes also played a role. According to a small proportion of Bolivians—particularly antiabortion activists and Catholic clergy—abortion, and even contraception, endangered the economic and social progress of the Bolivian nation. When I interviewed him in La Paz in 2010, antiabortion activist Leandro Rubén worked for a group that sought to locate women who were searching for abortion providers and convince them to continue their pregnancies.[90] While Leandro and his colleagues held religious and moral objections to abortion, they also opposed the procedure because they believed it contributed to Bolivia's underpopulation vis-à-vis more developed nations. Remarked Leandro, "The defense of life is not just a moral issue, it is a social issue, because the greater the population of a country, the more possibilities it has to progress. . . . If we had more population in Bolivia, we could think about creating companies—and there would be a larger labor force to meet the demand of these companies." After our interview, Leandro showed me a U.S.-produced documentary entitled *The Demographic Winter* that warned against the long-term impact of abortion and contraceptive use. "Abortion is causing a serious problem around the world," remarked Leandro as we watched the film. "We're talking about almost a billion human beings who now do not exist." Leandro also told me that aborted fetuses are commonly eaten in China. Catholic priest Mariano Solana, who cited the same documentary, contended that the widespread availability of birth control and abortion in Europe had aged the region's population considerably. "The largest portion of Europe's budget is spent on health care," remarked the priest, "and 80 percent of this budget is spent on diapers for the elderly."[91]

Social stigma against abortion and western-derived contraceptive use in La Paz and El Alto was often associated with broader anxieties about changes in women's roles over the previous few decades. Many interviewees blamed waves of economic crisis, coupled with changes in women's aspirations leading some women to favor career over family, for a perceived increase in abortion rates in recent years. When I asked her why she thought some women in Bolivia might choose abortion, antiabortion activist Carolina Llano remarked, "I think it's because of the economic situation, you know? . . . And I think that also nowadays, women want to study and be professionals, they want to quote un-quote 'realize their dreams.'"[92] For one female social worker employed with the La Paz police department, the broader danger of women seeking professional careers—beyond its impact on abortion rates—was that they no longer saw themselves as wives and mothers. Recalling the case of a male police officer whose wife was a city councilwoman in La Paz, the social worker recounted,

> Since [the establishment of] International Women's Day, women have been liberated from the yolk of the family. But what does this mean? It means she has turned into a libertine. I worked on a case of one policeman whose wife was a councilwoman. The wife often came home late from work because she said she was in meetings. This situation ultimately led to the dissolution of their family—why? Because he [the policeman] caught her with another man. The woman distorted her own situation terribly, she was no longer a mother or a wife, rather, she was a *woman*—and this situation happens a lot.[93]

It is worth noting that this social worker, who appeared to be in her fifties, made her comments in a "focus-group" style interview in which several of her male colleagues were present. (My access to interviews with police officers was more restricted than some of the other individuals I interviewed, and on this occasion, the officers I interviewed insisted on speaking with me as a group.) Nevertheless, the comments of Carolina and the social worker resonated with several individuals I interviewed, suggesting a deep ambivalence among some sectors of the population with changes in women's economic and political roles in La Paz and El Alto. By opting to be "women" and to seek careers, rather than "mothers" and "wives" oriented toward family life—and by sometimes choosing abortion as a means of fulfilling this goal—upwardly mobile women were viewed as a threat to the constitution of the family and of society at large.

Other interviewees felt that adolescent girls, particularly the daughters of working women, were to blame for rising abortion rates. In the context of economic crisis, some individuals faulted women for choosing to work outside the home and leaving their teenage daughters unsupervised. Others noted that the economic situation forced both parents to work and did not necessarily blame mothers for the abortions that ostensibly resulted from the lack of parental control. "I think that unwanted pregnancy occurs because now, young people have a lot of freedom and are not supervised by their parents," noted one male police officer, "because both [parents] have to work out of economic necessity."[94] Carolina, quoted earlier, asserted that abortion rates were high in Sucre because young women who moved to the city to pursue university education were living on their own and went unsupervised by their parents. For most interviewees, the role of poor parental supervision in contributing to abortions among adolescents was exacerbated by other problems at home, such as domestic violence, divorce, and alcohol abuse by both parents and young people. "Disorder [*desface*] in the home is what makes kids go out to the street," remarked Father Mariano Solana. "'My home is hellish, so where should I go?' they ask themselves. And they go looking for love elsewhere"—which, the priest continued, ultimately leads to unwanted pregnancy and abortion.

A number of interviewees blamed a general "loss of values" for increasing rates of unwanted pregnancy and abortion among both adolescent and adult women. Jumila Quiroga, who worked as an educator at a different home for pregnant youth than did Idelia, said that over the eight years she had worked at the refuge, more and more young women ended up at the home as a result of incestual rape.

> JQ: Things are changing because before, there weren't so many cases of this—of rape within the family unit, whether we're talking about the uncle, the father, the stepfather—lately, we're seeing a lot of cases like this.
>
> NK: And why do you think there are more cases like this recently?
>
> JQ: I don't know, I think because people have lost respect, they have lost values [*ya ha perdido los valores*]. At least before, people were a bit scared, they'd say to themselves, "No, that's a sin," or "God is watching," but now people have lost this—they couldn't care less [*les da lo mismo*]. It's about three years that we've been running into this.
>
> NK: Hmm. And how do you think values are lost, how might that happen?
>
> JQ: I don't know, look—maybe education, science, all that stuff makes it so that people do not value others and that we do not value ourselves. The Catholic Church doesn't have so much power anymore. Because here in Bolivia, people were really Catholic—but the Church has been losing influence, and this makes people do things they otherwise wouldn't.[95]

Although it is unclear what kind of education worked to erode values in Jumila's estimation, the educator's emphasis on the rising influence of scientific ideas vis-à-vis religious ones suggests that she believed that the secularization of education played a role in rising rates of intrafamilial rape. Daniel Báez, who worked for the Ekklesía Evangelical Christian Church in La Paz, also associated the loss of values with the reduced influence of religious ideologies in the country. To Daniel, the decline of religious values led to abortions among the upper classes and to large families among the poor.

DB: A great many abortions occur in the upper classes. There's a loss
of values—an ignorance with respect to what could happen during
an abortion, ignorance about what sexual relations mean, ignorance
on the part of parents to teach their kids how to be careful [*el cui-
dado que podrían tener*]. . . . And, among the poor, there is not a full
understanding of sexuality. So, girls get together with boys and they
get pregnant and then, usually, in the countryside or the suburbs
people end up having a lot of children because they don't know how
to take care of themselves. . . . People don't marry, they live a disor-
dered life, there aren't principles, there aren't values, and they live
life as it comes. . . .

NK: And what do you think that the government should do with
respect to education?

DB: I think the state should place much more emphasis on what life
is. . . . And I think it should start in schools, teaching what it means
to protect oneself, to take care of oneself. . . . And allow the Church
to enter these spaces to impart more values and more principles.

Daniel repeatedly used the term "*cuidarse*" to refer to what young people
should do with respect to negotiating their sexual and reproductive behavior, a term that often implies employing some form of fertility regulation.
When I asked Báez to clarify the position of his church on western-derived
birth control methods, in particular, he replied, "Well, contraceptive methods are microabortives [*microabortivos*], so we're against that."[96]

Finally, some individuals I interviewed believed that the attitudes
of rural-dwelling indigenous people toward abortion contributed to the
stigmatization of the procedure throughout the country. Several interviewees asserted that rural-dwelling indigenous women suspected of terminating their pregnancies were ostracized by community members, chiefly
because their abortions were believed to bring misfortune on the community at large. According to interviewees, this misfortune typically takes
the form of a hailstorm or other climatic event that damages the commu-

nity's harvest, and thus, threatens members' survival. Carla Yupanqui, an Aymara woman who grew up in Coro Coro, remarked, "When I was little, my mother often said that when it hailed a lot, it was because some woman had aborted. . . . It was like a punishment not just for her, but for the whole community. I also heard this in mining centers."[97] Juana Choque, who described herself as *Quechua urbana*, and Adela López, mestiza, produced a documentary on traditional birth practices in a rural community in the Department of La Paz. Juana and Adela noted that when a poor harvest befell the community, the female leaders would, "take all the young women and examine their breasts to see if there is milk."[98] Both Juana and Adela asserted that abortion was only believed to cause misfortune to a community if the aborted fetus was buried within the boundaries of that settlement; thus some women would inter any fetus they passed in a neighboring community. The activists also claimed that midwives were sometimes interrogated following climatic catastrophes to determine if they had performed an abortion on a woman in the community. According to Juana and Adela, as well as some other interviewees, female members of indigenous communities were sanctioned more often than men for actions considered to be morally suspect. Reflected Adela, "It's interesting to ask why it doesn't hail [in an indigenous community] when a man rapes a woman, you know?"

While the conversations cited here were insightful in highlighting what some urban Bolivians knew or believed they knew about abortion in the rural sphere, they shed less light on the actual attitudes and practices of the individuals living there. Based on his decades-long engagement with residents of the Aymara-speaking community of Wila Kjarka, Andrew Canessa described abortion as a common practice in the community, although one that is not often openly discussed (particularly by men). In Wila Kjarka, burying a fetus (or an unnamed baby) in a cemetery, or really in any plot of earth, would constitute sin, and could bring lightning as a punishment from the *achachilas*, or "tutelary spirits of the earth and mountains."[99] Instead, residents deposit fetuses off the embankment of a nearby river, where they can more quickly rejoin the ancestral world. According to Wila Kjarkeños, it is the Christian God ("God the Father") who punishes communities with hailstorms—but not for improperly burying a fetus or deceased infant, rather, for failing to baptize a child.[100] According to Libbet Crandon-Malamud's study of Kachitu, Bolivia, a woman who has aborted and buried a fetus in community soil does not face social stigma so long as she financially compensates campesinos who have lost crops to hail—an expense that may, nevertheless, "[cripple] her and her family for years."[101] In his study of one Quechua-speaking community in the Bolivian highlands, Tristan Platt found that aborted fetuses are converted into violent and vengeful *duendes* (goblins) that can cause health problems for women in childbirth.[102] According to Platt, fetuses, whether aborted or expelled during birth, are animated by "pre-Christian ancestral souls . . . that live within the earth (*ukhu pacha*) and enter women's wombs to give life and energy to the gestating human embryos."[103] Ineke Dibbits and Ximena Pabón note that residents of indigenous communities in a range of Andean settings report that unbaptized fetuses become duendes, the characteristics and meanings of which vary.[104] What may be consistent among these various conceptualizations of abortion by rural-dwelling Andeans is a key distinction between what constitutes a fetus versus a fully formed human being. As Lynn Morgan described in her study of rural Ecuador, "The unborn are imagined as liminal, unripe, and unfinished creatures. Nascent persons are brought into being slowly, through processes rife with uncertainty and moral ambiguity. Adults are slow to assign individual identity and personhood to the not-yet-born and the newly born."[105] Thus these scholars find that abortion, while rich in meaning, is not widely stigmatized in the rural Andes—nor are women necessarily ostracized for terminating pregnancies. In contrast, urban-dwelling interviewees tended to emphasize stigmatization to the exclusion of other, more complex understandings of abortion at work in the rural sphere.

Many individuals I interviewed in La Paz and El Alto who supported women's access to safe abortion (such as Juana and Adela, cited earlier) often said that women should have the "right" to decide to terminate or to continue a pregnancy; in addition, some felt that indigenous communities did not do enough to protect the reproductive and social rights of their female members. The interviews that I conducted with female activists who identified as Aymara or Quechua and a review of literature on these themes highlight the contentious nature of competing rights claims shaping understandings of abortion in Bolivia—as well as in other geographical contexts marked by significant ethnic and cultural diversity. As Morgan and Roberts explain, "The concept of 'indigenous rights' may trump reproductive rights in places such as Bolivia and Peru, where the new constitution has bestowed rights upon indigenous people, and where women's rights are framed as a movement to eliminate ethnic discrimination and to humanise medical care for all women, rather than on the right to bodily autonomy. This is a very different model than US-based rights claims about the 'choices' to which individual women should be entitled."[106]

Key to the conflict between understandings of indigenous and reproductive rights in the Andes are the notions of communal versus individual rights. While the former is rooted in Andean understandings of the rights of minority, cultural, and community groupings, the latter are based on western, Enlightenment-era concepts of liberalism.[107] Within Andean conceptualizations of the community, relations between the sexes are considered complementary. Silvia Rivera Cusicanqui defines gender complementarity as, "a dynamic and contentious equilibrium, normatively oriented by the model of the Andean couple."[108] The Andean couple (or *chachawarmi*, consisting of the union of a man and a woman), constitutes, "a socioeconomic and moral unit that accomplishes the basic social functions in a household and at the community level."[109] The functions that women and men perform within this unit are distinct. While the specific distinctions between the activities that each sex performs vary by region, "women are primarily responsible for the reproduction of the social order, for bringing children into social being."[110] (This does not mean, however, that indigenous communities in the Andes are pronatalist, and there is, in fact, considerable evidence that couples in many such communities take measures to limit the size of their families.[111])

In her chapter "The Peace Corps, Population Control, and Cultural Nationalist Resistance in 1960s Bolivia," Molly Geidel unpacks the ways that, "the ability to talk about women's rights in Bolivia is always a separate question from birth control and reproductive freedom."[112] Geidel describes the racism and elitism of the modernization theory that undergirded the Peace Corps's population control efforts in Bolivia, which simultaneously targeted rural indigenous women and dehumanized them in an attempt to quash the supposed overpopulation of the poor indigenous majority. Critics of population control, such as Domitila Barrios de Chungara, who mobilized mining housewives' committees in the 1970s, often articulated "resource-centered and territory-based nationalist discourses" in which "it remain[ed] the work of women to hand over their bodies to populate the country in order that their children might live to extract and fight for its natural resources."[113] Geidel cites an interview she conducted with then minister of health Nila Heredia, a medical doctor and anti-imperialist activist in Bolivia. Remarked Heredia, "The notion of women's rights is Western, here those rights come into conflict with the rights of the community. If a woman has all the rights to her body, to marry, to have twenty kids or not have kids at all, where is the right of the community in all that? But I'm also not in favor of patriarchal rule. It's a very difficult issue."[114]

Rosalva Aída Hernández and Andrew Canessa emphasize that the model of gender complementarity is based on sexual difference rather than equality, and that it can "give rise to egalitarian relations, but also can operate within a framework of hierarchical relations."[115] The authors summarize the positions of other scholars who have questioned whether notions such as multiculturalism and community rights are "bad for women" in subsuming women's individual rights to those of an indigenous community or ethnic group.[116] While Hernández and Canessa criticize the Eurocentrism of these claims, they also acknowledge that complementarity has sometimes been invoked in order to shut down indigenous women's attempts to mobilize for their own interests and those of their daughters.[117] According to some scholars, it is precisely the "frustrating and contradictory nature of Bolivian modernity" that has disrupted the ideal of gender complementarity among Andeans.[118] As Stéphanie Rousseau explains, "Gender relations have been profoundly transformed by colonialism; capitalist development; and, lately, neoliberal reform and globalization."[119]

One solution to the rift between the women's rights and communal rights camps in Bolivia has been posed by the radical "communitarian feminist" group, Mujeres Creando Comunidad, which formed after its leader, Julieta Paredes, split from Mujeres Creando—a group she began alongside María Galindo in 1985. Since its beginning, the Mujeres Creando collective, "question[ed] essentialist feminism and western bourgeois morality alongside Indianist discourses . . . [for failing] to open sufficient space to interrogate indigenous conceptualizations of gender."[120] In its book on communitarian feminism, Mujeres Creando Comunidad and Paredes write, "It is necessary to demystify the *chacha—warmi* (man-woman), which impedes the analysis of the reality of women in our own country."[121] According to Anders Burman, communitarian feminism as it is articulated by Mujeres Creando Comunidad is not widely accepted by Aymara activists in the country. "The crucial question in this debate is whether chachawarmi is a notion that conceals mechanisms of women's subordination or a notion that opens up possibilities for indigenous women to reclaim rights by denouncing the breach between discourse and practice."[122]

While aspects of the split between some women's and indigenous rights movements in Bolivia are understandable and palpable, in practice, the realities of ethnic and cultural identification in the country—and of women's experiences with unwanted pregnancy—blur this distinction. On the one hand, there is considerable overlap between female and indigenous constituents and activists who are served by, and who form part of, these two movements. (In other words, many women's rights organizations in La Paz and El Alto are staffed by Aymara- and Quechua-speakers and serve indigenous populations, while many indigenous rights groups in the region include women and organize around women's issues.) Further, the supposed distinction between the indigenous and women's rights camps implies that indigenous women may not experience, or are not particularly concerned with, unwanted pregnancy and abortion—which is in fact not the case. Both my own interview data and a 2009 study on ethnicity and desired fertility rates in the country reveal that women who self-identified as indigenous experienced more, not less, unwanted pregnancy than mestiza and European-descendant women.[123] Furthermore (and as chapter 3 explores), the personal narratives of indigenous women who have experienced unwanted pregnancy, which invoked both individual and social factors in deciding whether to continue or terminate a pregnancy, complicate any clear division of reproductive understandings along competing rights camps.[124]

Despite the relatively outspoken opposition of many sectors of the urban population to abortion, most individuals in La Paz and El Alto believed that the procedure should be permitted in some circumstances. While some interviewees merely hinted at finding abortion acceptable in some cases, others offered particular circumstances in which they believed it should be allowed. Manuela Pacari, a thirty-six-year-old Aymara woman who dressed de vestido, remarked that, "If you don't have a way to make it [salir adelante], it's better, I think, to abort a pregnancy than to toss it in the street once it's born."[125] Maita Perez, a thirty-one-year-old woman from the town of Viacha, believed a friend should have had access to abortion when the woman became pregnant after her health care provider failed to adequately teach her how to use the contraceptive method she had selected.[126] Broader, city- and nationwide surveys suggest that many Bolivians, including men, shared the conviction that abortion should be allowed in some cases. One 2008 survey of fifty male residents of El Alto found that twenty-eight of the men believed that abortion should be permitted in some circumstances.[127] In addition to economic difficulties, those surveyed found abortion acceptable in cases of rape, when a woman's health was threatened by a pregnancy, or when a fetus suffered congenital defects.

The experience of one receptionist at an El Alto clinic that provided abortions suggests that, even when to do so might provide them with much-needed employment, many Bolivians may be deterred by their fear of social stigma to admit to accepting abortion. Muriel Rodríguez, who was friendly and talkative at our interview, was in her twenties when she applied for the receptionist job. To interview for it, Muriel and eleven other candidates were assembled in a hotel lobby, where they were collectively questioned by clinic staff.

> They started to ask us questions—but not really things about work. Rather, they asked about our ways of thinking, and eventually, they raised the question of our thoughts on abortion. Well, since I was a child, I always thought abortion was a person's decision, despite being very Catholic. So, they asked us that question and I—just as I respond to you now—said openly that I supported it. But all the others said no, that they were against abortion. The majority of people at the interview were scared to talk and I think that they just said to themselves, "If I respond that I agree, they are going to think that I am a woman who is not dignified, a woman who could commit a murder." So, maybe they responded like that even though they actually feel the way I do.[128]

Muriel, the only job candidate to publicly declare her acceptance of abortion, received a call the following month and had worked at the clinic ever since.

CHAPTER 3

Feelings, Attitudes, and Decisions

REPRODUCTIVE DECISION MAKING IN THE URBAN ANDES

Paula Rojas was eighteen years old in 1986 and lived in the highland mining town of Siglo XX with her parents and nine brothers and sisters when she found herself facing an unexpected pregnancy. Although she had been dating (*enamorando*) with her boyfriend for four years and the two were sexually active, she did not realize that missing a menstrual period might mean she was pregnant. Terrified of how her parents and siblings would react, Paula hid the pregnancy from her family for seven months. "The first month that I didn't get my period, my friends and I even talked about drinking tea [to provoke an abortion]," explained Paula. "We went to buy the tea, but we got scared. . . . and I didn't end up buying it." When I asked if she considered getting an abortion a few years later, when she and her then husband faced a third pregnancy they felt came too soon after the birth of their second child, Paula remarked, "No. When I'm already pregnant, I say to myself, 'Ok, it doesn't matter—what can I do?' Since getting married, I never thought about it [abortion] again."[1]

Drawing on the testimonies of thirteen women who faced unwanted pregnancies in Bolivia between the mid-1950s and 2008, this chapter explores the emotional complexity of women's experiences with pregnancy, miscarriage, and abortion. I examine the variety of factors that influenced these women's feelings about their pregnancies, including their relationships with partners and family members and their economic circumstances and life goals. I also investigate the range of these women's responses to their pregnancies, including procuring abortion, considering abortion and deciding against it, attempting to seek abortion without success, and continuing a pregnancy without ever considering abortion.[2] Both women who had abortions and those who carried their unwanted pregnancies to term navigated complex emotions and life circumstances to decide how to best confront their reproductive experiences and, ultimately, plan their lives. This chapter reveals the multifaceted and sometimes contradictory nature of women's feelings toward their pregnancies. Fear, shame, and guilt surrounded many women's experiences with pregnancy termination, due in part to a deep-seated social stigma against abortion in the urban Andes, but also to personal factors, such as the tenor of women's relationships with family members, friends, and partners. For some women, abortion's prohibited status heightened the emotional difficulty of deciding to procure it, since the fear of legal repercussions and the sensation that they were doing something "wrong" shaped the experience as a whole. Feelings of guilt and shame were also common for women who ended up continuing pregnancies they described as unwanted, especially for women who had become pregnant outside the bounds of cohabitation. At the same time, many women experienced feelings of determination, and responded with strength and clarity, when met with unwanted pregnancies.

This chapter, like the book as a whole, wrestles with an uncomfortable and slippery notion—that of unwanted pregnancy (*embarazo no deseado*). Although both statistically significant and relevant to some women's reproductive experiences, this concept is obviously insufficient to describe the range of emotions that women feel toward their pregnancies. Many women unequivocally state that they have experienced unwanted pregnancy, whereas others may be hesitant to do so. This may be particularly true for women who decided to continue pregnancies they did not expect and are now raising children with distinctive personalities. For this reason,

I make an effort to distinguish between women who, at some point during an interview, described one or more of their pregnancies as
unwanted, those who said they had mixed feelings about being pregnant,
and those whose pregnancies were unplanned, but not unwanted. At the
same time, I utilize other terms that women employed to describe their
pregnancies, such as inopportune, and reference emotional reactions that
women had toward being pregnant, including sadness, uncertainty, disappointment, and fear. Even when these questions are approached with
care, women's experiences may not be fully explainable or may not fit
comfortably into scholarly or ethnographic paradigms for doing so. In
short, women's feelings toward their pregnancies may not always be easily
classified in terms of "wantedness"—nor may it be desirable to do so, particularly if such categorization hides from view other aspects of women's
experiences. Throughout the chapter, I simply endeavor to capture as fully
as possible the complexity of women's feelings toward their pregnancies,
while still reflecting patterns characterizing unplanned and unwanted
pregnancy in Andean Bolivia over the past several decades.

The reproductive experiences of the women whose testimonies appear
here were unique and varied, as were their feelings about them—yet their
idiosyncrasy does not detract from their ability to enlighten us about the
broader history of unwanted pregnancy and reproductive decision making in urban Bolivia. Instead, the diversity of these experiences highlights
the error of making assumptions about the ways in which women feel
about, and make choices regarding, their reproductive lives. This chapter
suggests that the ways in which women conceptualize their experiences
with unwanted pregnancy may demand a reevaluation of the language
with which reproductive rights activists and other sectors speak about
abortion more broadly. The polemical nature of debates around abortion's legalization often leads activists in Latin America (and elsewhere) to
frame discussions of abortion in a language of "rights" and of "choice"—
specifically, of women's right to control their reproductive lives by choosing when, and if, to bear a child. This chapter, like scholarship exploring

women's reproductive experiences elsewhere in the world, suggests that these legal and political frameworks are too limited to capture women's personal experiences with unwanted pregnancy and abortion.

THE EMOTIONAL TERRAIN OF REPRODUCTIVE DECISION MAKING

At seventeen years of age in 1955, Magda Cusi was one of five children being raised in the highland city of Potosí by her mother—a market vendor who "carried the family forward [*nos sacó adelante*]" by selling beer, bread, fruit, and other items—and her father, an injured veteran of the Chaco War. Magda's mother was insistent that she and her siblings continue their schooling; however, the girl often helped her mother at the market in her free time, particularly since their father was unable to work. One day, while selling a drink made of dried peach boiled with cinnamon, Magda met the man who would later become her husband and the father of her four children. "I saw him and he said, 'to your health,' raising the drink, and I immediately fell in love with him. . . . The following year we got married . . . and in 1956 my oldest child was born." When I asked her how she felt when she discovered she was pregnant, Magda said, almost by way of confession, "That was before I got married. . . . Because I had fallen in love in such a way that in the end, going to bed didn't matter. . . . Well, I felt bad—imagine, I was just a little kid still. Just seventeen years old and already pregnant!" Although she "felt panic at the idea of marriage," Magda and the boy married at the insistence of Magda's older brother, and the following year, their first child was born.[3]

Magda's and Paula's feelings of ambivalence toward their pregnancies echoed those of other women I interviewed who became pregnant for the first time unexpectedly. The single most important reason women reported not wanting their first pregnancies was the unstable nature of their relationships with male partners—particularly that these were not formalized with marriage, or at least cohabitation. This was equally true regardless of when a woman was born; however, women who became pregnant between the 1950s and the early 1990s preferred to be formally married, while those whose pregnancies occurred more recently were content to cohabitate with the father of their children. In part, women preferred more stable partnerships because they felt that live-in mates would demonstrate a greater sense of commitment to the pregnancy and to the relationship, compelling them to accompany and assist their girl-friend or wife during and after pregnancy. Women also sometimes pre-ferred to avoid pregnancy outside of marriage or cohabitation because they feared their families' disapproval or becoming the subject of neigh-borhood gossip.

Belinda López, a sixty-four-year-old, Catholic, mestiza woman, said that she did not want her first pregnancy in 1972 because she was not mar-ried to the child's father. I met Belinda at the same workshop where I met Magda; both women lived in Ciudad Satélite, a relatively upwardly mobile neighborhood of El Alto with a large daily market, paved roads, and homes made from stable structures like concrete and brick.[4] Belinda, who was born and raised in La Paz, was twenty-seven years old when she first became pregnant. That she was an adult woman with a stable job when she realized she was pregnant may explain why Belinda was less concerned with her mother's reaction to the pregnancy than was Magda. "I didn't want to be pregnant because my greatest wish was to get married in a church, in white, everything beautiful. So, my mom always told me, 'You have to take care [to not get pregnant]'; but sometimes the devil tempts us, and I ended up pregnant."[5] Like many women I interviewed, Belinda used the phrase *cuidarse* (to take care of oneself) to indicate taking steps to prevent pregnancy; what is less clear is whether Belinda's mother gave her specific instructions on *how* she should avoid pregnancy. Very few of the women I interviewed of any age, ethnic background, or geographical region reported having detailed conversations with their parents about sex or fertility regulation. More typically, women were simply warned to avoid certain behaviors because they could lead to pregnancy or other unidentified problems—advice that sometimes made women feel a vague sense of fear and shame when navigating sexual or romantic relationships. Instead, women usually learned on their own or from friends how to regulate their fertility—sometimes only after they had experienced an unexpected or unwanted pregnancy.

While Belinda stated that she did not want to be pregnant because she preferred to be married first, she also implied that, were the father of her child interested in forming a more stable union, she too would have been glad to do so.

> He was a good person but everything is partial, you know? People appear and they disappear, but leave a poor image [*todo es parcial, ¿no? Aparecen y desaparecen pero con mala imagen*]. . . . He didn't want [the child] either; our problems began when he discovered I was pregnant. . . . He was unhappy, he told me, "I didn't think about this." My uncle and aunt told him, "You have to marry her," and he said, "Yes, I'm going to formalize it [*sí, voy a arreglar*]" but he wasn't interested. I loved him a lot, he also loved me too much, but he didn't want more family. He was divorced and had two daughters. So, my daughter has two step-siblings.[6]

Maura Choque's first pregnancy occurred in 1995 when she was twenty-two years old. Although she first became pregnant four decades after Magda did, her feelings about the pregnancy were also shaped by a fear of how her parents might react. Maura was born in Viacha, a small city about twenty-two kilometers southwest of La Paz, which she said conformed to the stereotype of "*pueblo chico infierno grande* [small town, big hell]." She still lived there at the time of our interview. At that time, Maura was thirty-six years old and described herself as Aymara; she dressed de vestido (in pants, skirts, or dresses, rather than the pollera).

> I got together with him [her husband] when I was pregnant. . . . I was worried because my parents were going to find out, they were going to

scold me and hit me [*me iban a reñir a pegar*], and that's why I got
together with him [*me he juntado*]. . . . I was already three months pregnant and then we . . . formalized it. Now, he says that I was pinning it
on him [*que yo a él le estaba acusando*], that I was obligating him to get
together with me. He always said . . . that I had lied to him: "In order to
be with me you pinned it [the pregnancy] on me." I was worried, you
know? And then all of a sudden, I lost it [had a miscarriage]. With my
daughter, the second pregnancy, it wasn't like that; it was good. I mean,
I was happy, because I was with my husband.

Like many of the women I interviewed, Maura described having significant problems with her partner.[7] Yet these conflicts did not color all of
Maura's memories or feelings about her husband; instead, she felt content
becoming pregnant the second time because her relationship with her husband had become more stable.

Women facing unwanted pregnancy sometimes preferred to be in formal relationships because they believed that husbands and concubinos
(partners) were likely to make better fathers and partners than were casual
boyfriends. According to women's testimonies, good partners were those
who demonstrated a firm commitment to the relationship and to the pregnancy; who were emotionally supportive; who assisted with household
tasks; and who contributed financially to the family. Alma Tarqui, a
twenty-year-old Aymara woman who was born and raised in El Alto, was
fifteen years old when her first partner left her to confront a pregnancy on
her own. "When I became pregnant he didn't want to assume his responsibility. . . . He left me. 'It isn't my daughter,' he said, so we separated. He
abandoned me." After that experience, Alma initially felt panic when she
became pregnant eight months later by another man. "My first thought
was to leave him before he could leave me," recalled Alma, who believed
her partner had intentionally misguided the couple's use of the rhythm
method in order to get her pregnant. "But then I thought, maybe since he's
a bit older he'll assume his responsibility." At forty-five years of age, Alma's

partner was more than two decades her senior. "I began to see how he took care of everything . . . even bringing me food in bed—for me, this was the best, because the first time [I was pregnant] I was on my own." After the birth of her son, Alma and her partner were content with the two children they had, but tragically, their infant died when Alma fell asleep while breastfeeding and the child was smothered. "After that misfortune, I snapped myself out of it [*he vuelto a animarme*], I said, 'I want a baby,' and I got pregnant again within a month." While Alma described her relationship with her partner as "solid," she still hopes the two marry formally someday: "If something were to happen to my husband, I would have some guarantees."[8]

Some women felt ambivalent about their first pregnancies because they had to abandon other activities they valued—especially pursuing education. Women further worried that they would disappoint their parents by quitting school in order to raise their children. Magda, quoted earlier, felt disappointed when she became pregnant, not only because she enjoyed being a student but because her mother had sacrificed a lot in order for her and her siblings to study. (While Magda did not say that she would be forced to withdraw from school, Ida Torralba, an activist in La Paz, told me that, until recently, students who became pregnant in Bolivia were not allowed to attend.[9] Alma also left high school when she became pregnant but said that she did so because her partner was jealous and preferred that she stay at home.) Magda was seventy-five years old when I interviewed her in 2010 and described herself as Catholic and of Quechua ethnicity. Magda and her mother were, in some respects, uncharacteristically close compared to other women I interviewed. Recalling the conversation in which she was forced to admit to her mother that she was pregnant, Magda remarked: "'Mom, I am not going to continue [studying],' I said. 'Why, what's wrong? I don't want you to work. Leave everything else aside and keep studying! What, so your brothers and sisters are going to prepare themselves, but not you?' So, I had to confess [the pregnancy] to my mother. I knew what my mother was like—she wasn't going to beat me up or anything [*no me iba a matar pegando*], she was going to understand me because she was my mom. Who else was I going to trust?"[10]

While women who described their first pregnancies as unwanted typically did so because of the instability of their relationships or a desire to seek further education, interviewees whose second, third, or subsequent pregnancies were unwanted usually cited additional concerns. Some women felt ambivalent about their pregnancies because they were experiencing problems in their relationships and were hesitant to raise additional children with their partners or, alternatively, to do so alone. Other women preferred not to be pregnant because they were unhappy with the spacing of the pregnancy or sex of the fetus in relation to their other children, or worried about the impact of an additional child on the family's finances. A few women said they did not want to be pregnant because having children was never in their life plans, or because their pregnancies resulted from acts of sexual coercion or assault. As they reflected on their experiences, a number of women expressed frustration at the trajectory of their reproductive lives, saying they wished they had "known more" about sex and pregnancy, or that they had been able to speak more openly with their parents and partners about these matters. This was true of women of all ethnicities and from all geographical regions but was particularly prevalent among women in their thirties or older.

Jazmín Cahuana, a forty-five-year-old Aymara woman who wore the pollera, gave birth to eight children between 1984 and 2001, the last four of which she described as unwanted due primarily to her unhappy relationship with her partner. "I didn't want to be pregnant anymore, but my husband would come home drunk and obligate me to have sex. I didn't want to, because many times he would then deny being my children's father. . . . My son who is now eighteen . . . and my daughter who is eleven, he denies—'Whose kids are they?' he asks me. 'We didn't have sex! [*Acaso teníamos relaciones?*].' . . . He didn't remember sleeping with me, and that hurt a lot. . . . I always suffered being pregnant and he didn't care." Born in Murillo province, Jazmín was raised in the rural community of Alto Yanari alongside her eight siblings until the children's mother died when Jazmín was just six years old. Like her own partner years later, Jazmín's father denied being her biological parent, particularly after her mother's death. This eventually resulted in Jazmín being sent to La Paz to live with a family member. At twenty-three, Jazmín met the man who would become her husband and the father of her children. "He was an orphan by his father, I by my mother, so I said, 'He's an orphan, he's going to understand me, we're going to get along. . . .' But no, it wasn't good. We must have lived together well for five years—until my daughter was five—then he started to change." The problems Jazmín faced with her partner made her concerned that her daughters would also suffer poor relationships with men. "I have six daughters and two sons," remarked Jazmín. "'Until you reach a certain age, stay single,' I tell my daughters. . . . And they must have listened, because they are still single."[11]

Several women who became pregnant in La Paz and El Alto during these years reported not wanting their pregnancies because they were concerned with the impact of an additional child on the economic situation of their families. While some women hoped to delay having children until they achieved greater financial stability, others wanted to limit the size of their families due to their economic troubles. Simona Pinto, a thirty-two-year-old Aymara woman from Viacha, had two children, ages five and one, when she became pregnant a third time in 2004. "I felt bad," remarked Simona. "My husband has a job but he doesn't earn much, and we often don't have enough to get by." After the birth of her third child, her husband continued to want more kids, but Simona refused. "It's my decision and I have three children already, so no. In this life, there is so much suffering. . . . Sometimes when I have to buy bread, I can only buy it for my children and can't buy it for myself. . . . And the children still ask for more. This is why I don't want more children. This is my worry—I don't want them to suffer."[12] Simona, like several women I interviewed, engaged in activities like washing clothing and selling beverages in their El Alto neighborhood of Amor de Dios to earn extra money for her household without telling her partner that she did so.

Some women who experienced unwanted pregnancy felt that, because of the circumstances in which they became pregnant, they did not have the chance to adequately assess their situations and decide if they wanted to have children; instead, it seemed that motherhood had happened to them. When describing her first pregnancy, which occurred when she was young and unsure how to regulate her fertility, Pilar Mendoza remarked that she became pregnant unexpectedly [*aparecí embarazada*]. Pilar was raised in Cochabamba, a city in Bolivia's central valleys. She lived with her father, who worked as a police officer, until she was fourteen, when she moved to La Paz to live with an aunt. When Pilar left one evening to attend a quinceañera birthday party and failed to come home in the morning, her aunt sent her to a reformatory. Pilar said that this event contributed to her desire to find a partner who she could move in with and thus escape her aunt's tutelage. When I asked how she felt when she became pregnant with the partner she eventually met, Pilar corrected me, saying, "I didn't *get* pregnant. When he took me to his house to live, that's when I became pregnant— I turned up pregnant at his house [*No me he embarazado. Cuando ya me trajo a su casa a vivir, recién me embaracé—allí he aparecido embarazada*]." Looking back on the experience, Pilar suggested that her youth was particularly important in shaping her feelings about the pregnancy.

> I was sixteen years old, so I didn't look at it as others did. When you're already grown, you say, "Wow, I am going to be a mother!" But for me, well, I had already had [sexual] relations and hadn't gotten pregnant, and I wasn't using a method or anything. It was only after I moved in with him that it happened. . . . For me it was a little like a game, like having a doll. When a person is older, they think about having a child and giving that child all of their love and care—but it wasn't like that for me. For me it was like a dream; I wasn't prepared.[13]

A number of interviewees who continued pregnancies that they did not want or about which they had mixed feelings worried that their feelings of sadness, anger, or frustration had negatively impacted their experiences with pregnancy or childbirth, or the resulting children. Noel Terrazas was twenty-nine years old and had a child less than a year old when she became pregnant unexpectedly in 1987. "When I found out I was expecting my second child, it was difficult from the very beginning," remarked the fifty-one-year-old woman of Quechua descent. "It seemed as if I was rejecting it, I didn't want to have my baby. And the baby responded as if to say, 'Since you are rejecting me, I won't let you sleep.' Lying down, I couldn't sleep. Sitting up, sometimes I could."[14] Maura worried that two of her sons perceived the rejection she felt toward them during her pregnancies. "There are times I ask myself, 'Why did I cry so much over my sons?'—Because, you know, they say that children can feel this when they are in the womb. I think that perhaps they might hate me, my two sons, because I did not want them."[15] Women sometimes found themselves the targets of blame for failing to shield their unborn children from the sadness or anxiety that they experienced while pregnant. According to staff at the hospital where Margot Suárez delivered her child, Margot's feelings of sadness and her frequent "complaining" caused her to require a cesarean birth.

> I had my child by emergency cesarean section at seven months because of my sadness. They say when you are pregnant, you can't be sad and you can't complain. I had all these symptoms, though. I felt a lot of sadness and I cried and complained a lot [*lloraba mucho, renegaba mucho*]. . . . I thought I was going to be able to hold my child, but they put him in the incubator, and they [the hospital staff] told me it was because of that—that if I had carried the pregnancy normally, calmly, without complaining, without arguments, it would not have happened . . . But I let myself be carried away by sadness [*me he dejado . . . llevar por la tristeza*].[16]

The concerns of women I interviewed with the impact of their troubled feelings on their pregnancies and the personalities of their children echo the findings of other scholars working on emotions and health in the region. Individuals living in the Andes (and elsewhere in Latin America) often understand a range of emotions, such as rage, fright, and sadness, to be linked to illness, including problems in pregnancy.[17] Writes Maria Tapias of the relationship between emotions and miscarriage in Punata, Bolivia, "During pregnancy a mother's emotions could pass to her infant through her uterus and, in extreme cases, could cause miscarriage. Fetuses were said to be particularly vulnerable to the emotions a mother felt because they were still developing and their bodies were not yet strong."[18] In her examination of breastfeeding in the region, Tapias found that mothers who felt anger or sadness were sometimes blamed for transmitting an illness known as *arrebato* to their children through their breast milk. "During my fieldwork certain women became indexed as 'bad mothers' when their infants were affected with this ailment or when the mother failed to 'control' her emotions."[19] For Tapias, these discourses of "mother-blame," which sometimes discouraged women from breastfeeding in certain circumstances, often clashed with biomedical discourses that faulted women for *failing* to breastfeed either exclusively, or for as long as local development programs advised. These competing discourses demonstrate the scrutiny of mothers and motherhood both in western contexts, "because of [mothers'] role in the biological and social reproduction of society,"[20] and in Andean settings, where, "the work of making people . . . is specifically considered women's work."[21] At the same time, ideas about motherhood are remarkably varied even within western and community settings, and are shaped by broader hierarchies related to gender, class, and ethnicity.[22] The testimonies of women I interviewed in Bolivia further illustrate the multiple sources of, and negotiations surrounding, ideas about appropriate motherhood. Thus women's assessments of the quality of their own parenting were influenced by a complex intersection of women's relationships with partners and family members, their interactions with medical personnel, and their own experiences with health and illness.

Women's feelings of ambivalence toward their pregnancies were also deeply entwined with the broader social and economic circumstances in which these pregnancies took place. Noel and Maura, for instance, had mixed feelings about being pregnant because their pregnancies followed closely after their other children—conditions they knew could strain their families' financial resources and make their lives more difficult. These household economic dynamics were further embedded in larger, national trends—particularly, growing poverty following the implementation of neoliberal policies between the mid-1980s and late-1990s. During this period, neoliberal restructuring drew thousands of migrants to Bolivia's urban centers while shrinking the budgets for social services and opportunities for formal employment necessary to support the cities' newest residents.[23] It is more than likely that the consequences of neoliberalism in urban Bolivia impacted the lives of some of my interviewees; only five of the fifty-eight women I interviewed had what they described as formal employment, and almost all of the women reported that the most difficult challenge they faced in La Paz and El Alto was making ends meet. Perhaps because the interviews took place in 2009 and 2010, however, most individuals situated their financial troubles in the global economic crash of a few years before—itself a consequence of capitalism and of Bolivia's position of exploitation within this system.[24]

Women also felt ambivalent about their pregnancies because of their relationships with their partners and their families of origin, some of whom blamed the women for falling prey to sexual temptation and dishonoring their families with pregnancy out of the bounds of matrimony or cohabitation. These social attitudes toward gender and sexuality intersected with the broader conditions of women's subordinated status in urban Bolivia, and obviously colored women's (and men's) lives in a variety of ways. Most relevant to women's feelings about their pregnancies was the frequency with which men abused their partners and abandoned them while they were pregnant. While conducting research for this project, most activists I met who were engaged in organizing around issues impacting women were focused on femicide, rather than unsafe abortion. This was because of the terrible heights to which the murder of women for being women in Bolivia had reached by the first decade of the twenty-first century. The organization CIDEM found that 464 femicides occurred in Bolivia between 2009 and 2013, of which over 22 percent took place in El Alto.[25] The same machista ideologies that resulted in nearly a hundred murders of women per year due to "jealousy" (as male perpetrators often contend), also made possible men's abuse and abandonment of their pregnant partners. In short, women's lives were valued less than those of men. This reality, and its impacts on relationships between women and their male partners, were integral components of women's feelings of ambivalence toward their pregnancies.

INTO ACTION: DECIDING BETWEEN ABORTION AND KEEPING THE CHILD

Considering the complexity of women's feelings toward their unplanned and unwanted pregnancies, it is not surprising that they attempted to resolve these in a number of different ways. In general, interviewees who continued their pregnancies either considered abortion and decided against it, sought abortion but were turned away by doctors or other medical providers, attempted to abort on their own or at a clinic unsuccessfully, or never considered abortion. The ways in which women responded to their pregnancies remained fairly constant over the past several decades but were influenced by a wide range of factors, such as women's relationships with their partners and family members, and their religious beliefs, occupations, and life goals.

Women's comments about abortion—whether or not they thought about procuring the procedure themselves—were often marked by ambivalence. Women who considered terminating their pregnancies sometimes recalled feeling fearful of the procedure or of the ordeal of seeking it, and/or articulated moral, ethical, or religious concerns with abortion. Some women who attempted to provoke miscarriage on their own expressly stated that they had done so, while others implied that they had played sports or lifted heavy items in hopes that the vigorous activity might relieve them of an unwanted pregnancy. At the same time, women who never considered terminating their pregnancies often raised moral or ethical objections to abortion while simultaneously expressing frustration with or resignation to their unwanted pregnancies. Women who considered abortion but decided against it typically did so for one or more of the following reasons: partners or family members reacted unfavorably to their intentions to abort; they were concerned about the health risks the procedure might pose; or they were too scared to approach an abortion provider. A few women worried that abortion might contradict a higher order of events. Women who considered abortion but decided against it varied widely by age, marital status, ethnicity, educational level, and religion. In addition, the year or decade in which a woman became pregnant had little bearing on whether or not she considered having an abortion.

Simona's husband played an important role in her decision to keep her unwanted pregnancy, which occurred in 2004. "I went to the herbalists [*chifleras*] who sell tea and asked, 'What should I take, señora? My period's late and I don't want to have it—look, my other child is still just a baby.'"[26] Chifleras are female market workers who sell medicinal and ritual herbs and other items.[27] When she told her husband of her plan, however, he said, "'Do whatever you want. If you abort this child, though, forget about me. . . . I'm going to take my two kids and I'll leave you all alone.'" Initially, her husband's ultimatum angered Simona, who plotted to abort the pregnancy and go into hiding with her two children. After having a startling dream, however, Simona changed her mind. "One day I had a serious argument with my husband and I decided, 'I'm going to abort it and I'm going to go with my two kids where my husband will never find me—he can't take my kids away.' But one night I fell asleep crying and a lot of babies appeared in my dreams. . . . I got up in the middle of the night and started to cry, 'No, I can't abort it.' Maybe inside of me, there was something saying that I should not abort it. . . . So, I decided not to."

Unlike Simona's husband, who opposed her intention to terminate her pregnancy, Natividad Colque's aunt approached her niece and offered to help her procure an abortion when she became pregnant unexpectedly at age nineteen. Remarked the twenty-three-year-old alteña of Aymara descent, "I thought about it for a month. Part of me thought it would be best to interrupt the pregnancy, but finally, I decided not to. . . . My aunt said, 'Okay, you made your decision and now you have to carry on with your life [sobrellevar las cosas] and keep studying and everything.' So, that's how I had Daria." In part, Natividad decided not to terminate her pregnancy because she worried she might experience guilt or other psychological trauma. "There must be a feeling of guilt [following abortion] because in society, they put that on you—that you are killing a being that might have a soul," reflected Natividad. After she decided to continue her pregnancy, Natividad's aunt helped support her—although sometimes, that support took the form of tough love. "It was a stressful time for me because my aunt would pressure me sometimes. Actually, I am thankful that she pressured me, because that's how I continued studying," remarked Natividad. "With the little girl, the late nights, and the university, it was difficult. But my aunt has always helped me in that respect, economically— she's always helped both me and my mom."[28]

Several women considered seeking abortion but decided against it because they feared the procedure might pose serious risks to their health; even when they did not consider abortion themselves, many women feared or opposed the procedure for the same reason. Most commonly, women claimed that abortion, and in some cases incomplete miscarriage, caused gynecological problems later in life, including sterility; however, the procedure was also blamed for other conditions, such as cancer, body aches, urinary incontinence, and general physical malaise.[29] Yessica Ticona, who feared undergoing dilation and curettage procedures after her two miscarriages, remarked, "When they do abortions ... they always leave some tissue behind [in the uterus], and you don't realize this overnight ... it's probably five or ten years later when it finally hurts, and your womb is already spoiled [*malogrado*]."[30] One seventy-year-old Quechua woman I interviewed claimed that one of her neighbors in the Ciudad Satélite section of El Alto had undergone so many abortions that she was scarcely able to walk.[31]

Medical providers refused to assist Alma, Belinda, and Maura terminate their pregnancies, citing medical concerns with or ethical objections to abortion. When Alma became pregnant at fifteen and her partner abandoned her, Alma first tried intentionally falling in order to provoke a miscarriage. "I felt a kind of hate for my child, inside of my belly. It seems like I wanted to lose it. There were times I'd fall down, I wanted it to die." Eventually, Alma's mother took her to a clinic in El Alto, where the provider refused to perform an abortion, saying that, at three months, the pregnancy was too advanced. "He also spoke to me of how lovely it is; he said, 'You say that now, that you want to abort, but it's so beautiful. Instead, thank God for having given life to a child—you're going to have a baby!' ... So, I listened to him, and that's how my feelings changed."[32] When they sought abortion at private doctors' offices, both Belinda and Maura were turned away after being told their hearts would be unable to withstand the surgery. (While Belinda did have a history of heart trouble, Maura did not.[33])

Women's accounts of seeking abortion from western medical providers provide interesting insight into the dynamics of the doctor-patient relationship in Bolivia, and perhaps elsewhere in Latin America. Several women, activists, and medical personnel I interviewed asserted that doctors and nurses treated patients insensitively, dismissing their concerns, disregarding their explanations of their ailments, or approaching their patients with condescension. In a context marked by sociocultural and class hierarchies, western-educated (and often lighter-skinned) medical personnel are considered not only authorities on health but the social superiors of mestizo or indigenous patients. While an unequal power dynamic may characterize doctor-patient interactions in other world contexts, this may have a heightened impact in countries such as Bolivia, where the majority of the population is indigenous, and when it concerns access to services that are both prohibited and stigmatized, such as abortion. Thus (mostly male) medical doctors may attempt to utilize their perceived biomedical and sociocultural superiority to convince women of the moral, legal, or medical dangers of abortion—and in so doing, disempower women from exercising control over their reproductive lives. Belinda, for instance, whose doctor contended that abortion would pose a risk to her heart, ended up continuing her pregnancy—a decision that forever altered the makeup of her family. At other times, however, women used their relationships with their doctors to exercise greater control over their reproductive decisions—thus Noel convinced her family doctor to perform the three abortions she had during the course of her life.

Some women who experienced unwanted pregnancy during these years decided not to seek abortion because they were fearful of the procedure itself, or of approaching a provider to request the service. Rigoberta Justiniano, a twenty-nine-year-old mother of three, was seventeen years old and lived with her parents in El Alto when she discovered she was pregnant for the first time. "Things went through my head—that maybe I could get rid of it [*botarlo*], you know? But I didn't do it. I assumed my responsibility." When I asked why she had not sought an abortion, Rigoberta remarked, "I don't know—probably because I lacked the courage."[34] Other women, fearful of seeking abortion at a clinic and distraught at the prospect of having an unwanted child, attempted to abort on their own. When she became pregnant unexpectedly at age eighteen, Paula remarked that she routinely lifted heavy objects, saying, "I knew that this could make me expel it, or abort it, as they say. But maybe since I was still living with my parents, I wanted to do that, and that's why I didn't worry about lifting heavy things, or jumping—or even playing basketball," the then forty-year-old woman reflected. "I said to myself, 'It doesn't matter if I have a miscarriage, because my parents are going to kill me when they find out.'"[35]

Finally, some women who experienced unwanted pregnancy never considered abortion. Most women who planned to carry their unwanted pregnancies to term did so for one of three reasons: they did not agree with abortion for religious or ethical reasons; they felt that abortion was inappropriate considering the circumstances surrounding their pregnancies; or they were unfamiliar with the option of interrupting a pregnancy. Interestingly, only two women did not consider terminating their unwanted pregnancies, at least in part, because of their religious (particularly Catholic) faith. This was true despite the fact that thirty-nine of the fifty women I surveyed said they were Catholic. Scholarship on women's experiences with abortion further supports the notion that being Catholic does not necessarily "contribute to the difficulty of [women's] decision" to seek the procedure.[36]

A few women I interviewed did not consider terminating their unwanted pregnancies because they said they were unaware of this option at the time. As Jazmín explained, "I've recently heard people talk about this thing, abortion. On television, they also talk about it. But for me, it's bad, because it's like killing a child. It would be better to take care ahead of time to not get pregnant. I didn't know much about that [birth control], though." Despite her lack of familiarity with certain kinds of reproductive regulation, Jazmín did negotiate her fertility by avoiding sex. "One time, he [her husband] gave me a punch in the stomach and I had a miscarriage at three months, and at that point, I decided I didn't want any more children," recalled Jazmín. "Why would I bring more children in the world to suffer? So, I didn't accept my husband after that, and he didn't understand. He'd say, 'You're just rejecting me because you're sleeping with someone else.'" At the time I interviewed her in 2009, Jazmín was separated from her husband and shared a home in the El Alto neighborhood of Santa Rosa with several of her children. "Everything I have been through I explain to my daughters," she remarked. "And I also explain things to my sons—'You have to respect women,' I say to them, 'Think through your decisions.'"[37]

In looking back on their reproductive experiences, women often described their younger selves as "ignorant," saying they knew little about sexuality and pregnancy, or that they had had their children "without thinking." Jazmín, for instance, reflected, "Before, we just put up with it [pregnancy], we didn't use birth control. Now people take care of themselves. Now I tell my kids, 'I had my children thoughtlessly, one after another. . . . Have yourselves cured, daughters, don't be dumb like me' [*Antes uno se aguantaba nomás, no se cuidaba. Ahora ya se cuidan. A mis hijos yo mismo les digo, 'zonza he sido yo, en tener y tener hijos . . . se van a hacer curar hijitas no van a ser tonta como yo'*]."[38] The expressions "cure [*curación*]" and "to get cured [*curarse, hacerse curar*]" are commonly used to indicate abortion in the Andes. Throughout her interview, however, Jazmín employed the term to indicate surgical sterilization, which is likely what she means here. The tendency for women to refer to their younger selves as ignorant may emerge from, and suggest, a few different things. On the one hand, it is a relatively universal part of the human experience to look back on events that took place earlier in our lives and, with the benefit of hindsight, see our younger selves as ignorant or naïve. At the same time, the phenomena that shape individuals' perceptions of themselves vary according to one's specific life circumstances and social and cultural milieu. With respect to interviewees' attitudes toward their reproductive experiences, it is important to highlight the role that certain civil society institutions played in the lives of the women I interviewed. Since I relied on connections with a few organizations to meet most of my narrators, the majority of the women I interviewed had participated in (or were then participating in) workshops on themes like gender, sexuality, reproduction, or domestic violence led by one of such groups. Many women spoke positively about the influence of these workshops on their lives. Far from transmitting a set of objective facts about reproduction or other themes, however, civil society organizations and other development institutions craft, and are shaped by, specific value-laden narratives. These narratives may convey a range of messages to Bolivian women about "appropriate" ways of approaching health care, parenting, or romantic partnership. Thus these groups may privilege western-derived contraceptive methods over other types of fertility regulation, recommend certain methods of birth control while discouraging others, or suggest that a certain number of children or specific spacing between pregnancies is "ideal." These narratives, needless to say, also determine the themes of workshops offered to the local population and the specific topics included in these.

At the same time, civil society institutions may undervalue—and/or lead women to undervalue—other types of knowledge about sexuality and reproduction not represented in developmentalist narratives. In her study of contraception in Haiti, Catherine Maternowska found that when development organizations were unsuccessful in increasing birth control use among residents of Cité Soleil, staff chalked it up to Haitians' ignorance, rather than the considerable structural problems of, and discriminatory attitudes undergirding, their own programs.[39] Thus it is entirely possible that, after participating in educational initiatives held by organizations in La Paz and El Alto, some women I interviewed looked back on their experiences with pregnancy differently, wishing they had "known more" (i.e., possessed particular *kinds* of knowledge) about sex, relationships, or other phenomena in the past. At the same time, it is doubtful that women who participated in workshops on health or pregnancy accepted, wholesale, the recommendations advanced by these institutions—nor were their perceptions of their own experiences shaped solely by their contact with these groups. Instead, interviewees probably considered the information they learned at workshops alongside advice offered by friends and family members and lessons they learned during the course of their own lives. Overall, these testimonies suggest that women employed various forms of knowledge to figure out how to best plan their families, even if, reflecting back on these experiences years later, they might have wished they had done so differently.

The most common reasons that women cited for terminating, rather than continuing, their pregnancies included household economic problems and difficulties in their relationships with male partners, often in combination with a desire to limit or space their pregnancies. Women also terminated pregnancies in response to, or in anticipation of, negative reactions to their pregnancies on the part of partners or family members. One woman reported seeking abortion because she simply did not want to have children. Women often cited multiple reasons for seeking abortion. The reasons that women cited for having abortions remained fairly consistent over the years of this study, and across the age, ethnicity, and educational level of the woman. A woman's reasons sometimes varied, however, according to the health and stability of her relationship with her male partner. While women in live-in partnerships who described those relationships as functional and/or relatively happy cited economic concerns as the major motivating factor for their abortions, women who described their partnerships as conflictive stated that they had terminated their pregnancies due to these conflicts, sometimes in addition to financial concerns. Women who were dating their partners but not living with them when they became pregnant said that they sought abortion due not to economic concerns but because they feared—or had confirmed—that their parents or partners would react negatively to learning of their pregnancies.

Pilar and Marcela each terminated two pregnancies due to economic concerns and to problems in their marital relationships. Although they did not specifically intend to do so at the time, Pilar and Marcela ultimately utilized abortion to space their pregnancies; both women had additional children after at least one of their abortions. Pilar was married and nineteen years old in 1995 when she became pregnant with what would have been her third child. At that time, she and her partner decided together to terminate the pregnancy, since their income from working as small-scale merchants was already stretched thin. In subsequent years, Pilar and her partner had two more children. When she became pregnant a sixth time at age twenty-eight, Pilar again terminated the pregnancy, but this time she sought the abortion because her partner had taken up with another woman and she feared she could not support another child on her own. Pilar also complained that her partner faulted her for becoming pregnant and believed that she had done so intentionally in order to "trap" him in the relationship.[40]

Marcela Flores, a married mestiza woman who in 2009 worked as a medical assistant, sought abortions after her second and third children, at approximately twenty-six and thirty years of age. Marcela lived with her husband and their four children in a large house on Avenida Kollasuyo in La Paz. The house was divided into several apartments; her two younger brothers and their families occupied the other apartments. At first, Marcela remarked that financial concerns and her partner's rejection of her pregnancies led her to seek abortion; later, she added that her partner's excessive sexual appetite, and implicitly, abuse, occasioned the unwanted pregnancies and obligated her to terminate them.

> I became pregnant and I had to recur to abortion because economically, we were not doing well. . . . My husband has always rejected my pregnancies. I mean, I've suffered a lot—actually, economically, we were doing okay, but my husband was very into sex. . . . My husband thought only of his own satisfaction, he didn't think about me. So, I got pregnant two times, and both times I had to abort it because I couldn't have it. I argued with my husband, he said to me, "Then, why'd you get pregnant?" I responded, "I didn't ask you [for sex], you looked for me, I mean, you use me." . . . I think many women experience this in Bolivia because men use us sexually. . . . There's a lot of machismo, for that reason, yes, I've aborted two times. . . . At the moment that I found out I was pregnant, I did think about it—Should I have it? Should I not have it? But my husband also said to me, "What are we going to do? Another mouth to feed!" So, it was him that— well, all in all, we both decided.

While she draws parallels between her own coercive sexual experiences and those of other women in Bolivia's machista society, Marcela also struggles with how best to explain her decision to terminate her pregnancies. Although she alternately asserts that she "had to" have the abortions due to economic constraints and suggests that it was her husband's idea to seek abortion, she ultimately states that she and her husband decided together to terminate the pregnancies. At the same time, Marcela's comments suggest that these decisions, as well as the circumstances that led to her pregnancies, were fraught—and that the abortions may have been difficult events. This seems to have been true not only because the experiences themselves were trying, but because Marcela felt she had few people with whom she could share them. When I asked if she had ever spoken about her abortions with anyone, Marcela remarked, "No, parents here are very closed-minded. They just see that you ended up pregnant, they don't see what you might need going forward. It isn't easy to talk about stuff like this in Bolivia."[41] Interestingly, Marcela's daughter Graciela, who I also interviewed for this project, expressed the same sentiment about her own parents.[42]

The coercive sexual encounters that Marcela experienced with her husband, like those of other women I interviewed, point to the distressing commonality of women's mistreatment and abuse by intimate partners in Bolivia. In a 2003 national demographic survey, 68 percent of women reported having suffered physical, emotional, or sexual violence within a romantic relationship.[43] Although it is unclear how census takers framed this question or how individual women conceptualized their experiences with coercion or violence, this figure still suggests that mistreatment within romantic relationships is widespread. The conversations I had with women in Bolivia indicated that women's experiences and understandings of mistreatment occurred on a spectrum. While some women considered their experiences to form part of a "normal" relationship, others defined these as abusive. Still others reported that their views of their experiences had changed over time—particularly that they now saw as abusive experiences that, in the past, they might have considered normal. At the same time, although many women viewed abuse or violence within intimate relationships as common, they very rarely considered such behavior acceptable, even when they remained in these relationships. Sexual violence often results in pregnancy; six of the fifty-five women I interviewed became pregnant at least once as a result of acts of intercourse that they described as forced, coerced, or otherwise nonconsensual. Although in contemporary western settings "rape" is often defined as any sexual contact to which one party does not explicitly and verbally consent, women in Bolivia defined their own sexual experiences with more subtlety and did not necessarily feel they had been raped, even when they did not consent. Many women who suffer sexual assault in Bolivia, as elsewhere, do not report the incidents to authorities—and for understandable reasons. Women may fear that police will interrogate their sexual histories or deny their accusations of rape; or, if their attacker is a relative, women may be hesitant to upset the dynamics of their families.

Some women who terminated pregnancies were initially unsure how they felt about being pregnant, but eventually decided to seek abortion out of fear of their loved ones' reactions to their pregnancies. When she became pregnant at age eighteen, Adela López, who was single and had a one-year-old daughter, feared what her parents would say when they discovered she was pregnant yet again. Adela's fear of her family's reaction to her pregnancies led her to have two abortions, one in 1995 and a second in 1998. When we talked in 2009, Adela, a mestiza woman, was thirty-two years old and lived with her husband and two children in the Villa San Antonio neighborhood of La Paz. Adela worked as an activist in a local women's organization and said that her involvement with the group had significantly shaped her views on her past experiences with pregnancy and abortion.

> Both times I had an abortion, what most mattered was what my parents, and fundamentally my dad, were going to say. The first time, my daughter was a year old, so it was like, "What? So quickly, two kids?" . . .

Also, I felt ashamed. Who knows of what? Maybe because I didn't use a better contraceptive method. The second time, I also aborted because of what my parents might say. . . . I first thought of what everyone else would think before I thought of whether I wanted or did not want that baby. I mean, I didn't stop to think if I wanted it, if I really loved the father, or if I would've liked to be a mother again—no. First I thought of what my dad would say, then what my mom would say, and like that successively down to the neighbor on the corner.[44]

Like Adela, twenty-three-year-old Vania Condori was unsure if she wanted to be pregnant when she realized she had missed her period. An Aymara woman (de vestido) who was studying at the local university, Vania lived with her parents and seven younger siblings in the La Portada neighborhood of La Paz (where Marcela also lived). Although she worried how her parents might react to the news, the factor that most led Vania to seek abortion was her boyfriend's declaration that he wanted no part in the pregnancy.

We saw each other one day and I brought the pregnancy tests that I had done. He got scared, he took a few steps back and he started to cry, and the only thing that he said to me was that he was not prepared, that he was studying in the university. . . . that all of his courses were already paid for and that he was not going to risk that for a baby. I started crying, obviously, and he left. "Please excuse me, but I don't know you," he said, "and if you want to make problems for me . . . I will leave this very night for Tarija [a city in the south of Bolivia]." . . . I was sad; what was I supposed to do? . . . For a moment, yeah, I said to myself, "It must be nice, to have a baby." But no, I didn't want it—I didn't want it above all when he reacted this way. . . . I mean, it's not like I was fifteen years old—I was already in university, I was grown up, but . . . he said to me, "I don't know you, don't look for me, if you look for me, I'm going to act like I don't know you."

Even though she no longer wanted to be pregnant after her boyfriend reacted the way he did, Vania believed that if he had not repeatedly urged her to seek abortion—and eventually taken her to buy herbal abortifacients—she probably would have ended up continuing the pregnancy. "I was completely shocked. All I did was cry and sleep. I think that if I'd just stayed at home, I probably would have kept my baby. But he gave me all these options and alternatives. . . . He called me all the time, until finally we went up here to Santa Cruz Avenue and bought the tea."[45]

As the comments of Vania and other interviewees suggest, women's partners influenced their decisions to seek abortion in a number of ways. Some women, feeling uneasy about the strength or stability of their relationships or worried their partners would reject the pregnancies, sought abortion on their own. Other women decided jointly with their partners to seek abortion after sometimes long and difficult conversations. At times, women emerged from these conversations feeling confident about their decisions to terminate their pregnancies; at others, women felt they had been pressured or coerced into procuring abortion. Although they did not explicitly report feeling pressured to seek abortion, both Pilar and Marcela, quoted earlier, said they felt obligated by their partners' lack of support and sexual proclivities to terminate their pregnancies. Whether directly or indirectly, women's partners, and the status of their relationships with these, played a significant role in their decisions to seek abortion.[46]

Unwanted Pregnancy, Abortion, and "Choice"

As the foregoing testimonies suggest, while many women cited reasons or motivating factors that led them to seek abortion, few felt that they unequivocally "decided" or "chose" to do so. Interviewees used a number of expressions to describe how they came to terminate their pregnancies. While some women said they decided to have abortions—either on their own or together with their partners—other women said that they "had to" have abortions or were "obligated" or "forced" to do so. Lupe Colque, a woman of Aymara and Quechua descent who had an abortion in the early 1980s, did not explicitly use the term "decision" to describe her abortion experience; yet she knew from a young age that she never wanted to have children. "I aborted because, since I was about fifteen, I said to myself, 'I am never going to have children, I don't want to have children, I want to do other things.' I did not want to repeat what my mom was going through because she suffered a lot. . . . I did not want to be a mother, I did not want to be a housewife."[47]

Pilar and Marcela said at one point during their interviews that they decided to have their abortions, and then at another point that they were obligated to do so. While Pilar felt that her partner's poor reaction to her pregnancy and his relationship with another woman obligated her to seek her second abortion, Marcela explained that she had to have her two abortions because of her difficult economic situation and her husband's sexual abuse. Noel, who had three abortions, alternately explained that she terminated her pregnancies because her partner convinced and obligated her to do so, but also because she had planned to have only two children and was concerned with her family's economic situation.

> NT: I was not in a good situation to have my child. . . . My partner did
>   not earn enough to have another baby . . . and I only planned to have
>   two children, so because of this I interrupted the three pregnancies.
> NK: And at that time, did you speak with your partner about the
>   abortions?
> NT: I did want to have the children; it was him that didn't want to.
>   But he also convinced me. And the truth is I saw my situation—that
>   we barely had enough to eat. He said to me, "Look, the situation is
>   critical—where are we going to get money? . . . What are we going
>   to do?" . . . I was surprised, I said, "How are you going to do this if
>   God is sending us another child?" But he obligated me; he said, "No,

we can't have it because where are we going to get money to pay for food?" I mean, he convinced me, you know? And I also thought about it and said yes. . . . But I have a lot of guilt and I always ask God for forgiveness for all of the things I have done wrong, because I'm a Catholic and God says, "Do not kill; it isn't your decision." I already said that it wasn't my decision. But it was the situation that led us to do these bad things.

Torn by the desire to provide her existing children with a better life and her objections to abortion on religious grounds, the path that led Noel to terminate her pregnancies was clearly fraught. In part, Noel's conflicted attitude about her abortions related to the condition of her youngest child. Born in 2001 when Noel was forty-three years old (after her third abortion), Noel's son Marco had Trisomy 21, commonly known as Down syndrome. Noel often wondered if "God brought [her] a child with the syndrome" because she had abortions earlier in life.[48]

For Adela, the economic, political, and social challenges that she and other women face in Bolivia made it difficult for her to consider that women ever truly "decide" to abort their pregnancies.

I think that the conditions that society presents you with as a woman nowadays—economic and political conditions—it's impossible to think that it is your decision, right? Because, economically, you can want to have a baby, but you don't have the money nor the conditions to have one, and politically, I mean, everyone exercises power over your body, so everyone else decides if you should or should not have a child. There's a particular age, particular conditions to meet to have a baby—to be married, for example, or at least that the guy with whom you're going to have it be your formal partner. You can't say that one night you met a friend and you became pregnant—I mean, that would be a total taboo. So, there's an exercise of power over your body, so you decide to not have it, but *you* don't decide, right? Others decide, because you haven't met those requirements. No, in neither case did I feel that it was my

decision—but that doesn't mean that I regret having them either. I think
that abortion gives you the possibility to decide about your body, and
that women have a right to abort. . . . But the fact that you see a woman,
like in my case, who aborts more than one time, it shows you not that
I like to abort, right? Rather, it's society that is pushing women to abort.[49]

Tragically, two women I interviewed were unambiguously forced to
terminate their pregnancies—one by her mother and the other by her
husband. The testimony of one of these women, Olga Mollo, appears
next. When I sat down to interview Olga, a forty-year-old Aymara
woman (de vestido), I did so to learn about her work as a nurse at a clinic
providing abortions in La Paz. Several minutes into the interview, I asked
Olga to describe the characteristics of the women who sought abortion at
the clinic where she worked. It was then that she shared with me her own
experience with abortion, which took place in 1989.

> I'm going to tell you an anecdote of mine, that I went through, that
> I lived, and that perhaps made me enter into this field. . . . Well, when
> I was very young, about eighteen years old, just like every young girl has
> her boyfriend and things happen, I got pregnant—but I didn't know that
> I was pregnant. I didn't have that trust with my mother, so that she could
> give me advice on how I should take care of myself [to not get pregnant]
> once I started having sex. So, it had already been about three months . . .
> and my mother—mothers are wise, my mother wasn't a doctor or any-
> thing, she was a humble, poor woman—she said to me, "You seem
> strange, daughter, I think you are pregnant." And this surprised me,
> because I was happy that I hadn't gotten my period. She took me to a
> doctor who she said was her own doctor, on Buenos Aires Avenue. . . .
> The doctor . . . told me that I was three months pregnant . . . and my
> mother said to me, "You cannot have this child because you have to
> be a professional. I don't see a good future for you with this boy. You're
> both young. No . . . I am going to have you *cured*," she said—because
> that was her form of saying it. And since I was very young and relied

on her financially, I couldn't—she made decisions *for* me, practically. Nor did my partner ever know that I was pregnant. So, she took me there. . . . They gave me anesthesia, they did it [performed the abortion], I woke up from the anesthesia, I vomited. . . . It was a terrible experience for me. . . . I think that everywhere, it must happen like that. I think about how many women must have lived what I lived. . . . But here [at the clinic where she worked], I see certain differences. . . . Here, they demand quality of us. . . . Here, we cannot yell at a patient—she must be treated as if she is the best person that exists.

Olga's experience undergoing an abortion that she did not want at a clinic the quality of which she doubted bolstered her own commitment to provide quality care at the facility where she then worked. At the same time, Olga's experience was deeply painful—particularly since, when I interviewed her, Olga and her husband desperately desired a child but were having difficulty conceiving. "Sometimes I wonder, why didn't I resist my mother's decision?" remarked Olga tearfully. "I've had the fertility treatments and I can't get pregnant. . . . I've studied and everything, I'm a professional—and as a professional, I am successful. But as a woman and as a mother, I am not." For Olga, the experience of motherhood formed a central part of what it meant to be a woman. Having not had the opportunity to decide whether to pursue motherhood, Olga's experience with abortion and the subsequent trajectory of her life left her with a feeling of loss.[50]

Reflecting back on their abortions anywhere from three to thirty years earlier, women I interviewed in La Paz and El Alto had a variety of feelings about these. Some felt relief, while others were troubled by guilt and religious concerns. Most women fell somewhere in between, feeling both sadness, as they wondered how their child might have turned out, but also the desire to *salir adelante* (move on). About three-quarters of interviewees who had abortions disagreed with abortion in principle, and yet most also felt that in specific situations—such as prior to the last ten to fifteen years, when birth control was largely unavailable, or in dire economic circumstances—abortion represented the best alternative. Not one interviewee who terminated a pregnancy took into account the procedure's prohibited status when making her decision to seek abortion, nor did those women who felt guilt following their abortions attribute these feelings to having broken the law. Instead, social factors— particularly the stigmatization of abortion and of particular "types" of pregnancy and motherhood—shaped women's feelings about pregnancy termination. On the one hand, the social and religious stigmas attached to abortion—stigmas shaped by abortion's legal prohibition, by the strength of the Catholic Church and other religious institutions, and by closed-minded attitudes toward sexuality—contributed to the stress and difficulty of women's experiences with the procedure. Women who ter- minated pregnancies worried that they had committed an unethical act, or that others would judge them for seeking abortion. At the same time, societal stigmas attached to particular "types" of pregnancies—such as those that occurred when a woman was single or "too" young—often led women to seek abortion in the first place. Thus negative social attitudes surrounding abortion and pregnancies that occurred in particular cir- cumstances sometimes meant that both abortion and its alternatives represented difficult options that were laden with conflict.

Overall, there were more similarities than differences between the reproductive experiences of the various women I interviewed in La Paz and El Alto. Regardless of education, ethnicity, or marital status, women who faced unwanted pregnancy in urban Bolivia during these years often expressed frustration at the trajectories of their reproductive lives and their experiences with sex and pregnancy. Sometimes, this frustration led women to state or to imply that they had not really had the chance to "decide" whether to bear their unwanted children, but that they had instead "ended up" doing so. While some of these women characterized their attitudes toward their pregnancies as ones of resignation, others referenced God or a higher order of events to explain how they came to

accept these. Even when they expressed a sense of frustration or pessi-
mism toward their reproductive histories, however, women's comments
reveal the strength, determination, and resilience they often brought
toward their experiences confronting pregnancies that occurred in adverse
circumstances.

At first glance, it may be difficult to discern why some women facing
unwanted pregnancy during these years opted to continue, rather than
terminate, their pregnancy. When asked why they did not want to be
pregnant, women who kept unwanted pregnancies and those who
sought abortion cited similar, if not identical, factors. The factors that
most influenced women's feelings and reactions toward their pregnancies also remained the same across the last several decades, suggesting
that there has been little change over time in women's responses toward
unwanted pregnancy. Considering these similarities, why, then, did
some women facing unwanted pregnancy in Bolivia during these years
end up keeping their children, while others sought abortion? The conversations I shared with women in Bolivia suggest that the answer primarily came down to whom women knew. Women who sought abortion
typically knew someone—such as a cousin, friend, or sister—who had
interrupted a pregnancy and had told them about it. If she did not know
someone who had terminated a pregnancy, a woman who sought abortion usually had someone in her life willing to assist her in the abortion
process—helping her locate a provider, for instance, or accompanying
her to the clinic. On the other hand, women who continued their pregnancies often lacked these social connections, knowing neither individuals who had procured abortion in the past, nor people willing to assist
them in the process. In addition, women who were particularly young
when they became pregnant (under about twenty years old) were more
likely to keep their children than to seek abortion. This may have
been because younger women depended more heavily on their families
of origin, who might have opposed women's decisions to terminate their
pregnancies.

While women who continued their unwanted pregnancies and those who sought abortion may not have had the same social connections, their feelings about their reproductive experiences were often similar. When explaining why they kept or terminated their pregnancies, women cited a range of factors and life circumstances that shaped or constrained their decisions, or even superseded these. In other words, women did not typically conceive of their reproductive experiences as events about which they could articulate and exercise a personal "choice." This despite the tendency for some activists and policy makers to characterize the abortion debate as one about women's right to *choose* "whether to bear or beget a child."[51] For Rickie Solinger, whose work focuses on the United States, the capacity of women to make choices about their reproductive lives is heavily constrained by popular—and, as it turns out, limited—understandings of what "kind" of woman legitimately bears the right to choose. "The right to choose," writes Solinger, "has come to be intimately connected to the possession of resources. Many Americans have developed faith in the idea that women who exercise choice are supposed to be ... women with money."[52] For women in the United States, this restricted definition of who possesses the right to reproductive choice has far-reaching implications, underlying experiences as diverse as the coercive sterilization of poor women and women of color across much of the twentieth century, as well as contemporary debates about abortion and child welfare.[53]

Women in a range of geographical contexts, of course, face limitations to the capacity to define their reproductive lives; for most, the web of factors shaping their ability to choose abortion or other reproductive outcomes is embedded in local economic and social conditions. While the constraints that informed women's reproductive decisions in La Paz and El Alto were in part economic, other social, cultural, and demographic factors seemed to be nearly as important. In a country where more than half of the population lives below the national poverty line, a woman's age or relationship status, her ethnicity and form of dress, the number and ages of her children, or the social circle to which her parents belong may significantly influence society's assessment of her "right to choose."

The notion that reproductive decisions are shaped by not only personal factors but also structural ones may seem intuitive or even obvious—and yet these broader dimensions of reproductive decision making are often overlooked within political debates on abortion's legal status. Instead, these discussions of abortion tend to portray the decision to terminate a pregnancy as a choice made by some idealized, autonomous woman (who is likely white and at the very least, middle class); these discussions further seem to characterize the decision itself as one between two lives—that of the mother and that of the fetus. The testimonies featured here suggest that reproductive decisions in fact comprised a number of lives, including those of partners, family members, and women's existing children. Recognizing that the decision to continue a pregnancy or to seek abortion is highly complex, comprising dimensions both personal and structural, may necessarily require us to view this decision—and the woman making it—with greater compassion and respect.

CHAPTER 4

Navigating Unwanted Pregnancy in La Paz and El Alto, 1950s–1980s

Magda Cusi was a high school student living in the city of Potosí in 1955 when she found herself facing an unexpected pregnancy. Explaining her boyfriend's reaction upon learning about it, Magda remarked, "He was scared and he said, 'Oh, my parents, what will they say now? Let's go to . . . a clinic, a midwife [*matrona*], who knows,'—he surely wanted to have me abort." When I asked her if she knew of abortion providers operating in Potosí at that time, Magda told me she had a high school friend who had successfully procured an abortion a year or two before. Although she did not know who performed the young woman's abortion, Magda remarked that her friend, who was concerned with the symptoms she was experiencing after the abortion, told her, "I went to a clinic and they did a 'scraping' [*raspaje*] for me and now I am having bleeding."[1] Magda decided to continue her pregnancy, and in early 1956 she gave birth to her son at home with the assistance of a midwife. Other women facing unwanted or unexpected pregnancies in Bolivia during these years opted for abortion, either by visiting providers or recurring to any number of strategies to terminate their pregnancies on their own.

This chapter examines women's experiences with unwanted pregnancy and abortion between the early 1950s and the early 1980s. Drawing on medical records, oral interviews, and a variety of secondary sources, I investigate what it was like for a woman with an unexpected or unwanted pregnancy to give birth, undergo miscarriage, or experience abortion during these years; what sorts of individuals and facilities women turned to for help; how women felt about the care they received; what complications women experienced during these reproductive events and how they resolved these complications.

The first section of the chapter draws primarily on secondary sources to provide an overview of the reproductive health practices and traditions upon which women relied during the time period, including both western and Andean forms. The second section of the chapter analyzes medical records to illuminate the experiences of women who received pregnancy-related care at the "Natalio A. Aramayo" Maternity Institute (INA). Created in 1955 under the auspices of the MNR party's efforts to create more inclusive health systems and to reduce levels of maternal and infant mortality, the INA was designed to provide women with prenatal care and treat them in childbirth.[2] Medical records from the facility, however, reveal that INA personnel also sometimes treated women suffering complications from abortion or miscarriage; staff also recorded information on the pregnancies these women had experienced prior to visiting the facility. Personal testimonies provide richer and more comprehensive information regarding women's reproductive experiences during these decades. In the final section of the chapter, I draw on oral interviews with women who gave birth to or miscarried pregnancies that they described as unwanted between 1955 and 1982. (All of the women I interviewed who terminated their unwanted pregnancies did so after 1982; thus their stories are examined in chapter 5.)

This chapter reveals that women in La Paz and El Alto used both Andean and clinical facilities and practices to navigate their reproductive lives. This was true despite the efforts of doctors and policy makers to foster women's use of western medical facilities and practices to the exclusion of Andean health forms. It further demonstrates that women pushed the boundaries of periods of pronatalism in Bolivia. In the face of rhetorical opposition to and restrictive policies on contraception and abortion,

women negotiated their reproductive lives by using a variety of forms of
fertility regulation and by terminating pregnancies.

REPRODUCTIVE HEALTH CARE IN THE URBAN HIGHLANDS

Providers of reproductive health care in La Paz and El Alto between the
1950s and the 1980s were diverse in scope, and included a variety of kinds
of midwives, traditional doctors and herbalists, as well as western-trained
health care workers, such as biomedical doctors, nurses, and medical students, working in the public and private spheres.[3] When seeking assistance
in childbirth, most women turned either to trusted family members experienced in delivering infants or to midwives.[4] There were at least three
kinds of midwives active in La Paz and El Alto during the period: (1) indigenous parteras, who drew on Andean medicine to assist women in pregnancy and with any number of gynecological conditions; (2) criolla or
mestiza matronas, who utilized some combination of biomedical training and home remedies acquired through experience; and (3) parteras
empíricas, who drew on personal experience acquired informally and
employed home remedies to attend women in pregnancy. The techniques
of parteras empíricas were generally derived from western medical traditions.[5] The boundaries between these groups of midwives were somewhat
blurred with respect to their specific practices and clientele, yet matronas
typically served upper-class, urban-dwelling women, while indigenous
parteras and parteras empíricas usually tended to indigenous and mestiza women in both rural and urban areas.[6] At the turn of the twentieth
century in La Paz, criolla matronas, who worked with both state health
officials and western medical practitioners, could enjoy considerable power
and status. Many shared connections with elite families and were called
upon by upper-class women to deliver children in their homes; some also
held positions of authority at local maternity institutes. The municipal government also sometimes relied upon matronas to provide childbirth
assistance to poor women.[7] Yet the majority of the population in La Paz,

who did not pertain to elite sectors, likely relied on family members, indigenous parteras, and parteras empíricas for assistance in childbirth, probably without significant oversight from government authorities.

Biomedical doctors and nurses had less control over reproductive health care than did midwives in early twentieth-century La Paz and held little professional power or prestige. The few hospitals that existed were often administered by groups of nuns, some of European extraction, who managed the facilities' finances and personnel and cared for patients.[8] Physicians had little success in competing with midwives for authority over childbirth and infant care, in part, because of the failure of their treatments for common infections and, concomitantly, their inability to reduce high rates of maternal and infant death.[9] By the 1920s, however, physicians and policy makers began to pursue a number of initiatives designed to consolidate the position of the nascent obstetrical establishment over midwifery.[10] The struggle of obstetricians and gynecologists to eclipse the work of midwives was a contest taking place throughout Latin America (and indeed, the world), although it began later in Bolivia than it did elsewhere in the region.[11] In Bolivia, the efforts of the obstetric establishment to replace traditional birth attendants occurred alongside the consolidation of liberal rule and was intimately related to broader political and economic goals.[12]

Despite their own inability to reduce maternal and infant death, doctors in Bolivia partly justified their efforts to limit the practice of midwives by asserting that these were responsible for high infant and maternal mortality rates and for performing abortions.[13] Physicians' efforts to gain control of reproductive health care were further undergirded by racial and gender assumptions that targeted both indigenous mothers and medical practitioners as unhygienic, backward, and obstacles to liberal notions of progress and modernization. Cognizant of women's widespread recurrence to midwives, however, Bolivia's incipient obstetrical establishment sought to train young, mestiza midwives and subsume them to physicians' authority, rather than undertake the dubious project of phasing out these birth attendants completely. The ensuing training programs attempted to forge a tiered system of childbirth attendants that pitted university-trained criolla and mestiza matronas against indigenous parteras, while subordinating both to the authority of male medical practitioners.[14] The creation of the INA—and that of another important obstetrical facility during the period, the Instituto Maternológico 18 de Mayo, founded in 1952—was directly related to the efforts of the western medical establishment to consolidate its power over midwifery.[15] It is difficult to determine the impact of these attempts to reshape reproductive health practices on average Bolivians[16]; yet there is considerable evidence that women continued to rely on midwives and other traditional medical practitioners for pregnancy-related care throughout the twentieth century. Thus, by the 1980s, the Bolivian Society for Public Health estimated that only 10 percent of births in the country took place in hospital settings, while three times as many individuals used traditional medicine over biomedical forms.[17]

Bolivia's medical landscape during the period was richly peopled by a variety of kinds of Andean doctors and herbalists who provided health care to the majority of the country's population.[18] The precise names by which these providers were known and the specific services that they provided are likely to have varied over time and across geographical location, as well as according to whom you ask; many, however, possessed profound medical expertise and complex understandings of health and illness.[19] As described in the introduction, these practitioners and their clients conceived of health as consisting of physical, social, psychological, and spiritual elements, in which individual health was dependent upon a broader sense of balance in the natural world and the spiritual realm.[20] Practitioners of Andean medicine utilized a variety of different techniques to diagnose illness, including divination, examination of the body and its secretions, interpretation of dreams, and the dissection of animals. Treatments offered by Andean medical practitioners also varied, and included interventions into the patient's body, such as by administering herbal remedies, and solutions encompassing the broader social and physical environment, such as performing rituals for the Pachamama or mountain ancestors.[21] In the Andes, "home is the preferred site for curing because of its proximity to environmental and symbolic causes of illness."[22] Partly for this reason, some Andean medical practitioners traditionally traveled long distances to heal individuals at home, in their own ayllus (communities).

Among the most well-known healers of the Andes are the Kallawaya, skilled herbalists who originally formed part of an ethnic group from the Charazani region of the province of Bautista Saavedra (Department of La Paz). Kallawaya healers, who are predominantly, but not exclusively, men, traveled throughout Chile, Argentina, Bolivia, and Peru (and perhaps even farther afield) as early as A.D. 500 providing care for medical, psychological, and spiritual ailments.[23] The medical traditions of the Kallawaya, "draw analogies between the geographical areas occupied by their ayllus and the human body, referring to a properly functioning ayllu as similar to a healthy human body."[24] In this conception, the movement of rivers through the ayllu is analogous to the circulation of fluids through the human body; bodies in which these fluids are out of balance are subject to illness. The principle bodily fluids in Kallawaya medicine are blood, fat, and air, which are characterized as hot, cold, wet, or dry.[25] The *sonco* (heart) is responsible for the circulation of bodily fluids, and illness is typically caused by the disruption of this circulation.[26] The Kallawaya also characterize specific illnesses, herbs, and foods as being hot or cold (or, alternatively, "cordial"—a classification that, according to Joseph Bastien, is less important than hot and cold).[27] Hot ailments (e.g., liver and kidney problems) and cold illnesses (e.g., pneumonia and bronchitis) are treated by administering an herb or food of the opposite quality to restore balance.[28] Following colonization, Andean medical practitioners were exposed to Greek humoral theories, which share similar notions of the importance of bodily fluids to overall health. As noted by Ann Zulawski, while anthropologists disagree on the precise degree to which Andean and European conceptualizations intersect, similarities between their theories, in addition to the widely acknowledged efficacy of many Kallawaya remedies, may help explain why these were visited by mestizo and creole Bolivians.[29] Despite treating individuals across ethnic lines, the Kallawaya did not often share their techniques with outsiders; instead, they passed knowledge down to other young men from their kinship groups through traveling apprenticeships.[30]

What could be considered the female equivalent of the Kallawaya are herbalists known as K'awayu, although they have not been as widely investigated as their male counterparts.[31] Like the Kallawaya, K'awayu healers, who traditionally hail from the Tomás Frías Province (Department of Potosí), are understood to constitute an ethnic group, and their members transmit knowledge to other young women via kinship networks. In contemporary La Paz and El Alto, the K'awayu operate market stands offering herbal remedies, where they are visited by residents seeking medical guidance on any number of ailments. K'awayu healers trace their expertise to an origin story in which they were visited by a bird bearing medicinal herbs that was transformed into an angel, who granted them the gift of healing. According to this story, only women received this specialized medical knowledge. K'awayu healers also sometimes employ non-kin-related, Aymara-speaking women to work at their market stands, to whom they impart their knowledge of herbal remedies.[32]

From at least the 1950s, but likely much earlier, Kallawaya and K'awayu healers practiced in cities, including La Paz.[33] According to a 2008 interview with Walter Álvarez Quispe, a Kallawaya, biomedical doctor, and president of the Sociedad Boliviana de Medicina Tradicional (Bolivian Society of Traditional Medicine, or SOBOMETRA), "Fifty-five years ago, Kallawaya could be found alongside the San Francisco Church [in central La Paz], where they are now. Prior to that, they wanted to gather around the Church, but people made them leave—the authorities, the homeowners, and the [Franciscan] priests. They harassed them, calling them witches. . . . People would come up to them secretly, and get them to accompany them to their houses."[34] Today, a few streets near the sixteenth-century church, which are lined with the stands of Kallawaya and K'awayu, are known as the "witches' market" and are frequented by tourists. Prior to its construction, however, the area around the Church constituted an important pre-Columbian nucleus of the city and thus has long attracted the presence of Kallawayas and K'awayu, making the zone an important center of local medicine in La Paz.[35]

As the comments of Álvarez Quispe suggest, traditional medical practitioners in Bolivia have suffered persecution by state and religious authorities. Efforts to eradicate Andean medicine began in the colonial period, as part of broader attempts to exterminate non-Catholic religious practices in the region.[36] The authorities who implemented the Campaign to Extirpate Idolatry in the seventeenth century viewed Andean healers and religious specialists, who paid tribute to the Pachamama and to natural forms such as mountains and rivers, as practitioners of witchcraft who were consorting with the devil. Women healers, who were viewed as particularly vulnerable to manipulation by the devil, were especially targeted for persecution.[37] By the early twentieth century, western doctors and policy makers in Bolivia, concerned with the underdeveloped nature of the country's biomedical establishment vis-à-vis other Latin American nations, began to pursue measures designed to stamp out the practice of Andean healers and unlicensed empirics of all kinds. Local medical journals, in which physicians published partly to bolster their professional reputations, published articles during the period with titles such as, "Granting of degrees and the illegal exercise of the profession" and "Direct assault on empiricism."[38] In line with these concerns, the Ministry of Health passed a statute in 1938 restricting the practice of medicine to individuals with a diploma from a Bolivian university and requiring all medical providers to register with the Ministry.[39] In the second half of the twentieth century, Kallawaya were prevented from practicing in a number of locations—and some were even arrested and imprisoned.[40] As with the campaign of obstetricians to wrest control of reproductive health care from indigenous midwives, physicians' efforts to eradicate unlicensed medical practitioners reflected their own anxieties about building a professional medical establishment at a time when most individuals utilized Andean providers. They also revealed broader concerns of medical and state authorities about the so-called problem that Bolivia's indigenous populations ostensibly posed to the country's achievement of modern standards of public health, economic vitality, and political stability. Yet the foregoing measures were far from successful in cementing the hegemony of biomedicine over traditional forms, and urban residents continued to rely on Andean medical practitioners and empirics throughout the twentieth century.[41]

Elements of Andean understandings of health and the body, including the notion that human health is dependent on the larger natural and social world, and the importance of the circulation of bodily fluids and of hot and cold classifications, are evident in descriptions of reproductive practices in both rural and urban areas of Bolivia.[42] Denise Arnold and Juan de Dios Yapita found that, in the ayllu of Qaqachaka (Department of Oruro), understandings of fertility and pregnancy were undergirded by conceptualizations of linkages between individuals, animals, and celestial beings. Knowledge surrounding one such being, a Celestial Black Llama that was considered integral to the circulation of fluids in the natural world and in the human body, shaped many local practices concerning maternal health.[43] Aymara-speaking women often carried to urban settings the reproductive knowledge and practices that they developed in the rural communities in which they were raised.[44] Of these practices, Elvira Llanos Cervantes writes, "the recommendations received by the *usur warmi* (pregnant woman) are undergirded by the concept of equilibrium between the body and the spirit. Medicinal plants, utilized by women during and after childbirth, attempt to achieve a state of stability, since during pregnancy the body is conceived of as 'warm [*cálido*],' and during childbirth, as cold."[45]

Women in La Paz and El Alto took a number of measures in childbirth to ensure the appropriate heating of the body, including ingesting hot broth, chocolate, and mate (tea), and covering the body in blankets, in order to help the cervix dilate and facilitate delivery. Guillermina Arcani, an Aymara midwife who attended women in childbirth in La Paz and El Alto in the 1980s and 1990s, told me that the first thing she did when assisting a woman in labor was "to make her a good broth. She drinks her broth until she [her cervix] is well dilated."[46] Scholars also note that, in some locations, a man will fill the room in which his partner gives birth with smoke in order to help contractions progress.[47] Carla Yupanqui, an Aymara woman I interviewed in El Alto, told me that "women have to be very careful to not get too cold or too hot. It is said that if you expose your back to the sun when you're pregnant, the placenta can become stuck to the wall of the uterus, and then in childbirth you're going to have difficulty passing the placenta. . . . So, there are a series of rituals."[48] Following birth, indigenous women in both rural and urban areas often request the placenta so that it may be buried in the earth. Writes Andrew Canessa of this practice in the rural community of Wila Kjarka, Bolivia, "As the child enters the world of humans, the physical link with the spirits below must be cut. The placenta, part of the world of spirits, must be carefully returned. After the birth, the placenta is taken at night to a place in the stream where the stream spirits, the *sirinus*, dwell, and there it is washed (*sirintaña*). Then it is returned to the home, where it is buried in a corner of the house of the kunturmamani, the house spirit."[49]

When seeking to terminate unwanted or unexpected pregnancies, women in La Paz and El Alto between the 1950s and the 1980s sought the assistance of midwives, herbalists, and western medical practitioners. According to what medical anthropologists deem a "hierarchy of resort,"[50] or the order of options to which individuals recur for medical care, women in Bolivia would often first attempt to terminate pregnancies on their own or by visiting an herbalist before seeking the assistance of a provider who might employ a more invasive method. A common method was to procure from a K'awayu, or from a medicinal vendor called a chiflera, herbal remedies to induce abortion.[51] Women ingested as teas or inserted as vaginal suppositories herbal abortifacients made of oregano, fig leaves, basil, parsley, rue, or orange blossom—or a combination of several herbs—to terminate pregnancies. Some of these herbs were also used to stimulate contractions during a normal delivery or to assist the course of a miscarriage in progress.[52] In addition, or as an alternative, to utilizing herbal remedies, women might lift and carry heavy items, insert objects into their vaginas, or attempt to cause physical trauma to their own abdomens in an effort to abort. Sometimes these methods were successful in provoking abortion. Other times, they were not, and women tried still other methods or sought out providers to perform the procedure utilizing a more invasive method.

By the early 1980s, the most well-known providers of clinical abortion were situated in busy commercial districts, specifically in the Max Paredes district of La Paz and around the La Ceja, or the "eyebrow," of El Alto. Perched in offices above or alongside stores selling foodstuffs, clothing, or small electronics, these private clinics offered a range of health care services to individuals at a relatively low, out-of-pocket cost; they did not typically accept health insurance. It is difficult to know exactly when these market-district clinics began to operate, but interviewees remarked that they began to hear that some of them provided abortion in the 1970s. Usually, the only indication that such a clinic might be willing to perform an abortion were signs outside their offices offering pregnancy tests or curaciones (cures) "in a minute."[53] When I asked people in 2009 and 2010 where one could procure an abortion in La Paz or El Alto, a great majority of individuals—including not only women and activists but also government and police officials—referred to specific streets in these areas.[54] Evidence suggests that the abortion care provided by many of the market-district clinics was substandard, and in some cases, seriously deficient. Marcela Flores, who had an abortion at one such clinic in La Paz in the 1980s, remarked that, "It isn't sterile—they stick you in this office, they say they are performing the procedure cleanly, but it isn't true."[55] When I asked the receptionist of a clinic I had heard provided quality abortion care what she knew of the providers in market zones, she remarked, "One patient told me that they placed her on a regular wooden table covered with a sheet. Many women emerge from those places with infections."[56] According to María Silvia Elizabeth Benitez Reyes, abortion clinics in market zones were characterized by "inadequate infrastructure and unqualified personnel."[57]

Clinical providers of abortion during the period typically terminated pregnancies by using one or more of the following techniques: introducing an object into the cervix, or a liquid through the cervix into the uterus (which the body would then—it was hoped—expel, along with the pregnancy); dilating the cervix and removing the contents of the uterus (a procedure known as a dilation and curettage or "D and C"), or, after it became available in the late 1980s or early 1990s, giving an injection of methotrexate.[58] Dilation and curettage procedures were referred to by several different terms. Throughout this book, women who described their abortions with the following terms, or medical records that listed abortion methods in the following ways, have all been translated here as "D and Cs" (or surgical abortions): *raspaje, curetaje,* and *legrado uterino instrumental* (sometimes abbreviated LUI). The term *limpieza* (literally "cleaning") may refer to a D and C or to an abortion performed through vacuum aspiration, a technique widely used in Bolivia after the late 1990s and described in more detail in chapter 5. Providers with western medical training were probably more likely than those without to perform dilation and curettage procedures; however, dilation and curettage and placing an object or liquid into the cervix were likely the two most commonly used abortion methods by all types of providers until the late-1990s, if not longer.[59]

The abortion methods just described vary in efficacy according to the gestational age of the pregnancy and other factors; they also carry various degrees of risk. While some methods, when used correctly, can be relatively safe, others can be quite dangerous, causing uterine perforation, infection, poisoning, and death—particularly when performed in substandard conditions or by an individual lacking the necessary training. In particular, surgical procedures, which involve the insertion of objects into the cervix and uterus and likely remain the most commonly performed abortion procedures in La Paz and El Alto, carry significant risk of infection and uterine perforation. (The risk of sepsis, a life-threatening infection of the blood, is greater with insertion-based abortions than those induced by medications because these procedures dilate the cervix, opening a pathway to the body through which bacteria may more easily travel.[60]) Furthermore, most surgical abortions performed by providers in La Paz and El Alto probably took place in facilities ill-equipped to handle these procedures. Instead, abortions took place in medical offices, called consultorios (rather than clinics), or in private homes—either that of the patient, of the woman's partner or friend, or of the person performing the abortion. In fewer instances, abortions were performed in hospitals and clinics equipped to handle surgical procedures.[61] Although few abortion procedures took place in health facilities during the period, women sometimes visited these for help once an abortion or miscarriage began, or after it occurred. The following section examines what medical records reveal about women facing these circumstances.

Unwanted Pregnancy through the Lens of the "Natalio A. Aramayo" Maternity Institute

For most of its history, the "Natalio A. Aramayo" Maternity Institute (INA) was housed in the Hospital General de Miraflores (known today as the Hospital de Clínicas)—a facility that provided gynecological care, including treatment for pregnancy loss.[62] In 1994, the gynecological department of the Miraflores Hospital and the obstetrical INA joined to form La Paz's Hospital de la Mujer, which continues to operate today.[63] Despite the INA's focus on obstetrical care, the facility also sometimes saw patients suffering pregnancy loss; in addition, its staff recorded information on patients' previous pregnancies. While for some years this information was limited to the number of births, abortions, or miscarriages a woman had experienced in the past, for other years, these data were much more detailed, and included the years in which a woman's previous pregnancies took place, the method used to provoke an abortion, the location at which a birth or pregnancy loss transpired, and who, if anyone, had assisted her (e.g., a midwife, doctor, or family member). Variations in the kinds of data collected by medical personnel over these years seemed to correspond primarily to changes in the design of the medical record forms. While few women seen at the INA between 1955 and 1983 admitted to (or were recorded as) having intentionally terminated a pregnancy, many others had experienced some form of pregnancy loss—whether they described this as miscarriage or abortion or, most frequently, did not specify how the pregnancy was lost (referred to hereafter as unexplained miscarriage). Thus, while only 221 women whose medical records I examined were diagnosed with either current or previous provoked abortions, more than seven times as many patients—1,745 women—had lost at least one pregnancy through spontaneous, accidental, or unexplained miscarriage.[64]

According to medical records, women who sought abortion during these years visited a range of different kinds of providers; others terminated pregnancies on their own. Between 1955 and 1965, the design of medical record forms prompted staff to record the location of a woman's previous birth or abortion, as well as who had assisted the woman in the experience. Of the twenty-eight women recorded as having had abortions during this decade and who reported where the procedures took place, most underwent the experience at home; their pregnancies, however, were terminated by a diverse array of individuals. Eight women had their first abortions performed by a doctor, five by family members, and one by a nurse. One woman provoked her own abortion.[65] Eleven women said that one of a number of kinds of midwives had performed their abortions. Thus seven women procured abortions with matronas, while four women were assisted by one of the following providers: a *practicante* (practitioner); a partera; an empírico; or a *profano* (layperson, literally "profane"). Medical records demonstrate that women in La Paz and El Alto looked to mid-wives and other empirically trained birth attendants (often family members) for a range of pregnancy-related care in these decades. Thus at least 210 women seen at the INA between 1955 and 1965 reported that at least one of the aforementioned categories of providers assisted them with some aspect of pregnancy-related care, including childbirth and treat-ment following pregnancy loss.

Medical records suggest that women's use of herbal remedies to pro-voke abortion during these years, as well as to assist in miscarriage or childbirth, was common. In December 1968, a thirty-five-year-old, mar-ried, mestiza woman visited the INA after ingesting oregano and parsley teas to provoke an abortion. The woman, who had four children and lived in the San Pedro neighborhood of La Paz, passed the pregnancy before arriving at the medical facility but was suffering from a retained placenta. The record suggests that the woman brought the fetus with her to the med-ical facility; although staff was unsure about its gestational age, the fetus was determined to be male, weighed 320 grams, and was twenty-seven cen-timeters in length. According to the record, the woman's husband was fifty-five years old, and neither member of the couple had formal employ-ment—a difficult situation for a family with four children.[66] In March 1981, a single, eighteen-year-old mestiza student living in Ciudad Satélite arrived at the INA with her brother; she was in the process of passing a pregnancy of twenty-seven weeks' gestational age. According to medical staff, the young woman, who had never been pregnant before, had intentionally ingested "abortive teas" in order to terminate the pregnancy. After pass-ing a female fetus in breach position, the young woman was treated by medical staff before being released a few days later.[67]

Medical staff sometimes believed that the herbal remedies that women had ingested in order to assist in labor or to treat other health conditions had unintentionally led to stillbirths or miscarriages. In August 1966, a thirty-five-year-old, married woman living on Buenos Aires Avenue arrived at the facility to give birth to a full-term pregnancy. Upon exam, staff were unable to hear a fetal heartbeat, and the child was born dead a few hours later. According to staff, the stillbirth was a result of the woman ingesting teas made from oregano and orange blossom (*azahar*). The woman, who worked as a merchant and whose mother was listed as an agricultural worker, had previously given birth to five children, all of whom died within one to three days.[68] In 1973, a thirty-six-year-old, indigenous woman was transferred to the INA from the mining town of Corocoro when, at thirty-one weeks in pregnancy, she began to experience vaginal bleeding that persisted for several days. According to medical staff, the woman, who worked as a merchant and lived with her partner (*concubino*), was malnourished, anemic, and possibly suffering from "hepatic poisoning as a result of herbs (home remedy)."[69] After passing the fetus at the facility, medical staff ordered additional blood tests to assess whether the woman had also suffered from placenta previa—a condition that might have caused her bleeding.[70]

While the majority of visits to the INA during these years consisted of women giving birth, 138 visits corresponded to women seeking treatment in the course of losing a pregnancy (including by spontaneous or accidental miscarriage, incomplete abortion, and unexplained miscarriage). Medical personnel at the INA described just six of these cases as induced abortion; twenty-one cases were described as miscarriages caused by accidents of various kinds.[71] Of these, eleven were caused by abdominal trauma, eight by falls, and two by engaging in physical exertion. One thirty-five-year-old, indigenous woman said that, at five months in pregnancy, she had been subjected to rough movements as she traveled in a truck through the countryside over unpaved roads. A day after returning from the trip, the woman suffered two hours of labor pains before passing the deceased fetus and placenta in her home; she later sought follow-up care at the INA.[72] Another twenty-eight-year-old woman living in the Miraflores neighborhood of La Paz reported that a fall "on irregular terrain" in March 1961 caused intense vaginal bleeding, which she continued to experience when she arrived at the INA the next day. The woman passed her five-month pregnancy at the Institute and was released a few days later.[73] Most women who visited the INA with pregnancy loss during these years (and whose gestational histories are known) were pregnant at least once prior to the miscarriage or abortion, suggesting that many of these women had living children.

Although it would have been difficult for medical personnel to prove if a patient had intentionally provoked her abortion, INA staff sometimes doubted the veracity of women's reports of miscarriage. In 1955, a twenty-year-old, single, white woman claimed that the miscarriage she was experiencing occurred after she suffered an unspecified accident. Personnel wrote, "She says she felt her water break due to a traumatic accident, which is obviously false," and diagnosed the event as an, "incomplete spontaneous (?) abortion at two months in pregnancy."[74] A year later, a twenty-three-year-old, white woman from the Sopocachi neighborhood of La Paz visited the INA after experiencing two days of vaginal bleeding. The married woman reported having taken a "drastic purgative" two weeks before and, after several days of carrying her young child in her arms, began to experience abdominal pain and vaginal bleeding. After performing a dilation and curettage, medical personnel noted on the woman's chart, "The patient did not remember or did not realize that she was pregnant."[75]

Medical records at the INA only prompted personnel to ask a woman the cause of her abortion or miscarriage between approximately 1959 and 1966. One twenty-nine-year-old, white woman from La Paz who visited the INA in 1963 cited medical reasons for having terminated four pregnancies over the course of her reproductive life. After having two children by age twenty-two, the married woman then sought four provoked abortions, all performed by medical doctors (two of the procedures took place in her home and two in consultorios). When asked what led her to terminate her pregnancies, the woman stated "hardening of the aorta"; medical personnel, however, seemed not to understand the relationship of this ailment to the abortions, and followed the notation with a question mark in the medical chart. After the abortions, the woman went on to have three more full-term deliveries.[76] Another woman (whose own mother died in childbirth) was twenty-three years old when she gave birth to her fifth child at the INA in 1965. The mestiza woman reported having had one provoked abortion in the past because she already "had many children."[77]

Records suggest that women who terminated pregnancies utilized the procedure as a means of family planning—that is, of delaying their first pregnancy, or of limiting or spacing their pregnancies. Thus about half of the women who had abortions during these years already had children at the time of their first pregnancy termination, and many women had been pregnant several times before interrupting a pregnancy. This suggests that women who sought abortion may have done so in order to better care for their existing children (a phenomenon supported by interview data for these and later decades). One twenty-three-year-old, married, mestiza woman from La Paz experienced two pregnancy losses before giving birth to her first child at the INA in 1956. The woman reported having suffered the first of these losses, a spontaneous miscarriage, at age nineteen. A year later, the woman induced an abortion in her own home with the assistance of a matrona, effectively delaying the experience of motherhood.[78] The gestational history of a thirty-year-old, mestiza woman from Sucre who had an abortion in 1955 suggests that she may have recurred to abortion to space her pregnancies. The laundress, who at the time of her visit in 1960 described herself as single, had her first child in 1952 at the age of twenty-two; a few years later, she had a second child. When she became pregnant again the following year, the woman provoked an abortion by herself at home. Although it is unclear what method she utilized to terminate the pregnancy, the woman luckily experienced no complications from the procedure. After the abortion, the washerwoman went on to have two more children, both at the INA.[79]

In most cases in which women sought treatment at the INA for pregnancy loss, it is unclear what caused the symptoms, since medical personnel did not document this information in the medical chart. In part, doctors and nurses may have been more interested in providing care to a patient than in recording how her symptoms began; in addition, staff were likely unable to determine with certainty the cause of a woman's symptoms. Medical personnel attest to the difficulty of discerning the difference between a spontaneous miscarriage and an induced abortion by physical exam alone. As one doctor I interviewed explained, "It's a bit difficult [to tell the difference between these phenomena].... Because usually, the only symptom that the patient presents is genital bleeding. So, occasionally we would find a brass sound [dilator] stuck in the uterine cavity, despite the fact that the patient had categorically denied having been operated on.... But, those are very exceptional cases.... The majority say they have experienced traumas or accidents."[80] A review of cases of pregnancy loss during these years suggests that when records prompted personnel to note the cause of a woman's abortion or miscarriage, many more pregnancy losses were attributed to accidental causes than when records did not request this information.[81] This suggests that medical personnel were more likely to record the cause of a woman's miscarriage when prompted, *and* that many more miscarriages during the period were caused by accidents than data for other years suggest.

Of course, another reason why medical personnel do not often know the cause of a pregnancy loss is because the woman may be reticent to discuss it—and understandably so. Regardless of the cause of an interrupted pregnancy or a woman's feelings about it, a woman may feel that her experience of abortion or miscarriage is too private to discuss with hospital staff—particularly if members of the personnel are men, or if she feels she has been treated insensitively. Some women may have induced their abortions, but fearing moral judgment or legal repercussions, claim to have suffered an accidental miscarriage.[82] In other words, the complexities surrounding the experiences of pregnancy and its loss, in addition to the state's prohibition of abortion, may prevent women from discussing these phenomena openly with their health care providers; thus the causes of abortion and miscarriage may be absent from medical records.

Intimate Experiences with Unwanted Pregnancy

Ten women I interviewed in La Paz and El Alto became pregnant sometime between 1952 and 1982. The following pages highlight the stories of five of these women, some of whom navigated their reproductive experiences at home with the assistance of traditional birth attendants or family members, and others who did so in hospital settings. Women's decisions about where to pass their pregnancies were influenced by their family members' knowledge of health care providers in the areas where they each lived, as well as by concerns about insurance coverage (which was not widely available before 1989). Women's assessments of the care that they received were shaped in part by their own degree of familiarity with pregnancy when they became pregnant, and in part by knowledge and beliefs they had acquired about reproduction during subsequent decades.

The pregnancies of Magda Cusi and Camila Quelca occurred earliest among the women I interviewed. Magda and Camila were seventy-five and seventy years of age, respectively, when I interviewed them in El Alto in 2010. Both women were Catholic, spoke Quechua and Spanish, and dressed de vestido (in pants, skirts, or dresses, rather than the pollera). I met the two women at a workshop convened by a local organization that met in a classroom on the grounds of a Catholic Church in the neighborhood of Ciudad Satélite. Magda was born in 1934 in Potosí, a mining town of about 48,000 inhabitants as of the 1950 census.[83] Magda described her childhood as one of "tremendous poverty" and credited her mother for working tirelessly to raise her and her five siblings while her father was away fighting in Bolivia's Chaco War against Paraguay and later, left disabled from a gangrened leg. Camila was born five years later in Sucre, one of Bolivia's capital cities. Before her first birthday, Camila's family moved to the mining center of Siglo XX-Catavi, where Camila's father was employed at a mineral refinery and served as a leader of the mine workers. The family stayed in Siglo XX until 1951, when they were forced to flee to La Paz in the wake of a labor dispute. Recalling her family's sudden move, Camila said, "My father had to leave without compensation.... They brought us here and we suffered gravely; we didn't have money and my mother had to work at whatever she could find."[84] Thus, while Magda described her upbringing as poverty stricken from an early age, Camila said her family had fallen into poverty only after migrating to La Paz.

While Magda felt ambivalent about the pregnancy she confronted as a teenager, she opted to continue the pregnancy. When it came time for her to give birth, Magda's family called a partera to the home.

MC: Nowadays, people go to the clinic—everything is well monitored from the moment a child is in its mother's womb.... There are checkups, and I hadn't done any. I don't know if this was carelessness on the part of my parents—my mom could have said to me, "You have to go for your checkup"—or maybe those things didn't exist back then. But when my oldest son was about to be born ... I almost died in childbirth because I was skinny.... The birth took place at six months and the baby is supposed to be in the womb for *nine* months. It was the activities I engaged in—I had to help my mom, and by then I'd also gotten work, I worked with a Spanish guy in Potosí and he would tell me, "Señorita, you have to go to the station to pick up the packages." I used to do that, and this activity is what made my water break. The baby was in there without any liquid, and that's *never* supposed to happen. And then, when he was just about to be born, I couldn't take the pain anymore and a señora came.

NK: To the house?

MC: Yes, to the house. We used to call them matronas, but I don't think they were professionals. She came and said, "Ay! What happened? The baby doesn't even have liquid in there, how is he still alive? Why didn't you tell me?" Maybe because I was young and everything, I was scared—I didn't say anything, and because I wanted to keep doing things, I forced it. . . . After a lot of suffering, about eight hours, the baby was born—but it was almost suffocated. The partera lifted it up by the foot—oh, *that's* what they're called, parteras!—and I'm half-conscious watching the baby, and she says, "It's dead." She gave it a few smacks on the bottom and then it started crying. Then she said to me, "What were you thinking, working? You almost made this baby a martyr!" The umbilical cord was wrapped around its little neck. And they say that when one is forcing it too much in pregnancy, when one doesn't even take a moment of rest, that babies are born that way—that's what they say.[85]

As she told her story, Magda continually asserted that childbirth was different "back then" than it was at the time of our interview—particularly, that women did not have the same degree of western medical intervention into their birth experiences in the 1950s as they did in the early twenty-first century. At moments, Magda seemed almost apologetic about not having had formal prenatal care during her pregnancy. Despite the faith in clinical prenatal care that Magda's comments imply, she also portrayed the midwife that assisted in her delivery as knowledgeable and competent, if somewhat chiding. Magda also accepted the possibility that her child may have been born early and with the umbilical cord wrapped around its neck as a result of her having maintained an active lifestyle during the pregnancy.

Camila was in her mid-twenties in 1965 when she found herself facing what she described as an unexpected and inauspicious, though not entirely unwanted, pregnancy. Camila was employed at a chocolatery owned by a German couple who had fled to La Paz after the Second World War; on her breaks, she used to visit her brothers at the nearby factory where they worked. On one of these occasions, Camila met the factory's manager—the man with whom she would have her first child.

> CQ: I don't know if it was my destiny or something, but I met this manager . . . and you know what it's like when you fall in love, right? I wasn't that ugly when I was young, either. I met him and had my first child with him.
>
> NK: And the man you met at the factory—
>
> CQ: He was married.
>
> NK: Yes? How long were you together?
>
> CQ: Fourteen years. . . . Although you may not believe me, sweetie [*reina*], I like to be respectful and to have people respect me—he told me he was getting divorced. . . . And yes, in effect they *were* getting divorced, but what happened? He found another girl and he married her instead of me.

When I asked her how she felt when she discovered she was pregnant, Camila remarked, "Well, I was already twenty-five years old when I got pregnant, so, I wasn't scared. . . . But my mom said to me, 'How are you going to solve your problem, daughter? Why don't you tell him to formalize it?'" While Camila's mother's anxiety may have been motivated in part by a desire to protect the family's reputation, it may also have reflected worries about the impact of the status of "illegitimate" on the child's social rights. According to legal definitions at the time, "illegitimate" children were those conceived, "from adulterous or incestuous unions or relationships with priests"[86]; had the child been born of a union of two individuals who could marry, it would have held the status of a "natural" child. While Bolivia's 1938 constitution had improved protections for both illegitimate and natural children, the effect of these measures on questions of financial support, such as inheritance, was left unclear by the legislation.[87] In amendments to Bolivia's 1962 *Código Civil* (which was still applicable at the time of Camila's daughter's birth in 1966), a presumptive father could request an investigation of paternity if he was not married to the child's mother.[88] Despite the precariousness that the situation posed for Camila's daughter, the manager of the factory ended up recognizing the child voluntarily; he also provided Camila with financial support—until he married another woman and cut off further contact with Camila and their daughter.

In 1980, Camila entered a new relationship and became pregnant again, this time with what she described as an unwanted pregnancy. When I asked her how she met the child's father, Camila told me the following anecdote:

> My mom was dying in the hospital . . . and one day my father calls me and says, "Your mother wants to speak with you, daughter; go to her, and anything she tells you to do, you must obey her." I went and . . . sat on the edge of the bed, and my mom says to me, "Daughter, I'm going to die. There won't be anyone to take care of you and I don't want you to be alone. . . . It doesn't matter if it's just the security guard on the corner—but get yourself a husband. Your daughter is a young woman; tomorrow, the next day, what are they going to say about you? They're going to treat you poorly, they're going to say that you're a floosy, that you're with all kinds of men [*que eres una tal, una cual, que estás con todos*]—you need to have a husband." "Okay mom, I promise." Six months went by . . . and I met him. . . . But honestly, love, I never married him to this day, and we have lived together for thirty years.

Camila gave birth to her two daughters at what was then one of the largest public obstetrical facilities in La Paz, the Instituto Maternológico 18 de Mayo. "I was treated very well, I can't complain. I've always been treated well at every hospital I've visited, sweetie, maybe because I am not annoying or disagreeable." Camila's comments imply that she believed that she received quality care at the Maternológico because she "behaved well"—implicitly suggesting that other, more "demanding" patients are sometimes mistreated at western health facilities.

A number of tensions emerge in the testimonies of Magda and Camila. Both women suggest that they have faith in the western medical practices that were encouraged by the revolutionary and military regimes, but not necessarily to the exclusion of indigenous birth attendants. Both women's reproductive lives were also heavily influenced by their families of origin, who weighed social ideas about extramarital sex and out-of-wedlock birth, as well as legal considerations concerning children's status and inheritance rights, when advising the women on how to confront their pregnancies. Based on the tenor of Magda's and Camila's stories, it appears that the ideal trajectory of family formation in urban Bolivia in the 1950s and 1960s consisted of finding a man who had no other sexual partners or offspring and having children only once marriage was formalized. Yet neither Magda nor Camila conformed to this ideal, and while they both suggested that they feared stigma in the past, neither woman was shy about sharing with me her divergence from this idealized script of family formation by the time of our interviews.

Insurance coverage was an important factor shaping some women's decisions of where to turn for reproductive health care between the 1950s and the 1980s. Elsa Canqui and Nelly Mamani, both Aymara women who wore the pollera, gave birth to their first few children at home and sought hospital care later. Nelly delivered seven children between 1972 and 1998. "I had my child at home," said Nelly, speaking of the birth of her first child. "No one helped me at home; I was on my own. I had a week of labor pains. . . . I had three [children] at home and four in the hospital. There wasn't any insurance before, you had to pay. Since I gave birth to my daughter, there's been insurance."[89] After the passage of the Seguro Básico de Salud (Basic Health Insurance, SBS) in 1989, Nelly delivered her children at the Hospital Juan XXIII in the Munaypata neighborhood of La Paz. Nelly did not share details of her experiences at the hospital, saying simply that the care was "fine [bien, nomás]." Elsa gave birth to her first two children at home, in 1982 and 1983. Recalling her first delivery, Elsa remarked, "It was complicated, because my daughter was born at seven months. . . . A partero helped me [deliver], a man. . . . It took eight days. When it isn't time to give birth, the woman's cervix won't dilate . . . so, we really had to struggle in the delivery, I was in so much pain."[90] When Elsa became pregnant again in 1997, she gave birth at a clinic: "I had . . . the last one at the Virgen Copacabana clinic where my husband worked. . . . Earlier, my husband didn't have insurance; he wasn't working, so I couldn't have my other kids at the clinic." When I asked her if she preferred having children at home or at the medical facility, Elsa said, "The clinic is much better than the partero because suppose you have a hemorrhage— you're not really sure how the partero is going to stop it, but at the clinic, they'd put you in the operating room and get it under control."

Nelly and Elsa (fifty-nine and fifty years of age, respectively, at the time of our interviews) were both born and spent their early years in Pacajes Province in northwestern Bolivia and migrated to La Paz at age ten. While Nelly passed her childhood in the rural municipality of Calacoto where her parents worked raising livestock, Elsa grew up in the mining center of Coro Coro. Nelly ran away from home in approximately 1961 and ended up working as a domestic employee for a family in La Paz; she never had the opportunity to finish primary school, which she regretted. Elsa moved to La Paz in 1969 to work with a group of nuns and priests who later helped her obtain a scholarship to study sewing and other crafts at a local technical school. After graduating, Elsa returned to Pacajes as a *promotora* (educator) with the school, where she taught women macramé, sewing, and baking. I met Elsa at a weekly gathering of women who got together for knitting classes; the group met in a school classroom in the Alto Chijini neighborhood of La Paz. I met Nelly several months later at an organization in El Alto, where she was seeking legal assistance in a dispute against her husband.

My interview with Nelly took place in a small office space on a cold morning in March 2010. When I asked how she came to live in El Alto, Nelly began by telling me about her experience attending school in Pacajes as a child. "I came here because they [my parents] didn't put me in school; it was only when I was ten years old that they placed me in kindergarten, and the other kids abused me, they made fun of me—so I ran away [*me he k'itau*]. . . . I regret it now, I should have stayed and learned. But I was embarrassed; I was an older kid there with all the little ones in kindergarten—so, because of this embarrassment, I came here to work. I worked as a domestic servant [*empleada*]."[91] Nelly worked for a family in La Paz for nine years until she met the man who would become her first husband. While most of Nelly's answers to my questions were brief, she responded at length when I asked how long the couple had seen each other before marrying.

NK: How long were you two dating [*enamorando*]?

NM: Almost no time at all. Look, it was at a party—I was young still, only twenty-two years old, and at this Carnival party they drugged me and carried me off. He made me take these pills that put you to sleep—you know the ones, right? That's what he made me take and he made me appear in his house [*Eso me había hecho tomar y en su casa me ha hecho aparecer*]. So, we got married, we lived together, we had four kids—but he'd always been a womanizer [*cholero*] and he was running around with another woman. His family permitted this. My family didn't like him, either, so I ended up alone. I traveled to the mines on my own and I earned good money; I left my three daughters with my sister. But people talk about a woman like this who is on her own. . . . A lady accused me of going after her husband for no reason—I had nothing with her husband, he'd just buy stuff from me [*una mujer me ha prestado su marido sin motivo, no era nada ese su marido, solamente venía a comprarme*]. That's when my second husband showed up, and so I got together with him. It turns out he already . . . was married. So, now he's back with his wife, he abandoned me after breaking my hand; that's why I am here [at the organization]. . . . All on my own I am getting my education, and here they've helped me with the legal order; with this,

I've put him [her husband] in San Pedro [prison]. Until now, he hasn't paid me a cent.

Nelly's story made me realize the presumptuousness of my practice of asking women how long they had "dated" their partners. Clearly, there were experiences with courtship taking place in the Andes that did not fit easily into my limited understanding of dating or *enamorando*. I would later learn that *warmi suway*, or the practice of "stealing" a woman, often from Carnival parties, was common in some parts of the rural Andes, in particular. Writes anthropologist Krista E. Van Vleet of the Quechua-speaking community of Sullk'ata, Bolivia, "Stealing a woman, or initiating a marriage without the consent of parents, is the most typical way for marriages to begin in the region. . . . Sullk'atas [residents of Sullk'ata] recognize a range of circumstances when they use the phrase, from a young woman who is taken against her will and raped or forced to spend the night at the home of a young man to a couple that plans for months before eloping during a fiesta."[92] Warmi suway is complex, and linked to local understandings of ancestral connections, supernatural forces, fertility, sexuality, and drunkenness. As it is practiced in Sullk'ata, "women are agents in the process of marriage but are at the same time constrained differently than young . . . men."[93] While warmi suway is commonly accepted in the community, it may also provoke the anger of a woman's parents, as well as be experienced as traumatic by the woman involved.[94] Scholarship on partnership in other parts of the rural Andes suggests that, even where warmi suway is not commonly practiced, couples do not typically speak of their unions in terms of love or romance. Instead, women and men describe getting together after meeting and talking, or at the behest of their parents (as in the case of Elsa, discussed in the coming pages).[95]

Nelly's relatively negative assessment of her first marriage seemed to stem from her husband's womanizing, conflict with his family, and her own family's disapproval of the man, rather than from her feelings about the experience of warmi suway, necessarily. When I asked Nelly about how she met her first partner (before asking how long they had dated), Nelly remarked: "Going to parties, that's how I met him. He was from the same town and one of my kin, too [*era mi paisano nomás, uno de mi familiar nomás también era*]. His family was always getting involved in our lives, he worked as a driver and it didn't go well. Then he went off with another woman to live." At the same time, Nelly expressed frustration with not having had the chance to plan her romantic liaisons or her pregnancies; this frustration, which seemed to stem from a feeling of powerlessness, did seem connected to her experience of warmi suway. During interviews, I usually asked a woman how she felt about each of her pregnancies in turn, as she began to tell me of the circumstances surrounding them. When Nelly caught on to this strategy, she interrupted my line of questioning and remarked, "I never wanted to be pregnant. I wanted to be on my own. Like I said, I never had boyfriends or anything, they made me take those pills. . . . If it were up to me, perhaps I would never have had children [*por mí, capaz no tener hijo era*]." In an effort to prevent pregnancy, Nelly took birth control pills for a time without success. "I took pills and I still got pregnant. Then I wanted to get the copper T [IUD] but people told me, 'Your *wawa* [child] will be born out the back end.' When I got pregnant on the pill, I was worried, 'Maybe he'll be infected, messed up,' but no— thank God he was born okay." When I asked if she ever considered terminating a pregnancy, Nelly told me, "No. 'It's prohibited,' my mom always used to say." Nelly's frustration with her reproductive experiences may also reflect attitudes toward pregnancy and child-rearing that are common in some areas of the rural highlands, where Nelly was raised. For instance, Andrew Canessa found that, in the community of Wila Kjarka, "many people share [a] sense of frustration and the desire to have fewer children. It is very rare for people to speak of the joys of having children."[96]

Elsa was one of a minority of women I interviewed who never experienced unwanted pregnancy, a fact that she emphasized and attributed to her cooperative relationship with her husband. Elsa was grateful she ended up with a man with whom she was happy, particularly since she, not unlike Nelly, did not know her husband before they got together.

NK: How did you meet your husband?

EC: I went to his town in Pacajes Province, . . . I neither met nor fell in love with my husband. . . . He was studying at the university and one Saturday I and the other promotoras went to play basketball and then we were drinking a soda—nothing of alcohol at all—and the woman who is now my mother-in-law went to the mine and said [to my mother], "Your daughter is with my son." And my mom—my father was the boss at the mine—she *lived* for what people said. She said, "What are people going to say? How did that happen?" So, I got together with my husband and thank God I am happy with him— without dating, without even saying "Hello."

NK: Did your parents obligate you to marry?

EC: They didn't obligate me, they just said, "What are people going to say? Your future mother-in-law came and told us about you, and I don't think she's lying." They didn't believe me; they believed *her* more than me. At that time, I had never dated—I was still young. So, I said to my dad, "You live for what people say, Dad. If it goes poorly for me, it's going to be your fault." My dad said, "It hasn't gone poorly for any of your brothers or sisters"—there are twelve of us. So, I got together with the man who is now my husband. He's a good man. I didn't know how to cook; he taught me. His mother gave me two kilos of vicuña wool. . . . I stopped going to work because he said to me, "No, don't work anymore, I'll go work. You knit." I applied myself to learning to sew and I liked the work; I continue to do it. I encouraged my husband to study. Then I started having children. I had my oldest daughter, then the second a year later, because he always said to me, "Look: I want two children who are close in age; then, let's sacrifice to let them grow up, because if not we're going to have another, and then another a year later. No—that's bad for you, and it's bad for me." So, we agreed to have our second baby. Now they're professionals, the two girls. The oldest is twenty-seven and the younger twenty-six; they are both lawyers.

When I asked how she felt when she discovered she was pregnant, Elsa told me that using the rhythm method and periodic abstinence had success-fully allowed her to plan when and how she became pregnant. She pre-ferred to regulate her fertility by relying on cooperation with her husband rather than using western-derived contraceptive methods—particularly since Elsa knew other women who had suffered infections as a result of using methods such as the IUD.

> NK: Did you want to be pregnant at the time you became so?
>
> EC: Well, when you do your family planning yes, but not by force or without wanting to—but in my case, we've always planned when and how we wanted our children. . . . I never accepted [western-derived birth control] methods. After my [youngest] daughter was fifteen years old I had another baby, but I didn't use any of those things. My husband just said to me, "Look: You always get pregnant fast. Let's take care of ourselves, I'm not going to obligate you. . . ." When we were ready to have another child, we talked, and I said to him, "Let's have another baby, our daughters are young ladies." So, we had my littlest.

Elsa's description of her relationship suggested that she believed her situ-ation was relatively unique, and that most women faced coercion in their sexual relationships and lacked the support of their partners when taking measures to plan their families. When I asked if she knew women who had become pregnant when they did not want to, Elsa remarked, "Oh yes, many times. . . . They say, 'My husband obligated me to have this baby. I didn't consent; he obligated me [*no era de mi consentimiento porque él me ha obligado*].' I'll say to them, 'It's a blessing from God—but you should talk with your husband.' 'No, he doesn't understand,' they'll say. 'My husband is a dog, every night he wants to be with me. . . .' But thank God this never happened to me."

While the stories of Nelly and Elsa share some similarities, the women's assessments of their experiences with sexuality and pregnancy were markedly different. First, while Nelly experienced unwanted pregnancy and said if it were up to her, she'd never have had children, Elsa was fortunate that her efforts together with her partner to plan their family had allowed her to become pregnant only when she desired it. Nelly and Elsa both entered partnerships without enamorando, but the relationship both began and progressed in a more positive way for Elsa than for Nelly. The women's feelings about their respective relationships at the time of our interviews were also undoubtedly shaped by the circumstances each was then experiencing—while Elsa seemed relatively content with her husband, Nelly was actively engaged in a legal battle against her former partner.[97] At the same time, both Nelly and Elsa credited education as integral to the process of bettering their lives. While Nelly emphasized that she had sought education on her own, Elsa repeatedly mentioned that her husband had only studied and achieved better employment because of her encouragement.

Elba Claros was one of several women I interviewed who experienced a miscarriage after becoming pregnant unexpectedly. When I interviewed her in September 2009, Elba was fifty-nine years old, married, and living in the Alto Chijini neighborhood of La Paz. A Catholic woman, Elba had two children who were born in 1978 and 1980. Elba was one of the few women I interviewed who had advanced education and described herself as a professional; she declined to identify her ethnicity. Elba grew up in La Paz and described herself as a solitary child, which she attributed in part to unpleasant sexual experiences in her adolescence.

From twelve years old, I no longer lived with my mom, only with my dad. That period raises a lot of memories for me. When I started to become a young woman, I was very solitary because my father held me very close; he took care of me. During my youth, at around fourteen, things happened that now I realize should not have. . . . When a young woman begins to mature, people of the opposite sex start to notice her more, right? So, now I realize all of that and these are very offensive memories to me. That's why I hold tight to my little ones, I don't want anyone to touch them because I was touched. So, when I was younger, I was very introverted, I didn't like having friends, I was very quiet. But a moment came when I met my husband, who was the first man and the first boy and the first male friend I had.[98]

Elba met her future husband when she was eighteen and he twenty-one, but they did not begin a serious relationship until later, after Elba became pregnant. Elba described her first pregnancy as inopportune because the relationship she had with her boyfriend at the time, "was not the kind of relationship to become pregnant in." In the following passage, Elba describes miscarrying the pregnancy at five months.

EC: Before I got married I became pregnant with his child, but at five months I was frightened by a dog and I had a miscarriage. . . . Honestly, I didn't sense or feel the pregnancy. It was an inopportune pregnancy and when I had the miscarriage I didn't take it too hard either.

NK: How did that happen, exactly?

EC: A dog from the street scared me and as a consequence of that fright [susto], my stomach started aching for a week and my temperature went up and down, up and down, and what I didn't realize was that a miscarriage was beginning.

NK: When you had the miscarriage did you go to a hospital or—?

EC: No. . . . It was three in the morning and I lived with my older sister. I said to her, "Sister, I don't know what's going on, my stomach is hurting, something is coming out." So, she says to me, "I'll look at you and see what's happening." And it turns out his little feet were coming out. She says, "Wait a minute sister, lay down in bed, I'm

going to call the matrona," because a matrona lived nearby. But by
the time she had gone and come back the baby had already been
born. It was born in the chamber pot [bacín], as they say, and he was
alive; but, he sighed, raised his little hand to his head, and died—
and the placenta came out too.

According to Elba, the fright she experienced after encountering a dog in
the street eventually led her to miscarry her pregnancy. It was unclear during the course of the interview whether Elba felt that her miscarriage
resulted from the generalized trauma she sustained from the encounter
with the dog, or from susto, "a folk illness . . . [that] develops after a profound fright that causes a person's soul, or ánimo, to leave the body."[99] The
latter is cited as a common cause of infant death and of a variety of ailments in adults in a number of places in the region, including Bolivia,
Ecuador, and Mexico.[100] In the context of her unexpected pregnancy, Elba
did not find the miscarriage particularly troubling, despite the fright that
she experienced prior to passing the pregnancy. Remarked Elba, "When
I had the miscarriage, I did not take it very seriously, it did not hurt me
that much. After I got married my oldest son arrived, so I accepted that
more, but the earlier pregnancy, no."

Most women whose experiences are highlighted here utilized some
combination of biomedicine and Andean medicine when seeking assistance with their pregnancies; women's testimonies further suggest that
their ideas about pregnancy were shaped by both western and traditional
knowledge systems. This "dual use" of medical traditions is consistent with
the findings of scholars working in the Andes and in other geographical
regions where multiple health systems exist.[101] In the contemporary world
the phenomenon of medical pluralism, which is most common in societies that are stratified by class, "is characterized by a pattern in which biomedicine exerts dominance over alternative medical systems."[102] Yet, as
William C. Olsen and Carolyn Sargent write of medical pluralism in sub-
Saharan Africa, "Efforts by state and global health authorities to eliminate

or restrict nonbiomedical practices . . . have achieved partial success at best."[103] In Bolivia between the 1950s and the 1980s, most women's experiences with unwanted pregnancy and abortion took place outside the purview of the state. Even in the urban settings of La Paz and El Alto where the presence of state and medical authorities was comparatively greater, officials' efforts to phase out the practice of midwives and herbalists did not prevent women from recurring to these providers for assistance with reproductive health care, nor did the pronatalist positions of national governments dissuade women from taking measures to terminate pregnancies and regulate their fertility. At the same time, the invasive nature of some of the medical technologies available to women seeking care after abortion or miscarriage, in addition to the stigmatized status of sexuality and abortion in La Paz and El Alto, meant that women often suffered complications as a result of their pregnancy losses. Following the return to democracy in 1982, the persistent demand of women for abortion and organizing on the part of women's groups, as well as broader social, economic, and political processes, paved the way for significant changes in reproductive health care in La Paz and El Alto between the mid-1990s and 2010. These changes are explored in the next chapter.

Informal medical clinic in Max Paredes.

Example of medical record from the Instituto de Maternidad "Natalio A. Aramayo."

Commercial area in Macrodistrito II, Max Paredes.

La Paz.

Linares Street, near San Francisco Church and "witches' market."

CHAPTER 5

Unwanted Pregnancy and Abortion in the Wake of Democracy, 1982–2010

Let me make a comparison for you—between 1993 and 1997, we saw all kinds of complications due to unsafe abortion: uterine perforations, intestines emerging through the vagina, women who died. But since introducing the AMEU, the aspiration device, all this has decreased. Rare, very rare, is the woman who shows up at a hospital with severe complications.

—Medical doctor Emma Alvarez, speaking in 2009

Notwithstanding the significant decrease in rates of maternal mortality in the country since the 1990s . . . Bolivia remains one of the few countries where the probability of dying of pregnancy-related death continues to be unacceptably high, especially considering that nearly all of these deaths would be preventable if access to basic health care were available at a reasonable cost. The major problems responsible for [these high rates of maternal death] are, without a doubt, those associated with inequality, discrimination, abuse, abandonment, and violence, which tend to fall on the backs of women—particularly young, indigenous women with few resources and little education.

—National Strategic Plan for Sexual and Reproductive Health, 2009–2015

This chapter examines women's experiences with unwanted pregnancy and abortion in La Paz and El Alto since 1982, when democracy was restored to Bolivia after eighteen years of military rule. The first section of the chapter draws on government reports, interviews, medical records, and secondary sources to trace continuities and changes in the reproductive health services available to, and used by, women in these cities. The second section of the chapter draws on personal testimonies to examine women's experiences with unwanted pregnancy and abortion over the last few decades. At different points throughout the chapter, I also employ material from personal medical records representing the experiences of women who sought follow-up care after miscarriage or abortion at one of two public hospital facilities: La Paz's Women's Hospital (HM, 1994–2008), and the Bolivian-Dutch Municipal Hospital in El Alto (HMBH, 2005–2007).

This chapter argues that, while developments in reproductive health care services since the early 1980s helped reduce maternal mortality due to abortion and other forms of pregnancy loss, these changes did not benefit all women. Women who lacked the social or economic resources to access new, higher-quality services still faced a significant risk of medical complications and abuse. The lack of effective regulatory mechanisms, both for medications and for health care providers, also placed women who were seeking to regulate or terminate their pregnancies in a precarious position. Finally, women's testimonies highlight the ongoing impact of legal, social, and structural factors in shaping the ways in which women experienced their pregnancies. Ultimately, the state's prohibition of abortion and concomitant failure to regulate the procedure, societal stigma against abortion and sexuality, and economic and sociopolitical structures like poverty and patriarchy continued to make the experience of navigating an unwanted pregnancy difficult for many women.

Reproductive Health Care in
La Paz and El Alto, 1980s–2010

In February 2010, I interviewed Emilia Santana, an obstetrician-gynecologist, about her experiences treating women seeking care after miscarriage and abortion in the first decade of the twenty-first century.

NK: I'd like to ask about some of those cases, of women arriving with incomplete abortion and in which you believe they might have provoked their bleeding.

ES: These cases do come up. Generally they are women of lower or middle classes, and occasionally upper classes, who, number one, have a lot of children, and two, perhaps do not have knowledge about family planning methods. The latter is particularly true of women from the lower and middle classes. For this reason, they decide to go to so-called "pharmacies" where they are told what medications to take and how to take them [to provoke abortion]; many patients come with these tablets in the vagina. . . . So, we ask the patient, "What happened? Is it possible that you inserted some medication?" And eventually, the patient will tell us, "Yes, doctor, I provoked an abortion." Their motives? They can be economic. In many cases, women are obligated to have sex. In El Alto there is a lot of machismo. The man will arrive at home and sometimes, he'll not only obligate his partner to have sex, he'll also beat her. So, to avoid getting beat up, the woman will sometimes give in to having sex when she doesn't want to. . . . Many times, the woman knows when her fertile days are, but when the man insists, the woman becomes pregnant, and often the couple will have a lot of children that they cannot take care of because of the economic situation, and so they opt for abortion. They'll go to clinics in El Alto or to La Paz and they'll learn of medications that they can insert into their vaginas. And then they come here scared of the amount of bleeding that they are experiencing, and we have to take care of them, because it is the purpose of [this clinic] to give quality care to all patients without any kind of discrimination.

NK: And women arrive here scared of the amount of bleeding they are having?

ES: Of course—because, let's say they go to a pharmacy or to some clinic to consult about this; typically, they are not given complete information. They'll tell them, "This is going to provoke abortion," but they don't explain to them [the women] exactly what will happen after they insert the medication. The women will come here and say, "I have been having a lot of bleeding and I'm passing clots. They did not tell me this was going to happen, they just said I was going to abort." Perhaps this is because of the lack of knowledge of the way that the medication works, because the pharmacy doesn't explain what's going to happen.

NK: And can these medications be purchased without a prescription?

ES: Very often. Because, it's often just a consult between two people. So, they'll be told, "Here it is, but don't tell anyone who gave it to you." And if it's a clinic, from what I understand, they often have this medication and the doctor must give it secretly to the patient. Generally, you're supposed to have a prescription; it's sometimes prescribed because this medication is also used in cases of anembryonic pregnancy. . . . And sometimes they'll also tell them what traditional remedies to use, like oregano or orange blossom tea, which are natural oxytocics that can achieve the same objective.

NK: Do some women use the two methods?

ES: Of course, especially among the lower and middle classes. . . . Sometimes, women will tell me that they took large quantities of fig leaves, which causes the same symptoms as the tablets. Sometimes they'll go to the naturista, who will explain the two things to them, how to take the tea and how to insert the tablets.

NK: Why do you think that it is more among the lower classes that you see the use of natural methods?

ES: Why? For one, because of culture. It could be a friend who heard about or used the method. Or, they'll go to the naturista, who is often a bit more affordable, and they'll ask, "What can I do to provoke an abortion? This is the situation I am in." And the naturista will tell them, "Well, you can use this." Or, they'll go get a prescription some-

where. The naturista can't give a prescription, but they can give a
woman the name of the pharmacy where they can get the tablets.

NK: And when women arrive here with an incomplete abortion, how
do you treat them? With the AMEU?

ES: We use the AMEU or dilation and curettage, depending on the
gestational age [of the pregnancy] and the height of the uterus.[1]

Santana's comments highlight a number of patterns characterizing
women's experiences with unwanted pregnancy and reproductive health
care in twenty-first-century La Paz and El Alto. Some of these patterns represent continuities with women whose pregnancies took place in earlier
decades. For instance, men's widespread sexual and physical abuse of
women, embedded in broader systems of machismo and patriarchy, has
long constituted a central factor leading to unwanted and unexpected
pregnancies—as economic uncertainty has long been cited by women
as a reason they seek abortion. Santana's assertion that women visit clinics
and naturistas and make use of pharmaceutical and herbal medications to
terminate pregnancies also highlights the fact that women's recurrence to
both western and Andean medical practices, so common in earlier decades,
has continued in more recent years. While Santana acknowledges that
women across socioeconomic class terminate pregnancies, she cites class,
and implicitly ethnicity (or "culture"), as factors determining whether a
woman facing unwanted pregnancy chooses to visit a naturista or a phar-
macist in her search for abortifacients. An additional, and distressingly
long-standing, pattern characterizing pregnancy termination in the urban
Andes is the fact that seeking abortion represents, in many respects, a roll
of the dice. Faced with the ongoing legal prohibition of abortion, providers
of the procedure are unable to advertise their services, which leaves women
to navigate a complicated landscape of options, the quality of which is
uncertain. Ultimately, women with greater economic resources are more
easily able to obtain safe abortions than those who are poor.

The long-standing uncertainty that women face when seeking abortion has coupled with other, relatively new phenomena that, since the 1980s, have shaped women's experiences with unwanted pregnancy and abortion in contradictory ways. In particular, the development of pharmacology and the accelerated commercialization of bio- and herbal medications have made abortifacients more easily accessible, allowing women to terminate their pregnancies on their own in relative privacy without being forced to recur to the potentially more dangerous surgical methods of inserting instruments into their own bodies. At the same time, in the absence of effective regulatory mechanisms for health providers and the abortion remedies that they offer, women still face the risks of poisoning and hemorrhage. On the other hand, the existence of clinics such as the one where Santana works—which the doctor claims provides comprehensive and nonjudgmental care regardless of the circumstances that caused a woman to lose her pregnancy—is a relatively new phenomenon in La Paz and El Alto.

The pages that follow first outline developments in the relationship between traditional medical practitioners and biomedical systems, particularly as this impacted the provisioning of pregnancy-related care. The discussion then turns to the evolution of clinical care concerning unwanted pregnancy and abortion in La Paz and El Alto. Each section concludes by discussing the varied, and sometimes contradictory, consequences of these developments for women facing unwanted pregnancy in the urban highlands.

Traditional Medicine, the State, and Pregnancy-Related Care

In its 1989 history of public health in the country, the Bolivian Society of Public Health remarked that "it is true that Bolivian pharmacology has evolved in the last fifty years; however, the presence of native medicine is undoubtable. It would certainly constitute a valuable endeavor to hybridize professional doctors and pharmacists, who were trained in university classrooms, with traditional medicine, so that both together could provide services to the large campesina community that has inherited valuable knowledge and practices over thousands of years—knowledge and practices that have remained solidly locked away among the mountains of the Andes, which jealously guard these impassioned secrets."[2] The impassioned secrets of traditional medicine notwithstanding, the comments of the Society illustrate what was, at the time, an incipient but growing interest on the part of some biomedical doctors and policy makers in Bolivia in integrating the practices and providers of Andean medicine into national health systems. These efforts were partially undergirded by the World Health Organization's 1978 Alma-Ata Declaration, which articulated that global health problems could be best resolved through an emphasis on primary, preventive care and the incorporation of traditional medical practitioners into local institutional health systems.[3] Independent of the state's efforts toward integration, Andean healers since the late-1970s mobilized on their own for greater recognition and autonomy on a number of fronts, achieving the decriminalization of traditional medicine and institutional representation by autonomous organizations between the 1980s and 2000s. A central challenge facing Andean medical practitioners in Bolivia over the last several decades has been to maintain the sacred and expert nature of their customs and practices in the face of the growing institutionalization (and some contend, cooptation) of traditional medicine by the state.

Some of the earliest efforts of state officials to integrate Andean birth practices into national health systems during the period consisted of training programs for indigenous parteras, which were carried out in several areas of the country beginning in the late-1970s. The trainings, which would come to be called *parto limpio* (clean birth) programs, were designed to reduce infant and maternal mortality by instructing parteras in biomedical techniques, such as the use of obstetric tools and alcohol for sterilization.[4] One such training program implemented in 1982 took place at the El Alto facility that would later come to be called the HMBH, from which some of the medical records in this chapter are drawn.[5] According to Kathryn Gallien, parto limpio programs represented a departure from the Ministry's previous strategy of training mestiza midwives in biomedical techniques in hopes that these would eventually replace Andean birth attendants. At the same time, support for the programs within the medical establishment was inconsistent, and the trainings in many ways represented yet another phase in ongoing efforts to subordinate Andean medicine to western forms in line with broader political and economic goals, particularly quieting the politically mobilized indigenous majority.[6] In this, medical and government officials were ultimately unsuccessful: "There is little indication that parteras or their clients were more willing to set aside cultural practices or political activism. Furthermore, instead of reinforcing women's position within the home, health programs . . . allowed nurses and midwives access to important mid-level positions within the public health system."[7]

Some women and parteras criticized both the logic undergirding, and the implementation of, parto limpio programs for their discriminatory nature. As Denise Arnold and Juan de Dios Yapita write, "Many women expressed that they feel offended by the racist and derogatory jargon inherent in the use of current terms such as 'parto limpio,' with its implicit implication that the practices of rural individuals are 'dirty.'"[8] In February 2010, I interviewed Guillermina Arcani, an Aymara woman who participated in the training programs for parteras in the late-1980s at a health center in the La Portada neighborhood of La Paz. "Doctors gave us courses, so that's how we learned; the señoras didn't trust the doctors, they felt more comfortable with us."[9] Arcani's comments suggested that part of the purpose of the training programs was to draw women into public health centers, by casting parteras as liaisons between doctors and women. If convincing women to give birth at health centers was part of what ministry officials intended, however, they did not always succeed: "The pregnant women would get together once a week. They learned where I lived in La Portada, they would come get me at two or three in the morning . . . and I would deliver the children at their homes."

When I asked Arcani why many of the women she assisted as part of the parto limpio programs preferred not to visit hospitals for reproductive health care, the partera said that women often complained of being mistreated by medical personnel; she then shared with me her own experience of giving birth in a hospital in La Paz.

> I had seven children in the hospital. . . . With my last son, I was passing fluid and I was in the bathroom when two nurses came in. I knew my baby was about to be born and I said to them, "let's get me into bed and please bring me a bedpan because I am passing water"; I was also vomiting. "Okay," they told me, and brought me a bedpan. There was a doctor attending and I told her, "Doctor, I'm about to have my baby, he's about to be born." She says to me, "No, not yet. [To the nursing staff:] Give her some fluids; around eight the baby will be born." "Doctor: It's coming!" I told her. "No, no, it's not, señora—not yet." So, they're putting fluids in my IV, and I shout, "My baby!" And it just came out on its own. And I said, "See? I told you it was coming! I knew, I am also a partera." I said to them, "Don't quarrel with me [no me van a reñir], if you yell at me, I'll yell right back at you."

Many women in Bolivia report experiencing mistreatment at public health facilities when seeking pregnancy-related care, including an explicit disregard for the Andean traditions that they prefer to practice in childbirth. Leticia Quispe, a thirty-three-year-old Aymara woman, said she was very unhappy with the care she received at one La Paz hospital because "the pre-delivery room is cold, cold, cold, and that place should be hot, since we have to dilate!" When I asked about her interactions with medical personnel at the facility, Leticia remarked, "They treated me so poorly. They yell at you, demoralize you. . . . The doctors there are really wicked."[10] Carla Yupanqui, an Aymara woman in her fifties who grew up in the mining community of Coro Coro, remarked, "You must have seen how terrorized women feel in hospitals and health centers, no? . . . A woman will give birth and she'll say, 'Give me my placenta,' and [medical personnel] will tell her, 'No, we throw that away.' Or she'll say, 'I'm hungry, I'm cold,' and the personnel will say, 'No, you can't be like that'—because those are the hospital's norms. At home, she'd be visited by a partera. . . . The midwife would speak with her, chew coca, chat in Aymara. It wouldn't be this traumatic thing of 'Lay down, get up, stand up, open your legs.'"[11] Andean practices valued by women in childbirth and often denied them in western health facilities include giving birth in a vertical or squatting position, taking measures to ensure the heating of the body, and having the placenta returned to them for burial, rather than being discarded.[12]

The work of activist healers in the 1970s and 1980s to decriminalize traditional medicine and develop institutions devoted to its study and practice ushered in a new era of visibility and political influence on the part of traditional medical practitioners in the country. Efforts to decriminalize traditional medicine began in earnest in 1978 but did not achieve much headway until after the democratic opening. Walter Álvarez Quispe was a key player in this process, initially in his role as the first secretary of health of the newly formed Confederación Sindical Unica de Trabajadores Campesinos de Bolivia (CSUTCB), and later as a National Deputy of Parliament. In January 1984 (Supreme Resolution 198771), the Bolivian government officially recognized SOBOMETRA, and with it became the first country in Latin America to decriminalize the practice of traditional medicine. Three years later, the Parliament passed a bill creating the Instituto Boliviano de Medicina Tradicional Kallawaya (INBOMETRAKA); the measure also designated as the capital of traditional medicine Bautista Saavedra Province, from which Kallawaya healers traditionally hailed.[13] In the wake of these measures, the 1990s witnessed the emergence of a number of organizations of indigenous medical practitioners, "fighting for ethnic recognition and inclusion in the public health system."[14] The grassroots efforts of Andean medical practitioners in Bolivia for the decriminalization and free practice of traditional medicine gained national and international recognition and support across subsequent decades, although opposition to traditional medicine among some sectors, at times quite strong, has persisted.

Further state-led attempts to incorporate traditional medicine into national health systems were undertaken in 2002, when the Gonzalo Sánchez de Lozada administration passed the Seguro Universal Materno Infantil (Universal Maternal and Child Insurance, SUMI) and, shortly thereafter, reached a strategic agreement with the CSUTCB to bring primary health care to rural populations. Passed in November 2002 and implemented the following month, SUMI explicitly acknowledged the need for intercultural care in maternal health. Reads Article 8 of Supreme Decree 26874, "The services provided by SUMI at all three levels of health care must be adapted to the practices, customs, languages, and dialects of indigenous, campesino, and original peoples, with respect for their identity [and] cultural foundation, and with attention to gender."[15] In December 2002 as part of its agreement with the CSUTCB (Supreme Decree 26875, Article 10), the government planned to implement an accreditation system for traditional medical providers and to incorporate these into national health networks; however, due to the bloody confrontations of October 2003 and Sánchez de Lozada's subsequent flight from the country, this process never reached fruition.[16]

The months of indigenous-led protests over rising taxes and the export of natural gas were joined by an auspicious moment for traditional medicine when, in November 2003, the United Nations Educational, Scientific, and Cultural Organization (UNESCO) accepted a petition presented by Kallawaya healers and supported by Bolivia's Viceministry of Culture to "[proclaim] as a Masterpiece of the oral and intangible heritage of humanity the science of the Kallawaya."[17] This was followed in 2004 with the opening of the Hospital Kallawaya Boliviano Español in Curva, the capital of Bautista Saavedra Province. The hospital was designed to provide equal parts traditional and western medicine under one roof, a measure designed in part to decrease maternal and infant mortality.[18] Kallawaya healers also began to provide care at a new health center in Amarete, a town in the same province. Finally, the early 2000s witnessed a number of state- and nongovernmental organization (NGO)-led projects to integrate traditional birth practices and providers in health centers, including projects in Patacamaya and Huarina in La Paz Department, and in various localities within the Department of Potosí. Projects included direct services, such as the implementation of birth rooms staffed by parteras who assisted women in childbirth according to Andean practices, as well as workshops and conferences where health providers and activists exchanged ideas and strategies concerning intercultural health.[19]

The ascendance of Aymara political leader and coca farmer Evo Morales to the presidency in 2006 represented an important show of support for traditional medicine. Shortly after taking office, the Morales administration created and incorporated into the Ministerio de Salud y Deportes (Ministry of Health, MSD) the Viceministry of Traditional Medicine and Interculturality; a few years later, the Ministry launched Salud Familiar Comunitaria e Intercultural (Intercultural Community and Family Health System, SAFCI).[20] Promulgated through Supreme Decree 29601 in June 2008, the stated objectives of SAFCI were to eliminate unequal access to health care; foment community participation in decisions regarding health; provide health services that take into account the needs of individuals, families, and the community; and respect and value both biomedicine and traditional medicine with the broader purpose of improving health outcomes and improving the quality of life of the population in general.[21] The SAFCI model shares two broader concepts underlying the Morales administration—decolonization and interculturality—and is applied at all levels of the health system, including national (via the MSD); departmental, through the Servicios Departmentales de Salud (Departmental Health Services, SEDES) in each of Bolivia's nine departments; municipal, through autonomous or municipal indigenous authorities; and local, at the level of primary health care centers in individual communities and neighborhoods.[22] The SAFCI system has two principle foci, "participatory management and medical attention"; while the first aims to ensure community participation in health care decisions impacting residents, the second seeks to change how medical care is provided.[23] As such, this second aim has the potential to improve the experiences of women seeking reproductive health care in the country. Writes Brian Johnson,

> the reforms are directly related to the perceived necessity of a change in outlook and behavior on the part of medical personnel and the quality of attention provided. Rudeness and disrespect for clients and misunderstanding and rejection by physicians of traditional medicine and the cultural beliefs of the population have long been identified as the most frequent obstacles to a fluid physician-patient dialogue. . . . SAFCI calls for recognition of the strengths and limitations of both biomedicine and traditional medicine . . . [which] requires a significant ideological shift on the part of those with deeply ingrained beliefs and prejudices on both sides of the medical divide.[24]

The MSD has sought to implement these changes by introducing mobile units in rural areas and establishing medical residency programs wherein personnel commit to work in the countryside and to receive training in traditional medicine and other aspects of indigenous history and culture.[25] Other recent programs of the Morales administration impacting pregnant women included the Bono Juana Azurduy de Padilla, implemented in 2009, "which pays women directly for prenatal checkups during pregnancy, delivery in a state medical facility, and infant medical checkups,"[26] and Law 475, titled Servicios Integrales de Salud (Integral Health Services, SIS), which expanded health coverage to individuals not covered by SUMI and who lacked access to other forms of insurance.[27] Among the groups and services covered under the 2013 SIS program were "women of reproductive age for care related to sexual and reproductive health."[28] According to MSD officials, these measures contributed to an 85 percent increase in women who received at least four prenatal visits relative to 2009, a change that was reflected in the 2016 Demographic and Health Survey.[29]

Also in 2013, Bolivia's Plurinational Legislative Assembly instituted Law 459, the primary objective of which was "to regulate the practice of traditional ancestral Bolivian medicine and its articulation with the National Health System."[30] The law created a registry of traditional medical practitioners, including doctors, parteras, spiritual guides, and naturistas, through which providers could legalize their practice and be formally authorized to practice both on their own and alongside biomedical providers. As of August 2016, the Ministry of Health had formally registered 4,778 traditional medical practitioners in the country. The viceminister of traditional medicine in 2016, Germán Mamani Huallpa, remarked that authorities were still developing appropriate sanctions for traditional providers who failed to formally register their practice.[31] Traditional practitioners working in public health posts were also asked to keep a registry of the numbers of patients that they attended and the ailments for which individuals commonly sought treatment. In August 2017, the Associated Press reported that 500 parteras had been trained by the MSD, twenty-two of whom had been officially licensed to provide care in hospitals.[32] By October, Ministry officials estimated that 18,000 patients had been treated by traditional practitioners in health posts around the country, "attesting to the preference of the Bolivian population for traditional medicine."[33]

The logic undergirding and the practices involved in the implementation of SAFCI, and of the institutionalization of interculturality more broadly, have drawn criticism for a variety of reasons.[34] On the one hand, some health institutions and biomedical personnel see SAFCI as a threat to their hegemony in the Bolivian medical sphere and to the autonomy of their practice.[35] Additional critiques of SAFCI and of interculturality have come from those sectors that oppose Movimiento al Socialismo (Movement for Socialism, MAS) more generally (particularly the "Media Luna" regions of the country) and some international agencies, notably USAID. Finally, some members of and allies to the traditional medical community remain wary of SAFCI and the politics of interculturality for their vertical and hierarchical nature, and for excluding from the decision-making process those practitioners of traditional medicine who were active long before official recognition of traditional medicine by the state.[36]

According to Carmen Beatriz Loza, who represents one of the most vociferous critics of this latter group, intercultural health itself constitutes a foreign concept, the central purpose of which is to draw indigenous residents into western health centers and ultimately assert the hegemony of biomedicine over traditional medical systems. Loza argues that interculturality was initially elaborated in the late 1990s and early 2000s as a strategy for improving health outcomes. Codified in and supported by international organizations, such as the Pan American Health Organization (PAHO) and WHO, which saw in interculturality the possibility of integrating traditional and biomedical practices in a number of countries, Loza describes how interculturality became the subject of a number of anthropological studies and degree programs that facilitated the formation of an "intercultural elite" that would end up dominating positions in public administration. The author goes on to outline a number of problems with the concept of interculturality as it operates in the Bolivian health sphere.[37] "Interculturality is an imported concept whose significance is determined by the very institutions that work and intervene in the field of health from different perspectives that are not necessarily coincidental nor always compatible when it comes to their implementation on the ground in Bolivia. The opacity of the category only deepens the longer that it is coopted by biomedical [providers], who are converting it into an official state discourse."[38] Of the SAFCI program that resulted from this discourse, Loza writes, "SAFCI is proof that the Bolivian National Health System intends to absorb, control, and subordinate local indigenous medicine with the purpose of 'enriching' and aggrandizing Bolivian biomedicine."[39]

Critics also contend that many of the practitioners seated at the top of the state hierarchy lack both the spiritual tenets and the medical expertise of legitimate traditional medical providers. In 2014, Álvarez Quispe, in his capacity as executive director of INBOMETRAKA, argued that providers of traditional medicine were being systematically excluded from administrative positions within the Viceministry by practitioners who self-identified as naturistas. "Naturistas say that traditional medicine is associated with a pagan, Andean religion. They are evangelical Catholics and they have international support from the Church, so they are trying to marginalize us. We are in a secular state and they must respect us."[40] Undergirding Álvarez's critique is a rift between "natural medicine" and "traditional medicine" in contemporary Bolivia. In general, the ideas and practices of *medicina natural* or *naturismo* draw from European ideas of health rather than Andean traditions and, while those who practice it may claim that it shares much in common with traditional medicine, "generally natural medicine is an outgrowth of the processes of commercialization."[41] This new brand of natural medical doctors, Loza remarks, "have emerged from the globalizing public health policies currently applied in Bolivia. . . . Some urban professionals, in the face of unemployment, have started to call themselves amawtas and kallawayas to insert themselves into the labor market and climb the . . . ranks of the state, serving in . . . positions from which they . . . prepare offerings for the most trivial acts of public administration, and in so doing trivialize symbolic curative practices while at the same time coopting them for their own use."[42] Thus many traditional healers and their allies emphasize that naturismo does not engage in the ritual practices that are inextricable from the practice of traditional medicine and is primarily "academic," taught in courses rather than passed down through kinship ties via oral and experiential teachings.[43]

Further complicating the politics of interculturality in Bolivia, according to Loza, are the significant presence of Cuban doctors in the country's health centers, who lack knowledge of "local languages and cosmovision."[44] For the reasons already enumerated, Loza uses the term "labyrinth" to characterize the landscape of medical services in the cities of La Paz and El Alto through which individuals must navigate in order to obtain health care. "We are referring to a great medical market functioning outside the control of the state," writes Loza. "The health system is organized simply and plainly according to the will of providers (or those who claim to be so), and according to the support and legitimacy granted to these by consumers of health services."[45] As the following pages detail, the term is also strikingly apt when applied to the experiences of women seeking clinical abortion care in these cities. Amid a proliferation of health providers, and in a broader context of economic crisis and a landscape of largely unregulated health services, women confronting unwanted pregnancy face a wealth of options for care—the quality of which is uncertain.

The Evolution of Clinical Care Concerning Unwanted Pregnancy and Abortion

The challenges that individuals faced in traversing the labyrinth of health services in contemporary La Paz and El Alto seems to have been equally true in 1989, when the Bolivian Society of Public Health used the term "anarchy" to describe the state of the medical system in the country.[46] In the early 1980s, the primary institutions providing health services to residents of La Paz and El Alto included public hospitals and health centers dependent on the national health ministry (then named the Ministerio de Previsión Social y Salud Pública, or MPSSP); facilities run by the various *cajas* (social security funds), which provided care to individuals and their families through employers, unions, or the national fund, the Caja Nacional de Salud (CNS, then named the Caja Nacional de Seguro Social, or CNSS); a variety of privately funded centers, including those owned and operated by individual doctors and pharmacists and those administered by religious organizations and corporations; and, health institutions operated by NGOs, many of which received partial or total financial support from foreign governments.[47] The administration of and care provided by these facilities and individuals were theoretically regulated by the 1978 Health Code, but the Society of Public Health had little faith in its actual implementation. "Article 10 . . . [of the Health Code] says that, 'Every person and legal entity is subject to the mandates of this Code, [and to the] regulations . . . dictated by the health authorities,' but in reality almost none of these provisions are met."[48] Also of concern to the Society was the widespread, over-the-counter availability of medications, arguing that most were not adequately studied.[49] The lack of effective regulatory mechanisms for the sale, use, and commercialization of pharmaceutical and herbal medications has continued in more recent years. Remarked one 2018 study, ominously titled *The Business of Death*, "The contraband and falsification of medications continues to represent a significant public health threat to the Bolivian population."[50]

While the system within which clinical care operated faced significant challenges, the period since the early 1980s saw improvements in medical technologies and the services provided within this system for women facing unwanted pregnancy in La Paz and El Alto. The earliest of these changes consisted of improvements implemented since the mid-1990s in the quality of abortion care provided at many of the clinics in commercial areas of these cities. I am unable to provide details about the circumstances in which these improvements were implemented; however, in general terms, medical personnel were trained to treat women compassionately and to take steps to determine that a woman who visited the facility was requesting abortion on her own terms and was not being coerced into terminating her pregnancy. Among the most significant of the medical changes implemented at these clinics was the adoption by staff of a safer method of performing abortions, consisting of manual vacuum aspiration (aspiración manual endo-uterina, AMEU). The method, which is performed with an inexpensive and reusable plastic device (also referred to as the AMEU), reduces the risk of uterine perforation associated with other surgical abortions, such as the more invasive dilation and curettage method. The AMEU also constitutes a safer method of treating incomplete miscarriage and abortion. According to interview data, the introduction of the AMEU improved the ease, efficacy, and safety of both abortion and the treatment of incomplete pregnancy loss. Explained David Estrada, a medical doctor at a public hospital in El Alto, "The resolution [of cases of incomplete abortion] is simpler, less costly, and ambulatory—and not only can specialists perform the procedure, but also family practice doctors. Nurses could also be trained to do it."[51] (In describing abortion care as ambulatory, Estrada means that patients may be treated and released from medical facilities in a short time and do not require lengthy hospital stays.)

Just a few years after the AMEU began to be used in Bolivia, the MSD, in partnership with the U.S.-based manufacturer of the AMEU device, Ipas, introduced two policies that further improved the landscape of clinical care for pregnancy loss. With its Programa por el Tratamiento de Hemorragias en la Primera Mitad del Embarazo (Program for the Treatment of Hemorrhages in the First Half of Pregnancy, HPME), the Ministry of Health began to train medical personnel at public health facilities in the country to use the AMEU to resolve cases of incomplete pregnancy loss.[52] "The first workshop to introduce the AMEU [took place] in La Paz in 1999," recalled medical doctor Alessandra Muñecas. "Post-abortion care has improved remarkably since that time."[53] The aim of the program was to reduce maternal deaths due to abortion and to other types of pregnancy loss not only by promoting the AMEU method but also increasing women's willingness to seek care at public hospitals, by eliminating discrimination against women who might have provoked their abortions. "There was a lot of mistreatment of women with incomplete abortion," remarked medical doctor Daisy Serrato. "Many clients would go to hospitals and say to themselves, 'Darn! They treated me so poorly, I don't want to go back ever again.'"[54]

Changes to insurance coverage may have further empowered women to seek clinical care after their abortions. In 1999, the Seguro Básico de Salud (Basic Health Insurance, SBS) was expanded to include the treatment of complications related to pregnancy loss, making the AMEU procedure free of charge for all women. Two years later, with SUMI, coverage

was expanded even further to include medical attention for, "all conditions related to pregnancy and childbirth and care for the child up to age
five."[55] "Before the insurance programs," recalled one doctor, "if a patient
arrived with vaginal bleeding, she had to pay between 400 and 500
Bolivianos,"—about US$60.00 to US$70.00 in 2009—"in addition to paying for any medications."[56] Another doctor who completed his residency
at a public hospital in La Paz concurred, saying, "Treatment for women
in these situations was far from free—not the least because, to do a dilation and curettage procedure, a patient had to be hospitalized for more
than one day."[57] The doctors' comments are further supported by medical records from La Paz's HM and from the HMBH in El Alto; after the
introduction of the AMEU, the length of a woman's hospital stay was
shortened from between two to several days, to just hours.[58] While in
theory, the hemorrhage treatment and insurance programs were designed
to improve care for women suffering spontaneous miscarriage, in practice the policies guaranteed care for any woman experiencing symptoms
of a pregnancy loss—including those who might have provoked their
abortions.

The 1990s also saw the growing utilization of a pharmaceutical medication to provoke abortion, called misoprostol (or Cytotec, for the name
of its manufacturer). Although its earliest use in pregnancy termination
in Bolivia probably dates from around the mid-1990s, misoprostol—
which can be used to treat ulcers, in addition to other ailments—may
have been available in the country a great deal earlier. "Before the
1990s," remarked David Estrada, "misoprostol was already being used in
Brazil to terminate pregnancies, but people didn't start using it here
until later—and it's totally changed the epidemiology of abortion."[59]
Although the first studies on the use of misoprostol to induce abortion
date from the early 1980s, medical abortion was not approved until 1988 in
France and 2000 in the United States. In these countries, misoprostol—
a prostaglandin that functions by inducing contractions of the uterine

muscles—is used in combination with mifepristone, a more expensive medication that stops the growth of a pregnancy and detaches it from the uterine wall.[60] Although in countries where abortion is legal the regimen is only approved for use early in a pregnancy (up to about nine weeks), in Bolivia and elsewhere in Latin America, women often take misoprostol alone, without mifepristone, and many use it throughout pregnancy, even at a more advanced gestational age.[61]

Medical records provide some (albeit limited) insight into women's use of misoprostol as an abortifacient. Out of 1,017 clinical histories representing visits by women to the HM and HMBH between 1994 and 2008 for conditions related to pregnancy loss, 12 included references to misoprostol. In 10 of these cases, medical personnel administered the medication to treat symptoms women were experiencing following miscarriages or incomplete abortions caused by other phenomena. (Since the medication causes uterine contractions, it can be used to facilitate the passage of retained tissue after any form of pregnancy loss, in addition to provoking abortion.) In only two cases did women allegedly use misoprostol on their own to intentionally terminate pregnancies.[62] The paucity of these cases should not be taken as evidence that few women in La Paz and El Alto recurred to misoprostol in an attempt to abort; instead, most women who used the medication probably miscarried on their own and did not seek follow-up care at a medical facility.

Far more common than misoprostol was women's recurrence to herbal teas for pregnancy-related care. Since certain mates may be taken to facilitate vaginal bleeding, it is usually unclear in medical records whether a woman drank these to initiate an abortion or to treat symptoms that resulted from a miscarriage. Of the same sample of clinical histories already cited, forty-three women seen at the HM or HMBH between 1994 and 2008 used mates *caseros*, or teas brewed at home, for relief of the symptoms they were experiencing in association with pregnancy loss. In most of these cases, women reported drinking infusions made from oregano, anise, parsley, chamomile, *paico* (epazote), rue, or a combination of herbs, after bleeding in pregnancy began spontaneously or accidentally or after a surgical abortion. In at least one case, a woman used herbal tea alone, specifically mate infused with oregano, to terminate a pregnancy.[63]

An additional phenomenon that contributed to transforming the landscape of reproductive health care during these decades was the growing presence of clinical abortion providers who offered safe, affordable procedures and were committed to protecting women's reproductive health and rights. While these high-quality, ideologically motivated abortion providers may have always existed in the urban Andes to some extent, interviewees date the emergence of many to the late-1990s. "Today, there's an important number of high-quality, sensitive doctors that before did not exist," remarked one interviewee who mobilizes on issues concerning women.[64] These clinics are, without exception, operated by licensed medical doctors and nurses that are trained not only in the most effective abortion technologies (including the use of the AMEU and misoprostol), but also in providing nonjudgmental and patient-centered care.[65] "Women have very bad experiences seeking abortions and are coerced," explained Miguel Ramírez. "Instead, the service that we provide is different—totally personal, very human, very sensitive—and the cost is low."[66] For a nurse at one such clinic in La Paz who herself visited a market-district clinic for an abortion in the 1980s, the central difference between the two types of facilities lies in their "values," which are particularly visible in their attitudes toward patients.[67] Most, if not all, personnel of these establishments believe that abortion should be legal—a conviction staff members describe as arising from their concern for women, rather than from political or ideological motives. "You shouldn't have to go get an abortion full of fear, knowing that your uterus could be perforated, that you could get an infection, or that you could be raped," remarked one doctor when I asked if she felt the procedure should be legal. "So yes, I think it should be legal so that we can all, rich or poor, have the chance to access safe services. . . . As a mother, I am convinced of this. And

I hope my daughter finds a clinic and a doctor like me, should she ever need it."[68]

Recent estimates suggest that the various developments that have taken place in abortion care over the last few decades have had important impacts for many women. The first decade of the twenty-first century saw a reduction in medical complications and death due to abortion and other types of pregnancy loss vis-à-vis earlier years. While in 1994, Bolivia's maternal mortality rate was measured at 390 maternal deaths per 100,000 live births, 37 percent of which were due to pregnancy loss, by 2011, this number had decreased to 160 per 100,000 live births, for which pregnancy loss was responsible for 13 percent.[69] Despite this, many individuals I interviewed in Bolivia worried that women's access to safe, comprehensive abortion care remained limited. First, not all women possessed the social connections that facilitated access to the new, higher- quality abortion clinics; instead, many ended up recurring to the better-known medical offices located in market districts or terminating pregnancies on their own.[70] According to one 2012 study, women in Bolivia who induced their own abortions were more likely to suffer complications than those who saw providers—although more than a third of all women who had abortions experienced some type of complication, including fever, infection, excessive bleeding, and the failure of the method to terminate the pregnancy.[71] As of 2011, abortion still represented the third-highest cause of maternal mortality in the country (after hemorrhage and hypertension),[72] and MSD officials continued to remain concerned about maternal death, as evidenced by their declaration of 2018 as, "the year of vigilance for maternal and neonatal mortality."[73]

The availability of misoprostol, for its part, changed the landscape of abortion care in Bolivia in contradictory ways. On the one hand, the medication made some abortions safer, by eliminating the need to insert an object into the uterus, and thus, the risk of uterine perforation. Misoprostol also made the abortion experience more private—giving a woman a greater degree of control over her abortion—and more accessible, since the pills may be purchased over the counter at many pharmacies, on the street from some chifleras, or over the Internet.[74] On the other hand, the unregulated use of misoprostol may pose additional challenges to women. By using the medication without the supervision of a health care provider, women may be unsuccessful in terminating their pregnancies and, worse, may be putting their lives at risk. Bury et al. found that the thirty-four women in their study who used misoprostol to terminate a pregnancy took the medication thirty-three different ways (i.e., methods of administration and dosages); in addition, of all the methods survey participants utilized to terminate pregnancies, medication abortion caused the greatest number of complications.[75] Furthermore, while misoprostol may be relatively widely available, the high demand for and lack of regulation of the medication means that its cost varies considerably; thus misoprostol may remain inaccessible for many women.[76] While the cost of a single pill of misoprostol in the United States is estimated at US$0.25, women in La Paz and El Alto may pay anywhere from US$3.00 to US$70.00 for the regimen.[77] According to Ipas, the cost of misoprostol is higher in Latin America than any other world region.[78]

Finally, medical personnel disagreed as to the overall impact of government policies combatting mistreatment of postabortion patients in La Paz and El Alto. While some believed that discrimination against women seeking postabortion care had improved in recent years, others asserted that it was still a significant problem.[79] For Daisy Serrato, the overall quality and safety of a woman's abortion experience depended both on her ability to pay a skilled provider to perform the procedure *and* on the care she received after her abortion (if she required follow-up care).[80] Stigmatization of abortion and closed-minded attitudes toward sexuality in La Paz and El Alto, coupled with cultural values that engendered unequal power dynamics between medical personnel and their patients, meant that health care workers who opposed abortion may have continued to treat women harshly in the early twenty-first century—and may have been able to do so with relative impunity. In other words, while the landscape of abortion provisioning improved over the last several years, women seeking abortion in the region still face significant challenges.

Intimate Experiences with Unwanted Pregnancy

Alma Tarqui, an Aymara woman born and raised in El Alto, was fifteen years old when she discovered she was pregnant in 2004. "I worked a lot during the pregnancy, but my mom was always there for me, taking care of me." When it came time for her to give birth, Alma continued to rely on the support and guidance of her family in navigating the delivery.

> AT: My grandmother is a partera, so she and my mother helped me.
>
> NK: How did you decide to have your child at home?
>
> AT: It just happened, I didn't decide. I mean, I didn't know what the pain was going to be like, so, my belly started to hurt, and I started pacing back and forth. When my grandma arrived that day—she is from the countryside—she told me, "You're about to have your child." So, according to their customs from the countryside, they made me drink hot teas to speed things up and warm my body. . . . My grandma gave me hot water with oregano, soap, and oil . . . and I drank it without complaining.
>
> NK: And you had your second child at home as well?
>
> AT: Yes. That time I was also taken by surprise, because we were on our way to the hospital. . . . My husband and I were walking down the stairs here in our neighborhood and I felt like something was coming out. So, I said to my husband, "I feel like pushing," and he said to me, "Let's go back to the house." So, I had it at home—it was quick.
>
> NK: And your partner stayed and helped you?
>
> AT: Yes, yes. He took care of everything. He ran around, he carried me, lifted me, he helped me in every respect.
>
> NK: Was your mom also there the second time?

AT: No, just my mother-in-law and my husband.

NK: Did your mother-in-law also help?

AT: After the birth, yes. . . . It is their custom to give you hot food right after giving birth, so that's what she did, she looked after me and also after my little daughter.

NK: Your grandma is a partera; but your mother-in-law and your partner, how did they know what to do?

NK: My mother-in-law, she's also from the countryside, and they didn't have doctors or anything, they just took herbs. So, she knows what she's doing, she has her own kids, her husband, she knows what it is to have a child and what you need to do, how to wash the child after birth—that's their custom, to wash the baby very well after birth.[81]

Alma's experiences in childbirth share several commonalities with those of other women I interviewed. Forty-eight of the women I interviewed became pregnant sometime between 1982 and 2010; most of these women confronted at least one pregnancy that they did not want, or about which they felt strongly ambivalent. Together, these women experienced 173 pregnancies, of which 137 resulted in childbirth, 19 in miscarriage, and 17 in abortion; one woman had an ectopic pregnancy. Most women's decisions about where to turn for medical care were heavily influenced by the individuals in their support networks and by the broader circumstances and cultural landscapes of their lives. The economic, social, and health care resources to which women had access, either on their own or through friends, family members, and partners, shaped their experiences at home or at the clinic or hospital. The structural features of the neighborhoods through which women moved on a day-to-day basis (such as the availability of health posts and parteras in these areas), as well as broader societal attitudes toward women, sexuality, and pregnancy, further affected women's reproductive options and their assessments of their lives. The power of machismo emerges often in women's testimonies; thus of thirteen women who experienced miscarriage during these years, physical violence played a role in those of six women, most of whom lost their pregnancies after they were assaulted by intimate partners. Psychological and sexual violence against women, as well as women's abandonment by intimate male partners, were also distressingly common. As international and local attention to and resources for domestic violence grew in the 1980s and 1990s, however, women who suffered violence had more options for places to turn for support.

Women seeking reproductive health care during these years typically used some combination of western, Andean, and empirical medicine, seeking assistance from parteras and herbalists, giving birth at home with the help of family members, and/or visiting western facilities. Some aspects of women's experiences with reproductive health care reflected changes that took place in policies and technologies across the period—for instance, a woman who terminated a pregnancy may have undergone the AMEU procedure rather than a dilation and curettage, taken misoprostol, or received an injection of methotrexate to terminate her pregnancy. She may also have sought care at a hospital or other western health facility following a pregnancy loss after insurance programs were expanded. In other cases, women were unable to access newer methods of abortion and ended up terminating pregnancies on their own, with or without seeking follow-up care from a clinical facility. In most cases, women used whatever was most readily available to them given their specific cultural background and preferences, as well as those of their support networks—the individuals who were willing and available to assist, or in some cases encourage, them to terminate their pregnancies.

Twelve women I interviewed terminated pregnancies during these years. These women often succeeded in locating abortion providers only after some difficulty, and the quality of the abortions they received was sometimes questionable. Once she succeeded in obtaining an abortion, it was not unusual for a woman to experience medical complications following her procedure. While at times these complications resulted from

poorly performed abortions, at others they occurred due to poor care overall, such as when a woman was not counseled on how to best care for
herself afterward. Not all women who had abortions experienced complications, but this did not necessarily mean that they were satisfied with the
care they received. Even when women reported few problems during or
after their abortions, women often described the experience itself as logis-
tically difficult, expensive, or emotionally taxing.

Noel Terrazas, a Quechua woman who was fifty-one years old at the
time of our interview, convinced her family doctor to perform the three
abortions she had over her reproductive life, the first in approximately 1987.
"I cried, I begged him, I told him please, if he knew where someone would
do me the favor of . . . of . . . that I didn't want to have any more children.
And he told me, 'If you like I'll do it for you, but don't tell anyone.' . . . At
that time there weren't health posts everywhere like there are now, you
know? So, I went to him, he charged little and the care was good."[82] Lorena
Mercado and her husband had two children, ages three and four, when
they decided to terminate an unexpected pregnancy in 1997. Not comfortable asking someone directly about where she might find an abortion
provider, Lorena instead feigned curiosity to ask her sister-in-law where
she had secured her abortion a few years before. "She didn't *give* me the
information—I also didn't ask her, she doesn't know [about my abortion]—
I just said to her, 'Where did you go?' Like that I asked her. 'To this place,'
she told me. So, my husband and I went to look for it. Neither she nor anyone else knew; rather, she more or less told me the location [of the clinic]
involuntarily."[83]

Marcela Flores and Pilar Mendoza, who both had two abortions, relied
on their partners to help them locate providers the first time that they
sought the procedure; the second time, they found providers on their own.
When her family's economic situation led her to seek an abortion in the
late 1990s, Pilar and her partner walked around the Garita neighborhood
of La Paz, where abortion clinics were known to exist, until they located

a medical office that would perform the procedure. When I asked her how she knew which clinics in the area to approach, Pilar remarked, "Because they are offices that say, 'We can tell you right away if you are pregnant.' They are like normal offices with their normal doctors. So, we went by chance. We spoke with the doctor, saying that I was pregnant and that we did not want to have the baby. He made us sign a document saying that we were both in agreement. He didn't want to do it just like that [without a legal release] because he said, 'Perhaps I could have problems later.'" At first glance, it may seem odd that the abortion provider asked Pilar to sign a legal document about her abortion, since the procedure is against the law in most circumstances. According to interviewees, however, providers sometimes request such documents as a security measure to protect themselves in the event that the couple later quarrels and one of the pair (usually the man) denounces the provider. In those cases, the document could not only exonerate the provider from additional jail time if convicted but also implicate the couple for the abortion. Marcela described finding an abortion provider this way: "The first time [in approximately 1989], my husband said to me, 'Let's go to this place—I met a doctor and we're going to go there,' and he took me. The second time I needed an abortion [in 1994], I had to go by myself. By that time, I was a nurse and knew more about these things, so I knew where to look." Marcela described the places that are widely known to perform abortions as, "offices on Buenos Aires [Avenue] and Tumusla [Avenue], with signs that say, 'Gynecology,' 'Pregnancy Test,' or 'We'll solve it in twenty-four hours [*en veinticuatro horas lo solucionamos*],' that kind of thing."[84]

Some women, citing societal stigma, kept their plans to terminate their pregnancies largely to themselves, which—together with the conditions created by abortion's illegality and economic factors—may have limited their ability to locate better-quality providers. Adela López, a mestiza woman who was thirty-two years old at the time of our interview, had two abortions over the course of her life. Adela's second experience with abortion, which took place in 1998 when she was visiting a city far from home, highlights the terrible consequences some women face when they are unable to locate reliable providers.

> My second abortion experience was disastrous. [The provider] was a doctor, but because his clinic charged him money to do the abortion there, he decided—well, we both decided, since I didn't have money— to do the abortion in a hotel. So, we went in pretending that we were lovers. . . . He wasn't prepared to do the abortion, the anesthesia he used wasn't the same kind that they used the first time, so I felt things, it was terrible. And then after doing the abortion, since I was still anesthe- tized, he ended up raping me. Then, after that, I had to keep seeing him because I was in pain—and I couldn't denounce him [to police]. . . . I was in Santa Cruz; I had tried to find help in a clinic, but obviously the first thing they say to you is, "We don't do that, go away." . . . This doc- tor also created a lot of obstacles for me—he told me, "No one else is going to do your abortion and if someone finds out, they'll take you to prison. But me, since I'm your friend and I'm young, I understand what you're going through and I'm going to help you." So, he didn't let me look [for other places]—he scared me away from looking for more information.[85]

Adela's terrible experience represents a reality of unregulated abortion care in Bolivia, as well as in other countries where the procedure is pro- hibited; it is also important context for understanding the fear that women often express when they need to find someone willing to help them ter- minate a pregnancy. The Romanian film *4 Months, 3 Weeks, and 2 Days* addresses exactly this phenomenon of sexual assault against women seek- ing abortion.[86] Women I interviewed in La Paz and El Alto were well aware of the risks associated with visiting an unknown clinic or abortion provider. When Lupe Colque was forced to recur to asking a stranger on a La Paz street if she knew of any places that performed abortions in the area, she felt she was, "risking her life"—which was not, considering stories like Adela's and high rates of death due to unsafe abortion in the country, an unreasonable fear.[87]

Fortunately, no other woman I interviewed faced an assault by an abortion provider; still, it was not uncommon for women to suffer medical complications following their procedures. As Lorena recounted, "After [the abortion], a week went by and I was unwell. The bleeding increased and my abdomen inflated. So, I went back to the doctor and he told me that not all of it [the fetal tissue] had been removed. So, he did the 'cleaning' a second time."[88] Pilar remembered the care she received at her two abortion appointments more positively than did Lorena; however, the details of her testimony suggest that the quality of this care was less than excellent. "I wasn't supposed to have lifted weight and I lifted as I usually did. . . . Then I felt a pain in my womb. The doctor had said to me, 'If you feel anything wrong, come back, don't be afraid.' So, I went back to the doctor and . . . he says, 'Were you resting in bed?' 'No, I went to the market,' I said to him. 'It [your uterus] filled up again with blood, that's what's causing you the pain,' he told me. So, again they had to remove the blood." Thus Pilar's provider failed to advise her to rest following the procedure, which required her to undergo surgery a second time. The second time that Pilar had an abortion, in 2004, the experience could have ended disastrously. She returned to the provider she had visited a few years before, but he turned Pilar away, saying the pregnancy was too advanced. Distraught, Pilar located another provider on nearby Tumusla Avenue, a medical office sandwiched between a cake shop and a tailor in the Max Paredes district of La Paz. Desperate to end the pregnancy, Pilar deliberately misled the provider, telling him that she was two, rather than four months pregnant. Instead of verifying the gestation of the pregnancy—as most providers would in countries where abortion is legal—the provider went ahead with the procedure in a doctor's office ill-equipped to handle terminations of sixteen weeks. "I guess it's because we did the abortion at a consultorio, rather than a clinic. The doctor said we should have done it at a clinic and that I was in real danger."[89] Even if the medical office Pilar visited lacked equipment to determine the age of a pregnancy (such as an ultrasound machine), the provider could have performed a bimanual exam—a simple test that would easily reveal that Pilar's pregnancy was more advanced than she claimed.

Market-district clinics in La Paz and El Alto were often blamed for the majority of abortion-related complications; some also say they offered the procedure primarily for financial gain (despite the fact that their services were sometimes cheaper than those offered by higher quality providers). "There are doctors who profit from abortion, unfortunately," remarked Miguel Ramírez.[90] As of 2010, interviewees reported that the fee for an abortion at a market-district clinic ranged from US$10.00 to over US$100.00, with prices depending not only on the method used or gestational age of the pregnancy but also on the whim of the individual provider. (Dr. Ramírez, for his part, charged US$25.00 for an abortion at a clinic known for providing comprehensive, high-quality care.) Muriel Rodríguez, who worked as a receptionist at a reputable abortion clinic in a residential neighborhood of La Paz, said that she had heard stories about the market-district clinics from the patients where she works. "One girl told me, 'If you want the cleaning to be done *well well well*, it's going to cost you 600 [Bolivianos]"—the equivalent of about US$85.00 in 2010— "but if you want to just help yourself to some abortion pills, it'll cost 300."[91] The tendency for some clinics in La Paz and El Alto to offer abortions that were cheaper, but also riskier, than those offered by higher-quality clinics meant that poorer women likely faced the brunt of postabortion complications and death. Cati Molina, a middle-class mestiza woman, said that few women in La Paz and El Alto were able to access abortions that they could be sure were performed safely. "I paid US$300.00 to have a safe abortion in one of the best clinics of La Paz, because I could. But most women can't do that and they go . . . to clandestine places, and that's where women die."[92]

The cost of the abortions that interviewees obtained in La Paz and El Alto varied widely. Lupe does not remember the exact price of the abortion she had in the early 1980s, recalling only that it seemed inexpensive to her and her partner, who were both university students in their early twenties.[93] Pilar's two abortions in the late 1990s and 2004, both at market-district clinics, cost approximately US$85.00 and US$35.00, respectively. Earning an average monthly income of less than US$200.00 in 2009, for Pilar, these abortions cannot have seemed "cheap"—neither did they seem to correspond to differences in the type of procedure that was performed. While Pilar's first abortion was performed with the relatively cheaper aspiration device, her second abortion, for which she was administered a medication (probably misoprostol) *and* received a dilation and curettage, amounted to less than half the cost.[94] Lorena's dilation and curettage procedure in approximately 1997 cost around US$28.00—a bit less than Pilar's—while Nina Rojas paid about US$12.00 for her injection-induced abortion in 2000.[95]

Some women complained not of the quality of the abortions they obtained but the indifferent or cold attitude of the individuals performing them. When I asked her if the medical staff performing her abortion talked with her before or during the procedure, Lupe said, "No, not much: 'How far along are you?' and I don't know what else. . . . We [referring to the other women in the waiting room] were like—I don't know—like animals, I think, you know? That they had to do it [perform an abortion] for, and that's it."[96] Reflecting on her first experience of abortion in 1995, Adela wondered whether the insensitive attitude of the personnel that performed her procedure might have been due to abortion's illegal status—since providers may have been concerned they would be detected by authorities.

> It's something that I suppose is complicated for them because what they are doing is illegal, right? So, they treat you like a patient but they want to do everything fast—and they want to be done with you fast, to avoid problems. . . . With my first abortion, the anesthesia hadn't even worn off when they said, "You have to get dressed and leave." On top of it, I was in a hidden part of the clinic where you entered and left by the

door where they took out the garbage. "Be careful that no one sees you," they said. So, after all that, I even had to hide.[97]

Two women I interviewed, Vania Condori and Celestina Chambi, ended up provoking their own abortions—Vania by purchasing and ingesting herbs she acquired from an herbalist, and Celestina by lifting and carrying a heavy bag of cement. Both women were moved to induce abortion at the urging of their male partners—a pattern that illustrates the powerful influence that women's partners could have on their experiences with pregnancy. Celestina, an Aymara woman (de pollera) born in the community of Wilkunkani near Desaguadero, was twenty-nine years old and living in El Alto with her husband and two young daughters when she discovered she was facing an unexpected pregnancy in 1989.

> My daughter was a year and seven months old and I was having vomiting . . . and the doctor told me, "You're expecting." I said to myself, "What am I going to do? My child is so small still!" . . . My husband said to me, "Women shouldn't go around like that [with two small children], they can just get rid of it! Carry this cement." So, I carried the cement from the market all the way to the house. And I felt a big pulling and a pressure in my lower back, and a feeling of bursting— I couldn't go on, and I fainted. My daughters were crying out; my husband was nowhere to be found. They [her daughters] got me into bed and for three days I had bleeding until one day they called a doctor, I think he was a naturista, to come see me. He gave me an injection and said, "You aborted—look, it was a little boy"; but I couldn't look. Then, finally, my husband appeared; I guess he was out working. That's what happened to me.[98]

Celestina was tearful as she recounted her story, describing her abortion experience as something to which she had been subjected, rather than having chosen to do it on her own.

This feeling was shared by Vania, a twenty-five-year-old Aymara woman (de vestido) who was pressured to have an abortion by her then boyfriend in 2007. Vania was the second-oldest of eight children and lived with her parents in the La Portada neighborhood of La Paz; she devoted her time to studying social work at the large public university, Universidad Mayor de San Andrés (UMSA), and to taking care of her younger sisters and brothers.

VC: I wasn't very far along [in the pregnancy]. He would call me all the time, he'd come by my house. . . . He always talked to me about other possibilities [rather than keeping the pregnancy]. . . . "What if you take some mate?" he told me. . . . So, finally one day we got together and went to Mariscal Santa Cruz [Avenue] and asked around to see if there was some mate or something, and a señora told us there was.

NK: In the street? Or was it in some office?

VC: In the street, in the street. The only plant I recognized was fig leaves; . . . the rest of it I couldn't recognize. They gave it to us in a little envelope made of newspaper, just enough for one cup of tea, and she just told me, "Take it like a mate and that's it." He begged me, *begged* me to do it. And he was pestering me so much, constantly calling me—it made me so angry—that I just took it. And nothing happened! I mean, I took it and, in the afternoon, went to a big amusement park and thought nothing would happen. But we went—a friend, my brother, and I—because I was so sad, I hadn't been getting out of bed. I was spending all day in bed—morning, afternoon, and night, and I wasn't eating anything, I was so worried. So, we went to this park and at some point a señora came up to me and said, "Miss, your pants are stained, you should be careful." My period had come just at that moment. I don't know if the mate had finally taken effect after all the movement my body had been through at the park, because we'd gotten on a number of rides. . . . That night

when I got home, it felt like it was my normal period. But the next
day . . . when I got out of bed and stood up, a rush of blood came
out. . . . The only thing I could do was call a friend . . . and her mother
told me to take anise tea, that this was going to clean me out. . . . And
to this day, I've never seen my friend's mom again—it's been I don't
know *how* many years, and I'm just too ashamed to see her, I don't
want to see her. It's just that, I know I did something wrong [*yo sé que
he hecho mal*], that I shouldn't have taken that mate knowing that
I was pregnant. But he pestered me so much.

The changes that took place in abortion care in Bolivia after 1982 were
spurred by a number of interconnected phenomena at the local, national,
and international levels. On the one hand, concern with the public health
impact of unsafe abortion surged both domestically and internationally
beginning in the 1970s and 1980s. This concern coalesced with an increase
in political mobilization after Bolivia's democratic opening, creating the
willingness on the part of activist doctors and lawmakers to improve abortion care in specific, if limited, ways. The drive to improve abortion services also arose from intensely personal experiences—particularly women's
ongoing recurrence to abortion. While women's need to limit their pregnancies has always been present, their demand for abortion likely increased in
the mid-1980s, partly as a result of neoliberal policies. These policies spurred
migration to El Alto from mining centers and the countryside, putting additional pressure on an already underdeveloped medical system and on families
struggling to make ends meet. Women's demand for abortion ultimately
encouraged policy makers and sympathetic medical professionals to adopt
new strategies for providing safe abortion and for better treating women
who suffered the consequences of those procedures that were unsafe. At
the same time, abortion's stigmatized status, as well as its legal prohibition,
posed continuing challenges to the women who needed the procedure
and the providers who performed it. The complexities of abortion's legal
status in Bolivia are explored in the next chapter.

CHAPTER 6

Abortion and the Law
in La Paz and El Alto

Law is a discourse of absolutes, and yet it is beset by ambiguities. Legality is inevitably identified with morality, and yet there is in all legal systems a zone where the legal and the non-legal become hard to distinguish.

— *Olivia Harris*

Our society coexists harmoniously with the interruption of pregnancy. I mean, no one says anything. The police know where abortions are performed and they know who performs them; the judges know too—everyone knows. It's not a real secret. But no one does anything. Why? Because abortion is necessary. So, the police usually extort doctors, but they do not necessarily put them in jail.

— *Betina Águilar, a psychologist who worked*
with abortion providers in 2009

When I asked him about the potential legal consequences for a woman who provokes her own abortion or who solicits an abortion from another individual, Eduardo Castillo of the Fuerza Especial de Lucha Contra el Crimen (Special Force of the Fight Against Crime, FELCC), the crime unit of the police department in El Alto, pulled out a tattered copy of the country's penal code and read aloud, "'Abortion: imprisonment of one to three years for the woman who consents to having the abortion performed.' I mean, there are different gradations of punishment depending on the case." When I pressed him to explain why women in Bolivia are rarely imprisoned for abortion, Castillo protested in a somewhat exasperated tone, "But who are we supposed to punish?" After a somewhat awkward silence, he continued, "This is a very complicated situation. In this case the complaint is left in the hands of the Attorney General's Office [Ministerio Público], which investigates crimes requiring public prosecution in which the complaining victim desists. It would be advisable for you to ask *them* why more arrests are not made."[1]

The tenor of Castillo's comments regarding the relative scarcity of arrests in connection with abortion in La Paz and El Alto matched that of conversations I had with other law enforcement officers, medical doctors, and government officials shouldered with the responsibility of policing abortion in these cities. Sometimes, interviewees deflected responsibility for policing the procedure to individuals in other government agencies. At other times, public officials cited the seemingly insurmountable obstacles to upholding the country's abortion laws, such as the difficulty of proving that an abortion has occurred. On the one hand, officials asserted that it was difficult to arrest a woman for procuring an abortion, since it is nearly impossible to determine if a pregnancy loss has resulted from a provoked abortion or a spontaneous miscarriage, even upon physical exam. Authorities protested that it was equally tough to prosecute abortion providers because in order to meet the burden of proof, these must be caught in the act of performing the procedure. The complaints of Bolivian authorities notwithstanding, interview and medical record data suggest that, even when proof of an intentional abortion existed, medical doctors and police officers rarely denounced or arrested abortion providers or their patients.

This chapter highlights the selective nature of arrests and prosecutions in connection with abortion in La Paz and El Alto, and the failure (until very recently) of the legal system to provide women access to abortion in circumstances that *were* allowed by law. Drawing lessons from scholarship elsewhere in Latin America, it further reflects on some of the broader implications of the distance between law and practice concerning reproductive regulation and raises questions regarding the challenges faced by women for which legal reform may be an insufficient solution—particularly without deep and concerted attention to underlying inequalities of race, gender, and class.

The ensuing discussion is not meant, in any way, to suggest that I believe that more should be done to arrest or prosecute women or providers in connection with abortion. As this book and scholarship on abortion in other world contexts make clear, abortion's illegality significantly impacts women and society more broadly. While abortion's prohibition poses significant medical and legal risks for women and contributes to the stress and strain of an already difficult experience, widespread moral condemnation of the procedure shrouds society as a whole in an atmosphere of secrecy and shame.[2] Yet the contradictions between abortion's ubiquity and its ongoing legal prohibition raise a number of questions: Why do authorities choose to prosecute women for seeking abortion or doctors for performing the procedure only in limited cases? Alternatively, considering the lack of political will of authorities in the country to police abortion, why does the procedure continue to be prohibited—whose interests does abortion's illegality in Bolivia serve? Finally, which of the many consequences of abortion's legal prohibition for women and society might legislative change assuage, and which may depend upon broader, structural changes?

THE SELECTIVE NATURE OF ABORTION-RELATED PROSECUTION IN LA PAZ AND EL ALTO

Denunciations and arrests of abortion providers in Bolivia were infrequent over the last several decades, but they did sometimes occur. In his 1980 thesis, one political scientist in La Paz found that fifty-three abortion complaints were filed with that city's police department between 1978 and 1979, which amounted to less than 1 percent of all crimes reported for that year.[3] Of these cases, 66 percent were still pending in 1980 and fewer than 2 percent had been passed on to the Attorney General's Office for prosecution.[4] Statistics from more recent years conform to this general pattern. In 1998 and 1999, Bolivian authorities investigated approximately eighty complaints of abortion nationwide each year, representing less than 1 percent of all crimes reported during those years.[5] In the first decade of the twenty-first century, arrests for abortion in La Paz and El Alto were similarly rare, with fewer than seven made each year between 2005 and 2009.[6] It appears that, nationwide, abortion-related arrests in Bolivia—at least, those of women—may have increased over the last decade. Between 2008 and 2013, some 775 women were arrested on suspicion of having induced their own abortions; of these, two women were imprisoned—one for eight months and the other for three days.[7]

According to interviewees and the press, arrests of individuals in connection with abortion in Bolivia typically take place only after a woman has suffered severe complications or death due to a poorly performed procedure. The four complaints for abortion that Eduardo Castillo handled in El Alto in 2008 came to the attention of authorities after women were discovered in public places with severe vaginal bleeding. "They were found in the street by a police vehicle and . . . taken to the hospital," remarked Castillo. "The doctor examined them and realized it was an abortion . . . and we went to the clinic and intervened."[8] The same year, the La Paz daily *El Diario* reported on the investigation of a clinic that performed an abortion on a woman who later had to undergo three surgeries to treat the injuries she suffered as a result. The reporter failed to mention if either the woman or the abortion provider were ultimately arrested.[9] In an "exposé" on abortion printed in 2009, La Paz's *El Diario* asserted, "Business of this type occurs constantly, and the law is only applied . . . when a patient dies or when there is some scandal involving a famous person, because when the problem concerns someone of few economic resources, the case isn't even addressed."[10]

Arrests of abortion providers may occur following poorly performed abortions in part because the complainant—usually the patient or one of her family members—hopes the legal case will force the provider to repay the costs of treating the complications that resulted from the procedure. (This may have been particularly true prior to 2003, when universal health insurance was expanded to include treatment of postabortion complications.) In one case from 1999, the aunt of twenty-two-year-old alteña María reported her niece's abortion provider to police after the provider, in a private meeting, refused to cover the costs the family incurred treating the injuries the young woman sustained during her procedure. After the aunt filed the complaint, however, a friend of the abortion provider—a police officer—threatened to arrest María and her boyfriend if the family pushed ahead with the case. When the aunt consulted La Paz police on the matter, officials ostensibly supported the other officer's story. Faced with the possibility of María's arrest, the family dropped the complaint against the abortion provider.[11] Explained the family's lawyer, "The aunt of the girl came and told me that . . . the police warned them that if we did not accept that the abortion provider pay just sixty percent of the medical costs, they were going to detain the boyfriend of the girl for complicity in the crime, and then when the girl was released from the clinic, she would also be detained. . . . With this argument, and with the fear that the other policeman had inspired in them, they arranged a deal behind my back—I think that the doctor [sic] paid sixty percent of the costs."[12]

Many abortion cases fail to go to trial because the parties involved reach agreements on their own—probably involving an exchange of money. In an interview he conducted with three Superior Court judges in La Paz in the late 1970s, political scientist Hugo Altamirano said the officials in question believed that, "the rate of legal cases [concerning abortion] was minimal because agreements were made between the parties to avoid lodging the complaint with the Attorney General's Office."[13] Although such agreements may spare a woman or abortion provider a trial and potential imprisonment, they are often reached only after a threat of additional legal action has been made, usually against the woman or her partner. Thus Castillo explained that when a woman denounces the individual who performed her abortion, the patient usually ends up dropping the complaint after the provider threatens to file a countersuit. "Once an investigation is opened to arrest an abortion provider, he [the provider] reminds the woman, 'But you came searching for me,' and the patient abandons the case—and when the victim desists, the police are left with our arms crossed."[14]

When police are unable to pursue an abortion case due to the lack of a clear complainant or victim, the report is passed on to the Attorney General's Office for prosecution. Article 14 of Bolivia's Law of the Attorney General's Office lists among the central functions of the Office, "to defend the interests of the State and Society as established by . . . the Laws of the Republic," and "to exercise public criminal proceedings."[15] Although it is unclear how often police authorities report cases of abortion to the attorney general, they must occasionally do so, since trials for abortion do sometimes occur—even if these rarely end in conviction. Altamirano reported that fourteen cases of abortion reached the La Paz Superior Court system during 1978 and 1979, which represented less than one quarter of 1 percent of all suits brought for those years.[16] More recent data affirm the infrequency of trials for abortion. La Paz law student Elvira Cruz Vera (evidently unaware of the cases from the late 1970s) could locate only two trials concerning abortion before 2004, both of which were dismissed by the Supreme Court for insufficient evidence.[17] "To prove the crime of abortion," writes Cruz Vera, "one must demonstrate the existence of a pregnancy, the interruption of the pregnancy, and the death of the being that was conceived"—requirements that are difficult to fulfill.[18] Numbers of abortion trials in Bolivia from the early part of the twentieth century are similarly scant; only nine cases concerning abortion were heard at the Supreme Court of Cochabamba between 1915 and 1960.[19]

While some abortion cases fail to end in conviction due to a lack of proof, others may never reach trial because authorities fail to thoroughly investigate complaints of abortion. One 1995 study on abortion in Bolivia noted that "denunciations of abortion are rarely followed by police or the Attorney General's Office, so consequently few cases make it to the courts and they do not end up receiving a condemnatory sentence."[20] A 2009 article from *El Diario* concurred, noting, "Unlicensed clinics that perform illegal abortions proliferate . . . in the country, but the authorities do not act to close them down as they should according to the current [legal] norms."[21] Rather than attempt to arrest or prosecute abortion providers, interviewees assert that authorities typically resort to blackmail. Remarked one doctor who had worked in gynecological and obstetric care in La Paz and El Alto for over twenty years, "I do not know of cases of illegal abortion that have been punished as the law dictates. . . . Instead, the first thing that the police do is arrange a bribe [*lo van a chantajear*]."[22]

Despite the infrequency of arrests of abortion providers in Bolivia, providers of the procedure still fear detection by police—and for good reason. If discovered, individuals who perform abortions are subject to harassment and bribes from police officers, public humiliation (since abortion is widely stigmatized in urban areas), and often, the permanent destruction of their careers. While in Bolivia, I interviewed three doctors who regularly performed abortions (in addition to a few others who implied that they might), plus several health care workers employed at abortion clinics in La Paz and El Alto. When I asked her whether police in these cities pursued cases concerning abortion, Daisy Serrato, a physician who performed the procedure in La Paz, told me that police monitored clinics frequently. "They raid clinics—that's why we're so scared. . . . Police officers sometimes come to ask for an abortion undercover, so we have to be careful. We can't just tell clients, 'Sure, I'll do your abortion right now.' We have to investigate a bit, figure out how she heard about us, who sent her—because if you don't, you're finished." Aware of the risks posed to providers of abortion in La Paz, Serrato warned her family long ago that she might end up in jail someday. "Many illegal abortion centers have been closed and many doctors have gone to prison. They don't stay in prison, obviously, but they have already fallen, you know?"[23] Medical doctor Miguel Ramírez, who also performed abortions, said that police had not attempted to infiltrate his practice—but he was well aware that authorities monitored clinics in central areas of the city. "Here, we don't get followed much by police. . . . The clinics downtown, though—the police are always there . . . threatening and trying to extort them."[24] Julián Costa, an employee at another local abortion clinic, insisted that facilities such as the one where he worked were "at permanent risk" of detection by police. Recounting the story of a provider who was arrested a few years prior, Costa implied that the most deleterious aspect of the arrest was its impact on the doctor's professional and personal life. "There was one case in which the police went to pick up an . . . abortion provider from his house. They accused him of being an abortionist and they put him in prison. Imagine! They destroyed his family and his professional credibility—this doctor had to dye and perm his hair to change his image because the press went and filmed him, they showed him on television. They destroyed his life, you know?"[25]

Arrests of women in connection with abortion were also infrequent, but they did sometimes occur. Since police statistics did not distinguish between reports against providers and patients, it was unclear how many abortion complaints over the past few decades concerned women. Medical record and interview data, however, suggest that doctors who treated women following abortion rarely denounced these to police. Of thirty-seven women treated at public hospitals in La Paz and El Alto between 1955 and 2007 for complications from abortions that medical personnel believed to have been provoked, not a single one was reported to police authorities by medical staff.[26] Even when police had direct contact with patients suffering abortion-related complications, they typically did not arrest them. In December 1995, police brought a twenty-four-year-old woman to La Paz's Hospital de la Mujer (Women's Hospital, HM) for treatment for the symptoms she was suffering following an abortion. After dropping the woman off at the medical facility, police evidently failed to pursue the case further—the woman was released from the hospital in the company of her husband four days later.[27] The selective nature of abortion-related policing in Bolivia resonates with events taking place in at least a few other Latin American countries where the procedure is prohibited. One 1991 article on abortion in Brazil remarked that there were "sporadic crackdowns" on the procedure in the country and quoted one researcher who said, "There is a silent acceptance of these clinics, and everyone knows where they are located."[28]

WHY DO AUTHORITIES CHOOSE TO PROSECUTE WOMEN FOR SEEKING ABORTION OR DOCTORS FOR PERFORMING THE PROCEDURE ONLY IN LIMITED CASES?

Interview data suggest that medical personnel often choose not to report women for having interrupted their pregnancies because they disagree with the law that requires them to do so or feel that reporting falls outside the responsibilities of their profession, or both. As one doctor working at a public hospital in El Alto remarked, "When we are absolutely certain that a patient induced her own abortion, we are supposed to report her. But this represents a conflict for us, because here, abortion is considered a family planning method of last resort. . . . And besides, once we called them, the first thing the police would do is arrange a bribe."[29] Doctors also opt not to report abortion patients because it is difficult to prove that their symptoms were caused by a pregnancy loss that was provoked. One doctor who worked at La Paz's public HM in 2009 remarked, "We've never had any relationship with the police. We wouldn't be able to prove it, anyway, even if we did suspect a voluntary interruption of pregnancy."[30] While I was unable to locate any doctor who admitted alerting police in the case of a suspected abortion, several doctors asserted that, prior to the last ten to fifteen years, this did sometimes occur. "In one case," explained Miguel Ramírez, "medical staff at La Paz's Women's Hospital reported a woman who had misoprostol tablets in her vagina . . . they even locked up her husband."[31] Another doctor who participated in an initiative to improve postabortion care in public hospitals in 1999 remarked, "When we entered medical facilities to do the first workshops, women who arrived with vaginal bleeding were treated very poorly—they were even reported to the police."[32]

Like medical doctors, police officers who handle complaints against women for provoking abortion also sometimes choose not to pursue the cases, either because they believe they will be unable to find sufficient proof or because they sympathize with the patient's plight. When I asked him to describe how police investigate such cases, Castillo remarked that authorities usually find women unconscious in the street and only learn later that they interrupted their pregnancies. "Some women faint in the street because of excessive blood loss, so the police take them to the hospital," remarked Castillo. "When the medical personnel come and tell us, 'This is a provoked abortion,' then it's considered a crime. At that point, homicide personnel go to the hospital to investigate." When I asked him to clarify how police carry out this investigation, Castillo remarked, "Well, we would interrogate the woman, but only if it is possible, because one must remember that she is suffering." Later, when I asked him how he believed the legal system should approach women who terminated pregnancies, Castillo stated, "There are very radical positions that hold that women must be penalized, but these do not take into account the social aspect, the economic aspect, the question of the mother's age. . . . There are many factors that we must analyze. It shouldn't be about saying, 'Let's give it to her rough.' So, of the different positions that exist, I am with the most lenient."[33]

Though it should not be overstated—particularly since many women complain of being mistreated in clinical health facilities—interview testimonies suggest that one factor shaping the responses of some medical and police authorities to abortion laws is sympathy toward women who may have interrupted their pregnancies. This sympathy, which often stems from an understanding that women will seek abortion regardless of the risks, is well understood by the authors of the 2006 book, *The Human Drama of Abortion: A Global Search for Consensus*. Between the late-1940s and 1960s, Aníbal Faúndes and José S. Barzelatto saw firsthand the consequences for women suffering from unsafe abortion while working as medical doctors in Chile. According to Faúndes, witnessing these human dramas shaped his perspective on abortion's criminalization. "I was moved by the social injustice of penalizing women who abort. It is impossible to hear their stories without concluding that these women, far from being criminals, *are victims of the ways in which societies are organized.* Their biggest sin is being poor, because even in countries where abortion is legally restricted, women of means can obtain clean, safe abortions."[34] The experiences of the doctors in Chile echo the findings of Raúl Necochea López for Peru, where the author argues that a number of societal factors shaped local understandings both of abortion and of the women who sought it, across the twentieth century. "Laws, medical and lay knowledge, cultural norms about proper behavior for men and women, and sexual violence shaped the understanding of abortion throughout the twentieth century. . . . Despite the fact that physicians witnessed many instances of pregnancy loss, they rarely instigated criminal accusations of abortion. Even when physicians and state authorities advanced such charges, several obstacles stood in the way of a conviction. Among these obstacles were socially sanctioned violence against women, as well as the precept that 'honorable women' who had abortions deserved forgiveness and reformation rather than punishment."[35]

An additional reason some doctors and police authorities in Bolivia chose not to report women and medical providers in connection with abortion is because they recognized that, at least until 2014 (when the requirement for judicial authorization was lifted), women were unable to access even those abortions that *were* permitted under the law—except, perhaps, in cases in which the woman concerned met particular moralistic and gender-related requirements. In 1973, Bolivia decriminalized abortion in cases of rape, incest, or when a pregnancy threatened a woman's life or health. In the four decades following the modification of the penal code, however, only a handful of legal abortions were ever performed—and these after much controversy. Fearing professional ostracism, judges and doctors called upon to authorize and perform legal abortions often declined, passing the request off to other professionals. In most cases, the wheels of justice turned so slowly that petitioners' children were born before they were able to secure legal abortions. As noted by Faúndes and Barzelatto with respect to legislation concerning abortion worldwide, "Too little emphasis has been placed on the implementation of existing laws"—a point echoed by many of the activists and medical personnel I interviewed in La Paz and El Alto.[36]

Despite the fact that legal codes permitted abortion in certain cases (called aborto impune) for over two decades, the first legal abortion did not take place in Bolivia until 1998—and then only after persistent mobilization by the young woman's family and local women's rights activists. That year in May, fourteen-year-old Olga became pregnant after her stepfather raped her in their home in the city of Sucre. By the time the girl's mother, Leonarda, discovered the pregnancy, Olga was ten weeks pregnant. It took Olga's family and activists at the Centro Juana Azurduy (Juana Azurduy Center) more than a month of diligent work to secure the judicial authorization for Olga's procedure.[37] Even with the judicial order in hand, medical authorities at Sucre's Jaime Sánchez Pórcel Hospital invented a number of pretexts to avoid performing the abortion; when Leonarda questioned one medical student why it was taking so long to perform her daughter's procedure, the student reportedly remarked, "No one wants to dirty their hands with her."[38] Only when the director of the Juana Azurduy Center approached the court to complain of the hospital's incompliance was Olga finally able to secure her abortion on August 19— some six weeks after Leonarda first reported her daughter's rape to police.

The determination of the young woman's family and local activists notwithstanding, Olga's petition likely reached fruition—at least in part— due to a few peculiarities of the case. Evidently, the young woman "possessed a physique that appeared to match that of a much younger girl"—a fact that drew sympathy for Olga and raised concerns that she could suffer complications in childbirth.[39] Secondly, Olga's mother Leonarda probably acted with particular haste and resolve in helping to secure her daughter's abortion because, at age sixteen, she herself had been raped and impregnated by a friend of the family for whom she worked as a domestic servant.[40] Having suffered that experience, Leonarda not only advocated tirelessly on her daughter's behalf but also gained the sympathy of the activists and government authorities handling Olga's case.

Typically, petitioners of legal abortion in Bolivia were not so fortunate. In the early 1990s, one mother in the city of Santa Cruz filed requests for legal abortions for her two teenage daughters, both impregnated by their father. After the request was passed between three separate court bodies and after two judges had recused themselves from the case, the girls—by then nearly five and eight months pregnant, respectively—were forced to keep the children.[41] "I am very concerned about the . . . justice system," remarked Julián Costa. "More than thirty years have passed [since the implementation of the legal abortion law] and there must have been only six or seven legal pregnancy interruptions. . . . The police, the judges—they must change their mentality."[42] According to one government health official I interviewed in 2009, Bolivian authorities were hesitant to handle cases of legal abortion because they "don't want to implicate themselves. At the moment that the legislation must be applied . . . everyone acts like a savior of the world," the official remarked, "and finally the patient opts for a clandestine abortion."[43] Even Olga was almost unable to secure her procedure legally; members of the medical personnel who initially refused to perform the young woman's abortion ostensibly advised Olga to insert an abortifacient into her vagina herself, "since the situation would be different if the patient arrived to [our] hands with the abortion already begun by another person."[44]

Overall, the failure of the law to guarantee women's access to aborto impune in Bolivia between the early 1970s and 2014 points to the strength of public opposition of abortion in urban society, even in cases involving rape and incest. On the other hand, the decisions of authorities not to report and arrest women and doctors in connection with abortion—as well as those of the many Bolivian citizens who opt not to report friends and acquaintances who seek the procedure—suggests a hidden tolerance and compassion for women facing unwanted pregnancy in the country, even as many authorities extract bribes in exchange for silence.

CONSIDERING THE LACK OF POLITICAL WILL OF AUTHORITIES IN THE COUNTRY TO PROSECUTE CASES OF ABORTION, WHY DOES THE PROCEDURE CONTINUE TO BE PROHIBITED—WHOSE INTERESTS DOES ABORTION'S ILLEGALITY SERVE?

Abortion's ongoing legal prohibition serves the interests of lawmakers seeking to maintain power by balancing personal and political relationships with dominant social and religious sectors. The public sacrifice of a limited number of abortion providers and women who procure the procedure further benefits legal and political authorities in Bolivia, who may use these cases to demonstrate their compliance with the law while extracting bribes behind the scenes from the many women and providers whom they opt not to prosecute. Widespread public opposition to abortion on the part of government and police officials also serves to cement the position of these individuals on what is widely believed in La Paz and El Alto to be the "right side" of morality.

As noted by Olivia Harris at the beginning of this chapter, there is an implicit relationship between the law and morality; yet the contours of this relationship are imprecise and sometimes contradictory, since the moral regimes undergirding legislation are pitted against those of the specific individuals charged with upholding, or conforming to, the law. Writes Harris, "Laws themselves often put social actors in difficult moral predicaments by the fact that they forbid, or even criminalize, actions which for the people concerned are acceptable or desirable within their own moral code."[45] For most of the last four decades, guaranteeing women's access to aborto impune in Bolivia involved a burdensome, and highly public, legal process with few direct social, political, or economic benefits to the authorities upon whose will this process relied. In places where legal processes are burdensome, "what is known as 'corruption' flourishes. However, it is important to spell out the ambiguities of corruption. To receive or offer money or other resources in return for facilitating a legal process is strictly against the law, but those involved usually deny that they are acting illegally. It is because they are poorly paid, it is because the law is unworkable anyway, it is because they wish to be helpful, or owe a favour to X or Y. . . . Thus in many contexts, at the very point of operation of the law, there is uncertainty as to whether those involved are inside or outside."[46]

To accommodate (and indeed, uphold) the coexistence of repressive laws on abortion and the widespread availability of the procedure, a double discourse of morality concerning sexual and reproductive behavior has developed in La Paz and El Alto—as it has, argues Bonnie Shepard, in a number of Latin American countries. "Thanks to the ubiquity of the double discourse, in most Latin American countries the reproductive and sexual choices open to citizens are much wider than the official policies would lead one to believe. . . . [P]rivate individual discourses [that tolerate abortion] are complemented by social and political mechanisms—laws or interpretations of laws providing escape valves, common practices, clandestine services, etc.—that make expanded choices possible."[47] In Bolivia, a number of practices and services have emerged since the mid-1990s to provide women facing unwanted pregnancy safer options to terminate them. While these developments contributed to reducing abortion-related complications, it is possible that they also slowed efforts to legalize abortion. Since part of the pressure on the state to decriminalize abortion emerges from the procedure's impact on maternal morbidity and mortality, recent improvements in abortion care may have diffused pressure applied by medical and feminist sectors to legalize the procedure. At the same time, while improvements in abortion care and the mechanisms sustaining access to these, "constitute an escape valve that expands citizens' sexual and reproductive choices, . . . because they are makeshift, illegal, or unofficial, neither availability, safety (in the case of services), nor protections of basic rights are guaranteed."[48]

While the scope of this book does not allow for a broader comparison, the distance between laws governing pregnancy termination in Latin America and their implementation on the ground is likely not unique to abortion, but instead characterizes the relationship between laws on, and practices concerning, a range of phenomena. As such, the slippage between legal norms and empirical realities may reflect broader institutional features of the legal and juridical systems in some Latin American countries (and perhaps in other world contexts). Scholarship has demonstrated the widespread existence of informal political institutions in Latin America, or "*socially shared rules, usually unwritten, that are created, communicated, and enforced outside officially sanctioned channels.*"[49] These diverse institutions include "clientelism in Brazil and Honduras, legislative 'ghost coalitions' in Ecuador, norms of executive-legislative power-sharing in Chile, illicit campaign finance in Brazil, norms of electoral accountability in Argentina, indigenous law in the Andes," and "norms underlying police violence in Brazilian cities," among others.[50] While abortion care in Bolivia does not constitute an informal political institution per se, the wealth of scholarship on the distance between legal norms and their implementation suggests the commonality of this distance with regard to a range of phenomena in a number of Latin American contexts.

In recent years, scholars have explored the gap between law and practice with respect to gender-related policies, in particular. Mala Htun and S. Laurel Weldon argue that, "patterns of policy implementation can shape the extent to which rights earned on the books are actually felt on the ground. Variation in the efficacy of rights may be a function of state capacity, unequal access to resources, civic organizing, or deliberate political choices."[51] According to the authors, disaggregating the examination of different kinds of gender-related policies can shed light on the "logics" underlying these policies and reveal why, and to what degree, some policies are implemented while others are not. "Our analysis helps to unravel these surprising phenomena. We disaggregated women's rights into different dimensions, mapped out which policies combat disadvantage along each dimension, and then identified the *logics*—the distinct histories, conflicts, actors, and ideas—surrounding each area of gender justice."[52] Scholars have further noted that laws—which are used to constitute legal personhood—also govern who, precisely, is defined as a citizen deserving of the rights that personhood entails, and who is not. Writes Harris, "It has often been argued that Western legal subjects are founded in an abstract, neutral, gender-blind individual developed from Enlightenment thought. . . . Certain categories of people by such criteria are almost *ipso facto* outside the law, and to a certain extent therefore deprived of the status of legal subject: women, homosexuals, the poorly educated."[53] Thus (and as demonstrated by the title of Jacqui Alexander's article on the then-illegal status of lesbians in Trinidad and Tobago), "not just anybody can be a citizen"—or, therefore, a person deemed deserving of the policies designed to constitute, or to defend, their legally afforded rights.[54]

The consequences of the distance between law and reality vary depending on what, specifically, is being regulated; yet, these consequences tend to fall hardest on the poor, the disenfranchised, and the marginalized—those whose legal personhood is ambivalently guaranteed, at best. In Bolivia, the consequences of abortion laws fall, unsurprisingly, on these same groups. Due to abortion's prohibited status, women—particularly those who are poor and indigenous—are forced to navigate an already difficult experience in a context of secrecy, while risking their physical and mental health on Bolivia's unregulated abortion market.

WHICH OF THE MANY CONSEQUENCES OF ABORTION'S LEGAL PROHIBITION FOR WOMEN AND SOCIETY MIGHT LEGISLATIVE CHANGE ASSUAGE, AND WHICH MAY DEPEND UPON BROADER, STRUCTURAL CHANGES?

One of the arguments developed in this book, long established by scholarship on abortion worldwide, is that abortion's legal prohibition works hand-in-hand with the lack of regulation of the procedure to subject

women to a range of medical, social, and economic consequences—
consequences that are legion and often severe.[55] Because where abortion
is illegal it officially does not exist, most abortions take place outside of
the purview of state regulatory systems in conditions that are largely
unsafe. At the same time, scholars have shown that, even when abortion
is decriminalized, it is often regulated in such a way that neither its safety
nor women's unburdened access to the procedure are guaranteed. A 2017
study on abortion in Cape Town, South Africa, found that while abortion
is permitted in pregnancies up to twelve weeks (and up to twenty weeks
in certain circumstances), most women did not seek abortion in the public facilities where the procedure was available legally and free of charge.
Instead, citing stigma and mistreatment at these facilities, over 80 percent
of women surveyed, "consumed home remedies, herbal mixtures from traditional healers, or tablets from an unregistered provider" to terminate
their pregnancies.[56]

In Bolivia, many women's experiences with a variety of forms of reproductive health care—not just abortion—take place outside the supervision of the state. Furthermore, some of the mechanisms recently instituted
to regulate Andean forms of reproductive health care have drawn apt criticism by traditional medical practitioners for their tendency to promote
charlatanry and to restrict the political power and free practice of legitimate Andean providers. These patterns raise the question of what might
be accomplished by decriminalizing abortion and by instituting stronger
regulatory mechanisms for both clinical and Andean reproductive health
care services and providers—and whether these mechanisms might, in
fact, hoist further burdens on women seeking to exercise greater autonomy over their reproductive lives.

On the one hand, decriminalizing abortion and regulating its provision could assuage some of the medical risks women face in seeking the
procedure. For instance, were abortion legal, its providers could openly
advertise their services, allowing women greater opportunity to locate safe
and high-quality abortion care. However, it remains unclear what effective

regulation of abortion might entail. What would regulation mean, for instance, for providers of traditional medicine, who are often geographically mobile and have spiritual tenets incorporated in their practice? And what might be some of the unintended consequences of regulation for the services provided by those providers who perform abortions in clinical settings? Considering the contemporary situation facing many states in the United States, where abortion has been regulated almost entirely out of existence due to requirements such as mandatory waiting periods, hospital-admitting privileges, and surgical theater–style operation rooms, these questions regarding the implications of regulatory practices raise serious concerns.[57]

Furthermore, neither abortion's decriminalization nor the regulation of reproductive health care would solve other, systemic issues leading to unwanted pregnancy and unsafe abortion, including poverty, patriarchy, racism, and closed-mindedness. The testimonies featured in this book suggest that these economic and social patterns permeating urban Andean society interfered more pervasively with women's access to abortion and to other methods of fertility regulation than did legal norms or regulatory mechanisms. Thus policies expanding women's reproductive autonomy would have to emerge from a broader place of understanding that women will have abortions regardless of its legal status, and some acceptance of that fact—as well as a larger acceptance of women's personhood and their capacity to make decisions about their reproductive lives. Such policies, furthermore, would have to work to, as Rosalind Petchesky contends, "transform the social conditions of choosing, working, and reproducing"—so that the landscape in which women's pregnancies occur were one in which choices were truly possible.[58]

Conclusion

[Abortion] is a very delicate topic, one that's addressed very much under the rug. . . . The fact that abortion exists, that it can be done by experts without risking your life, is just passed by word of mouth [va de oído en oído]. It's impossible that you'd hear about it on the radio or television; it's a secret. . . . But perceptions are changing—women can now define their own lives, their bodies, their decisions. I think if abortion is ever legalized in Bolivia, it's not going to be a big boom. At the same time, there's a lot of opposition on the part of many sectors of the population.

—Dr. Dolores Ticahuanca

The comments of Dolores and of other individuals I interviewed in La Paz and El Alto highlight the profound contradictions that surround both conversations about and experiences of unwanted pregnancy and abortion in urban Bolivia. In public discourse, abortion is a sensitive topic that is kept secret—and yet its practice is so common that its legalization might not provoke widespread social turmoil (at least, in this doctor's estimation). Individuals across a range of social sectors oppose abortion, but perceptions of the women who recur to it are shifting. Abortion is widely performed by experts; yet many women still must risk their lives in order to secure it.

This book has argued that the experiences of the women featured herein are important, because (1) women's experiences with unwanted pregnancy and abortion spurred changes in public policies on, and services concerning, reproductive health; (2) the tendrils of women's reproductive experiences elucidate, and were influenced by, a number of conflicted attitudes toward women and sexuality held by a variety of social sectors in the urban highlands; and (3) attention to women's lived experiences, and to the contours of how women felt about and negotiated these experiences, upset common misperceptions about how women make decisions about their reproductive lives. These experiences also place in stark relief the life-and-death impacts of both legal prohibitions and societal stigma against abortion. ⌐ ⌐

In arguing that the experiences of women in Bolivia with unwanted pregnancy and abortion matter, the book has also attempted to highlight the significance of women's experiences with phenomena adjacent to its immediate focus—such as sex, partnership, and family life—and the importance of such experiences taking place in other geographical locations. It is my hope that, in examining sexuality and reproduction from the perspective of women themselves, the book has more closely approximated some experiential historical "truth," while imbuing the discussion of the phenomena of unwanted pregnancy and abortion with greater depth, and perhaps, compassion.

Reproductive Health Policies and Services

In saying that women's reproductive experiences are important, I also mean that they are worthy of historical inquiry—but only in part because these experiences were inseparable from public life. As in so many other contexts, women's reproductive experiences in Bolivia were intimately tied up with larger political and social processes. In the 1950s and 1960s, policy makers seeking to further national progress and modernization looked to the country's women, the majority of whom were indigenous, and deemed them unfit for the task of reproducing a population of healthy citizens. They attempted to solve this "problem" by reforming indigenous women's mothering practices and by subordinating the medical traditions of Andean providers to those of the biomedical establishment. They pursued these measures as part of broader attempts to reduce levels of infant and maternal mortality and spur population growth, which policy makers believed would foster economic progress and bolster Bolivia's position on the world stage. Between the late 1960s and the 1980s, reformers in Bolivia joined with international organizations like USAID to institute measures designed to *limit* the population of indigenous women and men. This took place in the face of growing international concern with the ostensible overpopulation of poor people of color worldwide, and in the context of Cold War–era concerns that these individuals would be particularly susceptible to communist agitation. Measures to limit population growth in Bolivia were undergirded by developmentalist discourses that continued to cast indigenous people as partly responsible for the country's lagging public health record. In the wake of the democratic opening in 1982 and the international conferences in Cairo in 1994 and in Beijing in 1995, reformers developed a new discourse around sexual and reproductive health in Bolivia that sought to disentangle family planning initiatives from the coercive language of population control. At the same time, in focusing on what they perceived to be the "unmet need" of indigenous Bolivians for western-derived contraceptive methods and reproductive practices, reformers, "were limited by a failure to acknowledge . . . the internal racial . . . hierarchies that informed their own understandings of Bolivia's 'population problems.'"[1]

The history of unwanted pregnancy and abortion in La Paz and El Alto is multilayered, in that moments of change or continuity in reproductive health policies and services, and in women's personal experiences with these services, proceeded along somewhat distinct timelines. On the one hand, the attitudes concerning reproduction espoused by government and medical officials during Bolivia's revolutionary and military periods colored women's experiences in ways that were somewhat distinct from the years after democracy was restored. The Movimiento Nacionalista Revolucionario's (MNR's) revolutionary project, like those at work in other Latin American countries at midcentury, held "motherhood [as] central to state formation and nation building."[2] This fact, coupled with the MNR's dual efforts to expand access to health care and to promote western over Andean medical practices, led to the founding of new maternal and infant health facilities in a variety of areas of the country to which some women turned for medical care. Yet the pronatalism of the MNR, the ambivalent attitudes of revolutionary and military leaders toward Bolivia's indigenous population, patterns of foreign intervention, and restrictions placed on political organizing under military rule, all placed women facing unwanted pregnancy in a difficult position. Women seeking to terminate pregnancies or to limit births during these years were forced to do so largely on their own, or by relying on the support of a limited number of trusted friends, family members, or health providers.

The democratic opening marked a significant moment in changes to some reproductive health policies and in the availability of some forms of fertility regulation, but not others. Policies prohibiting the circulation of western-derived birth control methods and the practice of traditional medicine were lifted in the early 1980s. However, birth control was not widely available until much later. Traditional medicine, for its part, was omnipresent throughout the period—though its providers may have had more freedom in where they could practice following its official recognition by the state in 1984.[3] In the decade of the 1980s, limits in insurance coverage made hospital birth and clinical treatment for incomplete pregnancy loss out of reach for many women. Changes in policies concerning reproductive health care instead accelerated after 1989, when a national family planning program was first adopted, through the 1990s and 2000s, when policies were enacted to expand insurance programs covering women in pregnancy. Similarly, clinical technologies used to induce abortion and to treat women following abortion or miscarriage remained largely unchanged until the mid-1990s, when the aspiration method was adopted by clinical medical providers. Technologies for abortion shifted once more in the first decade of the twenty-first century, when misoprostol became available over the counter in pharmacies and at street markets (and, more recently, online). These improved technologies were employed by the new, higher-quality abortion providers who emerged in La Paz and

El Alto beginning in the mid-1990s. At the same time—and despite the availability of new, safer medical technologies and abortion providers— many women who procured abortions at the turn of the twenty-first century were unable to access these improved services. Ultimately, the results of the recent changes in policies and services concerning unwanted pregnancy and abortion have been contradictory. These results include decreased rates of abortion-related death and an increased ability for some women to control the outcomes of their pregnancies, alongside the persistent vulnerability of poor women to unsafe abortion in the wake of the ongoing prohibition of the procedure and the absence of effective regulatory mechanisms for health providers and medications.

The changes in reproductive health policies and services that occurred since the early 1950s were a direct result of the actions taken by women (and some men), both as individuals and in collective groups. While some of these actions were intentionally aimed at shaping policy, others constituted the ongoing measures that women employed to regulate their fertility. In the wake of the democratic opening and in a broader context of international movements for women's equality, activists and their constituents in Bolivia pursued a number of initiatives aimed at improving women's health and securing their rights more broadly. Measures pursued by those organizations whose leadership was largely mestiza included advocacy to decriminalize abortion and to bolster women's access to sexual and reproductive health care, efforts to increase women's political participation, and initiatives combatting domestic violence. Organizations led by indigenous Bolivians also pursued initiatives to quash domestic violence and expand women's political representation; in addition, these groups mobilized to secure rights to land and to educational opportunities, and to bolster Andean medicine and its practitioners. The pressures brought to bear by these groups on the country's medical and policy-making sectors led to improvements in laws and services concerning unwanted pregnancy and abortion; they also led to official recognition for

Andean medicine and more concerted efforts to integrate traditional medical practices into national health systems.

Women also shaped the trajectory of reproductive health policies and services on an individual basis, by taking actions concerning their fertility and their sexual and reproductive health. They did so by employing a variety of methods of fertility regulation, including abortion, despite the challenges posed by doing so. These challenges included periods of pronatalist rhetoric and policies imposed by state policy makers; religious and societal stigma against contraception and abortion in urban areas; legal prohibitions against contraception in the late 1970s and early 1980s, coupled with the ongoing criminalization of abortion; discrimination in medical centers against women suffering complications after pregnancy loss; and the structural factors shaping women's reproductive experiences. In terminating pregnancies, some women were forced to recur to painful and risky strategies in the absence of other alternatives, such as inserting objects into the cervix and causing physical trauma to themselves. Collectively, women's persistence in procuring abortion despite these risks raised attention to high rates of maternal mortality due to unsafe abortion, which coalesced with international concerns with this phenomenon to place pressure on the state to take measures to improve treatments for pregnancy loss. Women's ongoing recurrence to abortion further sparked sympathy among members of the medical and activist communities, who worked to improve abortion and postabortion care—despite the legal risks that some of these measures posed. Women further eschewed the state's efforts to emphasize western over Andean methods of reproductive health care, even in the cities, where biomedicine was more prominent. Women in La Paz and El Alto took herbal remedies as teas and vaginal suppositories, and worked with midwives, healers, and naturalists to regulate their fertility, give birth, terminate pregnancies, and treat pregnancy-related ailments.

While women's individual and collective experiences shaped reproductive health policies in Bolivia, the reverse was typically not the case.

Rather than responding to shifts in public policy, women's experiences
with unwanted pregnancy and abortion were more directly shaped by phenomena that were both broader and more intimate, such as national and
international social and economic trends, the quality of women's relationships with their families and partners, and women's life goals and aspirations. Periods of economic crisis brought on by neoliberalism, as well as
the neoliberal austerity measures that governments implemented in the
1980s and 1990s in response to these crises,[4] caused profound insecurity
for Bolivian families; they also placed additional pressure on women struggling to make ends meet—both in their own lives and in those of their
potential, or already existing, children. Shifting attitudes toward women
and indigenous Bolivians further shaped women's reproductive experiences. While for much of the twentieth century indigenous women and
families were conceptualized as obstacles to the achievement of Bolivia's
public health goals, by the early twenty-first century, several national
health programs in the country recognized access to safe childbirth,
whether practiced according to western or Andean traditions, as a key ele-
ment of "women's universal human rights."[5] Patriarchy, and especially its
expressions in machismo and gender-based violence, was a particularly
virulent force shaping women's experiences with unwanted pregnancy in
La Paz and El Alto. The persistence of stigma, silence, and shame that permeated discussions (or lack thereof) of sexuality in both family and
national life further shaped both the circumstances in which women
became pregnant, and how they ended up resolving their pregnancies—
usually through choices that were heavily constrained by patriarchy,
racism, and poverty. At the same time, women's engagement with
organizations mobilizing for their health and rights since the early 1980s
helped shift women's understandings of, and negotiations concerning,
their pregnancies. Some women, perhaps influenced by the developmentalist narratives espoused by some of these institutions, looked back
on their reproductive experiences wishing they had "known more" about
western-derived contraception or abortion. Others harnessed the discus-

sions of gender relations and of personal and political empowerment taking place in these organizations to improve their relationships with male partners, children, and families of origin, as well as with their health care providers.

AMBIVALENCE AND CONTRADICTION

Another reason that women's reproductive experiences are important—and further evidence of their inextricability from public life—is the widespread ambivalence that these experiences reveal in social attitudes toward women and sexuality in the urban highlands. In public, most individuals I interviewed professed to oppose abortion, the women who procured it, and the providers who performed it. People from a wide range of social sectors, conflicted over women's changing roles in urban society, implicitly or explicitly blamed women for what they perceived to be increased rates of unwanted pregnancy and abortion in recent decades. While some blamed the supposed rise in abortion rates on women who chose to pursue career over family, others pointed to economic crisis leading mothers to work outside the home, which they argued left adolescent daughters unsupervised and more likely to become pregnant unexpectedly. Individuals also contended that the secularization of urban Andean society and a general "loss of values" led to an increase in incestuous rape and men's abandonment of their pregnant partners, and, concomitantly, to abortion. Those who opposed abortion did so on religious grounds; less commonly, individuals articulated resource-oriented arguments that linked abortion (and sometimes contraception) to what they perceived to be Bolivia's underpopulation and lagging economic growth vis-à-vis other Latin American countries. In most cases, and regardless of the particularities of their arguments against abortion, individuals asserted that fetuses possessed a "right to life" that trumped both rights-based claims concerning women, and public health concerns about the impact of unsafe abortion on women's mortality. At the same time, most Bolivians were remarkably pragmatic about the need of women—as well as those of men and of families—for abortion. Thus, when an unwanted pregnancy impacted a friend or loved one, or when it occurred in one of a range of circumstances that an individual deemed appropriate, attitudes toward abortion were much more flexible—as long as these ideas, and the actions resulting from them, were articulated and took place in relative privacy.

The double discourse on abortion in Bolivia—which makes it difficult for individuals to publicly defend abortion rights, but nonetheless allows for the widespread tacit acceptance of abortion—mirrors, in some respects, the evolution of public policy concerning this phenomenon over the last several decades. Pressured by growing international concern over the impact of unsafe abortion on maternal mortality but limited by the opposition of religious groups and the broader public to decriminalize abortion, Bolivia's political authorities, like those elsewhere in Latin America, traverse difficult terrain. At present, the solution of public health reformers in the country has been to implement stop-gap medical and insurance policies to mitigate abortion's risks to maternal mortality, while leaving intact the procedure's prohibited status. This strategy suggests that most health professionals and political officials in Bolivia conceive of abortion primarily as an issue of public health, rather than one of rights. At the same time, abortion's continuing prohibition has allowed the procedure to remain both unregulated—and thus, a continuing threat to women's health—and a locus of secrecy and shame for women, families, and the individuals who perform the procedure.

Ambivalence also seemed to permeate attitudes toward sexuality in La Paz and El Alto, a fact that complicated any effort to empower women in their sexual encounters and, by extension, with respect to their reproductive choices. Sex, like abortion, was largely considered a private affair and was not widely discussed in families or schools. In general, interviewees remarked that they received little information about sex, sexual health, or pregnancy, either at home or in the classroom—and none at all with respect to pleasure, or even consent. Discussions of women in relation to sexuality tended to portray women who engaged in sex, or who took measures to control their fertility, as promiscuous and morally suspect. In other words, religiosity and colonial-era notions that link women's honor to their asexuality or sexual chastity remain, to some degree, persistent in twenty-first-century La Paz and El Alto. At the same time, some people I interviewed asserted that public attitudes toward sexuality were shifting (unlike those on abortion, which they argued remained closed-minded). This is perhaps evidenced by the fact that women who were single mothers, as well as those who were partnered, though unmarried, were widely believed to be more accepted by urban society in the early twenty-first century than they were several decades before. These changes may be due, in part, to initiatives pursued in the last few decades to expand public discussions of sexuality in La Paz and El Alto. On the one hand, some discussion of sex undoubtedly took place in the context of workshops on women and health pursued by civil society organizations in the years following the democratic opening. Far more visible initiatives centered on sexuality were undertaken in the last few decades by the anarcho-feminist group Mujeres Creando. These included a widespread urban graffiti campaign about sex and patriarchy, the publication of texts about sex and pleasure (including lesbian desire), and public performances and video projects concerning sexuality.[6]

Even among those sectors who wholeheartedly, and publicly, defended abortion, its providers, and its procurers, other forms of ambivalence lingered. In particular, some individuals who defended a woman's right to choose the outcome of her pregnancy espoused conflicted attitudes toward indigenous women and toward the rural communities to which some of them belonged, or from which they originated. These individuals perceived stigma against rural-dwelling indigenous women to be fierce—particularly with respect to the notion that improperly buried fetuses caused hail, ruining harvests and leading to the persecution of women suspected of terminating, or found to have terminated, their pregnancies. These individuals, furthermore, sometimes faulted indigenous communities for failing to support the rights of their women members in a variety of arenas. Particularly concerning to women's rights activists and other urban residents were patterns of domestic violence against women in rural areas, as well as what they perceived to be limits to women's political participation.

On the one hand, scholars who have examined gender relations in rural areas often assert that there is some distance between ideals of gender parity and complementarity in indigenous communities, and the actual relations between women and men taking place there.[7] On the other hand, efforts on the part of self-proclaimed women's rights activists (as well as some scholars in western spheres) to accurately assess discrimination against rural-dwelling women may be stymied by western biases and a broader ignorance of gender complementarity. Remarking on discussions of women's lagging participation in political assemblies in the rural Andes, for instance, "[Denise] Arnold claims that it is a Western bias that leads scholars to overestimate the importance of public rhetoric and to interpret silence in communal assemblies as a straightforward proof of discrimination."[8] Scholars exploring gender relations in the rural Andes have further shown how women actively intervene in communal life via forms of language that, in western contexts, do not typically "count" as political—such as singing and weaving.[9] Even more important to acknowledge is some scholars' contention that, largely responsible for *causing* unequal gender relations in the rural sphere are, precisely, western economic and cultural systems. Silvia Rivera Cusicanqui argues that gender complementarity in the rural Andes has undergone a process of "Westernization and patriarchalization" over the past several decades due to the penetration of development organizations into the countryside, migration to and from these regions, and historical patterns of capital accumulation and modernization.[10] In this view, it is perfectly understandable why indigenous groups, including women, would resist the notion of "women's rights"— emblematic as the concept is of larger processes of westernization that, for indigenous people, have resulted in a variety of forms of exploitation, from long-standing economic and political marginalization to the exclusion of traditional medical providers from recent attempts to integrate Andean medicine into national health systems. One of the broader arguments of this book is that models for understanding women's personal experiences with reproduction, and for bolstering women's reproductive autonomy, are most persuasive when they are embedded in (and, indeed, emerge from) local context. Understanding women's reproductive experiences in Bolivia, therefore, requires an explicit recognition of the legitimacy of the aforementioned critiques of western-derived rights claims. Initiatives to improve the ways that indigenous women experience their sexual and reproductive lives, for their part, are most likely to meet with success when they are designed and implemented by members of these same groups.

Paying attention to the local context surrounding personal experiences of reproduction further highlights the limitations of "choice" for understanding women's feelings about their pregnancies in the urban highlands, as well as the ways that women made decisions about their pregnancies. Like the concept of women's rights, reproductive choice is intimately tied to western notions of individual citizenship and personal autonomy, which may partially explain its inability to explain the reproductive experiences of many women living in Bolivia (and, perhaps, in other non-western locales). Yet the discursive model of choice is similarly inadequate for some women in western contexts—particularly those who lack the resources that implicitly undergird society's assessment of who has the right to choose.[11] Write Jael Silliman et al. of the U.S. context, "Women of color . . . negotiate their reproductive lives in a system that combines interlocking forms of oppression. As . . . Loretta Ross puts it: 'Our ability to control what happens to our bodies is constantly challenged by poverty, racism, environmental degradation, sexism, homophobia, and injustice.'"[12] In failing to take into account poverty and other intersecting forms of oppression, the rhetoric of individual choice—which was largely developed by the white, middle-class feminist movement—overlooks women's differential access to a range of forms of social and economic capital that has a direct bearing on women's capacity to make choices regarding their pregnancies (and other aspects of their lives).[13] Furthermore, local and foreign institutions implicated in the development and distribution of western-derived contraceptive methods may also exercise powerful constraints upon women's reproductive choices. In some sites in Asia and the Pacific, for instance, Margaret Jolly argues that reproductive choice operates as a gendered and market-oriented "globalizing rhetoric," in which international agencies and national governments "affirm or control" individuals' choices through the selective promotion of contraceptive options that grant power to biomedical officials, rather than consumers, and that target women, rather than men.[14]

Women's experiences with sexuality and pregnancy in La Paz and El Alto over the last sixty years reveal that reproductive choices, when they existed at all, were similarly limited by a range of intersecting inequalities and by personal considerations. To a lesser extent, women's reproductive options were constrained by the actions of domestic and foreign doctors and policy makers. While the programs implemented by medical and policy-making sectors may have drawn women into western health establishments, for instance, they rarely, if ever, prevented women from seeking abortion, or from visiting Andean medical practitioners. Similarly peripheral to women's reproductive decisions in Bolivia were discourses that focused on fetal life (rather than on women's rights or reproductive choice). While some women professed the belief that abortion constituted taking a life, the decisions they made with respect to their pregnancies—whether they chose to continue or to terminate these—demonstrated complex negotiations that concerned a number of lives. In other words, a woman's decision of whether or not to interrupt a pregnancy typically represented neither an autonomous choice nor the selection of one life over another, but a constrained choice that involved several interconnected, and often mutually dependent, lives. Examining the range of local forces informing women's reproductive decisions can help us, I hope, to consider abortion and unwanted pregnancy as human experiences, rather than solely (or even primarily) questions for political debate.

A final reason why women's experiences with unwanted pregnancy and abortion are important is that for many women, these exceedingly common events are also matters of life and death—particularly in places such as urban Bolivia, where abortion is prohibited (and thus often inaccessible and unsafe), as well as widely stigmatized. While I trust that the dangers posed to women by abortion's prohibited and unregulated status are by this point, markedly clear, a brief anecdote about one young woman perhaps serves to elucidate the ways that social stigma may exacerbate these risks. Miguel Ramírez was completing his residency at a hospital in La Paz in the 1980s when he was called to assist on a case involving a sixteen-year-old girl brought to the facility by her parents. "She was really sick; she had sepsis and we couldn't figure out why. So, [after] investigating, we discovered that she'd had a uterine perforation. . . . This poor young girl, in this situation! She had kept quiet; she hadn't told her parents what was going on. And in spite of the hysterectomy, in spite of all the other services that we performed—she died."[15] Too frightened to tell her family about the abortion that led to her symptoms, the young girl's condition worsened; ultimately, she paid the high costs of social stigma against abortion, as well as of silence surrounding sexuality, with her life.

In other words, we frankly "lack the right to turn away" from women's personal experiences with unwanted pregnancy and abortion—just as Marguerite Feitlowitz has argued of (other forms of) political violence.[16] Women's experiences with these phenomena are of intimate concern for a majority of Bolivia's female population; they are equally pressing for women living in other regions of Latin America and in parts of Asia and Africa, where the majority of the unsafe abortions that occur worldwide take place.[17] In La Paz and El Alto, the last six decades witnessed considerable changes in reproductive policy and services, as well as notable shifts in social attitudes toward unwanted pregnancy. Despite this, I was struck when conducting research for this project with the frequency with which interviewees referred to abortion in the urban highlands as a *secreto a voces* (an open secret). Although the procedure is safer and more widely available today than it was in the early 1950s, abortion in La Paz and El Alto still appears to be highly stigmatized and a frightening experience for many. At the same time, this book demonstrates the powerful influence that women, and some men, have brought to bear on the trajectory of public policy and on access to reproductive health care in the urban highlands. The shifts that women and their allies have effected in reproductive and gender-related policies and services over the past several decades suggest that the future may bring still further initiatives—likely of both the formal and informal varieties—to expand women's reproductive autonomy. This is true despite the obstacles posed by structural factors in urban Andean society—obstacles with which women have always had to contend.

Appendix: Interviewee Information

Idalina Achuta   Born in 1970, a married, Aymara woman (de
                     vestido) with some high school education, who
                     is Catholic. Four children, born in 1990, 1992,
                     1994, and 1999. Resides in Charapaqui Segundo,
                     El Alto, and has a household income of
                     US$114.00 per month.

Jazmín Cahuana   Born in 1964, a separated, Aymara woman
                     (de pollera) with some primary school educa-
                     tion who is Catholic. Eight children (one
                     deceased), born in 1984, 1986, 1987, 1991, 1994,
                     1996, 1998, and 2001, and one miscarriage,
                     year unknown. Resides in Santa Rosa, El Alto,
                     and has a household income of US$43.00 per
                     month.

Concepción Camacho   Born in 1983, a married, white woman with a
                     high school degree, who is Catholic. Two
                     children, born in 2007 and 2009. Resides in
                     Ciudad Satélite, El Alto, and has a household
                     income of US$116.00 per month.

Elsa Canqui

Born in 1959, a married, Aymara woman (de pollera), with a primary school education, who is Catholic. Three children, born in 1982, 1983, and 1997. Resides in Alto Chijini, La Paz, and has a household income of US$317.00 per month.

Celestina Chambi

Born in 1960, a separated, Aymara woman (de pollera), with a primary school education who is Christian. Seven children, born between 1985 and 2007, one abortion in 1989. Resides in El Alto and has a household income of US$7.00 per month.

Felicidad Chambi

Born in 1972, a cohabitating, Aymara woman (de pollera), with some primary school education, who is Catholic. Three children, born in 1999, 2001, and 2003. Resides in Alto Chijini, La Paz, and is unsure of her household income.

Beatriz Chasqui

Born in 1960, a separated, Aymara woman (de vestido) with some high school education, who is Catholic. Four children (two deceased), born in 1982, 1984, 1986, and 1988, one miscarriage, year unknown. Resides in Villa Adela, El Alto, and has a household income of US$116.00 per month.

Maura Choque

Born in 1973, a separated, Aymara woman (de vestido) with some high school education, who is Christian. Five children, born in 1996, 1998, 2000, 2006, and 2007, and one miscarriage, year unknown. Resides in Viacha (approximately 22 km from El Alto) and is unsure of her household income.

Elba Claros

Born in 1950, a married woman with a college degree who claims no ethnic identity and who is

Catholic. Two children, born in 1978 and 1980, and one miscarriage, year unknown. Resides in Alto Chijini, La Paz, and has a household income of US$116.00 per month.

Lupe Colque   Born in 1958, a single, Aymara and Quechua woman (de vestido) with a college degree and no religion. No children; one abortion in the early 1980s. Resides in Ciudad Satélite, El Alto, and has a household income of US$500.00 per month. Women's rights activist.

Natividad Colque   Born in 1986, a cohabitating, Aymara woman (de vestido) with some university education. Two children, born in 2005 and 2007. Resides in El Alto. Information regarding religion and household income not collected. Lupe Colque's niece.

Vania Condori   Born in 1984, a single, Aymara woman (de vestido) with some university education, who is Catholic. No children; one abortion in 2007. Resides in La Portada, La Paz, and has a household income of US$43.00 per month.

Magda Cusi   Born in 1934, a married, Quechua woman (de vestido) with some high school education, who is Catholic. Four children, born in 1956, 1958, 1960, and 1962. Resides in Ciudad Satélite, El Alto, and has a household income of US$207.00 per month.

Graciela Flores   Born in 1989, a single, mestiza woman (de vestido) with a high school degree, who is Catholic. No children. Resides in La Portada, La Paz, and is unsure of her household income (receives US$7.00 per month from her parents).

Marcela Flores

Born in 1964, a married, mestiza woman (de vestido) with a degree in nursing, who is Catholic. Four children, born in 1987, 1989, 1992, and 2003, and two abortions, in 1990 and in 1994. Resides in La Portada, La Paz, and has a household income of US$285.00 per month. Graciela Flores's mother.

Rigoberta Justiniano

Born in 1981, a married, Aymara woman (de vestido) with some high school education, who is Catholic. Three children, born in 1998, 2000, and 2004, and one miscarriage, year unknown. Resides in Romero Pampa, El Alto, and has a household income of US$214.00 per month.

Sandra Laura

Born in 1981, a married, Aymara woman (de vestido) with some university education, who is Catholic. Four children, born in 1993, 1994, 2002, and 2006. Resides in Alto la Alianza, El Alto, and has a household income of between US$71.00–$86.00.

Adela López

Born in 1978, a married, mestiza woman (de vestido) with some university education and no religion. Two children, born in 1994 and 2007, and two abortions, in 1995 and 1998. Resides in Villa San Antonio, La Paz, and has a household income of US$855.00 per month.

Belinda López

Born in 1945, a single, mestiza woman (de vestido) with some high school education, who is Catholic. Two children (one deceased), born in 1972 and 1985. Resides in Ciudad Satélite, El Alto, and has a household income of US$61.00 per month.

Nelly Mamani	Born in 1951, a separated, Aymara woman (de pollera) with no education, who is Catholic. Seven children, born in 1972, 1977, 1979, 1988, 1990, 1993, and 1998. Resides in Villa Adela, El Alto, and is unsure of her household income.
Pilar Mendoza	Born in 1976, a separated, white woman with some high school education, who is Christian. Four children, born in 1992, 1994, 2000, and 2002, and two abortions, the first in the late 1990s and the second in 2004. Resides in Villa Tejada Rectangular, El Alto, and has a household income of US$171.00 per month.
Lorena Mercado	Born in 1971, a married, Aymara woman (de vestido) with some university education, who is Catholic. Three children, born in 1991, 1993, and 2005, and one abortion, in 1997. Resides in Alto Mariscal Santa Cruz, La Paz, and has a household income of US$357.00 per month.
Manuela Pacari	Born in 1973, a married, Aymara woman (de vestido) with some university education, who is Catholic. Four children, born in 1993, 2006, 2008, and 2009, and two miscarriages, years unknown. Resides in Alto Mariscal Santa Cruz, La Paz, and has a household income of US$342.00 per month.
Maita Perez	Born in 1977, a separated, mestiza woman (de vestido) with some university education, who is Catholic. Two children, born in 1997 and 2005. Resides in Ciudad Satélite, El Alto, and has a household income of US$214.00 per month.
Vicenta Pilco	Born in 1977, a married, Aymara woman (de pollera) with some primary school education

and no religion. Three children, born between 1992 and 2004, and four miscarriages in unknown years. Resides in Alto la Alianza, El Alto, and has a household income of US$243.00 per month.

Simona Pinto   Born in 1978, a married, Aymara woman (de vestido) with a high school degree, who is Catholic. Three children, born in 1999, 2004, and 2005. Resides in Amor de Dios, El Alto, and has a household income of US$71.00.

Camila Quelca   Born in 1939, a married, Quechua woman (de vestido) with some primary school education, who is Catholic. Two children, born in 1966 and 1980. Resides in Ciudad Satélite, El Alto, and is unsure of her household income (she receives US$2.00 per day from her husband).

Mili Quisbert   Born in 1977, a separated, Aymara woman (de vestido) with a primary school education, who is Catholic. Two children, born in 1998 and 2004, and one miscarriage, year unknown. Resides in El Alto and has a household income of US$43.00 per month.

Leticia Quispe   Born in 1976, a married, Aymara woman (de vestido) with some high school education, who is Catholic. Four children, born in 1994, 2001, 2007, and 2009, and one abortion, in 1996. Resides in Rio Seco, El Alto, with a household income of US$150.00 per month.

Paula Rojas   Born in 1969, a married, mestiza woman (de vestido) with a high school degree, who is Catholic. Four children, born in 1987, 1989, 1992,

	and 1995. Resides in Ciudad Satélite, El Alto, with a household income of US$428.00 per month.
Nina Rojas	Born in 1963, a separated, mestiza woman (de vestido) with some university education, who believes in God. Two children, born in 1995 and 1998, and one abortion in 2000. Resides in Villa Tejada Rectangular, El Alto, with a household income of US$71.00 per month. No relation to Paula Rojas.
Margot Suárez	Born in 1981, a married, mestiza woman (de vestido) with some university education and no religion. One child, born in 2001. Resides in Ciudad Satélite, El Alto, with a household income of US$285.00 per month.
Alma Tarqui	Born in 1989, a cohabitating, Aymara woman (de vestido) with some high school education who is Catholic. Three children (one deceased), born in 2005, 2006, and 2007. Resides in Alto Tejar, La Paz, with a household income of US$57.00 per month.
Noel Terrazas	Born in 1959, a separated, mestiza woman (de vestido) with some university education, who is Catholic. Three children, born in 1985, 1986, and 2001, and three abortions between 1987 and 2000. Resides in Villa Tejada Triangular, El Alto, with a household income of US$128.00 per month.
Yessica Ticona	Born in 1979, a separated, Aymara woman (de vestido) with a high school degree, who is Christian. Two children, born in 2000 and 2006, and two miscarriages, years unknown. Resides

in Alto Lima, El Alto, and has a household
income of US$107.00 per month.

Betina Aguilar	Psychologist who works with abortion providers.
Lidia Alvarado	Journalist.
Emma Alvarez	Medical doctor.
Guillermina Arcani	Independently practicing midwife.
Daniel Báez	Representative of an evangelical Christian church in La Paz.
Fanny Barrutia	Activist at a women's rights organization in La Paz.
Eduardo Castillo	Representative of the Fuerza Especial de Lucha Contra el Crimen (Special Force of the Fight Against Crime, FELCC) in El Alto.
Juana Choque	Activist of a women's rights organization in La Paz.
Andrea Cima	Representative of the Child Welfare Department in El Alto.
Nika Coelho	Representative of the Sexual and Reproductive Health Division of the Departmental Health Service (SEDES) in La Paz.
Community Police	Four officers and one social worker of the Community Police Force, Max Paredes, La Paz.
Julián Costa	Employee at a clinic that provides abortions in La Paz.
Adrián Espinoza	Obstetrician and gynecologist at the public Women's Hospital (HM) in La Paz.

David Estrada	Obstetrician and gynecologist at the public Bolivian-Dutch Municipal Hospital (HMBH) in El Alto.
Carolina Llano	Representative of the antiabortion organization Apostolate of the New Evangelism (ANE) Pro-Life in La Paz.
Vanessa Lujo	Educator in sexual and reproductive health at the public Women's Hospital (HM).
Cati Molina	Activist at the Center for Information and Development of Women (CIDEM) who had two abortions, years unknown.
Olga Mollo	Nurse at a sexual and reproductive health clinic in La Paz who had one abortion in 1989.
Stefania Montoya	Social worker at a sexual and reproductive health clinic in El Alto.
Alessandra Muñecas	Obstetrician and gynecologist at a sexual and reproductive health clinic in La Paz.
Gabriela Ovando	Activist at a group mobilizing on issues concerning women in La Paz.
Idelia Parra	Social worker at a home for pregnant adolescents in La Paz.
Dina Preto	Activist at a group mobilizing on issues concerning women in La Paz.
Jumila Quiroga	Educator at a home for pregnant adolescents in La Paz.
Miguel Ramírez	Medical doctor who performs abortions, among other services, in La Paz.
Antonia Rocio	Medical doctor in La Paz.
Muriel Rodríguez	Receptionist at a sexual and reproductive health clinic in El Alto.

Leandro Rubén	Activist at Family and Human Life, an antiabortion organization in La Paz.
Emilia Santana	Obstetrician and gynecologist at a clinic in El Alto.
Daisy Serrato	Medical doctor who performs abortions, among other services, in La Paz.
Mariano Solana	Catholic priest serving in the Family Ministry at a Catholic Church in La Paz.
Dolores Ticahuanca	Medical doctor who performs abortions, among other services, in El Alto.
Ida Torralba	Activist at Catholics for a Free Choice in La Paz.

Acknowledgments

A number of people contributed to this project in ways ranging from the planting of intellectual seeds through seemingly offhand comments, to considerably shaping the scope and content of the book through ongoing conversations and support. My largest debt of gratitude is to each of the individuals I interviewed in La Paz and El Alto. The sensitivity of the topic prevents me from acknowledging most of these people by name, but their generosity with their time and their openness about their experiences made the book possible. Also in Bolivia, I would like to thank Verónica, Yamel, and María Eugenia, who introduced me to dozens of women who would later volunteer to be interviewed, and who made for lovely company as we climbed the hillsides of La Paz between research sites. Without the assistance provided by S. L., I would have been unable to learn about the relationship between abortion and the law; I am extremely grateful for both her time and her insights. The support of several anonymous medical doctors allowed me to access medical records and statistical data and helped facilitate numerous interviews; I am grateful to them, and also to dozens of activists, who shared with me their wealth of knowledge and experience, as well as personal and professional connections. The L. V. family provided encouragement and support of every kind—I would especially like to thank J. M. for his help and friendship. L. P. and Sayuri Loza deserve a particularly heartfelt thank you. L., desde que te conocí, has sido una amiga de corazón. Gracias por el aporto que siempre me has prestado, y por tu honestidad y amistad. Te quiero mucho. Sayuri Loza meticulosamente transcribed each of my interviews and patiently answered my questions about Aymara inflections and Andean culture; I am extremely grateful for her assistance. Finally, Molly Geidel and Gabi Kuenzli were great friends in La Paz during my longest research trip to the city (spanning 2009 and 2010), and both have provided valuable feedback in the years since.

Outside of Bolivia, a number of people were instrumental to the book in one way or another, either as writing buddies, friends, colleagues, or mentors (or all of the above). Individuals who helped make the years I spent in Pittsburgh most enjoyable include, from the history program at Pitt, Nicole Bourbonnais, Alejandra Boza (as well as her spouse, Scott Hergenrother), Matthew Casey, Isaac Curtis, John Feerick, John Galante, Tori Harms, Jamie Holeman, Lars Peterson, Kavin Paulraj, Katie Phelps Walsh, Oscar de la Torre, Kelly Urban, and Madalina Veres. I would especially like to thank my dissertation committee—George Reid Andrews, Lara Putnam, Kathleen Blee, Alejandro de la Fuente, and Laura Gotkowitz—for their gentle criticism and exceedingly helpful guidance. Reid and Lara, in particular, have become the kind of mentors whose ongoing support over the years has made me both a better scholar and a more compassionate and engaged human being. I am deeply grateful to them both. Other individuals from the yoga, capoeira, and spiritual communities filled my days in Pittsburgh with fun, reflection, movement, and song. These include Alana DeLoge, Jennifer Ferris-Glick, Olga Klimova, Nana Marfo, Kristi Rogers, Sara Valenzuela, Dorothy Washington, Becky Yacht, and Charlie Yhap.

A number of scholars and activists I met at conferences or in the course of other endeavors helped develop my thinking on this book. Conversations with Kathryn Gallien, Raúl Necochea López, Nicole Pacino, and Cassia Roth were particularly stimulating and helpful. I am also grateful to Elise Andaya for speaking with me (and my students) about conducting research and publishing, and to Ann Zulawski, who shared with me her experience working with medical records. I would also like to thank Marcy Bloom and Claire Keyes, activists in the field of reproductive autonomy, and scholar and activist Melissa Madera, who has single-handedly collected hundreds of women's abortion stories. These women have consistently inspired me with their work and their persistent dedication to it.

In Hamilton (New York), where I spent a year at Colgate University, I would like to thank Danny Barreto, Dan and Liz Bouk, Alan Cooper, Ray Douglas, Jennifer Hull, Paul Humphrey, Kathleen Poling, Barbara and David Regenspan, Heather, Clare, and John Roller, Mary Simonson, the Tai-Woolley Clan, and Jen and Tristan Tomlinson for their friendship and commiseration about the joys and challenges of research and writing. Students of the course, "History of Sexuality and Reproduction Worldwide," which I taught in the spring of 2014, provided valuable feedback on an early version of chapter 3 of this book. Since joining the faculty at the College of Staten Island (CSI) in the fall of 2014, a number of individuals have provided friendship, collegiality, or both. I would particularly like to thank Bryan Averbuch, Melissa Borja (now at the University of Michigan), Alyson Bardsley, Rafael de la Dehesa, Samira Haj, Anne Hays, Mark Lewis, Jane Marcus-Delgado, Donna Scimeca, and Susan Smith-Peter. Conversations with both undergraduate and graduate students at CSI also influenced my approach to a number of themes explored in the book.

Off campus, several people helped me create a home in New York City, in general, and in Bay Ridge (Brooklyn), in particular. A deep and heartfelt thanks to Ashley Brennan, Fran Cartwright, Deirdre Grady, Stef Ploof, Adam Slade, Margaret Stepien, and Karen Unger; I am tremendously grateful for the presence of these individuals in my life. I am especially grateful to Janet Cohen—who designed the maps for this book—and to Erin Hartje. Of all my friends, these two women most bore the emotional labor of keeping me afloat during the revision process (along with my dog, Judah). Also in New York, Kathi O. and Christina C. provided support of the spiritual variety, without which I would have been unable to finish this book (or do much else). At Rutgers University Press, I am very grateful for the work of two anonymous reviewers, whose comments greatly improved the book, and for the support and patience of my editor, Kimberly Guinta.

Finally, I am grateful for the love and support of those who have been with me the longest. My friends Jacob Durtschi, Carolyn Maret, and Stephanie Saldivar provided encouragement and laughter through many years of ups and downs. Thanks also to Kevin Bortfeld, who accompanied me during more than one research trip to Bolivia and who contributed to making me the person I am today. Finally, I would like to thank my father, William Kimball—who even in our short time together instilled in me a persistent intellectual curiosity and an awe for the human experience—and my mother, Dorothy (aka Dottie) Kimball. Dottie has trudged with me a road filled with love, honesty, and a great deal of much-needed silliness. This book is dedicated to them, and to each of the women I interviewed in La Paz and El Alto.

———

Material from chapters 3 and 4 was previously published in the edited collection *Transcending Borders: Abortion in the Past and Present*, by Palgrave Macmillan (2017). The research for and writing of this book were supported by an Andrew Mellon Predoctoral Fellowship, several summer research fellowships at the University of Pittsburgh, the Lillian B. Lawler Fellowship, two PSC-CUNY Research Awards, and the CUNY Office of Research's Book Completion Award (Proposal 315). I am extremely grateful for this financial support.

Notes

INTRODUCTION

1. Maura Choque, El Alto, 30 November 2009. The names of interviewees mentioned in the text are pseudonyms. To avoid interrupting the flow of the narrative with frequent, repetitive footnotes, I cite each narrator only once in a passage in which her testimony may appear multiple times. All interviews were conducted and translated by the author and recorded digitally.

2. Sandra Aliaga Bruch, *No fue fácil para nadie: Aproximaciones a una historia de la salud sexual y reproductiva en Bolivia siglo XX* (La Paz: UNFPA and CIDEM, 2004), 81; Instituto Nacional de Estadística (INE), *Encuesta Nacional de Demografía y Salud* (La Paz: INE, 2008), 127.

3. Zulema Alanes, *El aborto en Bolivia: Mitos y realidades* (La Paz: The Population Council and the Servicio de Información para el Desarrollo [SID], 1995), 8; Jean Friedman-Rudovsky, "Abortion under Siege in Latin America," *Time*, August 9, 2007, http://content.time.com/time/world/article/0,8599,1651307,00.html; Ipas Bolivia, *Las cifras hablan: El aborto es un problema de salud pública* (La Paz: Ipas, 2011); Ministerio de Salud y Deportes (MSD), *Manual de normas, reglas, protocolos y procedimientos técnicos para el manejo de las hemorragias de la primera mitad del embarazo* (La Paz: Ipas, 2006), 11.

4. An important exception is Sandra Aliaga Bruch, Mery Quitón Prado, and María Elena Gisbert, *Veinte historias, un mismo tema: El aborto* (La Paz: Population Council and the Taller de Estudios Sociales [TES], 2000).

5. See, for instance, Mark Adams, ed., *The Wellborn Science: Eugenics in Germany, France, Brazil, and Russia* (New York: Oxford University Press, 1990); Laura Briggs, *Reproducing Empire: Race, Sex, Science, and U.S. Imperialism in Puerto Rico* (Berkeley and Los Angeles: University of California Press, 2002); Matthew

Connelly, *Fatal Misconception: The Struggle to Control World Population* (Cambridge, MA: The Belknap Press of Harvard University Press, 2008); Nancy Leys Stepan, *"The Hour of Eugenics": Race, Gender, and Nation in Latin America* (Ithaca, NY: Cornell University Press, 1991); Alexandra Minna Stern, *Eugenic Nation: The Faults and Frontiers of Better Breeding in Modern America* (Berkeley and Los Angeles: University of California Press, 2005); Okezi Otovo, *Progressive Mothers, Better Babies: Race, Public Health, and the State in Brazil* (Austin: University of Texas Press, 2016); and Johanna Schoen, *Choice and Coercion: Birth Control, Sterilization, and Abortion in Public Health and Welfare* (Chapel Hill: University of North Carolina Press, 2005).

6. Ackerman et al., "'Every *Body* Has Its Own Feminism': Introducing Transcending Borders," in *Transcending Borders: Abortion in the Past and Present*, ed. Ackerman, et al. (Cham, Switzerland: Springer Nature, Palgrave Macmillan, 2017), 4.

7. See, among many others, Ackerman et al., *Transcending Borders*; Katherine E. Bliss, *Compromised Positions: Prostitution, Public Health, and Gender Politics in Revolutionary Mexico City* (University Park: Pennsylvania State University Press, 2001); Connelly, *Fatal Misconception*; Juanita De Barros, *Reproducing the British Caribbean: Sex, Gender, and Population Politics after Slavery* (Chapel Hill: University of North Carolina Press, 2014); Margaret Jolly and Kalpana Ram, eds., *Borders of Being: Citizenship, Fertility, and Sexuality in Asia and the Pacific* (Ann Arbor: University of Michigan Press, 2001); Ann Stoler, *Carnal Knowledge and Imperial Power: Race and the Intimate in Colonial Rule* (Los Angeles: University of California Press, 2002); and Luise White, *The Comforts of Home: Prostitution in Colonial Nairobi* (Chicago: University of Chicago Press, 1990).

8. Briggs, *Reproducing Empire*, 9. See also Homi Bhabha, "Of Mimicry and Man: The Ambivalence of Colonial Discourse," in "Discipleship: A Special Issue on Psychoanalysis," *October* 28 (Spring 1984): 125–133; Jennifer Morgan, *Laboring Women: Reproduction and Gender in New World Slavery* (Philadelphia: University of Pennsylvania Press, 2004); Ann Stoler, *Race and the Education of Desire: Foucault's History of Sexuality and the Colonial Order of Things* (Durham: Duke University Press, 1999); and Peter Wade, *Race and Sex in Latin America* (New York: Pluto Press, 2009), 15–60.

9. On the use of multiple medical traditions in health and healing, in general, see Vincanne Adams, Mona Schrempf, and Sienna Craig, eds., *Medicine between Science and Religion: Explorations on Tibetan Grounds* (Oxford: Berghahn Books, 2011); Diego Armus, *Entre médicos y curanderos: Cultura, historia, y enfermedad en la América Latina moderna* (Buenos Aires: Grupo Editorial Norma, 2002); Hans A. Baer, *Biomedicine and Alternative Healing Systems in America: Issues of*

Class, Race, Ethnicity, and Gender (Madison: University of Wisconsin Press, 2001); Joseph W. Bastien, *Drum and Stethoscope: Integrating Ethnomedicine and Biomedicine in Bolivia* (Salt Lake City: University of Utah Press, 1992); Daniela Bleichmar, Paula De Vos, Kristin Huffine, and Kevin Sheehan, eds., *Science in the Spanish and Portuguese Empires, 1500–1800* (Stanford: Stanford University Press, 2009); Marcos Cueto and Steven Palmer, *Medicine and Public Health in Latin America: A History* (New York: Cambridge University Press, 2015); Michael S. Goldstein, "The Persistence and Resurgence of Medical Pluralism," *Journal of Health Politics, Policy, and Law* 29, nos. 4–5 (August–October 2004): 925–945; Joan D. Koss-Chioino, Thomas Leatherman, and Christine Greenway, eds., *Medical Pluralism in the Andes* (New York: Routledge, 2003); Charles Leslie, "Medical Pluralism in World Perspective," *Social Science & Medicine* 14, no. 4 (November 1980): 191–195; William C. Olsen and Carolyn Sargent, eds., *African Medical Pluralism* (Bloomington: Indiana University Press, 2017); Steven Palmer, *From Popular Medicine to Medical Populism: Doctors, Healers, and Public Power in Costa Rica, 1800–1940* (Durham: Duke University Press, 2003); Londa Schiebinger, *Plants and Empire: Colonial Bioprospecting in the Atlantic World* (Cambridge: Harvard University Press, 2004); Merrill Singer and Pamela I. Erickson, eds., *A Companion to Medical Anthropology* (Oxford: Wiley-Blackwell, 2011); V. Sujatha and Leena Abraham, eds., *Medical Pluralism in Contemporary India* (Hyderabad: Orient Blackswan, 2012); and Ann Zulawski, *Unequal Cures: Public Health and Political Change in Bolivia, 1900–1950* (Durham: Duke University Press, 2007). For literature on plural medical systems shaping reproductive health, in particular, see, among others, Denise Y. Arnold and Juan de Dios Yapita, *Las wawas del Inka: Hacia la salud materna intercultural en algunas comunidades andinas* (La Paz: Instituto de Lengua y Cultura Aymara [ILCA], 2002); Denise Arnold and Juan de Dios Yapita, "Los caminos de género en Qaqachaka: Saberes femeninos y discursos textuales alterativos en los Andes," in *Ser mujer indígena, chola o birlocha en la Bolivia postcolonial de los años 90*, ed. Silvia Rivera Cusicanqui (La Paz: Ministerio de Desarrollo Humano, Subsecretaría Nacional de Asuntos Étnicos, de Género y Generacionales, Subsecretaría de Asuntos de Género, 1996), 303–392; Rosanne Cecil, ed., *The Anthropology of Pregnancy Loss: Comparative Studies in Miscarriage, Stillbirth, and Neonatal Death* (Oxford: Berg, 1996); Anne-Claire Defossez, Didier Fassin, and Mara Viveros, eds., *Mujeres de los Andes: Condiciones de vida y salud* (Bogotá, Colombia: Instituto Francés de Estudios Andinos and Universidad Externado de Colombia, 1992); Martha Few, *Women Who Live Evil Lives: Gender, Religion, and the Politics of Power in Colonial Guatemala* (Austin: University of Texas Press, 2002); Kathryn Gallien, "Delivering the Nation, Raising the State: Gender, Childbirth, and the 'Indian Problem' in Bolivia's Obstetric

Movement, 1900–1982" (PhD diss., University of Arizona, 2015); John D. O'Neil and Patricia Leyland Kaufert, "*Irniktakpunga!*: Sex Determination and the Inuit Struggle for Birthing Rights in Northern Canada," in *Conceiving the New World Order: The Global Politics of Reproduction,* ed. Faye D. Ginsburg and Rayna Rapp (Los Angeles: University of California Press, 1995), 59–73; Jolly and Ram, eds., *Borders of Being*; and Manigeh Roosta, coord., *Salud materna en contextos de interculturalidad: Estudio de los pueblos Aymara, Ayoreode, Chiquitano, Guaraní, Quechua, y Yuqui* (La Paz: Plural Editores, 2013).

10. See, for instance, Sanjam Ahluwalia, *Reproductive Restraints: Birth Control in India, 1877–1947* (Chicago: University of Chicago Press, 2008); Nicole Bourbonnais, *Birth Control in the Decolonizing Caribbean: Reproductive Politics and Practice on Four Islands, 1930–1970* (New York: Cambridge University Press, 2016); De Barros, *Reproducing the British Caribbean*; and Lara Putnam, *The Company They Kept: Migrants and the Politics of Gender in Caribbean Costa Rica, 1870–1960* (Chapel Hill: University of North Carolina Press, 2002).

11. See, for instance, Ginsburg and Rapp, *Conceiving the New World Order*; Jolly and Ram, eds., *Borders of Being*; Lynn M. Morgan and Elizabeth F. S. Roberts, "Reproductive Governance in Latin America," *Anthropology & Medicine* 19, no. 2 (August 2012): 241–254; Gita Sen, Adrienne Germain, and Lincoln C. Chen, eds., *Population Policies Reconsidered: Health, Empowerment, and Rights* (Boston: Harvard Center for Population and Development Studies, 1994); and Jael Silliman et al., eds., *Undivided Rights: Women of Color Organize for Reproductive Justice* (Cambridge: South End Press, 2004).

12. See, among many others, Elise Andaya, *Conceiving Cuba: Reproduction, Women, and the State in the Post-Soviet Era* (New Brunswick, NJ: Rutgers University Press, 2014); Sueann Caulfield, Sarah C. Chambers, and Lara Putnam, eds., *Honor, Status, and Law in Modern Latin America* (Durham: Duke University Press, 2005); Sarah C. Chambers, *Families in War and Peace: Chile from Colony to Nation* (Durham, NC: Duke University Press, 2015); Elizabeth Dore and Maxine Molyneux, eds., *Hidden Histories of Gender and the State in Latin America* (Durham, NC: Duke University Press, 2000); Silvia Federici, *Caliban and the Witch: Women, the Body, and Primitive Accumulation* (Brooklyn: Autonomedia, 2004); Carrie Hamilton, *Sexual Revolutions in Cuba: Passion, Politics, and Memory* (Chapel Hill: University of North Carolina Press, 2012); Minna Stern, *Eugenic Nation*; Morgan, *Laboring Women*; Jadwiga E. Pieper Mooney, *The Politics of Motherhood: Maternity and Women's Rights in Twentieth-Century Chile* (Pittsburgh: University of Pittsburgh Press, 2009); Putnam, *The Company They Kept*; Julia Rodríguez, *Civilizing Argentina: Science, Medicine, and the Modern State* (Chapel Hill: University of North Carolina Press, 2006);

Stoler, *Carnal Knowledge and Imperial Power*; Heidi Tinsman, *Partners in Conflict: The Politics of Gender, Sexuality, and Labor in the Chilean Agrarian Reform, 1950–1973* (Durham: Duke University Press, 2002); White, *The Comforts of Home*; and Zulawski, *Unequal Cures*.

13. Aliaga Bruch, *No fue fácil para nadie*, 11–21; Susanna Rance, *Planificación familiar: Se abre el debate* (La Paz: Secretaría Técnica del Consejo Nacional de Población and the Ministerio de Planeamiento y Coordinación, 1990), 1–27.

14. Molly Geidel, *Peace Corps Fantasies: How Development Shaped the Global Sixties* (Minneapolis: University of Minnesota Press, 2015), 187–229; Rance, *Planificación familiar*, 13–27.

15. Aliaga Bruch, *No fue fácil para nadie*, 17–21; Antonio Cisneros, *El aborto inducido: Un estudio exploratorio* (La Paz: Centro Nacional de Familia [CENAFA], 1976), 4–10.

16. Lara Putnam makes this argument in her book *The Company They Kept*, 19.

17. "Worldwide, an Estimated 25 Million Unsafe Abortions Occur Each Year," *Guttmacher News Institute*, September 27, 2017, https://www.guttmacher.org/news-release/2017/worldwide-estimated-25-million-unsafe-abortions-occur-each-year.

18. Hamilton, *Sexual Revolutions in Cuba*, 50.

19. Wade, *Race and Sex in Latin America*; Joan Wallach Scott, *Gender and the Politics of History*, rev. ed. (New York: Columbia University Press, 1999).

20. Mary Weismantel, *Cholas and Pishtacos: Stories of Race and Sex in the Andes* (Chicago: University of Chicago Press, 2001), xxx–xli. See also Andrew Canessa, "Introduction: Making the Nation on the Margins," in *Natives Making Nation: Gender, Indigeneity, and the State in the Andes*, ed. Andrew Canessa (Tucson: University of Arizona Press, 2005), 24–25.

21. Shellee Colen, "'Like a Mother to Them': Stratified Reproduction and West Indian Childcare Workers and Employers in New York," in *Conceiving the New World Order*, ed. Ginsburg and Rapp, 78–102; Kimberlé Crenshaw, "Demarginalizing the Intersection of Race and Sex: A Black Feminist Critique of Antidiscrimination Doctrine, Feminist Theory and Antiracist Politics," *University of Chicago Legal Forum* 1, no. 8 (1989): 139–167; Kimberlé Crenshaw et al., eds., *Critical Race Theory: The Key Writings That Formed the Movement* (New York: The New Press, 1995). For recent work that draws on these concepts, see, among others, Andaya, *Conceiving Cuba*; Jelke Boesten, *Intersecting Inequalities: Women and Social Policy in Peru, 1990–2000* (University Park: Pennsylvania State University Press, 2010); and Krista E. Van Vleet, *Performing Kinship: Narrative, Gender, and the Intimacies of Power in the Andes* (Austin: University of Texas Press, 2008).

22. Boesten, *Intersecting Inequalities*; Pascha Bueno-Hansen, *Feminist and Human Rights Struggles in Peru: Decolonizing Transitional Justice* (Chicago: University of Illinois Press, 2015); Mala Htun and S. Laurel Weldon, *The Logics of Gender Justice: State Action on Women's Rights around the World* (New York: Cambridge University Press, 2018); Cris Shore and Susan Wright, *Anthropology of Policy: Critical Perspectives on Governance and Power* (London: Routledge, 1997).

23. Morgan and Roberts, "Reproductive Governance in Latin America," 243. See also Mala Htun, *Sex and the State: Abortion, Divorce, and the Family under Latin American Dictatorships and Democracies* (New York: Cambridge University Press, 2003); Maxine Molyneux, *Women's Movements in International Perspective: Latin America and Beyond* (New York: Palgrave, 2001); and Bonnie Shepard, "The 'Double Discourse' on Sexual and Reproductive Rights in Latin America: The Chasm between Public Policy and Private Actions," *Health and Human Rights* 4, no. 2 (2000): 111–143.

24. Morgan and Roberts, "Reproductive Governance in Latin America," 241.

25. Morgan and Roberts, "Reproductive Governance in Latin America," 245. The turn toward a rights-based discourse was further related to an upturn of neoliberal political and economic policies in the region.

26. Morgan and Roberts, "Reproductive Governance in Latin America," 243.

27. David A. B. Murray, *Flaming Souls: Homosexuality, Homophobia, and Social Change in Barbados* (Toronto: University of Toronto Press, 2012), 14.

28. Anders Burman, "Chachawarmi: Silence and Rival Voices on Decolonisation and Gender Politics in Andean Bolivia," *Journal of Latin American Studies* 43, no. 1 (February 2011): 65–91; Geidel, *Peace Corps Fantasies*, 187–229; R. Aída Hernández and Andrew Canessa, eds., *Género, complementariedades y exclusions en Mesoamérica y los Andes* (Quito, Ecuador, and Copenhagen, Denmark: Ediciones Abya Yala and the International Work Group for Indigenous Affairs, 2012), 10–11; Ipas Bolivia, *El aborto desde la mirada de las organizaciones indígenas* (La Paz: Ipas, 2012); Morgan and Roberts, "Reproductive Governance," 246–247; Silvia Rivera Cusicanqui, "The Notion of 'Rights' and the Paradoxes of Postcolonial Modernity: Indigenous Peoples and Women in Bolivia," trans. Molly Geidel, *Qui Parle* 18, no. 2 (Spring/Summer 2010): 29–54; Stéphanie Rousseau, "Indigenous and Feminist Movements at the Constituent Assembly in Bolivia: Locating the Representation of Indigenous Women," *Latin American Research Review* 46, no. 2 (2011): 5–28.

29. See, among others, Ackerman et al., eds., *Transcending Borders*; Joan C. Chrisler, ed., *Reproductive Justice: A Global Concern* (Santa Barbara, CA: ABC-CLIO LLC, 2012); Linda Gordon, *The Moral Property of Women: A History of Birth*

Control Politics in America (Chicago: University of Illinois Press, 2007); Barbara Gurr, *Reproductive Justice: The Politics of Health Care for Native American Women* (New Brunswick, NJ: Rutgers University Press, 2015); Iris López, *Matters of Choice: Puerto Rican Women's Struggle for Reproductive Freedom* (New Brunswick: Rutgers University Press, 2008); M. Catherine Maternowska, *Reproducing Inequities: Poverty and the Politics of Population in Haiti* (New Brunswick, NJ: Rutgers University Press, 2006); Lynn M. Morgan and Meredith W. Michaels, eds., *Fetal Subjects, Feminist Positions* (Philadelphia: University of Pennsylvania Press, 1999); Jean Peterman, *Telling Their Stories: Puerto Rican Women and Abortion* (Boulder, CO: Westview Press, 1996); Rosalind P. Petchesky, *Abortion and Woman's Choice: The State, Sexuality, and Reproductive Freedom* (Lebanon, NH: Northeastern University Press, 1984); Silliman, et al., eds., *Undivided Rights*; Andrea Smith, "Beyond Pro-Choice versus Pro-Life: Women of Color and Reproductive Justice," *NWSA Journal* 17, no. 1 (Spring 2005): 119–140; Rickie Solinger, *Beggars and Choosers: How the Politics of Choice Shapes Adoption, Abortion, and Welfare in the United States* (New York: Hill and Wang, 2001); Chandra Talpade Mohanty, Ann Russo, and Lourdes Torres, eds., *Third World Women and the Politics of Feminism* (Bloomington: Indiana University Press, 1991); Carly Thomsen, "The Politics of Narrative, Narrative as Politic: Rethinking Reproductive Justice Frameworks through the South Dakota Abortion Story," *Feminist Formulations* 27, no. 2 (Summer 2015): 1–26; and Jo Wainer, *Lost: Illegal Abortion Stories* (Victoria, Australia: Melbourne University Press, 2006). On sexual partner choice, see Makiko Kasai and S. Craig Rooney, "The Choice before the Choice: Partner Selection Is Essential to Reproductive Justice," in *Reproductive Justice*, ed. John C. Chrisler, 11–28. On the relinquishment of children for adoption as a result of coercion, rather than choice, see Ann Fessler, *The Girls Who Went Away: The Hidden History of Women Who Surrendered Children for Adoption in the Decades before Roe v. Wade* (New York: Penguin Books, 2006). On questions of individual freedom and intimacy, see Elizabeth A. Povinelli, *The Empire of Love: Toward a Theory of Intimacy, Genealogy, and Carnality* (Durham: Duke University Press, 2006).

30. See also Joan C. Chrisler, "Introduction," in *Reproductive Justice*, 4.

31. República de Bolivia, Ministerio de Hacienda y Estadística, Dirección General de Estadística y Censos, *Censo Demográfico 1950* (La Paz: Editorial "Argote," 1950), Cuadro no. 1, n.p. On the history of land tenure, see, among many others, Laura Gotkowitz, *A Revolution for Our Rights: Indigenous Struggles for Land and Justice in Bolivia* (Durham: Duke University Press, 2007); Erick Langer, *Economic Change and Rural Resistance in Southern Bolivia: 1880–1930* (Stanford: Stanford University Press, 1989); Brooke Larson, *Trials of Nation-Making: Liberalism, Race,*

and Ethnicity in the Andes, 1810–1910 (New York: Cambridge University Press, 2004); and Silvia Rivera Cusicanqui, *Oprimidos pero no vencidos: Luchas del campesinado aymara y qhechwa de Bolivia, 1900–1980* (La Paz: Hisbol and CSUTCB, 2003 [1986]).

32. Herbert S. Klein, *A Concise History of Bolivia* (New York: Cambridge University Press, 2011), 270.

33. Instituto Nacional de Estadística, *Resultados del censo nacional de población y vivienda* (La Paz: INE, 1976), 28, 226; Klein, *A Concise History of Bolivia*, 235–236.

34. See, for instance, Caulfield, Chambers, and Putnam, eds., *Honor, Status, and Law in Modern Latin America*; Scarlett O'Phelan Godoy et al., eds., *Familia y vida cotidiana en América Latina: Siglos XVIII–XX* (Lima: Pontífica Universidad Católica del Perú, 2003).

35. Gloria Ardaya, *Política sin rostro: Mujeres en Bolivia* (La Paz: Editorial Nueva Sociedad, 1992), 26–29, 44–62; Gotkowitz, *A Revolution for Our Rights*, 117–120, 178–179, 280.

36. Gotkowitz, *A Revolution for Our Rights*, 176–179.

37. Laura Gotkowitz, "Trading Insults: Honor, Violence, and the Gendered Culture of Commerce in Cochabamba, Bolivia, 1870s–1950s," in *Honor, Status, and Law in Modern Latin America*, ed. Sueann Caulfield, Sarah C. Chambers, and Lara Putnam, 131–154; Ximena Medinaceli, *Alterando la rutina: Mujeres en las ciudades de Bolivia, 1920–1930* (La Paz: CIDEM, 1989); Marcia Stephenson, *Gender and Modernity in Andean Bolivia* (Austin: University of Texas Press, 1999).

38. INE, *Encuesta Nacional de Demografía y Salud*, 209–210.

39. The figure concerning violence is reported in the 2008 *Encuesta Nacional de Demografía y Salud*, 233. For broader measures of inequality, see United Nations Development Programme (UNDP), *Human Development Report 2011, Sustainability and Equity: A Better Future for All* (New York: Palgrave MacMillan, 2011), 139–142.

40. Alice Campaignolle, Irene Escudero, and Carlos Heras, "In Bolivia, a Backlash Against Women in Politics," *NACLA Report on the Americas*, November 19, 2018, https://nacla.org/news/2018/11/19/bolivia-backlash-against-women -politicsen-bolivia-una-reacción-violenta-contra-las; "Mujeres conquistaron el 48% de los escaños en el Legislativo," *La Razón*, October 22, 2014, http://www.la -razon.com/nacional/Mujeres-conquistaron-escanos-Legislativo_0_2148385212 .html.

41. Rossana Barragán, "Más allá de lo mestizo, más allá de lo Aymara: Organizaciones y representaciones de clase y etnicidad en La Paz," *América Latina Hoy* 43 (August 2006): 107–130; Andrew Canessa, *Intimate Indigeneities: Race, Sex, and*

History in the Small Spaces of Andean Life (Durham, NC: Duke University Press, 2012), 6–10; Gotkowitz, *A Revolution for Our Rights*, 13–14; Herbert S. Klein, "The Historical Background to the Rise of the MAS, 1952–2005," in *Evo Morales and the Movimiento Al Socialismo en Bolivia*, ed. Adrian Pearce (London: Institute for the Study of the Americas, University of London, 2011), xi–xiii; Brooke Larson and Olivia Harris, eds., with Enrique Tandeter, *Ethnicity, Markets, and Migration in the Andes: At the Crossroads of History and Anthropology* (Durham: Duke University Press, 1995); Stephenson, *Gender and Modernity*, 1–4; Weismantel, *Cholas and Pishtacos*, xxiv–xli; Zulawski, *Unequal Cures*, 10–11.

42. Rivera Cusicanqui, *Oprimidos pero no vencidos*, 139–160; Stephenson, *Gender and Modernity*, 111–157.

43. Rossana Barragán, "Entre polleras, lliqllas y ñañacas: Los mestizos y la emergencia de la tercera república," in *Etnicidad, economía, y simbolismo en los Andes*, ed. Silvia Arze et al. (La Paz: Hisbol, Instituto Francés de Estudios Andinos and SBH-ASUR, 1992), 85–127; Burman, "Chachawarmi," 86.

44. Burman, "Chachawarmi," 86–87; Ineke Dibbits, *Polleras libertarias: Federación Obrera Femenina, 1927–1964* (La Paz: Taller de Historia y Participación de la Mujer [TAHIPAMU], 1986); Olivia Harris, "Ethnic Identity and Market Relations: Indians and Mestizos in the Andes," in *Ethnicity, Markets, and Migration in the Andes*, 371–376; Rosaleen Howard, "Language, Signs, and the Performance of Power: The Discursive Struggle over Decolonization in the Bolivia of Evo Morales," *Latin American Perspectives* 37, no. 3 (May 2010): 176–194; Maria L. Lagos, comp., *Nos hemos forjado así: Al rojo vivo y a puro golpe. Historias del comité de amas de casa de Siglo XX* (La Paz: Plural Editores, 2006); Stephenson, *Gender and Modernity*; Ana Cecilia Wadsworth and Ineke Dibbits, *Agitadores de buen gusto: Historia del sindicato culinarias (1935–1958)* (La Paz: Taller de Historia y Participación de la Mujer [TAHIPAMU], 1989); Weismantel, *Cholas and Pishtacos*.

45. These recent shifts in Bolivia's social structure are owed, in part, to improvements in education and health and increased urbanization and social mobilization over the past three decades. Klein, *A Concise History of Bolivia*, 285–287. See also Larson, *Trials of Nation-Making*, 18–19.

46. Klein, *A Concise History of Bolivia*, 286.

47. Sian Lazar, *El Alto, Rebel City: Self and Citizenship in Andean Bolivia* (Durham, NC: Duke University Press, 2008), 31.

48. Lesley Gill, *Teetering on the Rim: Global Restructuring, Daily Life, and the Armed Retreat of the Bolivian State* (New York: Columbia University Press, 2000), 38; Lazar, *El Alto, Rebel City*, 30.

49. Geidel, *Peace Corps Fantasies*, 189–190; Gill, *Teetering on the Rim*, 38.

50. El Alto's 1976 population is recorded in Juan Manuel Arbona, "Dinámicas históricas y espaciales en la construcción de un barrio alteño," *Colombia Internacional* 73 (January–June 2011): 94. The country's 1976 census lists La Paz's population that year as 635,283. INE, *Resultados del censo nacional de población y vivienda*, 28.

51. Arbona, "Dinámicas históricas y espaciales en la construcción de un barrio alteño," 94.

52. Xavier Albó, "El Alto, la vorágine de una ciudad única," *Journal of Latin American Anthropology* 11, no. 2 (2006): 329–350.

53. Albó, "El Alto, la vorágine de una ciudad única"; Arbona, "Dinámicas históricas y espaciales en la construcción de un barrio alteño"; María Eugenia Choque and Carlos Mamani, "Reconstrucción del ayllu y derechos de los pueblos indígenas: El movimiento indio en los Andes de Bolivia," *Journal of Latin American Anthropology* 6, no. 1 (March 2001): 202–224; Lazar, *El Alto, Rebel City*; Pablo Mamani, *Microgobiernos barriales: Levantamiento de la Ciudad de El Alto (Octubre 2003)* (La Paz: Centro de Asesoramiento para el Desarrollo Social [CADES], Instituto de Investigaciones Sociológicas [IDIS] and UMSA, 2005). Lesley Gill reports that, as of 1992, 92 percent of El Alto residents were born either in La Paz or in the surrounding countryside. *Teetering on the Rim*, 26. Klein reports that 86 percent of El Alto's population was identified as indigenous in 2001. *A Concise History of Bolivia*, 286.

54. Mauricio Antezana Villegas, *El Alto desde El Alto II* (La Paz: UNITAS, 1992); Gill, *Teetering on the Rim*, 26; Klein, *A Concise History of Bolivia*, 286; Lazar, *El Alto, Rebel City*, 30–31; Ministerio de Desarrollo Sostenible, Viceministerio de Planificación, Secretaria Técnica del Consejo de Población para el Desarrollo Sostenible, *El Alto desde una perspectiva poblacional* (La Paz: Punto & Imagen, 2005).

55. Lazar, *El Alto, Rebel City*, 32.

56. Concejo Municipal de La Paz, *Mi barrio cuenta y yo cuento con mi barrio* (La Paz: Impresiones Gráficas "Virgo," 2009), 90.

57. Arnold and Yapita, *Las wawas del Inka*; Arnold and Yapita, "Los caminos de género en Qaqachaka"; Denise Arnold and Juan de Dios Yapita, *Río de vellón, río de canto: Cantar a los animales, una poética andina de la creación* (La Paz: Hisbol and ILCA, 1998); Denise Arnold and Juan de Dios Yapita, with Margarita Tito, *Vocabulario aymara del parto y de la vida reproductiva de la mujer* (La Paz: Family Health International and ILCA, 2000); Bastien, *Drum and Stethoscope*; Joseph W. Bastien, *Mountain of the Condor: Metaphor and Ritual in an Andean Ayllu* (Prospect Heights, IL: Waveland Press, 1978); Canessa, *Intimate Indigeneities*; Libbet Crandon-Malamud, *From the Fat of Our Souls: Social Change, Political*

Process, and Medical Pluralism in Bolivia (Berkeley and Los Angeles: University of California Press, 1991); Defossez, Fassin, and Viveros, *Mujeres de los Andes*; Ineke Dibbits and Ximena Pabón, *Granizadas, bautizos, y despachos: Aportes al debate sobre el aborto desde la provincial Ingavi*, Serie Estudios e investigaciones 4 (La Paz: Creativa, 2012); Gerardo Fernández Juárez, *Médicos y yatiris: Salud e interculturalidad en el altiplano Aymara* (La Paz: Ediciones Gráficas E. G., 1999); Gallien, "Delivering the Nation, Raising the State"; Olivia Harris, *To Make the Earth Bear Fruit: Essays on Fertility, Work and Gender in Highland Bolivia* (London: Institute of Latin American Studies, 2000); Koss-Chioino, Leatherman, and Greenway, *Medical Pluralism in the Andes*; Carmen Beatriz Loza, *El laberinto de la curación: Itinerarios terapéuticos en las ciudades de La Paz y El Alto* (La Paz: Instituto Superior Ecuménico Andino de Teología [ISEAT], 2008); Lynn M. Morgan, "Imagining the Unborn in the Ecuadoran Andes," *Feminist Studies* 23, no. 2 (Summer 1997): 322–350; Elizabeth F. S. Roberts, *God's Laboratory: Assisted Reproduction in the Andes* (Berkeley and Los Angeles: University of California Press, 2012); Roosta, *Salud materna en contextos de interculturalidad*; Tristan Platt, "El feto agresivo: Parto, formación de la persona y mito-historia en los Andes," *Estudios Atacameños* no. 22 (2002): 127–155; Maria Tapias, *Embodied Protests: Emotions and Women's Health in Bolivia* (Chicago: University of Illinois Press, 2015); Van Vleet, *Performing Kinship*; Zulawski, *Unequal Cures*.

58. Joseph W. Bastien, *Healers of the Andes: Kallawaya Herbalists and Their Medicinal Plants* (Salt Lake City: University of Utah Press, 1987), 38; Ineke Dibbits, "Población Aymara," in Roosta, *Salud materna en contextos de interculturalidad*, 77–79; Elvira Llanos Cervantes, "El embarazo en mujeres Aymaras migrantes: Un studio en zonas urbanopopulares al oeste de La Paz," in Defossez, Fassin, and Viveros, eds., *Mujeres de los Andes*, 116; Zulawski, *Unequal Cures*, 31–32.

59. Arnold and Yapita, "Los caminos de género en Qaqachaka"; Bastien, *Healers of the Andes*; Bastien, *Mountain of the Condor*; Canessa, *Intimate Indigeneities*; Crandon-Malamud, *From the Fat of Our Souls*; Harris, *To Make the Earth Bear Fruit*; Platt, "El feto agresivo"; Zulawski, *Unequal Cures*, 31–36.

60. Arnold and Yapita, "Los caminos de género en Qaqachaka," 339.

61. Arnold and Yapita, "Los caminos de género en Qaqachaka"; Bastien and Edens, "Midwives and Maternal and Infant Health Care," in Bastien, *Drum and Stethoscope*, 138–139; Canessa, *Intimate Indigeneities*, 120–128; Platt, "El feto agresivo."

62. Aliaga Bruch, *No fue fácil para nadie*; Sandra Aliaga Bruch et al., *Situaciones inevitables: Embarazos no deseados y abortos inseguros en cinco ciudades de Bolivia* (La Paz: Scorpión, 2011); Aliaga Bruch, Quitón Prado, and Gisbert, *Veinte historias, un mismo tema*; Louise Bury et al., "Hidden Realities: What Women Do

When They Want to Terminate an Unwanted Pregnancy in Bolivia," *Journal of Gynecology and Obstetrics* 118 (September 2012): S4–S9; María Elena Gisbert and Mery Quitón Prado, "Mujer sub-urbana y prácticas del aborto en la ciudad de El Alto de La Paz, Bolivia" (unpublished manuscript, December 1992); Erica Nelson, "Birth Rights: Bolivia's Politics of Race, Region, and Motherhood, 1964–2005" (PhD diss., University of Wisconsin-Madison, 2009); Rance, *Planificación familiar*; Sidney Ruth Schuler, María Eugenia Choque, and Susanna Rance, "Misinformation, Mistrust, and Mistreatment: Family Planning among Bolivian Market Women," *Studies in Family Planning* 25, no. 4 (July–August 1994): 211–221.

63. Canessa, *Intimate Indigeneities*, 129–130; Dibbits and Pabón, *Granizadas, bautizos, y despachos*, 56–65.

64. I am grateful to an anonymous reviewer for sharing this information.

65. Canessa, *Intimate Indigeneities*, 128–129; Dibbits and Pabón, *Granizadas, bautizos, y despachos*, 122–126.

66. Rance, *Planificación familiar*, 90; Schuler, Choque, and Rance, "Misinformation, Mistrust, and Mistreatment," 214–216.

67. Harris, *To Make the Earth Bear Fruit*, 185. See also Canessa, *Intimate Indigeneities*, 144.

68. Canessa, *Intimate Indigeneities*, 144; Harris, *To Make the Earth Bear Fruit*, 186.

69. Canessa, *Intimate Indigeneities*, 129–134; Harris, *To Make the Earth Bear Fruit*, 173, 186.

70. Bastien, *Mountain of the Condor*, 86–87, 113–127; Canessa, *Intimate Indigeneities*, 139–146; Harris, "Complementarity and Conflict: An Andean View of Women and Men" and "The Power of Signs: Gender, Culture, and the Wild," in Harris, *To Make the Earth Bear Fruit*, 164–200; Rivera Cusicanqui, "The Notion of 'Rights' and the Paradoxes of Postcolonial Modernity;" and Rousseau, "Indigenous and Feminist Movements at the Constituent Assembly in Bolivia."

71. Canessa, *Intimate Indigeneities*, 134.

72. Arnold and Yapita, "Los caminos de género en Qaqachaka," 318, 350; Canessa, *Intimate Indigeneities*, 128–134; Crandon-Malamud, *From the Fat of Our Souls*, 121–123; Dibbits and Pabón, *Granizadas, bautizos y despachos*, 83; Harris, *To Make the Earth Bear Fruit*, 45–46; Morgan, "Imagining the Unborn in the Ecuadoran Andes," 336–337; Platt, "El feto agresivo."

73. Canessa, *Intimate Indigeneities*, 121. See also Morgan, "Imagining the Unborn in the Ecuadoran Andes"; Morgan and Michaels, *Fetal Subjects, Feminist Positions*.

74. Canessa, *Intimate Indigeneities*, 134–135; Harris, *To Make the Earth Bear Fruit*, 182–183; Morgan, "Imagining the Unborn in the Ecuadoran Andes," 329–330; Roberts, *God's Laboratory*, 207–209.

75. Canessa, *Intimate Indigeneities*, 128. See also Morgan, "Imagining the Unborn in the Ecuadoran Andes," 340–345. Crandon-Malamud remarks that one of the souls recognized in the Andes (the *animu*) "does not become solidly entrenched in the body until adolescence." *From the Fat of Our Souls*, 133.

76. Canessa, *Intimate Indigeneities*, 139.

77. Denise Arnold, *The Metamorphosis of Heads: Textual Struggles, Education and Land in the Andes* (Pittsburgh: University of Pittsburgh Press, 2006), 126–130; Canessa, *Intimate Indigeneities*, 139; Harris, *To Make the Earth Bear Fruit*, 194–195.

78. Canessa, *Intimate Indigeneities*, 144–146.

79. See, for instance, Hans A. Baer, "Contributions to a Critical Analysis of Medical Pluralism: An Examination of the Work of Libbet Crandon-Malamud," in Koss-Chioino, Leatherman, and Greenway, *Medical Pluralism in the Andes*, 44–45; Mark Padilla, *Caribbean Pleasure Industry: Tourism, Sexuality, and AIDS in the Dominican Republic* (Chicago: University of Chicago Press, 2007), xi.

80. Loza, *El laberinto de la curación*, 16.

81. The expression "promise and dilemma" is taken from the title of Florencia Mallon's article, "The Promise and Dilemma of Subaltern Studies: Perspectives from Latin American History," *American Historical Review* 99, no. 5 (December 1994): 1491–1515.

82. Hamilton, *Sexual Revolutions in Cuba*, 4. Hamilton notes that this feature of oral history may be particularly useful when applied to the study of themes such as sexuality.

83. Susan Armitage, ed., with Patricia Hart and Karen Weathermon, *Women's Oral History: The* Frontiers *Reader* (Lincoln: University of Nebraska Press, 2002); Sherna Berger Gluck and Daphne Patai, eds., *Women's Words: The Feminist Practice of Oral History* (New York: Routledge, 1991); John Beverley, *Testimonio: On the Politics of Truth* (Minneapolis: University of Minnesota Press, 2004); Kathleen Blee, *Women of the Klan: Racism and Gender in the 1920s*, with a new preface (Berkeley and Los Angeles: University of California Press, 2009); Phillippe Bourgois, *In Search of Respect: Selling Crack in El Barrio*, 2nd ed. (New York: Cambridge University Press, 2003); Briggs, *Reproducing Empire*, 193–209; Julie Cruikshank, *Do Glaciers Listen?: Local Knowledge, Colonial Encounters, and Social Imagination* (Vancouver: University of British Columbia Press, 2015); Ranajit Guha, "The Small Voice of History," in *Subaltern Studies IX: Writings on South*

Asian History and Society, ed. Shahid Amin and Dipesh Chakrabarty (New Delhi: Oxford University Press, 1996), 1–12; Carrie Hamilton, "On Being a 'Good' Interviewer: Empathy, Ethics, and the Politics of Oral History," *Oral History* 36, no. 2, Connections (Autumn 2008): 35–43; Hamilton, *Sexual Revolutions in Cuba;* Daniel James, *Doña María's Story: Life, History, Memory, and Political Identity* (Durham, NC: Duke University Press, 2003); Mary Jo Maynes, Jennifer L. Pierce, and Barbara Laslett, *Telling Stories: The Use of Personal Narratives in the Social Sciences and History* (Ithaca: Cornell University Press, 2008); Luisa Passerini, *Autobiography of a Generation: Italy, 1968,* trans. Lisa Erdberg (Middletown, CT: Wesleyan University Press, 1996); Daphne Patai, "Ethical Problems of Personal Narratives, or, Who Should Eat the Last Piece of Cake?" *International Journal of Oral History* 8 (February 1987): 7–27; Alessandro Portelli, *The Death of Luigi Trastulli and Other Stories: Form and Meaning in Oral History* (Albany: State University of New York Press, 1991); Alessandro Portelli, *They Say in Harlan County: An Oral History* (New York: Oxford University Press, 2011); Elizabeth Porter, *Feminist Perspectives on Ethics* (New York: Longmans, 1999); Nancy Scheper-Hughes, *Death without Weeping: The Violence of Everyday Life in Brazil* (Berkeley and Los Angeles: University of California Press, 1993); Joan Wallach Scott, "The Evidence of Experience," in *Feminist Approaches to Theory and Methodology: An Interdisciplinary Reader,* ed. Sharlene Hesse-Biber, Christina Gilmartin, and Robin Lydenberg (New York: Oxford University Press, 1999), 79–99; Anna Sheftel and Stacey Zembrzycki, eds., *Oral History Off the Record: Toward an Ethnography of Practice* (New York: Palgrave Macmillan, 2013); Anna Sheftel and Stacey Zembrzycki, "Who's Afraid of Oral History? Fifty Years of Debates and Anxiety about Ethics," *Oral History Review* 43, no. 2 (2016): 228–366; Sistren with Honor Ford-Smith, *Lionheart Gal: Life Stories of Jamaican Women* (London: The Women's Press, 1986); Gayatri Chakravorty Spivak, "Can the Subaltern Speak?" in *Marxism and the Interpretation of Cultures,* ed. Cary Nelson and Lawrence Grossberg (Urbana: University of Illinois Press, 1988), 271–316; Paul Thompson, *The Voice of the Past: Oral History,* 3rd ed. (New York: Oxford University Press, 2000); Valerie Raleigh Yow, *Recording Oral History: A Guide for the Humanities and Social Sciences,* 3rd ed. (Lanham, MD: Rowman & Littlefield, 2015).

84. More detailed information on each of these individuals is available in the book's appendix.

85. As Alessandro Portelli notes, "instead of discovering sources, oral historians partly create them." *The Death of Luigi Trastulli,* 56.

86. Kathryn Anderson and Dana Jack, "Learning to Listen: Interview Techniques and Analyses," in Berger Gluck and Patai, *Women's Words,* 11–26; Sherna

Berger Gluck, "From California to Kufr Nameh and Back: Reflections on 40 Years of Feminist Oral History," in *Oral History Off the Record*, 26–27; Portelli, *They Say in Harlan County*, 7–8.

87. Berger Gluck, "From California," 38; Beverley, *Testimonio*, 38;Yow, *Recording Oral History*, 165.

88. Portelli, *They Say in Harlan County*, 8.

89. For a good discussion of shared authority and its limits, see Berger Gluck, "From California," 25–42.

90. Yow, *Recording Oral History*, 82.

91. A similar technique is discussed in Yow, *Recording Oral History*, 161.

92. See, among others, Julie Cruikshank, *The Social Life of Stories: Narrative and Knowledge in the Yukon Territory* (Lincoln: University of Nebraska Press, 2000); Clifford Geertz, *Local Knowledge: Further Essays in Interpretive Anthropology*, 3rd ed. (New York: Basic Books, 2000); Guha, "The Small Voice of History;" and Russell Thornton, *Studying Native America: Problems and Prospects* (Madison: University of Wisconsin Press, 1998). In Bolivia, among the most prominent efforts to rewrite dominant historical narratives can be found in the scholarly and activist initiatives pursued by the groundbreaking *Taller de Historia Oral Andina* (Andean Oral History Workshop, or THOA). Lucila Criales and Cristóbal Condoreno, "Breve reseña del Taller de Historia Oral Andina (THOA)," *Fuentes* 10, no. 43 (April 2016): 57–66; Marcia Stephenson, "Forging an Indigenous Counterpublic Sphere: The Taller de Historia Oral Andina in Bolivia," *Latin American Research Review* 37, no. 2 (2002): 99–118; Esteban Ticona Alejo, "Algunas experiencias metodológicas en Historia Oral," *Boletín de Historia Oral* 1 (November 1986): 1–10.

93. Maria Tapias, "The Intergenerational Embodiment of Social Suffering," in Tapias, *Embodied Protests*, 56–75.

94. Briggs, *Reproducing Empire*, especially 202–205; Bourgois, *In Search of Respect*, 342; Cruikshank, *Do Glaciers Listen?* especially 255–257; Guha, "The Small Voice of History."

95. Daphne Patai, "U.S. Academics and Third World Women: Is Ethical Research Possible?" in Berger Gluck and Patai, *Women's Words*, 137.

96. Hamilton, *Sexual Revolutions in Cuba*, 9.

97. This technique is also addressed in Hamilton, *Sexual Revolutions in Cuba*, 9.

98. Michael Gorkin, "Introduction," in *From Grandmother to Granddaughter: Salvadoran Women's Stories*, Michael Gorkin, Marta Pineda, and Gloria Leal (Berkeley and Los Angeles: University of California Press, 2000), 14; Thompson, *The Voice of the Past*, 173–189.

99. Victoria Sanford, *Buried Secrets: Truth and Human Rights in Guatemala* (New York: Palgrave MacMillan, 2003), 22.

100. Dominick LaCapra, *Writing History, Writing Trauma* (Baltimore: Johns Hopkins University Press, 2001), 78, quoted in Sanford, *Buried Secrets*, 22.

101. See also Ruth Behar's beautiful discussion of the anthropological encounter in *The Vulnerable Observer: Anthropology That Breaks Your Heart* (Boston: Beacon Press, 1996).

102. República de Bolivia, *Código Penal Banzer*, chapter II, art. 263 (La Paz, 1972).

103. Naming some individuals while anonymizing others would provide the opportunity to deduce "known" narrators and more easily identify those who are "unknown."

104. The dissertation on which this book is based originally included more details about abortion services in these cities; it was subsequently revised and resubmitted to ensure that any copies available online were stripped of potentially damaging information.

105. Raymond Gorden, *Interviewing: Strategy, Techniques and Tactics*, 4th ed. (Chicago: Dorsey Press, 1987), 16; Alessandro Portelli, *The Battle of Valle Giulia: Oral History and the Art of Dialogue* (Madison: University of Wisconsin Press, 1997), 55.

106. Yow, *Recording Oral History*, 160. See also Patai, "U.S. Academics and Third World Women"; Porter, *Feminist Perspectives on Ethics*, 25.

107. "Principles for Oral History and Best Practices for Oral History," Oral History Association, October 2009, http://www.oralhistory.org/about/principles -and-practices-revised-2009/#best.

108. Portelli, *The Death of Luigi Trastulli*, 50–51; Valerie Yow, "Ethics and Interpersonal Relationships in Oral History Research," *Oral History Review* 22, no. 1 (Summer 1995): 51–66. In accordance with requirements by the University of Pittsburgh's institutional review board, record numbers listed here can be traced only to a volume of medical records at La Paz's Archivo Histórico La Paz (La Paz Historical Archive, or ALP), and not to specific medical records, which contain women's names. The record number following the colon corresponds only to the number that is randomly assigned by the Endnote software program in which I documented information from medical charts.

109. See, among others, Berger Gluck, "From California," 40; Briggs, *Reproducing Empire*, especially 193–209; Gorkin, Pineda, and Leal, *From Grandmother to Granddaughter*, especially 13–15; Gluck and Patai, *Women's Words*; Sanford, *Buried Secrets*, especially 22–29; Sheftel and Zembzycki, "Who's Afraid of Oral History?"

110. Shepard, "The 'Double Discourse' on Sexual and Reproductive Rights in Latin America."

CHAPTER 1 — LEGISLATING UNWANTED PREGNANCY
AND ABORTION IN BOLIVIA

Epigraph: Dolores Ticahuanca, El Alto, 7 December 2009.

1. Klein, *A Concise History of Bolivia*, 159–160.

2. Larson, *Trials of Nation-Making*, 204–207.

3. Larson, *Trials of Nation-Making*, 202–229. See also Olivia Harris, "Ethnic Identity and Market Relations."

4. Larson, *Trials of Nation-Making*, 220–229.

5. Larson, *Trials of Nation-Making*, 215–217.

6. Larson, *Trials of Nation-Making*, 220–229. Among the most explosive conflicts of the period was the 1899 Federalist War. For a good discussion of the war, see Larson, *Trials of Nation-Making*, 229–245.

7. Larson, *Trials of Nation-Making*, 239–245; Deborah Poole, *Vision, Race, and Modernity: A Visual Economy of the Andean Image World* (Princeton: Princeton University Press, 1997).

8. Seemin Qayum, "Indian Ruins, National Origins: Tiwanaku and *Indigenismo* in La Paz, 1897–1933," in *Histories of Race and Racism: The Andes and Mesoamerica from Colonial Times to the Present*, ed. Laura Gotkowitz (Durham, NC: Duke University Press, 2011), 160. See also Harris, *To Make the Earth Bear Fruit*, 4–5.

9. Qayum, "Indian Ruins, National Origins," 161. See also Brooke Larson, "Capturing Indian Bodies, Hearths, and Minds: The Gendered Politics of Rural School Reform in Bolivia, 1920s–1940s," in *Natives Making Nation*, ed. Andrew Canessa, 36–39.

10. Brooke Larson, "Capturing Indian Bodies, Hearths and Minds: The Gendered Politics of Rural School Reform in Bolivia, 1910–52," in *Proclaiming Revolution: Bolivia in Comparative Perspective*, ed. Merilee Grindle and Pilar Domingo (London: Institute of Latin American Studies, 2003), 185. See also Larson, "Capturing Indian Bodies," in *Natives Making Nation*, ed. Andrew Canessa, 32–59; Brooke Larson, "Forging the Unlettered Indian: The Pedagogy of Race in the Bolivian Andes," in *Histories of Race and Racism*, ed. Laura Gotkowitz, 134–156; Leys Stepan, "*The Hour of Eugenics*"; Weismantel, *Cholas and Pishtacos*, 88–90.

11. Larson, "Capturing Indian Bodies," in *Proclaiming Revolution*, ed. Merilee Grindle and Pilar Domingo, 195.

12. Larson, "Capturing Indian Bodies," in *Natives Making Nation*, ed. Andrew Canessa, 41–42.

13. Larson, "Capturing Indian Bodies," in *Proclaiming Revolution*, ed. Merilee Grindle and Pilar Domingo, 201–202. See also Marcia Stephenson, "Fashioning

the National Subject: Pedagogy, Hygiene, and Apparel," in Stephenson, *Gender and Modernity*, 111–157.

14. Dibbits, *Polleras libertarias*; Stephenson, "Skirts and Polleras: Ideologies of Womanhood and the Politics of Resistance in La Paz, 1900–1952," in Stephenson, *Gender and Modernity*, 9–34; Wadsworth and Dibbits, *Agitadoras de Buen gusto*; Zulawski, *Unequal Cures*, 118–123.

15. Medinaceli, *Alterando la rutina*, 72–73; Stephenson, *Gender and Modernity*, 13.

16. Stephenson, *Gender and Modernity*, 12.

17. Stephenson, *Gender and Modernity*, 14. See also Zulawski, *Unequal Cures*, 120–121.

18. Stephenson, *Gender and Modernity*, 14–15.

19. Zulawski, *Unequal Cures*, 122. See also Federation of Women Workers, "A Woman's Work," trans. Alison Spedding, in *The Bolivia Reader: History, Culture, Politics*, ed. Sinclair Thomson et al. (Durham, NC: Duke University Press, 2018), 339–345.

20. Stephenson, *Gender and Modernity*, 11–24. See also Zulawski, *Unequal Cures*, 122–123.

21. Larson, "Capturing Indian Bodies," in *Natives Making Nation*, ed. Andrew Canessa, 43–44; Stephenson, *Gender and Modernity*, 24–26; Zulawski, *Unequal Cures*, 52–85.

22. Stephenson, *Gender and Modernity*, 24.

23. Stephenson, *Gender and Modernity*, 27–29.

24. Stephenson, *Gender and Modernity*, 30–31.

25. Stephenson, *Gender and Modernity*, 30.

26. Zulawski, *Unequal Cures*, 118–156.

27. Zulawski, *Unequal Cures*, 134.

28. Zulawski, *Unequal Cures*, 123–141.

29. Zulawski, *Unequal Cures*, 141–154.

30. Weismantel, *Cholas and Pishtacos*, 45. See also Lesley Gill, *Precarious Dependencies: Gender, Class, and Domestic Service in Bolivia* (New York: Columbia University Press, 1994), 19–20.

31. Weismantel, *Cholas and Pishtacos*, 20–21.

32. Gill, *Precarious Dependencies*, 74–76; Weismantel, *Cholas and Pishtacos*.

33. Ana María Condori, with Ineke Dibbits and Elizabeth Peredo, *Nayan Uñatatawi: Mi Despertar* (La Paz: HISBOL, TAHIPAMU, 1988); Lesley Gill, "Painted Faces: Conflict and Ambiguity in Domestic Servant-Employer Relations in La Paz, 1930–1988," *Latin American Research Review* 25, no. 1 (1990): 130; Stephenson, *Gender and Modernity*, 155–157.

34. Weismantel, *Cholas and Pishtacos*, 121.

35. Weismantel, *Cholas and Pishtacos*, 245–246. See also Gill, *Precarious Dependencies*, 105–108.

36. Geidel, *Peace Corps Fantasies*, 189.

37. Nicole Pacino, "Prescription for a Nation: Public Health in Post-Revolutionary Bolivia, 1952–1964" (PhD diss., University of California, Santa Barbara, 2013), 32.

38. Ardaya, *Política sin rostro*, 44.

39. Klein, *A Concise History of Bolivia*, 212–215.

40. Gotkowitz, *A Revolution for Our Rights*, 166–174; Silvia Rivera Cusicanqui, "Construcción de imágenes de indios y mujeres en la iconografía post-52: El miserabilismo en el Álbum de la Revolución (1954)," in *Discursos sobre (a) pobreza: América Latina y/e países luso-africanos*, ed. Martín Leinhard (Madrid: Iberoamericana, 1996), 171–208; Stephenson, *Gender and Modernity*, 111–157; Juliana Strobele-Gregor, Bert Hoffman, and Andrew Holmes, "From Indio to Mestizo . . . to Indio: New Indianist Movements in Bolivia," *Latin American Perspectives* 21, no. 2 (Spring, 1994): 106–123; Deborah Yashar, *Contesting Citizenship in Latin America: The Rise of Indigenous Movements and the Postliberal Challenge* (New York: Cambridge University Press, 2005), 156.

41. Pacino, "Prescription for a Nation," 37.

42. Gregorio Mendizábal Lozano, *Historia de la salud pública en Bolivia: De las juntas de sanidad a los directorios locales de salud* (La Paz: OPS/OMS, 2002), 191–194.

43. Gallien, "Delivering the Nation, Raising the State," 158.

44. Nicole L. Pacino, "Creating Madres Campesinas: Revolutionary Motherhood and the Gendered Politics of Nation Building in 1950s Bolivia," *Journal of Women's History* 27, no. 1 (Spring 2015): 62–87; Pacino, "Prescription for a Nation," 159–216.

45. "Creating Madres Campesinas," 64.

46. Hubert Navarro, *Informe estadístico de Bolivia* (La Paz: Departamento Nacional de Bioestadística, 1953), 5–6; Abelardo Villalpando, *Un año de experiencia de la reforma agraria en Potosí*, Bolivian Political Pamphlet No. 1110 (University of Pittsburgh), 35–36.

47. Navarro, *Informe estadístico de Bolivia*, 35–36.

48. Navarro, *Informe estadístico de Bolivia*, 12.

49. Gallien, "Delivering the Nation, Raising the State," 34, 150–155; Pacino, "Creating Madres Campesinas," 62–64.

50. Pacino, "Creating Madres Campesinas," 63. See also Pacino, "Prescription for a Nation," 159–216.

51. Pacino, "Creating Madres Campesinas," 63.

52. Gallien, "Delivering the Nation, Raising the State," 153–154.

53. Gallien, "Delivering the Nation, Raising the State," especially chapter 3, "Matronas, Miners, and Medical Knowledge: The Transnational Politics of Health and the Rise and Fall of University-Educated Midwives in Bolivia, 1950s–1970s," 132–176.

54. June Nash, *We Eat the Mines and the Mines Eat Us: Dependency and Exploitation in Bolivian Tin Mines* (New York: Columbia University Press, 1993 [1979]), 62.

55. Gallien, "Delivering the Nation, Raising the State;" Pacino, "Creating Madres Campesinas" and "Prescription for a Nation."

56. Ardaya, *Política sin rostro*, 61.

57. Navarro, *Informe estadística de Bolivia*, 14–15.

58. INE, *Resultados del censo nacional de población y vivienda*, 257–260.

59. Pacino, "Prescription for a Nation," 225.

60. Despite this, Domitila Barrios de Chungara, an activist of the miners' Housewives' Committee of Siglo XX, noted that the Barzolas were hostile to mine workers and their families who visited La Paz in 1961 to protest conditions in the mines. Domitila Barrios de Chungara with Moema Viezzer, *Let Me Speak! Testimony of Domitila, A Woman of the Bolivian Mines,* trans. Victoria Ortiz (New York: Monthly Review Books, 1978), 72–73.

61. See the testimony of Leonor Calvimontes, quoted in Ardaya, *Política sin rostro*, 73.

62. Ardaya, *Política sin rostro*, 78–83.

63. Klein, *A Concise History of Bolivia*, 209–216.

64. Pacino, "Prescription for a Nation," 160–162.

65. Pacino, "Prescription for a Nation," 212–216.

66. Klein, *A Concise History of Bolivia*, 222–238.

67. Montaño would later serve as Bolivia's first sub-secretary of gender issues from 1993 to 1995 and, as of 2011, was the director of the Division of Gender Issues for the UN Economic Commission for Latin America and the Caribbean (ECLAC). Cati Molina, La Paz, 18 June 2009.

68. *Amnesty International Report 1981* (London: Amnesty International Publications, 1981), 118.

69. Klein, *A Concise History of Bolivia*, 226–231.

70. Klein, *A Concise History of Bolivia*, 226–231.

71. Gallien, "Delivering the Nation, Raising the State," 176.

72. Gallien, "Delivering the Nation, Raising the State," 177–203; Klein, *A Concise History of Bolivia*, 230; Rivera Cusicanqui, *"Oprimidos pero no vencidos,"* 167–175.

73. Gallien, "Delivering the Nation, Raising the State," 180.

74. Gallien, "Delivering the Nation, Raising the State," 181; Geidel, *Peace Corps Fantasies*, 190–191.

75. Gallien, "Delivering the Nation, Raising the State," 182.

76. Gallien, "Delivering the Nation, Raising the State," 188.

77. Gallien, "Delivering the Nation, Raising the State," 183.

78. Gallien, "Delivering the Nation, Raising the State," 189–190.

79. Gallien, "Delivering the Nation, Raising the State," 190; Ministerio de Salud y Deportes, *Plan Nacional de Maternidad y Nacimiento Seguros (2004–2008)* (La Paz: MSD, Pan American Health Organization [PAHO], and United Nations Population Fund [UNFPA], 2004), 11; Sociedad Boliviana de Salud Pública, *Salud Pública en Bolivia: Historia y Perspectivas* (La Paz: Sociedad Boliviana de Salud Pública, 1989), 89.

80. Gallien, "Delivering the Nation, Raising the State," 188–191; Sociedad Boliviana de Salud Pública, *Salud Pública en Bolivia*, 89.

81. Geidel, *Peace Corps Fantasies*, 187–230; Molly Geidel, "'Sowing Death in Our Women's Wombs': Modernization and Indigenous Nationalism in the 1960s Peace Corps and Jorge Sanjinés' *Yawar Mallku*" *American Quarterly* 62, no. 3 (September 2010): 763–786; Nelson, "Birth Rights," 25–28; Rance, *Planificación familiar*, 14–15.

82. Nelson, "Birth Rights," 28–29.

83. Nelson, "Birth Rights," 33.

84. Geidel, *Peace Corps Fantasies*, xix–xx.

85. Nelson, "Birth Rights," 29.

86. Geidel, *Peace Corps Fantasies*, 204–208; Nelson, "Birth Rights," 39–40.

87. Gallien, "Delivering the Nation, Raising the State," 191.

88. Gallien, "Delivering the Nation, Raising the State," 190.

89. Rance, *Planificación familiar*, 15. See also Nelson, "Birth Rights," 123–124.

90. Nelson, "Birth Rights," 126–129. Nelson remarks that Kushner López was unclear on the exact date of the project launch. Rance places the start of this program in 1974. Rance, *Planificación familiar*, 15–19.

91. For the Department of Santa Cruz, this coverage was estimated at 1 percent of Bolivian women of fertile age during the first year, with a 2 percent increase each subsequent year. Rance, *Planificación familiar*, 16; Martín Sivak *El dictador elegido: Biografía no autorizada de Hugo Banzer Suárez* (La Paz: Plural Editores, 2001), 171. In La Paz Department, the program intended to reach 10,000 women in 1975 with an increase in subsequent years. Rance, *Planificación familiar*, 16.

92. Rance, *Planificación familiar*, 16; Sivak, *El dictador elegido*, 175–176.

93. Nelson, "Birth Rights," 135; Sivak, *El dictador elegido*, 176.

94. Aliaga, *No fue fácil para nadie*, 21; Interview with medical doctor Adrián Espinoza, La Paz, 8 October 2009; Geidel, *Peace Corps Fantasies*, 222. Aliaga contends that Banzer prohibited birth control provisioning in the country following the release of the 1976 national demographic and health survey, which estimated Bolivia's population at about a million fewer inhabitants than expected. Nelson does not explicitly mention Banzer's prohibition of birth control, but notes that, facing pressure from the Catholic Church, the dictator stripped birth control provisioning from the USAID/UNFPA project. Nelson, "Birth Rights," 129–130.

95. Gallien, "Delivering the Nation, Raising the State," 191.

96. Nelson, "Birth Rights," 96.

97. Nelson, "Mapping Mothers: Demography, Development, and the Regionalization of Reproduction," in "Birth Rights," 73–118. See also Gallien, "Delivering the Nation, Raising the State," 192.

98. Aliaga, *No fue fácil para nadie*, 21; Geidel, *Peace Corps Fantasies*, 220–229.

99. Aliaga, *No fue fácil para nadie*, 16–17; Nelson, "Birth Rights," 131.

100. Aliaga, *No fue fácil para nadie*, 47–87; Nelson, "Birth Rights," 196–207; Schuler, Choque, and Rance, "Misinformation, Mistrust, and Mistreatment," 211–221; interviews with Marcela Flores, La Paz, 22 September 2009; Cati Molina, La Paz, 18 June 2009; Emilia Santana, El Alto, 10 February 2010, and Miguel Ramírez, La Paz, 21 October 2009.

101. Cisneros, *El aborto inducido*, 11.

102. República de Bolivia, *Código Penal Bánzer*, 109.

103. Interviews in La Paz with medical doctors Emma Alvarez, June 2009; Alessandra Muñecas, 19 June 2009, and Daisy Serrato, 7 October 2009, and with activists Fanny Barrutia, 18 June 2009 and Lupe Colque, 29 June 2009, among others.

104. Emily Achtenberg, "For Abortion Rights in Bolivia, A Modest Gain," *NACLA*, February 27, 2014, https://nacla.org/blog/2014/2/28/abortion-rights-bolivia-modest-gain; Ipas, "Human Rights Committee to Bolivia: Stop Arresting Women for Abortion" November 5, 2013, http://www.ipas.org/en/News/2013/November/Human-Rights-Committee-to-Bolivia—Stop-arresting-women-for-abortion.aspx.

105. This quote is taken from the subtitle of Htun's book, *Sex and the State: Abortion, Divorce, and the Family under Latin American Dictatorships and Democracies*.

106. Htun, *Sex and the State*, 149. According to Htun, the relative tolerance of the Catholic Church toward legislative reform on the family began to change in the late 1970s and throughout the ensuing decades, with the election of conservative Pope John Paul II in 1978. Htun, *Sex and the State*, 151.

107. Htun, *Sex and the State*, 142–150.

108. Abortion was legalized in Cuba in 1979 but had been widely practiced in the two previous decades, while Uruguay and Mexico City have allowed the procedure in the first trimester of pregnancy since 2012 and 2007, respectively. "Abortion Legalised in Mexico City," *BBC News*, April 25, 2007, http://news.bbc.co.uk /2/hi/americas/6586959.stm; Hamilton, *Sexual Revolutions in Cuba*, 35; "Uruguay Senate Approves First-Trimester Abortions," *New York Times*, October 17, 2012, http://www.nytimes.com/2012/10/18/world/americas/uruguay-senate-approves -first-trimester-abortions.html?_r=0.

109. Argentina's abortion law went through subtle shifts first under military dictator Juan Carlos Onganía in 1967 and again in 1973 and 1976 under both democratic and authoritarian regimes—the same years that Banzer modified the Bolivian law. Htun, *Sex and the State*, 148.

110. Cisneros, *El aborto inducido*; interview with medical doctor Adrián Espinoza, La Paz, 8 October 2009; John M. Paxman, et al., "The Clandestine Epidemic: The Practice of Unsafe Abortion in Latin America," *Studies in Family Planning* 24, no. 4 (July–August 1993): 205–226; Benjamin V. Viel, "Latin America," in *International Handbook on Abortion*, ed. Paul Sachdev (Westport, CT: Greenwood Press, 1988), 320–322.

111. Cisneros, *El aborto inducido*, 11–12.

112. Cisneros, *El aborto inducido*, 10, 12.

113. Nelson contends that U.S. Embassy Population Offices in Bolivia, Chile, Ecuador, and Argentina pointed to high abortion rates in an effort to convince local authorities to establish national family planning programs. "Birth Rights," 46.

114. Gallien, "Delivering the Nation, Raising the State," 172, 177, 197–198; Sociedad Boliviana de Salud Pública, *Salud Pública en Bolivia*, 94.

115. Gallien, "Delivering the Nation, Raising the State," 179.

116. Gallien, "Delivering the Nation, Raising the State," 218.

117. Klein, *A Concise History of Bolivia*, 186, 232–238.

118. Gloria Ardaya, Participación política y liderazgos de mujeres en Bolivia (La Paz: Talleres Gráficos Creativa, 2001), 25; Elizabeth Monasterios P., "Introducción," in Elizabeth Monasterios P., ed., No pudieron con nostotras: El desafío del feminismo autónomo de Mujeres Creando (La Paz: Plural Editores, 2006), 17.

119. Cati Molina, La Paz, 18 June 2009.

120. Gill, *Teetering on the Rim*, 1–5; Germán Guaygua, Ángela Rivera, and Máximo Quisbert, *Ser jóven en El Alto: Rupturas y continuidades en la tradición cultural* (La Paz: Fundación PIEB, 2000), 13–15; Lazar, *El Alto, Rebel City*, 29–34.

121. Lazar, *El Alto, Rebel City*, 47.

122. Interview with medical doctor Antonia Rocio, La Paz, 26 May 2010. At its founding in the United States in the 1970s, Ipas was originally an acronym for "International Pregnancy Advisory Services," which the institution dropped in 1993. "The Ipas Story," http://www.ipas.org/en/Who-We-Are/The-Ipas-Story.aspx.

123. Rance, *La planificación familiar*, 25–26.

124. These developments are discussed in detail in chapter 5.

125. The World Bank was later forced to amend the document to exclude mention of population reform. Rance, *La planificación familiar*, 13, 19–22.

126. Aliaga, *No fue fácil para nadie*, 56–59; Nelson, "Birth Rights," 178.

127. Nelson, "Birth Rights," 178–179.

128. Nelson, "Birth Rights."

129. Ministerio de Previsión Social y Salud Pública (MPSSP), Secretaría de la Mujer, Salud, y Desarrollo, and the Conferencia Episcopal Boliviana (CEB), *Lucha contra el aborto: Seminario taller* (La Paz: Ministerio de Previsión Social y Salud Pública, 1989), 11. See also Nelson, "Birth Rights," 177–178.

130. MPSSP, Secretaría de la Mujer, Salud, y Desarrollo, and the CEB, *Lucha contra el aborto*, 11.

131. Interviews in La Paz with medical personnel and activists Emma Alvarez, 16 June 2009; Julián Costa, 3 July 2009; Vanessa Lujo, 26 March 2010; Alessandra Muñecas, 19 June 2009, and Miguel Ramírez, 21 October 2009, among others.

132. Emma Alvarez, La Paz, 19 June 2009.

133. Daisy Serrato, La Paz, 7 October 2009. See also Alanes, *El aborto en Bolivia*, 10–15 and Nelson, "Birth Rights," 209–210.

134. Aliaga, *No fue fácil para nadie*, 79–111; Htun, *Sex and the State*, 149–151; Nelson, "Birth Rights," 209–215.

135. Julián Costa, La Paz, 3 July 2009.

136. Eliana del Pozo and Juan Luis Alanes Bravo, *Marcando un hito en Bolivia: Experiencia. Atención de las hemorragias de la primera mitad del embarazo en servicios de primer nivel de atención* (La Paz: Ipas, 2007), 11.

137. Del Pozo and Alanes Bravo, *Marcando un hito en Bolivia*, 11.

138. Del Pozo and Alanes Bravo, *Marcando un hito en Bolivia*, 12; Ministerio de Salud y Deportes, *Plan Nacional de Maternidad*; Ministerio de Salud y Deportes, *Manual de normas, reglas, protocolos y procedimientos técnicos para el manejo de las hemorragias de la primera mitad del embarazo*, 11. The results of these policies are addressed in detail in chapter 5.

139. Cati Molina, La Paz, 18 June 2009.

140. See the Campaign's website, http://www.28deseptiembre.org/index.php ?option=com_k2&view=item&id=69:¿cuando-surgió-la-campaña-28-de -septiembre?&Itemid=210, accessed 1 December 2012. Cati Molina remembered

the campaign beginning five years earlier, at a conference in Brazil in 1985. Interview in La Paz on 18 June 2009.

141. Grupo de Trabajo sobre Embarazo no Deseado y Aborto, *Embarazo no deseado y aborto: Bibliografía* (La Paz: Secretaría Nacional de Salud and WHO, 1995), 13.

142. Grupo de Trabajo sobre Embarazo no Deseado y Aborto, *Embarazo no deseado*, 13. See also Aliaga, *No fue fácil para nadie*, 105–108, 11; Susanna Rance and Sandra Vallenas, coord., *Memoria de la reunion sobre embarazo no deseado y aborto en Bolivia y Perú* (La Paz: Population Council, 1999).

143. Cati Molina, La Paz, 18 June 2009. See also Zulema Alanes and Susanna Rance, coord., *Una alianza por la salud y los derechos: Memoria del Simposio Interamericano sobre Legislación en Salud Sexual y Reproductiva* (La Paz: Population Council, 1999), 24.

144. María Dolores Castro Mantilla and Silvia Salinas Mülder, *Avances y retrocesos en un escenario cambiante: Reforma en salud, mortalidad materna y aborto en Bolivia, 2000–2002* (La Paz: CIDEM, 2004), 114.

145. Cati Molina, La Paz, 18 June 2009.

146. Klein, *A Concise History of Bolivia*, 291–293. Legal rights for heterosexual couples in common-law marriages and for any children resulting from these unions were further expanded under Bolivia's Family Code in 2014. Guiomara Calle, "Unión libre será registrada sin la necesidad de un juez," *La Razón*, December 11, 2013, http://www.la-razon.com/sociedad/Union-libre-registrada-necesidad -juez_0_1959404080.html.

147. Constitución Política del Estado, 7 February 2009, Art. 4 and 66.

148. Cati Molina, La Paz, 18 June 2009.

149. Fanny Barrutia, La Paz, 18 June 2009. See also Rousseau, "Indigenous and Feminist Movements at the Constituent Assembly in Bolivia," 23. The formal proposal of the 28th of September Campaign to the Constitutional Assembly was known as "Desde el nuevo texto constitucional hacia nuestros cuerpos: Las propuestas femeninas a los derechos reconocidos en el proyecto de la nueva constitución política del estado."

150. The dominant proposal of the women's movement to the Constitutional Assembly was entitled, "De la protesta al mandato: Presentes en la historia, mujeres en la Asamblea Constituyente" and included the participation of both national organizations and smaller, local organizations. With respect to sexual and reproductive rights, the proposal defended a woman's right to bodily autonomy and to plan her family; however, it did not explicitly demand access to contraception or to abortion. Mujeres Presentes en la Historia, *De la protesta al mandato: Una propuesta en construcción* (La Paz: Proyecto Mujeres y Asamblea Constituyente, 2006), 6.

151. Fanny Barrutia, La Paz, 18 June 2009.

152. "Descartan debate sobre despenalización del aborto en Bolivia," *Los Tiempos*, November 6, 2010, http://lapatriaenlinea.com/index.php?t=descartan -debate-sobre-la-despenalizacion-del-aborto-en-bolivia&nota=47558.

153. Rousseau, "Indigenous and Feminist Movements at the Constituent Assembly in Bolivia." See also Ana María Bravo, *Democracia, paridad y participación de las mujeres: Desafíos de la asamblea constituyente* (Cochabamba: Fundación de Apoyo al Parlamento y a la Participación Ciudadana [FUNDAP-PAC] and Fundación Konrad Adenauer, 2005); Teresa Lanza Monje, "Proyecto Mujeres y Asamblea Constituyente," *Cotidiano Mujer* 4, no. 44 (November 2008): 48–53; Claudia G. Amonzabel Meneses and Rosario Paz Ballivián, *Las mujeres rumbo a la asamblea constituyente: Segundo ciclo de seminarios— taller "Participación política y ciudadanía de las mujeres," Noviembre a Diciembre de 2003* (La Paz: FUNDAPPAC and Fundación Konrad Adenauer, 2003); and Viceministerio de Género y Asuntos Generacionales and Cooperación Técnica Alemana, *Mujeres constituyentes* (La Paz: Gesellschaft für Technische Zusammenarbeit, 2007).

154. Rousseau, "Indigenous and Feminist Movements at the Constituent Assembly in Bolivia."

155. Rousseau, "Indigenous and Feminist Movements at the Constituent Assembly in Bolivia," 18.

156. Rousseau, "Indigenous and Feminist Movements at the Constituent Assembly in Bolivia," 19.

157. Rousseau, "Indigenous and Feminist Movements at the Constituent Assembly in Bolivia," 19–21.

158. Rousseau, "Indigenous and Feminist Movements at the Constituent Assembly in Bolivia," 21. See also Burman, "Chachawarmi," 69–70 and interview data.

159. Email correspondence with Fanny Barrutia, November 29, 2012. See also "Plantean ley de educación sexual en vez de la de aborto," *La Razón*, September 29, 2012, http://www.la-razon.com/sociedad/Plantean-ley-educacion-sexual-aborto _0_1696630346.html.

160. Gillian Kane, "After Jailing Women, Bolivia Weighs Legalizing Abortion," *The Atlantic*, June 24, 2013, https://www.theatlantic.com/international/archive /2013/06/after-jailing-women-bolivia-weighs-legalizing-abortion/277147/.

161. Gillian Kane, Beatriz Galli, and Patty Skuster, *Cuando el aborto es un crimen: La amenaza para mujeres vulnerables en América Latina* (Chapel Hill: Ipas, 2015), 5–6.

162. "MAS deja despenalización del aborto en manos del Tribunal Constitucional," *La Razón*, July 23, 2013, http://www.la-razon.com/nacional/despenalizacion

-aborto-manos-Tribunal-Constitucional_0_1874812576.html; Yuvert Donoso, "Los argumentos del fallo del Tribunal Constitucional sobre el aborto," *La Razón*, February 14, 2014, http://www.la-razon.com/sociedad/argumentos-fallo-Tribunal -Constitucional-aborto_0_1998400212.html.

163. Jennifer Zelmer, "Abort the System," *NACLA*, January 9, 2018, https://nacla .org/news/2018/01/09/abort-system; "A diciembre 2016 se registraron 120 abortos legales en seis departamentos de Bolivia," *Página Siete*, January 5, 2017, https:// www.paginasiete.bo/sociedad/2017/1/5/diciembre-2016-registraron-abortos -legales-seis-departamentos-bolivia-122739.html#!.

164. In some reports on the proposed changes to the penal code, the measure concerning abortion is described as Article 153, while in others, it is referred to as Article 157. See Fernando Molina, "Bolivia amplía los casos de aborto legal," *El País*, September 30, 2017, https://elpais.com/internacional/2017/09/29/america /1506707616_443555.html; Marcelo Tedesqui, "Abrueban el artículo 153 del Código de Sistema Penal referido al aborto," *El Deber*, September 29, 2017, https://www .eldeber.com.bo/bolivia/Camara-de-Diputados-aprueba-el-articulo-153-del -Codigo-de-Sistema-Penal-referido-al-aborto-20170928-0098.html; Jennifer Zelmer, "Abort the System."

165. "El anuncio de abrogación del código penal no frena las protestas en Bolivia," *Agencia EFE*, January 22, 2018, https://www.efe.com/efe/america /sociedad/el-anuncio-de-abrogacion-del-codigo-penal-no-frena-las-protestas -en-bolivia/20000013-3500305#; "Legal abortion access greatly expanded in Bolivia," *Ipas*, December 15, 2017, http://www.ipas.org/en/News/2017/December /Legal-abortion-access-greatly-expanded-in-Bolivia.aspx.

166. Alessandra Muñecas, La Paz, 19 June 2009. See also interviews in La Paz with Lupe Colque, 29 June 2009; Fanny Barrutia, 18 June 2009; Cati Molina, 18 June 2009; and Carla Yupanqui, 2 February 2010, among others.

167. Julián Costa, La Paz on 3 July 2009; Antonia Rocio, La Paz, 26 May 2010; Daisy Serrato, La Paz, 7 October 2009; and Dolores Ticahuanca, El Alto, 7 December 2009, among others.

168. Individual interviewees who held these positions are too numerous to cite here, but included members of the police, government officials, religious authorities, medical doctors and other health workers, and women's rights activists.

169. Interviews in La Paz with medical personnel, Olga Mollo, 7 October 2009 and Daisy Serrato, 7 October 2009, both of whom worked in health care facilities administered by the Catholic Church.

170. The La Paz–based organization Familia y Vida Humana (Family and Human Life) administers such courses, as does the Pastoral Familiar (Family Ministry) of the Catholic Church. Interviews in La Paz with Leandro Rubén, of

Family and Human Life, on 3 December 2009 and with Father Mariano Solana, of the Family Ministry, on 30 April 2010.

171. Interview in La Paz on 30 April 2010. The organization Apostolado de la Nueva Evangelización (ANE) Pro-Vida, which is affiliated with the Catholic Church, represents one of the more active bodies of the pro-life movement in La Paz. Interview with activist Carolina Llano in La Paz on 5 May 2010. La Paz's Catholic university, the Universidad Salesiana, also administers a pro-life organization by the name of Centro por la Vida (Center for Life, or CEPROVI). In October 2010, the organization held a national conference of pro-life supporters in the northern city of Riberalta. "'Centro Por la Vida' de la Universidad Salesiana de Bolivia realizó en Riberalta el 'Primer Encuentro por la Vida y la Familia,'" *Radio San Miguel*, 19 October 2010, http://www.bolivia-riberalta.com/blog.php/ ?p=6964. Finally, the organization Family and Human Life, mentioned above, has represented an important wing of the pro-life movement in La Paz and El Alto since its founding in 2005. Leandro Rubén, La Paz, 3 December 2009. The group held a conference in La Paz in 2009 at which participants condemned the World Health Organization (WHO) and other international organizations for "promoting programs and legislation on sexual and reproductive rights in order to legalize abortion." "Apoyan proyectos de salud sexual y reproductiva para legalizar el aborto," *El Diario*, 19 June 2009. To my knowledge, all of the pro-life organizations in Bolivia share affiliations with Human Life International, a U.S.-based pro-life organization with offices worldwide. Carolina Llano, La Paz, 5 May 2010; Leandro Rubén, La Paz, 3 December 2009. See also Htun, *Sex and the State*, 151.

172. Interview with Daniel Báez, La Paz, 6 April 2010; "Las iglesias evangélicas se instalan en el eje central," *La Razón*, July 10, 2011, http://la-razon.com/nacional /iglesias-evangelicas-instalan-eje-central_0_1428457149.html.

173. Conferencia Episcopal Boliviana (CEB), "Propuesta de la Iglesia Católica en Bolivia a la Asamblea Constituyente," 2007, http://www.iglesiacbba.org/descar gas/docs/cartacons.pdf, 2.

174. CEB, "Propuesta de la Iglesia Católica en Bolivia a la Asamblea Constituyente," 8.

175. Article 15 of the constitution declares that "Every person has a right to life and to physical, psychological, and sexual integrity." Constitución Política del Estado, February 7, 2009.

176. Daniel Báez, La Paz, 6 April 2010; Carolina Llano, La Paz, 5 May 2010. See also "Iglesias cristianas de Bolivia contrarias a muchos artículos de la constitución del MAS," *Hoybolivia.com*, January 13, 2009, http://hoybolivia.com/Noticia.php ?IdNoticia=9912.

177. "Plantean ley de educación sexual en vez de la de aborto." See also Mariano Solana, La Paz, 30 April 2010.

178. Catholics for a Free Choice, *Attitudes of Catholics on Reproductive Rights, Church-State, and Related Issues: Three National Surveys in Bolivia, Colombia and Mexico* (Washington, DC: Belden Russonello & Steward Research and Communications, 2003), n.p.

179. Catholics for a Free Choice, *Attitudes of Catholics*, n.p.

180. Daisy Serrato, La Paz, 7 October 2009.

CHAPTER 2 — DOUBLE DISCOURSES: SOCIAL ATTITUDES
ON SEXUALITY AND REPRODUCTION

Epigraphs: Julián Costa, La Paz, 3 July 2009; Briggs, *Reproducing Empire*, 201.

1. Daisy Serrato, La Paz, 7 October 2009.

2. Shepard, "The 'Double Discourse' on Sexual and Reproductive Rights in Latin America," 114.

3. Shepard, "The 'Double Discourse' on Sexual and Reproductive Rights in Latin America," 111. See also Pieper Mooney, *The Politics of Motherhood*, 51.

4. Cisneros, *El aborto inducido*, 12.

5. Cisneros, *El aborto inducido*, 12.

6. Paxman et al., "The Clandestine Epidemic," 206.

7. Viel, "Latin America," 321.

8. Ipas Bolivia, *Las cifras hablan: El aborto es un problema de salud pública* (La Paz: Ipas, 2011), 11. Interviews with a number of individuals also support this assertion.

9. Viel, "Latin America," 321. See Alanes, *El aborto en Bolivia*, 8 and Paxman et al., "The Clandestine Epidemic," 206.

10. World Health Organization (WHO), *Unsafe Abortion: Global and Regional Estimates of the Incidence of Unsafe Abortion and Associated Mortality in 2008* (Geneva: WHO, 2011), 19. WHO defines an unsafe abortion "as a procedure for terminating a . . . pregnancy carried out either by persons lacking the necessary skills or in an environment that does not conform to minimum medical standards, or both" (2).

11. Paxman et al., "The Clandestine Epidemic," 205–206; Viel, "Latin America," 318–319. Ann Zulawski notes that, as of 1928, high infant mortality in Bolivia continued to limit family size. Zulawski, *Unequal Cures*, 121.

12. Paxman et al., "The Clandestine Epidemic," 206.

13. Pieper Mooney, *The Politics of Motherhood*, 50; Paxman et al., "The Clandestine Epidemic," 206.

14. Pieper Mooney, *The Politics of Motherhood*, 51.

15. Viel, "Latin America," 321. See also Pieper Mooney, *The Politics of Motherhood*, 54.

16. Monica Weisner, "Induced Abortion in Chile, with References to Latin American and Caribbean Countries," paper presented at the annual meeting of the Population Association of America, cited in Paxman, et al., "The Clandestine Epidemic," 206–207.

17. Paxman et al., "The Clandestine Epidemic," 206.

18. In her review of the data for these years, Zulawski found that incomplete abortion represented "the single most important cause for admission" to the gynecological department of the hospital. Zulawski, *Unequal Cures*, 140. This figure likely included some cases of spontaneous miscarriage.

19. Cisneros, *El aborto inducido*, 12.

20. Cisneros, *El aborto inducido*, 55–57.

21. Cisneros, *El aborto inducido*, 58.

22. Cisneros, *El aborto inducido*, 58.

23. Luis Kushner López, Luis Llano Saavedra, and Patricia Elizabeth Bailey, *Investigación de los aspectos sociales y médicos de la pérdida de embarazo: Análisis de resultados* (La Paz: Sociedad Boliviana de Ginecología y Obstetricia and Family Health International [FHI], 1986), 10–14.

24. Kushner López, Llano Saavedra, and Bailey, *Investigación de los aspectos sociales y médicos de la pérdida de embarazo*, 13.

25. Kushner López, Llano Saavedra, and Bailey, *Investigación de los aspectos sociales y médicos de la pérdida de embarazo*, 20–21.

26. Kushner López, Llano Saavedra, and Bailey, *Investigación de los aspectos sociales y médicos de la pérdida de embarazo*, 32.

27. Susheela Singh and Deirdre Wulf, "The Likelihood of Induced Abortion among Women Hospitalized for Abortion Complications in Four Latin American Countries," *International Family Planning Perspectives* 19, no. 4 (December 1993): 134.

28. Kushner López, Llano Saavedra, and Bailey, *Investigación de los aspectos sociales y médicos de la pérdida de embarazo*, 13–14.

29. Singh and Wulf, "The Likelihood of Induced Abortion," 136.

30. Singh and Wulf, "The Likelihood of Induced Abortion," 134–136.

31. I am grateful to a hospital official for sharing these data. In these statistics, unlike those for the 1990s, pregnancy losses are defined as numbers of manual vacuum aspiration procedures (or *aspiración manual endo-uterina*, hereafter abbreviated AMEU) that were performed for each year. The AMEU procedure would only have been performed on incomplete pregnancy losses of twenty weeks' gestational age or less, which means that pregnancy losses of greater than twenty

weeks are not included in these figures. As for the data from the 1990s, numbers of visits do not necessarily equal numbers of patients.

32. I am grateful to a hospital official for sharing these data. Total numbers of pregnancy losses in HMBH data include all abortions, miscarriages, and unexplained miscarriages resolved by any treatment method.

33. Bury et al., "Hidden Realities," S4–S5.

34. This means that one in eight women who had engaged in sexual intercourse had also terminated a pregnancy. Bury et al., "Hidden Realities," S4–S5.

35. In the 1970s, WHO defined WRA as women between the ages of fifteen and forty-four; this was later expanded to include women up to the age of forty-nine. WHO, *Reproductive Health Indicators: Guidelines for Their Generation, Interpretation and Analysis for Global Monitoring* (Geneva: WHO Press, 2006). Researchers in Latin America measuring abortion incidence during these years did not always specify the ages of the women included in their studies. Cisneros employs the category of WRA in his 1976 study of abortion in Bolivian cities but does not mention the ages of the women he interviewed—which means that his estimates of abortion rates may not be comparable to those found in other studies. Kushner López et al. also employ WRA, remarking that their definition of the category matched the standards of Bolivia's 1976 census. It is unclear, however, how that census defined WRA. Bolivia's next demographic and health survey, conducted in 1989, defined WRA as women aged fifteen to forty-nine, in line with WHO's updated designation of the category.

36. In La Paz and El Alto, many of these providers, fearing detection from police, cannot safely maintain records of the abortions they perform.

37. Kushner López, Llano Saavedra, and Bailey, *Investigación de los aspectos sociales y médicos de la pérdida de embarazo,* 17; interview data.

38. Interview data.

39. Viel argues that rates of induced abortion decreased in Chile due to an increase in the use of birth control. "Latin America," 320–321.

40. Aliaga Bruch, *No fue fácil para nadie,* 47–87; Nelson, "Birth Rights," 196–207; Rance, *Planificación familiar;* Schuler, Choque, and Rance, "Misinformation, Mistrust, and Mistreatment"; interview data.

41. This study is cited in Rance, *Planificación familiar,* 77–79.

42. INE, *ENDSA* (1989), 42. The ENDSA includes among traditional methods periodic abstinence, withdrawal, and "other methods," likely herbal infusions.

43. Karina Felitti, "Family Planning in 1960s Argentina: An Original Latin American Case?" paper presented at the 15th Berkshire Conference on the History of Women, Amherst, Massachusetts, June 12, 2011, 5–10. For more on the development of contraceptive programs in Latin America, see Jorge Balán and

Silvina Ramos, *Las decisiones anticonceptivas en un contexto restrictivo: El caso de los sectores populares en Buenos Aires* (Liège, Belgium: International Union for the Scientific Study of Population [IUSSP], 1990); Sonia Correa, *Los derechos sexuales y reproductivos en la arena política* (Montevideo: Mujer y Salud en Uruguay [MYSU], 2003); Karina Felitti, "Derechos reproductivos y políticas demográficas en América Latina" *Iconos: Revista de Ciencias Sociales* no. 35 (September 2009): 55–66; Ximena Jiles and Claudia Rojas, *De la miel a los implantes: Historia de las políticas de regulación de la fecundidad en Chile* (Santiago: Corporación de Salud y Políticas Sociales, 1992); Juan José Llovet and Silvina Ramos, "La planificación familiar en Argentina: Salud pública y derechos humanos" *Cuadernos Médico- Sociales* 38 (December 1986): 25–39; Raúl Necochea López, *A History of Family Planning in Twentieth-Century Peru* (Chapel Hill: University of North Carolina Press, 2014), and Joana María Pedro, "A experiência com contraceptivos no Brasil: Uma questão de geração" *Revista Brasileira de História* 23, no. 45 (2003): 239–260, among others.

44. Rance, *Planificación familiar,* 88

45. This study is cited in Rance, *Planificación familiar,* 89.

46. Schuler, Choque, and Rance, "Misinformation, Mistreatment, and Mistrust," 214.

47. Schuler, Choque, and Rance, "Misinformation, Mistreatment, and Mistrust," 214.

48. INE, *ENDSA* (2003), 91.

49. Marcela Flores, La Paz, 22 September 2009. Interviews with women who feared the negative health impacts of contraception either in the past or currently are too numerous to cite here comprehensively.

50. Cited in Rance, *Planificación familiar,* 89.

51. Schuler, Choque, and Rance, "Misinformation, Mistreatment, and Mistrust," 211. See also Claudia de la Quintana, Gretzel Jové, and Carmen Velasco, *Salud reproductiva en población migrante: Estudio comparativo El Alto-Sucre* (La Paz: PROMUJER, 1998), 21–30.

52. Schuler, Choque, and Rance, "Misinformation, Mistreatment, and Mistrust," 211–221.

53. Women interviewees who report having experienced mistreatment at public health facilities are too numerous to cite here comprehensively but included women of Aymara and Quechua descent and mestizas. See also Bury et al., which found that women seeking postabortion care often experience mistreatment at health facilities. Bury et al., "Hidden Realities," S8.

54. Schuler, Choque, and Rance "Misinformation, Mistreatment, and Mistrust," 211; interview data.

55. Weismantel, *Cholas and Pishtacos*, 209. See also Bastien, *Healers of the Andes*, 47, 67–76; Crandon-Malamud, *From the Fat of Our Souls*, 119–121; Zulawski, *Unequal Cures*, 33.

56. Zulawski, *Unequal Cures*, 33.

57. Weismantel, *Cholas and Pishtacos*, 217.

58. Rachel K. Jones et al., "Better Than Nothing or Savvy Risk-Reduction Practice? The Importance of Withdrawal," *Contraception* 79 (June 2009): 407.

59. Marianne C. Burkhart et al., "Effectiveness of a Standard-Rule Method of Calendar Rhythm among Mayan Couples in Guatemala," *International Family Planning Perspectives* 26, no. 3 (September 2000): 134.

60. Schuler, Choque, and Rance, "Misinformation, Mistreatment, and Mistrust," 216.

61. Schuler, Choque, and Rance, "Misinformation, Mistreatment, and Mistrust," 216. The 1983 study also cited "the husband's opposition" as a central factor deterring women from using western-derived forms of birth control. Cited in Rance, *Planificación familiar*, 90.

62. Bury et al., "Hidden Realities," S5. See also Lidia Limachi, "Embarazos, anticoncepción y derechos sexuales y reproductivos," in Susanna Rance, coord., *Abriendo el paquete envuelto: Violencias y derechos en la ciudad de El Alto* (La Paz: Centro de Promocíon de la Mujer Gregoria Apaza and Solidaridad Internacional Bolivia, 2009), 45–52.

63. Forty-nine percent of women surveyed were utilizing some form of contraception, with 39 percent of these using a western-derived method. Bury et al., "Hidden Realities," S5.

64. Miguel Ramírez, La Paz, 21 October 2009.

65. Morgan and Roberts, "Reproductive Governance in Latin America," 241.

66. Matthew C. Gutmann, *The Meanings of Macho: Being a Man in Mexico City*, 10th Anniversary Edition (Berkeley and Los Angeles: University of California Press, 2007).

67. Judith Butler, *Gender Trouble: Feminism and the Subversion of Identity* (New York: Routledge, 1990); Gutmann, *The Meanings of Macho*, 222; Stoler, *Carnal Knowledge and Imperial Power*; Wade, *Race and Sex in Latin America*.

68. Canessa, *Intimate Indigeneities*, 220–228; Gill, *Teetering on the Rim*, 104–132.

69. Concepción Camacho, El Alto, 5 November 2009.

70. Paula Rojas, La Paz, 30 September 2009.

71. Elsa Canqui, La Paz, 19 October 2009.

72. Antonia Rocio, La Paz, 26 May 2010. Limachi also makes this argument in "Embarazos, anticoncepción y derechos sexuales y reproductivos," 52.

73. Idelia Parra, La Paz, 10 November 2009.

74. Dolores Ticahuanca, El Alto, 7 December 2009.

75. Idalina Achuta, El Alto, 10 March 2010.

76. Beatriz Chasqui, El Alto, 13 October 2009. The expression "to take care of oneself" has been translated from the Spanish, "*cuidarse*," which is commonly used to mean preventing pregnancy through the use of modern forms of birth control or other methods of fertility regulation.

77. Sandra Laura, El Alto, 13 October 2009.

78. Lorena Mercado, La Paz, 7 July 2009.

79. Fessler, *The Girls Who Went Away*; Ellen Messer and Kathryn May, *Back Rooms: Voices from the Illegal Abortion Era* (Buffalo: Prometheus Books, 1988); Peterman, *Telling Their Stories*; Wainer, *Lost*.

80. Fanny Barrutia, La Paz, 18 June 2009.

81. Ida Torralba, La Paz, 19 June 2009.

82. Muriel Rodríguez, El Alto, 7 December 2009.

83. Stefania Montoya, El Alto, 3 February 2010.

84. It is unclear which government ministry planned to distribute the condoms.

85. Gotkowitz, *A Revolution for Our Rights*, 121–122.

86. Belén Cuellar, La Paz, 30 September 2009.

87. Natividad Colque, El Alto, 16 June 2009.

88. Rigoberta Justiniano, El Alto, 10 March 2010.

89. Rosalind Petchesky, "Fetal Images: The Power of Visual Culture in the Politics of Reproduction," *Feminist Studies* 13, no. 2 (Summer 1987): 264.

90. Leandro Rubén, La Paz, 3 December 2009.

91. Mariano Solana, La Paz, 30 April 2010.

92. Carolina Llano, La Paz, 5 May 2010.

93. Julina López, La Paz, 18 March 2010.

94. Interview with several members of the Community Police Force in La Paz, 18 March 2010; this police officer was one of the members.

95. Jumila Quiroga, La Paz, 24 May 2010.

96. Daniel Báez, La Paz, 6 April 2010.

97. Carla Yupanqui, El Alto, 2 February 2010.

98. Juana Choque and Adela López, La Paz, 1 July 2009. This practice is also discussed in Dibbits and Pabón, *Granizadas, bautizos y despachos*, 102, and Filomena Nina Huarcacho, *Detrás del cristal con que se mira: Mujeres del Altiplano, órdenes normativos e interlegalidad* (La Paz: Editora Presencia, 2009), 72.

99. Canessa, *Intimate Indigeneities*, 52.

100. Canessa, *Intimate Indigeneities*, 52–53; 128–134. See also Arnold and Yapita, "Los caminos de género en Qaqachaka," 318, 350.

101. Crandon-Malamud, *From the Fat of Our Souls*, 122.

102. Platt, "El feto agresivo."

103. Platt, "El feto agresivo," 128.

104. Dibbits and Pabón, *Granizadas, bautizos y despachos*, 74–75.

105. Morgan, "Imagining the Unborn in the Ecuadoran Andes," 329. See also Canessa, *Intimate Indigeneities*, 128.

106. Morgan and Roberts, "Reproductive governance in Latin America," 246–247.

107. Hernández and Canessa, eds., *Género, complementaridades y exclusions en Mesoamérica y los Andes*, 10–11; Rousseau, "Indigenous and Feminist Movements at the Constituent Assembly in Bolivia," 17–18.

108. Rivera Cusicanqui, "The Notion of 'Rights' and the Paradoxes of Postcolonial Modernity," 31. See also Harris, *To Make the Earth Bear Fruit*, 164–179.

109. Rousseau, "Indigenous and Feminist Movements at the Constituent Assembly in Bolivia," 17.

110. Morgan, "Imagining the Unborn in the Ecuadoran Andes," 344.

111. Canessa, *Intimate Indigeneities*, 145; Harris, *To Make the Earth Bear Fruit*, 186.

112. Geidel, *Peace Corps Fantasies*, 223.

113. Geidel, *Peace Corps Fantasies*, 224.

114. Geidel, *Peace Corps Fantasies*, 226.

115. Hernández and Canessa, eds., *Género, complementariedades y exclusiones*, 13. See also Rousseau, "Indigenous and Feminist Movements at the Constituent Assembly in Bolivia," 17.

116. This quote is taken from an article by Susan Moller Okin, "Is Multiculturalism Bad for Women?" cited in Hernández and Canessa, eds., *Género, complementariedades, y exclusiones*, 11. See also Burman, "Chachawarmi"; Marisol de la Cadena, "'Women Are More Indian': Ethnicity and Gender in a Community near Cuzco," in Larson and Harris, *Ethnicity, Markets, and Migration in the Andes*, 329–348.

117. Moller Okin, "Is Multiculturalism Bad for Women?" 11. See also Burman, "Chachawarmi," 87.

118. Rivera Cusicanqui, "The Notion of 'Rights' and the Paradoxes of Postcolonial Modernity," 32.

119. Rousseau, "Indigenous and Feminist Movements at the Constituent Assembly in Bolivia," 17.

120. Freya Schiwy, "'No queremos ser un capítulo en tu libro': Notas sobre heterogeneidad, colonialidad, y zonas refractarias," in Monasterios, *No pudieron con nostotras*, 191. See also Raquel Alfaro, "Mujeres Creando Comunidad: Feminización de la comunidad," *Bolivian Studies Journal* 15–17 (2008–2010): 211–236; Julieta Paredes and Comunidad Mujeres Creando Comunidad, *Hilando fino: Desde el feminismo comunitario* (La Paz: Comunidad Mujeres Creando Comunidad, 2010); and interview data.

121. Julieta Paredes and Comunidad Mujeres Creando Comunidad, *Hilando fino*, 78.

122. Burman, "Chachawarmi," 85.

123. Catherine B. McNamee, "Wanted and Unwanted Fertility in Bolivia: Does Ethnicity Matter?" *International Perspectives on Sexual and Reproductive Health* 35, no. 4 (December 2009): 166. See also Geidel, *Peace Corps Fantasies*, 226.

124. In 2010, sexual and reproductive rights organization Ipas implemented an initiative to build consensus with indigenous organizations on the issue of abortion. Ipas Bolivia, *El aborto desde la mirada de las organizaciones indígenas* (2012).

125. Manuela Pacari, La Paz, 7 July 2009. *Salir adelante* is a common phrase in Bolivia that sometimes, but not always, has economic connotations.

126. Maita Perez, El Alto, 24 November 2009.

127. This survey, entitled "Masculinidades," was conducted by the La Paz–based organization CIDEM, whose representatives interviewed fifty men door-to-door in El Alto in 2008. I am grateful to the organization for providing me with transcripts of the interviews.

128. Muriel Rodríguez, El Alto, 7 December 2009.

CHAPTER 3 — FEELINGS, ATTITUDES, AND DECISIONS:
REPRODUCTIVE DECISION MAKING IN THE URBAN ANDES

1. Paula Rojas, La Paz, 30 September 2009.

2. Although there is evidence that some women facing unwanted pregnancy in the Andes end up relying on extended kinship networks to raise the resulting children, none of the women I interviewed told me that they did so. For more on kinship in the Andes, see Van Vleet, *Performing Kinship* and Mary Weismantel, "Making Kin: Kinship Theory and Zumbagua Adoptions," *American Ethnologist* 22, no. 4 (1995): 685–709.

3. Magda Cusi, El Alto, 28 January 2010.

4. Guaygua, Rivera, and Quisbert, *Ser jóven en El Alto*, 15.

5. Belinda López, El Alto, 22 October 2009.

6. Belinda López, El Alto, 22 October 2009.

7. See Maura's comments at the beginning of the introduction.

8. Alma Tarqui, La Paz, 7 July 2009.

9. Ida Torralba, La Paz, 17 June 2009.

10. Magda Cusi, El Alto, 28 January 2010.

11. Jazmín Cahuana, El Alto, 30 November 2009.

12. Simona Pinto, El Alto, 24 February 2010.

13. Pilar Mendoza, El Alto, 30 October 2009.

14. Noel Terrazas, El Alto, 17 November 2009.

15. Maura Choque, El Alto, 30 November 2009.

16. Margot Suárez, El Alto, 18 February 2010.

17. See, for instance, Arnold and Yapita, *Las wawas del Inka*; Dona L. Davis and Setha Low, eds., *Gender, Health, and Illness: The Case of Nerves* (New York: Hemisphere, 1989); Morgan, "Imagining the Unborn in the Ecuadoran Andes," 343–344; Platt, "El feto agresivo;" and Scheper-Hughes, *Death without Weeping*.

18. Tapias, *Embodied Protests*, 49.

19. Maria Tapias, "'Always Ready and Always Clean'? Competing Discourses of Breast-feeding, Infant Illness and the Politics of Mother-blame in Bolivia," *Body and Society* 12, no. 2 (June 2006): 84.

20. Tapias, "Always Ready," 95.

21. Morgan, "Imagining the Unborn in the Ecuadoran Andes," 345.

22. Tapias, "Always Ready," 83–108.

23. Gill, *Teetering on the Rim*, 2. See also Daniel Goldstein, *The Spectacular City: Violence and Performance in Urban Bolivia* (Durham: Duke University Press, 2004), 11–14.

24. Julio César Velasco, *La crisis mundial vista desde Bolivia: Lecturas económica y política (2008–2011)* (La Paz: Fundación Konrad Adenauer, 2011), 275–278.

25. Miguel Rivas, "En 5 años, El Alto registró 107 feminicidios, 21 por gestión," *La Razón* October 18, 2013, http://www.la-razon.com/ciudades/anos-Alto-registro -feminicidios-gestion_0_1927007316.html.

26. Simona Pinto, El Alto, 24 February 2010.

27. Bastien, *Healers of the Andes*, 24. Herbalists are discussed in greater detail in chapter 4.

28. Natividad Colque, El Alto, 16 June 2009. "Daria" is a pseudonym.

29. Marcela Flores, interviewed in La Paz on 22 September 2009, asserted that abortion caused urinary incontinence; Mili Quisbert, interviewed in El Alto on 16 November 2009, said the procedure caused body aches; Yessica Ticona, interviewed in El Alto on 9 November 2009, claimed abortion could lead to cancer; and Elsa Canqui and Felicidad Chambi, interviewed in La Paz on 19 October 2009 and 26 October 2009, respectively, stated that abortion caused unspecified physical problems.

30. Yessica Ticona, El Alto, 9 November 2009.

31. Camila Quelca, El Alto, 11 February 2010.

32. Alma Tarqui, La Paz, Bolivia, 7 July 2009.

33. Belinda López, El Alto, 22 October 2009; Maura Choque, El Alto, 30 November 2009.

34. Rigoberta Justiniano, El Alto, 10 March 2010.

35. Paula Rojas, La Paz, 30 September 2009. See also Maura's comments at the beginning of the introduction.

36. Peterman, *Telling Their Stories*, 3–4.

37. Jazmín Cahuana, El Alto, 30 November 2009.

38. Jazmín Cahuana, El Alto, 30 November 2009.

39. Maternowska, *Reproducing Inequities*.

40. Pilar Mendoza, El Alto, 30 October 2009.

41. Marcela Flores, La Paz, 22 September 2009.

42. Graciela Flores, La Paz, 22 September 2009.

43. INE, *ENDSA* (2003), 279.

44. Adela López, La Paz, 1 July 2009.

45. Vania Condori, La Paz, 2 December 2009.

46. Marcela Flores, La Paz, 22 September 2009; Pilar Mendoza, El Alto, 30 October 2009. See also Bury et al., "Hidden Realities," S6–S7.

47. Lupe Colque, La Paz, 29 June 2009.

48. Noel Terrazas, El Alto, 17 November 2009. "Marco" is a pseudonym.

49. Adela López, La Paz, 1 July 2009.

50. Olga Mollo, La Paz, 7 October 2009.

51. Roe v. Wade 410 U.S. 113 (1973).

52. Solinger, *Beggars and Choosers*, 6.

53. Minna Stern, *Eugenic Nation*; Schoen, *Choice and Coercion*.

CHAPTER 4 — NAVIGATING UNWANTED PREGNANCY IN LA PAZ AND EL ALTO, 1950S–1980S

1. Magda Cusi, El Alto, 28 January 2010.

2. Gallien, "Delivering the Nation, Raising the State," 111; Pacino, "Creating Madres Campesinas," 78.

3. Gallien, "Delivering the Nation, Raising the State;" Sociedad Boliviana de Salud Pública, *Salud pública en Bolivia*, 271–282.

4. Gallien, "Delivering the Nation, Raising the State;" Zulawski, *Unequal Cures*, 120.

5. However, indigenous *parteras* were sometimes erroneously referred to as *empíricas* in medical literature. Arnold and Yapita, "Los caminos de género en

Qaqachaka," 333; Gallien, "Delivering the Nation, Raising the State," 34–43; Zulawski, *Unequal Cures*, 136–141.

6. Gallien, "Delivering the Nation, Raising the State," 41–42; Zulawski, *Unequal Cures*, 31, 136–138.

7. Gallien, "Delivering the Nation, Raising the State," 48–52.

8. Gallien, "Delivering the Nation, Raising the State," 43–48; Zulawski, *Unequal Cures*, 25–28.

9. Gallien, "Delivering the Nation, Raising the State," 51; Zulawski, *Unequal Cures*, 119–120.

10. Gallien, "Delivering the Nation, Raising the State," 88–90.

11. Maria Lucia de Barros Mott, "Madame Durocher, modista e parteira," *Estudos Feministas* 2, no. 1 (1994): 101–116; Jean Donnison, *Midwives and Medical Men: A History of the Struggle for the Control of Childbirth* (New Barnet, England: Historical Publications, 1977); Barbara Ehrenreich and Deirdre English, *For Her Own Good: Two Centuries of Medical Experts' Advice to Women* (New York: Random House, 2005); Federici, *Caliban and the Witch*; María Soledad Zárate, *Dar a luz en Chile, Siglo XIX: De la 'ciencia de hembra' a la ciencia obstétrica* (Santiago: Centro de Investigaciones Barros Arana and the University of Alberto Hurtado, 2007); Zulawski, *Unequal Cures*, 6–7, 136–138.

12. Gallien, "Delivering the Nation, Raising the State," 52–53.

13. Gallien, "Delivering the Nation, Raising the State," 62, 74–83; Pacino, "Creating Madres Campesinas"; Zulawski, *Unequal Cures*, 138–139.

14. Gallien, "Delivering the Nation, Raising the State"; Zulawski, *Unequal Cures*, 138.

15. Gallien, "Delivering the Nation, Raising the State," 111; Mendizábal Lozano, *Historia de la salud pública en Bolivia*, 196; Pacino, "Creating Madres Campesinas," 77–78.

16. Pacino, "Creating Madres Campesinas," 66.

17. Sociedad Boliviana de Salud Pública, *Salud pública en Bolivia*, 90, 271–272.

18. Arnold and Yapita, "Los caminos de género en Qaqachaka"; Bastien, *Healers of the Andes*; Crandon-Malamud, *From the Fat of Our Souls*; Louis Girault, *Kallawaya: Curanderos itinerantes de los Andes* (La Paz: Impresores Quipus, 1987); Loza, *El laberinto de la curación*; Zulawski, *Unequal Cures*.

19. See, for instance, differences in how these practitioners are described in Bastien, *Healers of the Andes*, 21–26; Crandon-Malamud, *From the Fat of Our Souls*, 128–129; Loza, *El laberinto de la curación*, 20–25; and Lynn Sikkink, *New Cures, Old Medicines: Women in the Commercialization of Traditional Medicine in Bolivia* (Belmont, CA: Wadsworth, 2010), 24. According to Loza, while the differences between these providers are palpable, the institutionalization of traditional

medicine in recent years, as well as the tendency for individuals facing economic crisis to fraudulently claim the identities and expertise of some of these
healers, hinders an accurate and comprehensive understanding of these practitioners. The impact of the institutionalization on understandings of traditional
medical practitioners is described in more detail in chapter 5. Loza, *El laberinto
de la curación*, 21. Louis Girault asserts that Kallawaya healers complained of
imposters claiming Kallawaya identity and expertise as far back as the 1960s.
Girault, *Kallawaya*, 24–25. On regional variation in terms used for traditional
medical practitioners, see also Anders Burman, *Indigeneity and Decolonization
in the Bolivian Andes: Ritual Practice and Activism* (New York: Lexington Books,
2016), 36–37.

20. Bastien, *Healers of the Andes*, 38; Ineke Dibbits, "Población Aymara," in
Roosta, *Salud materna en contextos de interculturalidad*, 77–79; Llanos Cervantes,
"El embarazo en mujeres Aymaras migrantes," 116; Zulawski, *Unequal Cures*,
31–32.

21. Bastien, *Healers of the Andes*; Crandon-Malamud, *From the Fat of Our Souls*;
Loza, *El laberinto de la curación*; Zulawski, *Unequal Cures*, 31–36.

22. Bastien, *Healers of the Andes*, 39.

23. Bastien, *Healers of the Andes*, preface, unnumbered page, 24. Much has been
written about the medical knowledge and social and cultural history of the Kal-
lawaya. See, among others, Bastien, *Drum and Stethoscope*; Bastien, *Healers of the
Andes*; Crandon-Malamud, *From the Fat of Our Souls*, 42–43; Girault, *Kallawaya*;
Carmen Beatriz Loza, *Kallawaya: Reconocimiento mundial a una ciencia de los
Andes* (La Paz: Talleres Sagitario, 2004); and Loza, *El laberinto de la curación*.

24. Zulawski, *Unequal Cures*, 32. See also Bastien, *Healers of the Andes*, 1–6.

25. Bastien, *Healers of the Andes*, 38–55; Zulawski, *Unequal Cures*, 32–34.

26. Bastien, *Healers of the Andes*, 46.

27. *Healers of the Andes*, 51.

28. Bastien, *Healers of the Andes*, 45–52.

29. Zulawski, *Unequal Cures*, 33–34. See also Arnold and Yapita, "Los caminos
de género en Qaqachaka," 309.

30. Bastien, *Healers of the Andes*, 11, 28–29; Loza, *El laberinto de la curación*, 51.

31. Women have played central roles as providers of Andean medicine, although
Loza contends that this has often been overlooked in anthropological literature
on the subject as well as in official documents, which has contributed to a persistent
tendency toward their invisibility. Loza, *El laberinto de la curación*, 45–49. Scholarship from the 1990s sheds some light on women's roles as Kallawayas, *yatiris*,
and, especially, as providers of reproductive health care, including abortion and
childbirth. Chief among these are works by Denise Y. Arnold and Juan de Dios

Yapita, whose studies of various aspects of Aymara life in rural areas of the altiplano have been seminal in contributing to our understandings of women as providers (and users) of Andean medicine. See, for instance, "Los caminos de género en Qaqachaka"; *Las wawas del Inka*; *Río de vellón, río de canto*, and *Vocabulario aymara del parto y de la vida reproductiva de la mujer*.

32. Loza, *El laberinto de la curación*, 48–61.

33. Bastien, *Healers of the Andes*, 5, 25; Loza, *El laberinto de la curación*, 43.

34. Cited in Loza, *El laberinto de la curación*, 44.

35. Loza, *El laberinto de la curación*, 43–45; Sikkink, *New Cures, Old Medicines*, 27. There were a number of other providers of traditional medicine who operated in La Paz and El Alto across some portion of the twentieth century, including practitioners identified by the following names: *yatiri* and *amawta* (sometimes written *amauta* or *amaut'a*), who are typically known as traditional doctors and wise men; *ch'amakani*, who are spiritual providers, and *laika* (or *layqa*), often described as more malevolent spiritual practitioners. More general terms, such as *curandero, qulliri , espiritista , herbolaria* , and *naturista*, were also commonly used, sometimes as synonyms for one or more the above providers.

36. Irene Silverblatt, *Moon, Sun, and Witches: Gender Ideologies and Class in Inca and Colonial Peru* (Princeton, NJ: Princeton University Press, 1987).

37. Federici, *Caliban and the Witch*, 219–243; Loza, *El laberinto de la curación*, 47; Sikkink, *New Cures, Old Medicines*, 12; Silverblatt, *Moon, Sun, and Witches*, xvii–xxxii, 159–210.

38. Rolando Costa, Eduardo Estrella, and Fernando Cabieses, *Bibliografía anotada de medicina tradicional (Bolivia, Ecuador, Peru)* (Quito: Universidad Andina Simón Bolívar, 1998), 7–18. On the function of medical journals, see Zulawski, *Unequal Cures*, 36.

39. Gallien, "Delivering the Nation, Raising the State," 109.

40. Bastien, *Healers of the Andes*, 23–26; Loza, *El laberinto de la curación*, 44–45; Sociedad Boliviana de Salud Pública, *Salud pública en Bolivia*, 277.

41. Bastien, *Healers of the Andes*, 34–41; Gallien, "Delivering the Nation, Raising the State;" Girault, *Kallawaya*, 24; Loza, *El laberinto de la curación*, 44–45; Pacino, "Creating Madres Campesinas"; Zulawski, *Unequal Cures*.

42. Arnold and Yapita, "Los caminos de género en Qaqachaka;" Arnold and Yapita, *Las Wawas del Inka*; Bastien, "Birth Rituals," in Bastien, *Mountain of the Condor*, 85–102; Joseph Bastien and Nancy Edens, "Midwives and Maternal and Infant Health Care," in Bastien, *Drum and Stethoscope*, 137–169; Canessa, *Intimate Indigeneities*, especially 119–165 and 216–280; Dibbits and Pabón, *Granizadas, bautizos y despachos*; Llanos Cervantes, "El embarazo en mujeres Aymaras migrantes"; Nash, "Belief and Behavior in Family Life," in Nash, *We Eat the Mines and*

the Mines Eat Us, 57–86; June Nash, *I Spent my Life in the Mines: The Story of Juan Rojas, Bolivian Tin Miner* (New York: Columbia University Press, 1992), 115–120, 136–139; Platt, "El feto agresivo"; Roosta, *Salud materna en contextos de interculturalidad.*

43. Arnold and Yapita, "Los caminos de género en Qaqachaka," 309–311.

44. Llanos Cervantes, "El embarazo en mujeres Aymaras migrantes," 121.

45. Llanos Cervantes, "El embarazo en mujeres Aymaras migrantes," 122. See also Arnold and Yapita, "Los caminos de género en Qaqachaka," 311, 339; Bastien and Edens, "Midwives and Maternal and Infant Health Care," 138–141.

46. Guillermina Arcani, La Paz, 8 February 2010.

47. Canessa, *Intimate Indigeneities,* 125; Platt, "El feto agresivo," 139.

48. Carla Yupanqui, El Alto, 2 February 2010.

49. *Intimate Indigeneities,* 127.

50. Sikkink, *New Cures, Old Medicines,* 25. See also Baer, "Contributions to a Critical Analysis of Medical Pluralism," 45.

51. It is unclear what markers might differentiate a *chiflera* from a K'awayu in an urban market setting, although scholarship suggests that the latter have a distinct ethnic identity, cultural tradition, and degree of medical expertise not necessarily shared by all chifleras. Bastien characterizes most chifleras operating in La Paz in the 1980s as mestiza and differentiates these from both men and women Kallawaya herbalists who operated market stands in the city. Bastien, *Healers of the Andes,* 24. Sikkink notes the following of women vendors of traditional medicines at markets in rural areas: "Although not technically considered 'healers,' these vendors fill the primary role in a 'hierarchy of resort' for many lower-order ailments, and especially for 'women's complaints.'" Sikkink, *New Cures, Old Medicines,* 26.

52. Gisbert and Quitón Prado, "Mujer sub-urbana y prácticas del aborto en la ciudad de El Alto de La Paz, Bolivia," 19, and medical records and interviews with a number of women and medical providers. Many of these herbs were also used to induce abortion or to facilitate delivery in other geographical and historical contexts. See, for other areas of Bolivia, Arnold and Yapita, *Las wawas del Inka,* 225–229; Canessa, *Intimate Indigeneities,* 128–130; Nash, *We Eat the Mines and the Mines Eat Us,* 62–63. For other geographical regions, see John M. Riddle, *Eve's Herbs: A History of Contraception and Abortion in the West* (Cambridge: Harvard University Press, 1997) and Londa Schiebinger, "Exotic Abortifacients," in Schiebinger, *Plants and Empire,* 105–149.

53. Quoted in María Silvia Elizabeth Benitez Reyes, "El tortuoso camino de la mujer con aborto complicado: Entre la ley y los servicios de salud" (Licensure thesis, Universidad Mayor de San Andrés [UMSA], Sociología, La Paz, 2000)," 91.

NOTES TO PAGES 158–161

54. Several women I interviewed also obtained their abortions from providers in these zones.

55. Marcela Flores, La Paz, 22 September 2009.

56. Muriel Rodríguez, El Alto, 7 December 2009.

57. Benitez Reyes, "El tortuoso camino de la mujer con aborto complicado," 91.

58. Interviews with numerous individuals in Bolivia as well as medical record data support these assertions. These methods were used in a variety of Latin American countries in which the procedure is widely prohibited. Aníbal Faúndes and José S. Barzelatto, *The Human Drama of Abortion: A Global Search for Consensus* (Nashville, TN: Vanderbilt University Press, 2006), 22–24; Paxman et al., "The Clandestine Epidemic," 208.

59. Bury et al., "Hidden Realities," S7; Kushner López, Llano Saavedra, and Bailey, *Investigación de los aspectos sociales y médicos de la pérdida de embarazo*, 18–19; interviews with abortion providers.

60. Patricia E. Bailey et al., "Estudio hospitaliario del aborto ilegal en Bolivia," *Boletín de la Oficina Sanitaria Panamericana* 104, no. 2 (1988): 144–158; Kushner López, Llano Saavedra, and Bailey, *Investigación de los aspectos sociales y médicos de la pérdida de embarazo*; interviews with medical doctors.

61. Bury et al., "Hidden Realities," S7–S8; Bailey et al., "Estudio hospitaliario del aborto ilegal en Bolivia," 149–151; interview data.

62. Sociedad Boliviana de Salud Pública, *Salud pública en Bolivia*, 90. As of 2010, there were approximately 25,309 existing medical records from the INA spanning the years from 1955 to 1983; each of the records represents one or more visits by a woman to the facility. Most, or 274, of the books of records were housed at the Archivo Histórico La Paz (La Paz Historical archive, ALP); the remaining fifty-six books were housed in the statistics department at the HM. I was unable to locate any records for the years 1984–1993. During the course of my research, I examined approximately 12,386 of the records, or close to 49 percent—but this percentage did not hold steady across all of the years of the collection, since there were a different number of books of records available for each year. Of the 12,386 records that I reviewed, 2,033 (or about 16 percent) included evidence of a woman's current or previous experience with abortion, miscarriage, unexplained miscarriage, or stillbirth.

63. Adrián Espinoza, La Paz, 8 October 2009.

64. The difference between these figures could be due to a few different factors—and may suggest a few different things. Since the term *aborto* does not distinguish between abortion and miscarriage, some of the women included in the 1,745 figure may have intentionally terminated their pregnancies, rather than suffered accidental or spontaneous pregnancy loss. This could be true either

because women provided false information or were intentionally vague when reporting their reproductive histories or because medical personnel did not inquire about or document the type of *aborto* a woman experienced (or both). Throughout this chapter, I have relied on notations by medical personnel in counting and designating cases of abortion and of spontaneous, accidental, and unexplained miscarriage. (In other words, if a medical chart designates a woman's pregnancy loss as a spontaneous miscarriage, I have accepted that designation, regardless of the circumstances detailed in the chart.) Notations of *aborto provocado* and *aborto inducido* are counted as abortion; of *aborto espontáneo* as spontaneous miscarriage, and of *aborto accidentado* and *aborto traumático* as accidental miscarriage; reproductive experiences designated simply as *aborto* are counted as unexplained miscarriage. Spontaneous and accidental miscarriage are counted and referred to as "true" miscarriages; however, unexplained miscarriages are not. I have also designated as spontaneous miscarriages those pregnancy losses that were caused by medical conditions, such as placenta previa. The gestational histories of some women who visited the INA during these years were not recorded by medical staff—and thus, more women may have had abortions or miscarriages than appear here.

65. The remaining women either were not asked where their first abortions took place or declined to respond. I only report quantitative data on each woman's first abortion. ALP INA, 1955–1965.

66. ALP INA December 1968: 2503.

67. ALP INA February–March 1981: 3022.

68. ALP INA August 1966: 1493.

69. ALP INA October 1973: 2246.

70. ALP INA October 1973: 2246.

71. Most of the cases of pregnancy loss during these years constituted unexplained miscarriage, wherein medical personnel did not document the cause (or suspected cause) of the loss.

72. ALP INA May–June 1955: 51.

73. ALP INA March 1961: 853.

74. ALP INA May–June 1955: 44. The notation made by medical staff in Spanish reads, "Relata haber sentido la ruptura de la bolsa de las aguas, a consecuencia de un accidente traumático a todas luces falso." The question mark appears in the original handwritten document.

75. ALP INA May 1956: 139. This notation in Spanish reads, "La enferma no recuerda o no haberse dado cuenta [sic] el haber estado embarazada."

76. ALP INA January 1963: 1058.

77. ALP INA September 1965: 1386. It is unclear when this woman had her abortion or how many children she may have had at that time.

78. ALP INA December 1956: 262.

79. ALP INA April–May 1960: 731.

80. Adrián Espinoza, La Paz, 8 October 2009.

81. For instance, between 1959 and 1966, when medical charts asked personnel to record the cause of a patient's miscarriage or abortion, pregnancy losses that were reportedly caused by accidents reached over 64 percent, while for years during which charts did *not* ask the cause of the pregnancy loss, this figure amounted to less than 1 percent.

82. Kushner López, Llano Saavedra, and Bailey report that 42 percent of women in their study who were hospitalized for postabortion complications refused to tell medical personnel who had provoked the abortion due to the illegality of the procedure. *Investigación de los aspectos sociales y médicos de la pérdida de embarazo*, 17.

83. Dirección General de Estadística y Censos, *Censo Demográfico República de Bolivia* (La Paz: Ministerio de Hacienda y Estadística, 1950), 2.

84. Camila Quelca, El Alto, 11 February 2010.

85. Magda Cusi, El Alto, 28 January 2010.

86. Gotkowitz, *A Revolution for Our Rights*, 121.

87. Gotkowitz, *A Revolution for Our Rights*, 121.

88. Law No. 177, 15 January 1962. Accessed May 20, 2015. http://www.lexivox.org /norms/BO-L-177.xhtml.

89. Nelly Mamani, El Alto, 1 March 2010.

90. Elsa Canqui, La Paz, 19 October 2009.

91. Lesley Gill examines the experiences of women who migrated from the rural countryside to La Paz where they ended up working as domestic employees. Gill, *Precarious Dependencies.*

92. Van Vleet, *Performing Kinship*, 101.

93. Van Vleet, *Performing Kinship*, 103.

94. Van Vleet, *Performing Kinship*, 103–108.

95. Canessa, *Intimate Indigeneities*, 140–143. See also Luis Millones and Mary Louise Pratt, *Amor brujo: Imagen y cultura del amor en los Andes* (Lima: Instituto de Estudios Peruanos, 1989).

96. Canessa, *Intimate Indigeneities*, 130.

97. Oral historians note that interviewees' present emotional circumstances can shape the contours of their memories. See, for instance, Yow, *Recording Oral History*, 50–51.

98. Elba Claros, La Paz, 24 September 2009.

99. Tapias, *Embodied Protests*, 2.

100. See, for instance, Libbet Crandon-Malamud, "Why Susto?" *Ethnology* 22 (1983): 153–167; Morgan, "Imagining the Unborn in the Ecuadoran Andes," 343; Roberts, *God's Laboratory*, 96; and Arthur Rubel, *Susto: A Folk Illness* (Berkeley: University of California Press, 1984).

101. The term "dual use" is employed by Baer in "Contributions to a Critical Analysis of Medical Pluralism," 45.

102. Baer, "Contributions to a Critical Analysis of Medical Pluralism," 45.

103. William C. Olsen and Carolyn Sargent, "Introduction," in Olsen and Sargent eds., *African Medical Pluralism*, 3.

CHAPTER 5 — UNWANTED PREGNANCY AND ABORTION
IN THE WAKE OF DEMOCRACY, 1982-2010

Epigraphs: Emma Alvarez, La Paz, 19 June 2009; Estado Plurinacional de Bolivia and MSD, *Plan Estratégico Nacional de Salud Sexual y Reproductiva 2009–2015*, Serie: Documentos Técnico-Normativos (La Paz: Excelsior, 2010), 13.

1. Emilia Santana, El Alto, 10 February 2010.

2. Sociedad Boliviana de Salud Pública, *Salud pública en Bolivia*, 526.

3. Gallien, "Delivering the Nation, Raising the State," 177–179, 198–200.

4. Gallien, "Delivering the Nation, Raising the State," 177–179, 198–200.

5. Gallien, "Delivering the Nation, Raising the State," 215.

6. Gallien, "Delivering the Nation, Raising the State," 198–219.

7. Gallien, "Delivering the Nation, Raising the State," 218.

8. Arnold and Yapita, *Las wawas del Inka*, 22. See also Arnold and Yapita, with Tito, *Vocabulario aymara del parto y de la vida reproductiva de la mujer*.

9. Guillermina Arcani, La Paz, 8 February 2010.

10. Leticia Quispe, El Alto, 24 February 2010.

11. Carla Yupanqui, El Alto, 2 February 2010.

12. Arnold and Yapita, *Las wawas del Inka*, 13–15; Arnold and Yapita, "Los caminos de género en Qaqachaka"; Bastien and Edens, "Midwives and Maternal and Infant Health Care," 138–139; Canessa, *Intimate Indigeneities*, 127.

13. Deby Babis, "The Role of Civil Society Organizations in the Institutionalization of Traditional Medicine in Bolivia," *Social Science & Medicine* 123 (2014): 291; Bolivia, "Resolución Suprema: 198771," *Gaceta Oficial*, January 10, 1984, http://gacetaoficialdebolivia.gob.bo/index.php/resolucions/ultimasResoluciones/page:2080/ayuda:La%20búsqueda%20se%20realizará%20en%20el%20LISTADO%20DE%20ULTIMAS%20RESOLUCIONES; Loza, *Kallawaya*, 134–135; Loza, *El laberinto de la curación*, 89–90; WHO Unit on Traditional Medicine,

Legal Status of Traditional Medicine and Complementary/Alternative Medicine (Geneva: WHO, 2001), 44.

14. Babis, "The Role of Civil Society Organizations in the Institutionalization of Indigenous Medicine in Bolivia," 292.

15. Bolivia, "Decreto Supremo 26874," December 21, 2002, http://www.derechoteca.com/gacetabolivia/decreto-supremo-26874-del-21-diciembre-2002/.

16. Bolivia, "Decreto Supremo 26875," December 21, 2002, https://www.lexivox.org/norms/BO-DS-26875.xhtml; Loza, *El laberinto de la curación*, 93–94.

17. Loza, *Kallawaya*, 178.

18. Yolanda Vargas, "Salud Familiar Comunitaria Intercultural (SAFCI)," in *Salud materna en contextos de interculturalidad*, coord. Manigeh Roosta, 36–37.

19. Jobita Sandy Choque, Paulina Ramos, and Sergio Suxo Mamani, "Salud Familiar Comunitario Intercultural—SAFCI," in *Antecedentes, situación actual, y perspectivas de la salud intercultural en América Latina*, comp. Víctor Manuel del Cid Lucero (Managua, Nicaragua: Universidad de las Regiones Autónomas de la Costa Caribe Nicaragüense, 2008), 94–102; Ministerio de Salud y Deportes, *Guía de atención intercultural de la salud materna*, Serie: Documentos Técnicos Normativos (La Paz: MSD, 2005); Vargas, "Salud Familiar Comunitaria Intercultural (SAFCI)," 37–55.

20. Luca Citarella Menardi, "Desarrollo de la salud intercultural en Bolivia: Desde las experiencias locales a la políticas públicas de salud," in *Yachay tinkuy: Salud e interculturalidad en Bolivia y América Latina,* ed. Luca Citarella Menardi, Alessia Zangari, and Roberto Campos Navarro (La Paz: Editorial Gente Común, 2010), 5; Brian B. Johnson, "Decolonization and Its Paradoxes: The (Re) envisioning of Health Policy in Bolivia," *Latin American Perspectives* 37, no. 3 (May 2010): 145.

21. "Modelo de salud familiar comunitario intercultural," Decreto Supremo 29601, June 11, 2008, https://www.lexivox.org/norms/BO-DS-29601.xhtml. Like the earlier parto limpio programs, SAFCI was undergirded by the 1978 Alma-Ata Declaration and its emphasis on primary health care, community participation in health systems, and the integration of traditional medicine into biomedical models. Choque, Ramos, and Mamani, "Salud Familiar Comunitario Intercultural—SAFCI," 94–99; Johnson, "Decolonization and Its Paradoxes," 146; MSD, *Salud Familiar Comunitaria Intercultural: Documento técnico-estratégico* (La Paz: MSD, 2013), 9.

22. Johnson, "Decolonization and Its Paradoxes," 145–147; MSD, *Salud Familiar Comunitario Intercultural*, 41.

23. Johnson, "Decolonization and Its Paradoxes," 146.

24. Johnson, "Decolonization and Its Paradoxes," 147.

25. Johnson, "Decolonization and Its Paradoxes," 147–148.

26. Johnson, "Decolonization and Its Paradoxes," 148.

27. INE, *Encuesta de Demografía y Salud 2016 (EDSA 2016), Bolivia: Indicadores Priorizados* (La Paz: INE, 2017), 21.

28. INE, *EDSA 2016*, 21.

29. INE, *EDSA 2016*, 43; "En 9 años, el Bono Juana Azurduy benefició a mas de dos millones de madres y niños," *MSD Unidad de Comunicación*, May 22, 2018, https://www.minsalud.gob.bo/3271-9no-aniv-bja.

30. Ley 459, "Law of Traditional Ancestral Bolivian Medicine," December 19, 2013, https://www.minsalud.gob.bo/images/Documentacion/normativa/ley-459 -edicin-596nec.pdf.

31. Verónica Zapana Salazar, "Salud registra a 4.778 kallawayas en Bolivia y alista su legalización," *Página Siete*, August 11, 2016, https://www.paginasiete.bo /sociedad/2016/8/11/salud-registra-4778-kallawayas-bolivia-alista-legalizacion -105838.html.

32. Paola Flores, "Bolivia suma a parteras a lucha contra mortalidad materna," *Associated Press*, August 3, 2017, https://www.apnews.com/4ebe3102eda7417597a7 ea6c4bbba6b7.

33. "Bolivia: Parteras, guías espirituales, naturistas y médicos tradicionales iniciarán registro de pacientes," *MSD Unidad de Comunicación*, October, 10, 2017, https://www.minsalud.gob.bo/2765-bolivia-parteras-guias-espirituales -naturistas-y-medicos-tradicionales-iniciaran-registro-de-pacientes.

34. Johnson, "Decolonization and Its Paradoxes," 150–156.

35. Johnson, "Decolonization and Its Paradoxes," 151.

36. Johnson, "Decolonization and Its Paradoxes," 153–155; Loza, *El laberinto de la curación*; Carmen Beatriz Loza, Review of *Salud e Interculturalidad en América Latina: Antropología de la Salud y Crítica Intercultural*, coord. Gerardo Fernández Juárez, *Chungara: Revista de Antropología Chilena*, 42, no. 2 (2010): 543–547.

37. Loza, *El laberinto de la curación*, 76; Organización Mundial de la Salud (OMS), *Estrategia de la OMS sobre medicina tradicional 2002–2005* (Geneva: OMS, 2002).

38. Loza, *El laberinto de la curación*, 76.

39. Loza, *El laberinto de la curación*, 88.

40. "Denuncian que yatiris y naturistas se disputan cargos," *Erbol Digital*, October 21, 2014, http://www.erbol.com.bo/noticia/social/21102014/denuncian_que _yatiris_y_naturistas_se_disputan_cargos.

41. Sikkink, *New Cures, Old Medicines*, 137.

42. Loza, *El laberinto de la curación*, 21–22.

43. Loza, *El laberinto de la curación*, 75–104; Sikkink, *New Cures, Old Medicines*, 136–142.

44. Loza, *El laberinto de la curación*, 79.

45. Loza, *El laberinto de la curación*, 152.

46. Sociedad Boliviana de Salud Pública, *Salud pública en Bolivia*, 393.

47. Antonio J. Cisneros C., Germán La Fuente, and Carlos Koch, *La capacitación técnica de los farmacéuticos: Un studio evaluativo de aprendizaje* (La Paz: Centro de Investigaciones Sociales, 1985), 20; Sociedad Boliviana de Salud Pública, *Salud pública en Bolivia*, 390–393.

48. Sociedad Boliviana de Salud Pública, *Salud pública en Bolivia*, 394.

49. Sociedad Boliviana de Salud Pública, *Salud pública en Bolivia*, 526.

50. Gonzálo Mario Vidaurre Andrade, *El negocio de la muerte: Comercio informal de medicamentos en Bolivia* (La Paz: UPS Publicidad, 2018), 12. See also Loza, *El laberinto de la curación*, 17.

51. David Estrada, El Alto, 30 March 2010.

52. Del Pozo and Alanes Bravo, *Marcando un hito en Bolivia*; MSD, *Plan Nacional de Maternidad y Nacimiento Seguros (2004–2008)*; MSD, *Módulo de Capacitación para el Facilitador en Tratamiento a Mujeres con Hemorragias de la Primera Mitad del Embarazo* (La Paz: MSD, USAID, and Catalyst/Pathfinder International, 2005).

53. Alessandra Muñecas, La Paz, 19 June 2009.

54. Daisy Serrato, La Paz, 7 October 2009.

55. MSD, *Plan Nacional de Maternidad y Nacimiento Seguros (2004–2008)*, 11–12.

56. David Estrada, El Alto, 30 March 2010.

57. Adrián Espinoza, La Paz, 8 October 2009.

58. The length of hospital stays at the HM in cases of incomplete pregnancy loss were significantly reduced following the introduction of the AMEU in the late 1990s. At the HMBH, the AMEU was already widely used by 2005, and medical records reveal that most patients with incomplete miscarriage and abortion were treated and released on the same day.

59. David Estrada, El Alto, 30 March 2010. According to Ipas, the first reports of misoprostol's use in pregnancy termination in Latin America originated in Brazil in 1986. Ipas, *Misoprostol and Medical Abortion in Latin America and the Caribbean* (Chapel Hill: Consorcio Latinoamericano Contra el Aborto Inseguro [CLACAI] and Ipas, 2010), 3.

60. Between 1988 and 2000, a number of other countries legalized medical abortion, including Israel, Norway, Sweden, Taiwan, and South Africa. NAF, "Medical Abortion: History and Overview," http://www.prochoice.org/education/resources/med_history_overview.html.

61. Bury et al. "Hidden Realities," S4–S9; Ipas, *Misoprostol and Medical Abortion in Latin America and the Caribbean*; Jessica Cohen et al., "Reaching Women with Instructions on Misoprostol Use in a Latin American Country," *Reproductive Health Matters* 13, no. 26 (November 2005): 85; interview data.

62. HM November 1995: 2086; HMBH October 2007: 1487.

63. HM March 1998: 2639.

64. Lidia Alvarado, La Paz, 2 July 2009.

65. For confidentiality reasons, I am unable to provide additional details about these providers; however, testimonies of medical personnel who work at these facilities, as well as of activists and women who have procured abortions, illustrate the differences between these new, ideologically motivated clinics and many of the clinics that existed previously.

66. Miguel Ramírez, La Paz, 21 October 2009.

67. Olga Mollo, La Paz, 7 October 2009.

68. Daisy Serrato, La Paz, 7 October 2009.

69. The 1994 figure is reported in Del Pozo and Alanes Bravo, *Marcando un hito en Bolivia*, 14, while the 2011 figure is reported in Ministerio de Salud, Dirección General de Planificación, and Sistema Nacional de Información en Salud y Vigilancia Epidemiológica, *Estudio Nacional de Mortalidad Materna 2011: Resumen Ejecutivo*, Serie: Documentos de Investigación No. 44 (La Paz: Gráfika Leal, 2016), 13.

70. In their 2012 study of abortion in Bolivia, Bury et al. reported that, of 152 urban-dwelling women who had ever terminated a pregnancy, between 34 and 39 percent of these did so on their own (or attempted to do so) by ingesting medications or herbal infusions or inflicting physical trauma on themselves. "Hidden Realities," S7.

71. Bury et al., "Hidden Realities," S8.

72. Ministerio de Salud, Dirección General de Planificación, and Sistema Nacional de Información en Salud y Vigilancia Epidemiológica, *Estudio Nacional de Mortalidad Materna 2011*, 15.

73. "Bolivia declara el 2018 como año de la vigilancia de la muerte materna y lanza el Sistema Informático de Perinatal Plus," OPS/OMS Destacados, accessed September 22, 2018, https://www.paho.org/bol/index.php?option=com _content&view=article&id=2106:bolivia-declara-el-2018-como-ano-de-la-vigilancia -de-la-muerte-materna-y-lanza-el-sistema-informatico-de-perinatal-plus&Ite mid=481.

74. Bury et al., "Hidden Realities," S4; Ipas, *Misoprostol and Medical Abortion in Latin America and the Caribbean*, 4; Jhenny Nava B., "Casos de aborto suben

en los últimos seis años y se practican en casa," *Opinión.com.bo,* August 30, 2017, http://www.opinion.com.bo/opinion/articulos/2017/0830/noticias.php?id =228997.

75. Bury et al., "Hidden Realities," S7–S8.

76. "Salud investigará a las farmacias," *La Prensa,* March 19, 2007, 8a, cited in Loza, *El laberinto de la curación,* 92; Vidaurre Andrade, *El negocio de la muerte,* 67.

77. Bury et al., "Hidden Realities," S7; Margarita Palacios, "Abortos clandestinos se hacen por 300 a 1.000 bolivianos," *Página Siete,* October 5, 2013, https://www.paginasiete.bo/sociedad/2013/10/6/abortos-clandestinos-hacen -1000-bolivianos-2383.html. According to interview data, the cost of a single tablet of misoprostol at pharmacies in La Paz and El Alto may vary from about US$0.50 to US$15.00. David Estrada, El Alto, 30 March 2010; Stefania Montoya, El Alto, 3 February 2010, and Emilia Santana, El Alto, 10 February 2010.

78. Ipas, *Misoprostol and Medical Abortion in Latin America and the Caribbean,* 4.

79. Emma Alvarez, La Paz, 16 June 2009; David Estrada, El Alto, 30 March 2010; Alessandra Muñecas, La Paz, 19 June 2009; Miguel Ramírez, La Paz, 21 October 2009; Daisy Serrato, La Paz, 7 October 2009.

80. Daisy Serrato, La Paz, 7 October 2009.

81. Alma Tarqui, La Paz, 7 July 2009.

82. Noel Terrazas, El Alto, 17 November 2009.

83. Lorena Mercado, La Paz, 7 July 2009.

84. Marcela Flores, La Paz, 22 September 2009.

85. Adela Lopez, La Paz, 1 July 2009.

86. The procedure was banned in Romania for more than twenty years under the rule of Nicolae Ceaușescu, during which over 9,000 women died due to unsafe abortion. *4 Months, 3 Weeks, and 2 Days,* directed by Cristian Mungiu (BAC Films, 2007), DVD, 113 minutes; Ann Furedi, "On abortion, we should study Romanian history," *The Guardian,* January 15, 2013, https://www.theguardian.com/commentis free/2013/jan/15/abortion-romanian-history.

87. Lupe Colque, La Paz, 29 June 2009.

88. Lorena Mercado, La Paz, 7 July 2009.

89. Pilar Mendoza, El Alto, 30 October 2009.

90. Miguel Ramírez, La Paz, 21 October 2009.

91. Muriel Rodríguez, La Paz, 7 December 2009.

92. Cati Molina, La Paz, 18 June 2009.

93. Lupe Colque, La Paz, 29 June 2009.

94. Pilar Mendoza, El Alto, 30 October 2009.

95. Lorena Mercado, La Paz, 7 July 2009; Nina Rojas, El Alto, 16 November 2009.

96. Lupe Colque, La Paz, 29 June 2009.

97. Adela Lopez, La Paz, 1 July 2009.

98. Celestina Chambi, El Alto, 16 November 2009.

CHAPTER 6 — ABORTION AND THE LAW IN LA PAZ AND EL ALTO

Epigraphs: Olivia Harris, ed., *Inside and Outside the Law: Anthropological Studies of Authority and Ambiguity* (New York: Routledge, 1996), n.p.; Betina Aguilar, La Paz, 6 July 2009.

1. Eduardo Castillo, El Alto, 19 February 2010.

2. Bury et al., "Hidden Realities"; Messer and May, *Back Rooms*; Wainer, *Lost*.

3. Hugo A. Michel Altamirano, "El aborto" (Licensure thesis, UMSA, Facultad de Ciencias Jurídicas y Políticas, La Paz, 1980), 142.

4. Michel Altamirano, "El aborto," 142.

5. Benitez Reyes, "El tortuoso camino de la mujer con aborto complicado," Appendix 3.3. It is unclear how many of these complaints resulted in arrests or convictions.

6. This according to Eduardo Castillo, El Alto, 19 February 2010, and statistics provided to the author by the General Command of the Bolivian Police reflecting arrests for abortion from January 2005 to December 2009. The year 2008 saw the most arrests, with four in El Alto and seven in La Paz. In 2005 and 2006, there were no arrests made in either La Paz or El Alto for abortion.

7. Liliana Carrillo Valenzuela, "Este mes detuvieron a siete mujeres acusadas de abortar," *Página Siete*, August 28, 2017, https://www.paginasiete.bo/sociedad/2017/8/28/este-detuvieron-siete-mujeres-acusadas-abortar-149915.html.

8. Eduardo Castillo, El Alto, 19 February 2010.

9. "Abortos provocan daños y perforación de órganos," *El Diario*, August 28, 2008.

10. "Autoridades dejan de lado control de clínicas ilegales," *El Diario*, February 22, 2009.

11. Benitez Reyes, "El tortuoso camino," 93–122.

12. Quoted in Benitez Reyes, "El tortuoso camino," 114. The individual who performed María's abortion claimed to be a gynecologist, but La Paz's Medical School failed to locate any record of him, suggesting that he was not in fact a licensed doctor. Benitez Reyes, "El tortuoso camino," 92.

13. Michel Altamirano, "El aborto," 143.

14. Eduardo Castillo, El Alto, 19 February 2010.

15. *Ley Orgánica del Ministerio Público*, Ley 2175, February 13, 2001, http://bolivia.infoleyes.com/shownorm.php?id=304.

16. Michel Altamirano, "El aborto," 143.

17. Elvira Cruz Vera, "El aborto en la ciudad de La Paz" (Licensure thesis, UMSA, Derecho, La Paz, 2004), 28–30. Writing in 2007, Friedman-Rudovsky asserted that, "There is no record of any doctors or patients involved [in abortion cases] being prosecuted [in Bolivia]." Friedman-Rudovsky, "Abortion under Siege in Latin America."

18. Cruz Vera, "El aborto en la ciudad de La Paz," 28.

19. The outcome of these cases is unclear. I am grateful to Laura Gotkowitz for sharing this information.

20. Alanes, El aborto en Bolivia, 9.

21. "Autoridades dejan de lado control de clínicas ilegales," El Diario, February 22, 2009.

22. Davíd Estrada, El Alto, 30 March 2010. A number of interviewees asserted that police regularly bribe abortion providers. See, in La Paz, Betina Aguilar, 6 July 2009; Emma Alvarez, 16 June 2009; Miguel Ramírez, 21 October 2009; Daisy Serrato, 7 October 2009.

23. Daisy Serrato, La Paz, 7 October 2009.

24. Miguel Ramírez, La Paz, 21 October 2009.

25. Julián Costa, La Paz, 3 July 2009.

26. In these cases, women either admitted that their abortions were provoked or medical staff encountered physical evidence of the abortion, or both. It is unclear whether staff would make a notation in a woman's medical chart if they had reported her to police. However, a discharge date is noted in each of these records, suggesting that patients who provoked their abortions were allowed to leave the facility unhindered.

27. HM December 1995: 2210.

28. "Brazil Abortions: Illegal in Name Only," New York Times, July 21, 1991.

29. David Estrada, El Alto, 30 March 2010.

30. Adrián Espinoza, La Paz, 8 October 2009.

31. Miguel Ramírez, La Paz, 21 October 2009. It is unclear when this case occurred.

32. Alessandra Muñecas, La Paz, 19 June 2009.

33. Eduardo Castillo, El Alto, 19 February 2010.

34. Faúndes and Barzelatto, The Human Drama of Abortion, xv–xvi, emphasis added.

35. Necochea López, A History of Family Planning in Twentieth-Century Peru, 53.

36. Faúndes and Barzelatto, The Human Drama of Abortion, 140.

37. Soledad Domínguez, Cuando el valor rompe el silencio: Crónica del primer aborto legal realizado en Bolivia (Sucre: Centro Juana Azurduy, 1999), 6–34. It is unclear if the author altered the names of the individuals involved in this case; I have maintained the names that appear in the original text.

38. Quoted in Domínguez, *Cuando el valor rompe el silencio*, 32.

39. Domínguez, *Cuando el valor rompe el silencio*, 24.

40. Domínguez, *Cuando el valor rompe el silencio*, 9–10.

41. Cruz Vera, "El aborto en la ciudad de La Paz," 31–32.

42. Julián Costa, La Paz, 3 July 2009.

43. Nika Coelho, La Paz, 4 July 2009.

44. Domínguez, *Cuando el valor rompe el silencio*, 31.

45. Harris, "Introduction," in *Inside and Outside the Law*, 2.

46. Harris, "Introduction," 10.

47. Shepard, "The 'Double Discourse' on Sexual and Reproductive Rights in Latin America," 114.

48. Shepard, "The 'Double Discourse' on Sexual and Reproductive Rights in Latin America," 115.

49. Gretchen Helmke and Steven Levitsky, "Introduction," in *Informal Institutions & Democracy: Lessons from Latin America,* ed. Gretchen Helmke and Steven Levitsky (Baltimore: Johns Hopkins University Press, 2006), 5. Emphasis in original. See also Georgina Waylen, "Informal Institutions, Institutional Change, and Gender Equality," *Political Research Quarterly* 67, no. 1 (March 2014): 212–223.

50. Helmke and Levitsky, "Introduction," 3.

51. Htun and Weldon, *The Logics of Gender Justice*, 255.

52. Htun and Weldon, *The Logics of Gender Justice*, 246. Emphasis in original. See also Boesten, *Intersecting Inequalities*, 58–59; Bueno-Hansen, *Feminist and Human Rights Struggles in Peru*, 29.

53. Harris, "Introduction," in *Inside and Outside the Law*, 2. See also Nancy Leys Stepan, "Race, Gender, Science, and Citizenship," *Gender & History* 10, no. 1 (April 1998): 26–52.

54. M. Jacqui Alexander, "Not Just Any (Body) Can Be a Citizen: The Politics of Law, Sexuality and Postcoloniality in Trinidad and Tobago and the Bahamas," *Feminist Review*, no. 48 (Autumn 1994): 5–23.

55. See, for instance, Gilda Sedgh et al., "Induced Abortion: Incidence and Trends Worldwide from 1995 to 2008," *The Lancet* 379 (January 2012): 625–632.

56. Caitlin Gerdts et al., "Women's Experiences Seeking Informal Sector Abortion Services in Cape Town, South Africa: A Descriptive Study," *BMC Women's Health* 17, no. 95 (October 2017): 1.

57. "Targeted Regulation of Abortion Providers," *Guttmacher News Institute,* December 1, 2018, https://www.guttmacher.org/state-policy/explore/targeted-regulation-abortion-providers.

58. Petchesky, *Abortion and Woman's Choice*, 11.

CONCLUSION

Epigraph: Dolores Ticahuanca, El Alto, 7 December 2009.

1. Nelson, "Birth Rights," 269.

2. Pacino, "Creating Madres Campesinas," 65. See also Hamilton, *Sexual Revolutions in Cuba*; Tinsman, *Partners in Conflict*.

3. Loza, *Kallawaya*, 134.

4. Gill, *Teetering on the Rim*; Lazar, *El Alto, Rebel City*.

5. Gallien, "Delivering the Nation, Raising the State," 223.

6. Alfaro, "Mujeres Creando Comunidad;" Leonardo García-Pabón, "Sensibilidades Callejeras: El trabajo estético y político de 'Mujeres Creando,'" *Revista de Crítica Literaria Latinoamericana* 29, no. 58, Poesía y Globalización (2003): 239–254; Monasterios, *No pudieron con nostotras*; Julieta Paredes and María Galindo, *Machos, varones, y maricones: Manual para conocer tu sexualidad por ti mismo* (La Paz: Ediciones Mujeres Creando, 2000); Julieta Paredes and María Galindo, *Sexo, sexualidad, y placer: Manual para conocer tu sexualidad por ti misma* (La Paz: Ediciones Mujeres Creando, 1998).

7. See, for instance, Burman, "Chachawarmi"; Andrew Canessa, "The Indian Within, the Indian Without: Citizenship, Race, and Sex in a Bolivian Hamlet," in *Natives Making Nation*, ed. Andrew Canessa, 130–155; María Eugenia Choque, *Chacha warmi: Imaginarios y vivencias en El Alto* (El Alto: CPMGA, 2009); Harris, "Complementarity and Conflict" and "The Power of Signs" in *To Make the Earth Bear Fruit*; Hernández and Canessa, eds., *Género, complementariedades, y exclusiones*; Rivera Cusicanqui, "The Notion of 'Rights' and the Paradoxes of Postcolonial Modernity"; Rousseau, "Indigenous and Feminist Movements at the Constituent Assembly in Bolivia."

8. Burman, "Chachawarmi," 71. See Denise Arnold, "Introducción," in *Más allá del silencio: Las fronteras de género en los Andes*, Volume 1 of *Parentesco y género en los Andes* (La Paz: CIASE/ILCA, 1997), 47.

9. Denise Arnold, "Making Men in her Own Image: Gender, Text, and Textile in Qaqachaka," in Rosaleen Howard-Malverde, ed., *Creating Context in Andean Cultures* (New York and Oxford: Oxford University Press, 1997), 100; Burman, "Chachawarmi," 71–72; Harris, *To Make the Earth Bear Fruit*, 182–183.

10. Rivera Cusicanqui, "The Notion of 'Rights' and the Paradoxes of Postcolonial Modernity," 32. See also Burman, "Chachawarmi," 74–75; Canessa, "The Indian Within, the Indian Without"; Rousseau, "Indigenous and Feminist Movements at the Constituent Assembly in Bolivia," 17.

11. Nancy Leys Stepan, "Race, Gender, Science, and Citizenship," 26–52; Solinger, *Beggars and Choosers*, 6.

12. Silliman et al., *Undivided Rights*, 4.

13. Bourbonnais, *Birth Control in the Decolonizing Caribbean*, 171; Chrisler, *Reproductive Justice*; Gordon, *The Moral Property of Women*, 302.

14. Jolly and Ram, *Borders of Being*, 26. See also Maternowska, *Reproducing Inequities*.

15. Miguel Ramírez, La Paz, 21 October 2009.

16. Marguerite Feitlowitz, *A Lexicon of Terror: Argentina and the Legacies of Torture*, rev. ed. (New York: Oxford University Press, 2011), 58.

17. "El aborto, un gran dolor de cabeza para la salud púbica," *La Razón*, March 20, 1996, A11; Sedgh et al., "Induced Abortion."

Bibliography

ARCHIVES, HOSPITALS, AND COLLECTIONS

Archivo Histórico La Paz (ALP), Instituto de Maternidad "Natalio A. Aramayo" (INA)

Biblioteca y Archivo Histórico del Honorable Congreso Nacional (BAHCN)

Hospital de la Mujer (HM)

Hospital Municipal Boliviano-Holandés (HMBH)

NEWSPAPERS AND PERIODICALS

Agencia EFE

Associated Press

The Atlantic

BBC News

El Comercio

El Deber

El Diario

Erbol Digital

The Guardian

Guttmacher News Institute

Hoybolivia.com

New York Times

Opinión.com.bo

Página Siete

El País

La Prensa

Radio San Miguel

La Razón

Los Tiempos

Time

PERSONAL CORRESPONDENCE

Aguilar, Betina (pseud.). Electronic correspondence. 15 February 2011.

———. "Informe mensual." La Paz, July 2009.

Barrutia, Fanny (pseud.). Electronic correspondence. 30 November 2012.

Preto, Dina (pseud.). Electronic correspondence. 23 March 2012.

UNPUBLISHED MANUSCRIPTS AND REPORTS

Benitez Reyes, María Silvia Elizabeth. "El tortuoso camino de la mujer con aborto complicado: Entre la ley y los servicios de salud." Licensure thesis, Universidad Mayor de San Andrés (UMSA), Sociología, La Paz, 2000.

Carmona Cervantes, Julio. "Incidencia del aborto en Sucre como problema de salud años 1970–1979." Doctoral thesis, Universidad Boliviana Mayor, Real, y Pontífica de San Francisco Xavier de Chuquisaca, Médico Cirujano, Sucre, 1981.

Centro de Información y Desarrollo de la Mujer (CIDEM). "Masculinidades." La Paz, 2008.

Claure, Bernarda. "Tiempo de descuento en debate sobre aborto en la Asamblea Constituyente." 2007. Accessed December 4, 2012. http://www.lafogata.org /07latino/latino7/bol.4.8.htm.

Conferencia Episcopal Boliviana (CEB). "Propuesta de la Iglesia Católica en Bolivia a la Asamblea Constituyente." 2007. Accessed March 12, 2013. http:// www.iglesiacbba.org/descargas/docs/cartacons.pdf.

Cruz Vera, Elvira. "El aborto en la ciudad de La Paz." Licensure thesis, UMSA, Derecho, La Paz, 2004.

Federación Nacional de Trabajadoras del Hogar de Bolivia. "Propuestas hacia la Asamblea Constituyente." La Paz, 2006.

Gisbert, María Elena, and Mery Quitón Prado. "Mujer sub-urbana y prácticas del aborto en la ciudad de El Alto de La Paz, Bolivia." La Paz, December 1992.

Michel Altamirano, Hugo A. "El Aborto." Licensure thesis, UMSA, Facultad de Ciencias Jurídicas y Políticas, La Paz, 1980.

Villalpando, Abelardo. "Un año de experiencia de la reforma agraria en Potosí." Bolivian Political Pamphlet No. 1110. University of Pittsburgh.

GOVERNMENT DOCUMENTS

Dirección General de Estadística y Censos. *Censo Demográfico República de Bolivia*. La Paz: Ministerio de Hacienda y Estadística, 1950.

Estado Plurinacional de Bolivia. *Constitución Política del Estado*. La Paz, February 7, 2009.

Estado Plurinacional de Bolivia and Ministerio de Salud y Deportes (MSD). *Plan Estratégico Nacional de Salud Sexual y Reproductiva 2009–2015*. Documentos Técnico-Normativos. La Paz: Excelsior, 2010.

Instituto Nacional de Estadística (INE). *Censo nacional*. 1976.

———. *Encuesta de Demografía y Salud 2016 (EDSA 2016), Bolivia: Indicadores Priorizados*. La Paz: INE, 2017.

———. *Encuesta de hogares*. La Paz: INE, 2009; 2007.

————. *Encuesta Nacional de Demografía y Salud (ENDSA)*. La Paz: INE, 2008; 2003; 1994, 1989.

————. *Resultados del censo nacional de población y Vivienda*. La Paz: INE, 1976.

Ministerio de Desarrollo Sostenible, Viceministerio de Planificación, Secretaria Técnica del Consejo de Población para el Desarrollo Sostenible. *El Alto desde una perspectiva poblacional*. La Paz: Punto & Imagen, 2005.

Ministerio de Previsión Social y Salud Pública (MPSSP), Secretaría de la Mujer, Salud, y Desarrollo, and the CEB. *Lucha contra el aborto: Seminario taller*. La Paz: MPSSP, 1989.

Ministerio de Salud, Dirección General de Planificación, and Sistema Nacional de Información en Salud y Vigilancia Epidemiológica. *Estudio Nacional de Mortalidad Materna 2011: Resumen Ejecutivo*. Documentos de Investigación 44. La Paz: Gráfika Leal, 2016.

MSD. *Guía de atención intercultural de la salud maternal*. Documentos Técnicos Normativos. La Paz: MSD, 2005.

————. *Manual de normas, reglas, protocolos y procedimientos técnicos para el manejo de las hemorragias de la primera mitad del embarazo*. La Paz: IPAS, 2006.

————. *Módulo de Capacitación para el Facilitador en Tratamiento a Mujeres con Hemorragias de la Primera Mitad del Embarazo*. La Paz: MSD, USAID, and Catalyst/Pathfinder International, 2005.

————. *Plan Nacional de Maternidad y Nacimiento Seguros (2004–2008)*. La Paz: MSD, Pan American Health Organization (PAHO), and United Nations Population Fund (UNFPA), 2004.

————. *Salud Familiar Comunitario Intercultural: Documento técnico-estratégico*. La Paz: MSD, 2013.

Mujeres Presentes en la Historia. *De la protesta al mandato: Una propuesta en construcción*. La Paz: Proyecto Mujeres y Asamblea Constituyente, 2006.

Navarro, Hubert. *Informe estadístico de Bolivia*. La Paz: Departamento Nacional de Bioestadística, 1953.

República de Bolivia. *Código Penal Bánzer*. La Paz: Empresa Editora "Urquizo Ltda.,"1972.

————. *Código Penal Santa Cruz*. La Paz, 1834.

United States Supreme Court. Roe v. Wade. 410 U.S. 113 (1973).

Viceministerio de Género y Asuntos Generacionales and Cooperación Técnica Alemana. *Mujeres constituyentes*. La Paz: Gesellschaft für Technische Zusammenarbeit, 2007.

SECONDARY SOURCES

Achtenberg, Emily. "For Abortion Rights in Bolivia, A Modest Gain." *NACLA* (February 27, 2014). https://nacla.org/blog/2014/2/28/abortion-rights-bolivia -modest-gain.

Ackerman, Katrina, Kristin Burnett, Travis Hay, and Shannon Stettner, eds. *Transcending Borders: Abortion in the Past and Present.* Cham, Switzerland: Springer Nature, Palgrave Macmillan, 2017.

Adams, Mark, ed. *The Wellborn Science: Eugenics in Germany, France, Brazil, and Russia.* New York: Oxford University Press, 1990.

Adams, Vicanne, Mona Schrempf, and Sienna Craig, eds. *Medicine between Science and Religion: Explorations on Tibetan Grounds.* Oxford: Berghahn Books, 2011.

Ahluwalia, Sanjam. *Reproductive Restraints: Birth Control in India, 1877–1947.* Chicago: University of Chicago Press, 2008.

Alanes, Zulema. *El aborto en Bolivia: Mitos y realidades.* La Paz: Population Council and the Servicio de Información para el Desarrollo (SID), 1995.

Alanes, Zulema, and Susanna Rance, coord. *Una alianza por la salud y los derechos: Memoria del Simposio Interamericano sobre Legislación en Salud Sexual y Reproductiva.* La Paz: Population Council, 1999.

Albó, Xavier. "El Alto, la vorágine de una ciudad única." *Journal of Latin American Anthropology* 11, no. 2 (2006): 329–350.

Alexander, M. Jacqui. "Not Just Any (Body) Can Be a Citizen: The Politics of Law, Sexuality and Postcoloniality in Trinidad and Tobago and the Bahamas." *Feminist Review* no. 48 (Autumn 1994): 5–23.

Alfaro, Raquel. "Mujeres Creando Comunidad: Feminización de la comunidad." *Bolivian Studies Journal* 15–17 (2008–2010): 211–236.

Aliaga Bruch, Sandra. *No fue fácil para nadie: Aproximaciones a una historia de la salud sexual y reproductiva en Bolivia siglo XX.* La Paz: UNFPA and CIDEM, 2004.

Aliaga Bruch, Sandra, Mery Quitón Prado, and María Elena Gisbert. *Veinte historias, un mismo tema: El aborto.* La Paz: Population Council and the Taller de Estudios Sociales (TES), 2000.

Aliaga Bruch, Sandra, Ximena Machicao Barbery, Franklin García Pimentel, and Louise Bury. *Situaciones inevitables: Embarazos no deseados y abortos inseguros en cinco ciudades de Bolivia.* La Paz: Scorpión, 2011.

Amnesty International Report 1981. London: Amnesty International Publications, 1981.

Amonzabel Meneses, Claudia G., and Rosario Paz Ballivián. *Las mujeres rumbo a la asamblea constituyente: Segundo ciclo de seminarios—taller "Participación política y ciudadanía de las mujeres," Noviembre a Diciembre de 2003.* La Paz: FUNDAPPAC and Fundación Konrad Adenauer, 2003.

Andaya, Elise. *Conceiving Cuba: Reproduction, Women, and the State in the Post-Soviet Era.* New Brunswick, NJ: Rutgers University Press, 2014.

Antezana Villegas, Mauricio. *El Alto desde El Alto II.* La Paz: UNITAS, 1992.

Arbona, Juan Manuel. "Dinámicas históricas y espaciales en la construcción de un barrio alteño." *Colombia Internacional* 73 (January–June 2011): 91–120.

Ardaya, Gloria. *Participación política y liderazgos de mujeres en Bolivia.* La Paz: Talleres Gráficos Creativa, 2001.

———. *Política sin rostro: Mujeres en Bolivia.* La Paz: Editorial Nueva Sociedad, 1992.

Armitage, Susan, ed., with Patricia Hart and Karen Weathermon. *Women's Oral History: The* Frontiers *Reader.* Lincoln: University of Nebraska Press, 2002.

Armus, Diego. *Entre médicos y curanderos: Cultura, historia, y enfermedad en la América Latina moderna.* Buenos Aires: Grupo Editorial Norma, 2002.

Arnold, Denise. *Más allá del silencio: Las fronteras de género en los Andes.* Volume 1 of *Parentesco y género en los Andes.* La Paz: CIASE/ILCA, 1997.

———. *The Metamorphosis of Heads: Textual Struggles, Education and Land in the Andes.* Pittsburgh: University of Pittsburgh Press, 2006.

Arnold, Denise Y., and Juan de Dios Yapita. *Las wawas del Inka: Hacia la salud materna intercultural en algunas comunidades andinas.* La Paz: Instituto de Lengua y Cultura Aymara (ILCA), 2002.

———. *Río de vellón, río de canto: Cantar a los animales, una poética andina de la creación.* La Paz: Hisbol and ILCA, 1998.

Arnold, Denise Y., and Juan de Dios Yapita, with Margarita Tito. *Vocabulario aymara del parto y de la vida reproductiva de la mujer.* La Paz: Family Health International and ILCA, 2000.

Babis, Deby. "The Role of Civil Society Organizations in the Institutionalization of Traditional Medicine in Bolivia." *Social Science & Medicine* 123 (2014): 287–294.

Baer, Hans A. *Biomedicine and Alternative Healing Systems in America: Issues of Class, Race, Ethnicity, and Gender.* Madison: University of Wisconsin Press, 2001.

Bailey, Patricia E., Luis Llano Saavedra, Luis Kushner, Michael Welsh, and Barbara Janowitz. "Estudio hospitalario del aborto ilegal en Bolivia." *Boletín de la Oficina Sanitaria Panamericana* 104, no. 2 (1988): 144–158.

Balán, Jorge, and Silvina Ramos. *Las decisiones anticonceptivas en un contexto restrictivo: El caso de los sectores populares en Buenos Aires.* Liège, Belgium: International Union for the Scientific Study of Population (IUSSP), 1990.

Barragán, Rossana. "Entre polleras, lliqllas y ñañacas: Los mestizos y la emergencia de la tercera república." In *Etnicidad, economía, y simbolismo en los Andes,* edited by Silvia Arze, Rossana Barragán, Laura Escobari and Ximena Medinaceli, 85–127. La Paz: Hisbol, Instituto Francés de Estudios Andinos and SBH-ASUR, 1992.

———. "Más allá de lo mestizo, más allá de lo Aymara: Organizaciones y representaciones de clase y etnicidad en La Paz." *América Latina Hoy* 43 (August 2006): 107–130.

Barrios de Chungara, Domitila, with Moema Viezzer. *Let Me Speak!: Testimony of Domitila, a Woman of the Bolivian Mines.* Translated by Victoria Ortiz. New York: Monthly Review Books, 1978.

Bastien, Joseph W. *Drum and Stethoscope: Integrating Ethnomedicine and Biomedicine in Bolivia.* Salt Lake City: University of Utah Press, 1992.

———. *Healers of the Andes: Kallawaya Herbalists and Their Medicinal Plants.* Salt Lake City: University of Utah Press, 1987.

———. *Mountain of the Condor: Metaphor and Ritual in an Andean Ayllu.* Prospect Heights, IL: Waveland Press, 1978.

Behar, Ruth. *The Vulnerable Observer: Anthropology That Breaks Your Heart.* Boston: Beacon Press, 1996.

Berger Gluck, Sherna, and Daphne Patai, eds. *Women's Words: The Feminist Practice of Oral History.* New York: Routledge, 1991.

Beverley, John. *Testimonio: On the Politics of Truth.* Minneapolis: University of Minnesota Press, 2004.

Bhabha, Homi. "Of Mimicry and Man: The Ambivalence of Colonial Discourse." *October* 28 Discipleship: A Special Issue on Psychoanalysis (Spring 1984): 125–133.

Blee, Kathleen. *Women of the Klan: Racism and Gender in the 1920s,* with a new preface. Berkeley and Los Angeles: University of California Press, 2009.

Bleichmar, Daniela, Paula De Vos, Kristin Huffine, and Kevin Sheehan, eds. *Science in the Spanish and Portuguese Empires, 1500–1800.* Stanford: Stanford University Press, 2009.

Bliss, Katherine E. *Compromised Positions: Prostitution, Public Health, and Gender Politics in Revolutionary Mexico City.* University Park: Pennsylvania State University Press, 2001.

Boesten, Jelke. *Intersecting Inequalities: Women and Social Policy in Peru, 1990–2000.* University Park: The Pennsylvania State University Press, 2010.

Bourbonnais, Nicole. *Birth Control in the Decolonizing Caribbean: Reproductive Politics and Practice on Four Islands, 1930–1970.* New York: Cambridge University Press, 2016.

Bourgois, Phillippe. *In Search of Respect: Selling Crack in El Barrio,* 2nd ed. New York: Cambridge University Press, 2003.

Bravo, Ana María. *Democracia, paridad y participación de las mujeres: Desafíos de la asamblea constituyente.* Cochabamba: FUNDAPPAC and Fundación Konrad Adenauer, 2005.

Briggs, Laura. *Reproducing Empire: Race, Sex, Science, and U.S. Imperialism in Puerto Rico.* Berkeley and Los Angeles: University of California Press, 2002.

Bueno-Hansen, Pascha. *Feminist and Human Rights Struggles in Peru: Decolonizing Transitional Justice.* Chicago: University of Illinois Press, 2015.

Burkhart, Marianne C., Lidia de Mazariegos, Sandra Salazar, and Virginia M. Lamprecht. "Effectiveness of a Standard-Rule Method of Calendar Rhythm among Mayan Couples in Guatemala." *International Family Planning Perspectives* 26, no. 3 (September 2000): 131–136.

Burman, Anders. "Chachawarmi: Silence and Rival Voices on Decolonisation and Gender Politics in Andean Bolivia." *Journal of Latin American Studies* 43, no. 1 (February 2011): 65–91.

———. *Indigeneity and Decolonization in the Bolivian Andes: Ritual Practice and Activism.* New York: Lexington Books, 2016.

Bury, Louise, Sandra Aliaga Bruch, Ximena Machicao Barbery, and Franklin García Pimentel. "Hidden Realities: What Women Do When They Want to Terminate an Unwanted Pregnancy in Bolivia." *Journal of Gynecology and Obstetrics* 118 (September 2012): S4–S9.

Butler, Judith. *Gender Trouble: Feminism and the Subversion of Identity.* New York: Routledge, 1990.

Campaignolle, Alice, Irene Escudero, and Carlos Heras. "In Bolivia, a Backlash against Women in Politics." *NACLA Report on the Americas* (November 19, 2018). https://nacla.org/news/2018/11/19/bolivia-backlash-against-women-politicsen-bolivia-una-reacción-violenta-contra-las.

Canessa, Andrew. *Intimate Indigeneities: Race, Sex, and History in the Small Spaces of Andean Life.* Durham, NC: Duke University Press, 2012.

Canessa, Andrew, ed. *Natives Making Nation: Gender, Indigeneity, and the State in the Andes.* Tucson: University of Arizona Press, 2005.

Castro Mantilla, María Dolores, and Silvia Salinas Mülder. *Avances y retrocesos en un scenario cambiante: Reforma en salud, mortalidad materna y aborto en Bolivia, 2000–2002.* La Paz: CIDEM, 2004.

Catholics for a Free Choice. *Attitudes of Catholics on Reproductive Rights, Church-State, and Related Issues: Three National Surveys in Bolivia, Colombia and Mexico.* Washington, D.C.: Belden Russonello & Steward Research and Communications, 2003.

Caulfield, Sueann, Sarah C. Chambers, and Lara Putnam, eds. *Honor, Status, and Law in Modern Latin America.* Durham: Duke University Press, 2005.

Cecil, Rosanne, ed. *The Anthropology of Pregnancy Loss: Comparative Studies in Miscarriage, Stillbirth, and Neonatal Death.* Oxford: Berg, 1996.

Chambers, Sarah C. *Families in War and Peace: Chile from Colony to Nation.* Durham, NC: Duke University Press, 2015.

Choque, Jobita Sandy, Paulina Ramos, and Sergio Suxo Mamani. "Salud Familiar Comunitario Intercultural—SAFCI." In *Antecedentes, situación actual, y perspectivas de la salud intercultural en América Latina*, compiled by Víctor Manuel del Cid Lucero, 94–102. Managua, Nicaragua: Universidad de las Regiones Autónomas de la Costa Caribe Nicaragüense, 2008.

Choque, María Eugenia. *Chacha warmi: Imaginarios y vivencias en El Alto.* El Alto: CPMGA, 2009.

Choque, María Eugenia, and Carlos Mamani. "Reconstrucción del ayllu y derechos de los pueblos indígenas: El movimiento indio en los Andes de Bolivia." *Journal of Latin American Anthropology* 6, no. 1 (March 2001): 202–224.

Chrisler, Joan C., ed. *Reproductive Justice: A Global Concern.* Santa Barbara, CA: ABC-CLIO LLC, 2012.

Cisneros, Antonio. *El aborto inducido: Un estudio exploratorio.* La Paz: Centro Nacional de Familia (CENAFA), 1976.

Cisneros C., Antonio J., Germán La Fuente, and Carlos Koch. *La capacitación técnica de los farmacéuticos: Un studio evaluativo de aprendizaje.* La Paz: Centro de Investigaciones Sociales, 1985.

Citarella Menardi, Luca. "Desarrollo de la salud intercultural en Bolivia: Desde las experiencias locales a la políticas públicas de salud." In *Yachay tinkuy: Salud e interculturalidad en Bolivia y América Latina*, edited by Luca Citarella Menardi, Alessia Zangari, and Roberto Campos Navarro, 3–29. La Paz: Editorial Gente Común, 2010.

Cohen, Jessica, Olivia Ortiz, Silvia Elena Llaguno, Lorelei Goodyear, Deborah Billings and Imelda Martinez. "Reaching Women with Instructions on Misoprostol Use in a Latin American Country." *Reproductive Health Matters* 13, no. 26 (November 2005): 84–92.

Concejo Municipal de La Paz. *Mi barrio cuenta y yo cuento con mi barrio.* La Paz: Impresiones Gráficas "Virgo," 2009.

Condori, Ana María, with Ineke Dibbits and Elizabeth Peredo. *Nayan Uñatatawi: Mi Despertar*. La Paz: HISBOL, Taller de Historia y Participación de la Mujer (TAHIPAMU), 1988.

Connelly, Matthew. *Fatal Misconception: The Struggle to Control World Population*. Cambridge, MA: The Belknap Press of Harvard University Press, 2008.

Correa, Sonia. *Los derechos sexuales y reproductivos en la arena política*. Montevideo: Mujer y Salud en Uruguay (MYSU), 2003.

Costa, Rolando, Eduardo Estrella, and Fernando Cabieses. *Bibliografía anotada de medicina tradicional (Bolivia, Ecuador, Peru)*. Quito: Universidad Andina Simón Bolívar, 1998.

Crandon-Malamud, Libbet. *From the Fat of Our Souls: Social Change, Political Process, and Medical Pluralism in Bolivia*. Berkeley and Los Angeles: University of California Press, 1991.

———. "Why Susto?" *Ethnology* 22 (1983): 153–167.

Crenshaw, Kimberlé. "Demarginalizing the Intersection of Race and Sex: A Black Feminist Critique of Antidiscrimination Doctrine, Feminist Theory and Antiracist Politics." *University of Chicago Legal Forum* 1, no. 8 (1989): 139–167.

Crenshaw, Kimberlé, Neil Gotanda, Gary Peller, and Kendall Thomas, eds. *Critical Race Theory: The Key Writings That Formed the Movement*. New York: The New Press, 1995.

Criales, Lucila, and Cristóbal Condoreno. "Breve reseña del Taller de Historia Oral Andina (THOA)." *Fuentes* 10, no. 43 (April 2016): 57–66.

Cruikshank, Julie. *Do Glaciers Listen?: Local Knowledge, Colonial Encounters, and Social Imagination*. Vancouver: University of British Columbia Press, 2015.

———. *The Social Life of Stories: Narrative and Knowledge in the Yukon Territory*. Lincoln: University of Nebraska Press, 2000.

Cueto, Marcos, and Steven Palmer. *Medicine and Public Health in Latin America: A History*. New York: Cambridge University Press, 2015.

Davis, Dona L., and Setha Low, eds. *Gender, Health, and Illness: The Case of Nerves*. New York: Hemisphere, 1989.

De Barros, Juanita. *Reproducing the British Caribbean: Sex, Gender, and Population Politics after Slavery*. Chapel Hill: The University of North Carolina Press, 2014.

De Barros Mott, Maria Lucia. "Madame Durocher, modista e parteira." *Estudos Feministas* 2, no. 1 (1994): 101–116.

Defossez, Anne-Claire, Didier Fassin, and Mara Viveros, eds. *Mujeres de los Andes: Condiciones de vida y salud*. Bogotá, Colombia: Instituto Francés de Estudios Andinos and Universidad Externado de Colombia, 1992.

De la Quintana, Claudia, Gretzel Jové, and Carmen Velasco. *Salud reproductiva en población migrante: Estudio comparativo El Alto-Sucre.* La Paz: PROMUJER, 1998.

Del Pozo, Eliana, and Juan Luis Alanes Bravo. *Marcando un hito en Bolivia: Experiencia. Atención de las hemorragias de la primera mitad del embarazo en servicios de primer nivel de atención.* La Paz: Ipas, 2007.

Dibbits, Ineke. *Polleras libertarias: Federación Obrera Femenina, 1927–1964.* La Paz: TAHIPAMU, 1986.

Dibbits, Ineke, and Ximena Pabón. *Granizadas, bautizos, y despachos: Aportes al debate sobre el aborto desde la provincial Ingavi.* Estudios e investigaciones 4. La Paz: Creativa, 2012.

Domínguez, Soledad. *Cuando el valor rompe el silencio: Crónica del primer aborto legal realizado en Bolivia.* Sucre: Centro Juana Azurduy, 1999.

Donnison, Jean. *Midwives and Medical Men: A History of the Struggle for the Control of Childbirth.* New Barnet, England: Historical Publications, 1977.

Dore, Elizabeth, and Maxine Molyneux, eds. *Hidden Histories of Gender and the State in Latin America.* Durham, NC: Duke University Press, 2000.

Ehrenreich, Barbara, and Deirdre English. *For Her Own Good: Two Centuries of Medical Experts' Advice to Women.* New York: Random House, 2005.

Faúndes, Aníbal, and José S. Barzelatto. *The Human Drama of Abortion: A Global Search for Consensus.* Nashville, TN: Vanderbilt University Press, 2006.

Federici, Silvia. *Caliban and the Witch: Women, the Body, and Primitive Accumulation.* Brooklyn, NY: Autonomedia, 2004.

Feitlowitz, Marguerite. *A Lexicon of Terror: Argentina and the Legacies of Torture.* Revised and Updated with a New Epilogue. New York: Oxford University Press, 2011.

Felitti, Karina. "Derechos reproductivos y políticas demográficas en América Latina." *Iconos: Revista de Ciencias Sociales* no. 35 (September 2009): 55–66.

———. "Family Planning in 1960s Argentina: An Original Latin American Case?" Paper presented at the 15th Berkshire Conference on the History of Women, Amherst, Massachusetts, June 12, 2011.

Fernández Juárez, Gerardo. *Médicos y yatiris: Salud e interculturalidad en el altiplano Aymara.* La Paz: Ediciones Gráficas E. G., 1999.

Fessler, Ann. *The Girls Who Went Away: The Hidden History of Women Who Surrendered Children for Adoption in the Decades before Roe V. Wade.* New York: Penguin Books, 2006.

Few, Martha. *Women Who Live Evil Lives: Gender, Religion, and the Politics of Power in Colonial Guatemala.* Austin: University of Texas Press, 2002.

French, William, and Katherine Elaine Bliss. *Gender, Sexuality, and Power in Latin America Since Independence.* Lanham, MD: Rowman and Littlefield, 2007.

Gallien, Kathryn. "Delivering the Nation, Raising the State: Gender, Childbirth, and the 'Indian Problem' in Bolivia's Obstetric Movement, 1900–1982." PhD diss., University of Arizona, 2015.

García-Pabón, Leonardo. "Sensibilidades Callejeras: El trabajo estético y político de 'Mujeres Creando.'" *Revista de Crítica Literaria Latinoamericana* 29, no. 58, Poesía y Globalización (2003): 239–254.

Geertz, Clifford. *Local Knowledge: Further Essays in Interpretive Anthropology,* 3rd ed. New York: Basic Books, 2000.

Geidel, Molly. *Peace Corps Fantasies: How Development Shaped the Global Sixties.* Minneapolis: University of Minnesota Press, 2015.

———. "'Sowing Death in Our Women's Wombs': Modernization and Indigenous Nationalism in the 1960s Peace Corps and Jorge Sanjinés' *Yawar Mallku.*" *American Quarterly* 62, no. 3 (September 2010): 763–786.

Gerdts, Caitlin, Sarah Raifman, Kristen Daskilewicz, Mariette Momberg, Sarah Roberts, and Jane Harries. "Women's Experiences Seeking Informal Sector Abortion Services in Cape Town, South Africa: A Descriptive Study." *BMC Women's Health* 17, no. 95 (October 2017): 1–10.

Gill, Lesley. "Painted Faces: Conflict and Ambiguity in Domestic Servant-Employer Relations in La Paz, 1930–1988." *Latin American Research Review* 25, no. 1 (1990): 119–136.

———. *Precarious Dependencies: Gender, Class, and Domestic Service in Bolivia.* New York: Columbia University Press, 1994.

———. *Teetering on the Rim: Global Restructuring, Daily Life, and the Armed Retreat of the Bolivian State.* New York: Columbia University Press, 2000.

Ginsburg, Faye D., and Rayna Rapp, eds. *Conceiving the New World Order: The Global Politics of Reproduction.* Los Angeles: University of California Press, 1995.

Girault, Louis. *Kallawaya: Curanderos itinerantes de los Andes.* La Paz: Impresores Quipus, 1987.

Goldstein, Daniel. *The Spectacular City: Violence and Performance in Urban Bolivia.* Durham: Duke University Press, 2004.

Goldstein, Michael S. "The Persistence and Resurgence of Medical Pluralism." *Journal of Health Politics, Policy, and Law* 29, nos. 4–5 (August–October 2004): 925–945.

Gorden, Raymond. *Interviewing: Strategy, Techniques and Tactics,* 4th ed. Chicago: Dorsey Press, 1987.

Gordon, Linda. *The Moral Property of Women: A History of Birth Control Politics in America.* Chicago: University of Illinois Press, 2007.

Gorkin, Michael, Marta Pineda, and Gloria Leal. *From Grandmother to Granddaughter: Salvadoran Women's Stories.* Berkeley and Los Angeles: University of California Press, 2000.

Gotkowitz, Laura, ed. *Histories of Race and Racism: The Andes and Mesoamerica from Colonial Times to the Present.* Durham: Duke University Press, 2011.

———. *A Revolution for Our Rights: Indigenous Struggles for Land and Justice in Bolivia.* Durham: Duke University Press, 2007.

Grindle, Merilee, and Pilar Domingo, eds. *Proclaiming Revolution: Bolivia in Comparative Perspective.* London: Institute of Latin American Studies, 2003.

Grupo de Trabajo sobre Embarazo no Deseado y Aborto. *Embarazo no deseado y aborto: Bibliografía.* La Paz: Secretaría Nacional de Salud and WHO, 1995.

Guaygua, Germán, Ángela Rivera, and Máximo Quisbert. *Ser jóven en El Alto: Rupturas y continuidades en la tradición cultural.* La Paz: Fundación PIEB, 2000.

Guha, Ranajit. "The Small Voice of History." In *Subaltern Studies IX: Writings on South Asian History and Society,* edited by Shahid Amin and Dipesh Chakrabarty, 1–12. New Dehli: Oxford University Press, 1996.

Gurr, Barbara. *Reproductive Justice: The Politics of Health Care for Native American Women.* New Brunswick, NJ: Rutgers University Press, 2015.

Gutmann, Matthew C. *The Meanings of Macho: Being a Man in Mexico City,* 10th Anniversary Edition. Berkeley and Los Angeles: University of California Press, 2007.

Hamilton, Carrie. "On Being a 'Good' Interviewer: Empathy, Ethics, and the Politics of Oral History." *Oral History* 36, no. 2, Connections (Autumn 2008): 35–43.

———. *Sexual Revolutions in Cuba: Passion, Politics, and Memory.* Chapel Hill: University of North Carolina Press, 2012.

Harris, Olivia. *To Make the Earth Bear Fruit: Essays on Fertility, Work and Gender in Highland Bolivia.* London: Institute of Latin American Studies, 2000.

Harris, Olivia, ed. *Inside and Outside the Law: Anthropological Studies of Authority and Ambiguity.* New York: Routledge, 1996.

Helmke, Gretchen, and Steven Levitsky. "Introduction." In *Informal Institutions & Democracy: Lessons from Latin America,* edited by Gretchen Helmke and Steven Levitsky, 1–31. Baltimore: Johns Hopkins University Press, 2006.

Hernández, Aída R., and Andrew Canessa, eds. *Género, complementariedades y exclusions en Mesoamérica y los Andes.* Quito, Ecuador, and Copenhagen: Ediciones Abya Yala and the International Work Group for Indigenous Affairs, 2012.

Howard, Rosaleen. "Language, Signs, and the Performance of Power: The Discursive Struggle over Decolonization in the Bolivia of Evo Morales." *Latin American Perspectives* 37, no. 3 (May 2010): 176–194.

Howard-Malverde, Rosaleen, ed. *Creating Context in Andean Cultures*. New York and Oxford: Oxford University Press, 1997.

Htun, Mala. *Sex and the State: Abortion, Divorce, and the Family Under Latin American Dictatorships and Democracies*. New York: Cambridge University Press, 2003.

Htun, Mala, and S. Laurel Weldon. *The Logics of Gender Justice: State Action on Women's Rights around the World*. New York: Cambridge University Press, 2018.

Ijaz, Nadine, and Heather Boon. "Statutory Regulation of Traditional Medicine Practitioners and Practices: The Need for Distinct Policy Making Guidelines." *Journal of Alternative and Complementary Medicine* 24, no. 4 (April 2018): 307–313.

Ipas. *Misoprostol and Medical Abortion in Latin America and the Caribbean*. Chapel Hill: Consorcio Latinoamericano Contra el Aborto Inseguro (CLACAI) and Ipas, 2010.

Ipas Bolivia. *El aborto desde la mirada de las organizaciones indígenas*. La Paz: Ipas, 2012.

———. *Las cifras hablan: El aborto es un problema de salud pública*. La Paz: Ipas, 2011.

James, Daniel. *Doña María's Story: Life, History, Memory, and Political Identity*. Durham: Duke University Press, 2003.

Jiles, Ximena, and Claudia Rojas. *De la miel a los implantes: Historia de las políticas de regulación de la fecundidad en Chile*. Santiago: Corporación de Salud y Políticas Sociales, 1992.

Johnson, Brian B. "Decolonization and Its Paradoxes: The (Re)envisioning of Health Policy in Bolivia." *Latin American Perspectives* 37, no. 3 (May 2010): 139–159.

Jolly, Margaret, and Kalpana Ram, eds. *Borders of Being: Citizenship, Fertility, and Sexuality in Asia and the Pacific*. Ann Arbor: The University of Michigan Press, 2001.

Jones, Rachel K., Julie Fennell, Jenny A. Higgins, and Kelly Blanchard. "Better Than Nothing or Savvy Risk-Reduction Practice? The Importance of Withdrawal." *Contraception* 79 (June 2009): 407–410.

Kane, Gillian, Beatriz Galli, and Patty Skuster. *Cuando el aborto es un crimen: La amenaza para mujeres vulnerables en América Latina*. Chapel Hill: Ipas, 2015.

Klein, Herbert S. *A Concise History of Bolivia*. New York: Cambridge University Press, 2011.

———. "The Historical Background to the Rise of the MAS, 1952–2005." In *Evo Morales and the Movimiento Al Socialismo en Bolivia*, edited by Adrian Pearce, 27–61. London: Institute for the Study of the Americas, University of London, 2011.

Koss-Chioino, Joan D., Thomas Leatherman, and Christine Greenway, eds. *Medical Pluralism in the Andes*. New York: Routledge, 2003.

Kushner, Eve. *Experiencing Abortion: A Weaving of Women's Words*. New York: Haworth Press, 1997.

Kushner López, Luis, Luis Llano Saavedra, and Patricia Elizabeth Bailey. *Investigación de los aspectos sociales y médicos de la pérdida de embarazo: Análisis de resultados*. La Paz: Sociedad Boliviana de Ginecología y Obstetricia and Family Health International (FHI), 1986.

LaCapra, Dominick. *Writing History, Writing Trauma*. Baltimore: Johns Hopkins University Press, 2001.

Lagos, Maria L., comp. *Nos hemos forjado así: Al rojo vivo y a puro golpe. Historias del comité de amas de casa de Siglo XX*. La Paz: Plural Editores, 2006.

Langer, Erick. *Economic Change and Rural Resistance in Southern Bolivia: 1880–1930*. Stanford: Stanford University Press, 1989.

Lanza Monje, Teresa. "Proyecto Mujeres y Asamblea Constituyente." *Cotidiano Mujer* 4, no. 44 (November 2008): 48–53.

Larson, Brooke. *Trials of Nation-Making: Liberalism, Race, and Ethnicity in the Andes, 1810–1910*. New York: Cambridge University Press, 2004.

Larson, Brooke, and Olivia Harris, eds., with Enrique Tandeter. *Ethnicity, Markets, and Migration in the Andes: At the Crossroads of History and Anthropology*. Durham: Duke University Press, 1995.

Lazar, Sian. *El Alto, Rebel City: Self and Citizenship in Andean Bolivia*. Durham, NC: Duke University Press, 2008.

Leslie, Charles. "Medical Pluralism in World Perspective." *Social Science & Medicine* 14, no. 4 (November 1980): 191–195.

Leys Stepan, Nancy. *"The Hour of Eugenics": Race, Gender, and Nation in Latin America*. Ithaca, NY: Cornell University Press, 1991.

———. "Race, Gender, Science, and Citizenship." *Gender & History* 10, no. 1 (April 1998): 26–52.

Llovet, Juan José, and Silvina Ramos. "La planificación familiar en Argentina: Salud pública y derechos humanos." *Cuadernos Médico- Sociales* 38 (December 1986): 25–39.

López, Iris. *Matters of Choice: Puerto Rican Women's Struggle for Reproductive Freedom*. New Brunswick: Rutgers University Press, 2008.

Loza, Carmen Beatriz. *El laberinto de la curación: Itinerarios terapéuticos en las ciudades de La Paz y El Alto.* La Paz: Instituto Superior Ecuménico Andino de Teología (ISEAT), 2008.

———. *Kallawaya: Reconocimiento mundial a una ciencia de los Andes.* La Paz: Talleres Sagitario, 2004.

———. Review of *Salud e Interculturalidad en América Latina: Antropología de la Salud y Crítica Intercultural,* coord. by Gerardo Fernández Juárez. *Chungara: Revista de Antropología Chilena,* 42, no. 2 (2010): 543–547.

Mallon, Florencia. "The Promise and Dilemma of Subaltern Studies: Perspectives from Latin American History." *American Historical Review* 99, no. 5 (December 1994): 1491–1515.

Mamani, Pablo. *Microgobiernos barriales: Levantamiento de la Ciudad de El Alto (Octubre 2003).* La Paz: Centro de Asesoramiento para el Desarrollo Social (CADES), Instituto de Investigaciones Sociológicas (IDIS) and UMSA, 2005.

Maternowska, M. Catherine. *Reproducing Inequities: Poverty and the Politics of Population in Haiti.* New Brunswick: Rutgers University Press, 2006.

Maynes, Mary Jo, Jennifer L. Pierce, and Barbara Laslett. *Telling Stories: The Use of Personal Narratives in the Social Sciences and History.* Ithaca, NY: Cornell University Press, 2008.

McNamee, Catherine B. "Wanted and Unwanted Fertility in Bolivia: Does Ethnicity Matter?" *International Perspectives on Sexual and Reproductive Health* 35, no. 4 (December 2009): 166–175.

Medinaceli, Ximena. *Alterando la rutina: Mujeres en las ciudades de Bolivia, 1920–1930.* La Paz: CIDEM, 1989.

Mendizábal Lozano, Gregorio. *Historia de la salud pública en Bolivia: De las juntas de sanidad a los directorios locales de salud.* La Paz: Organización Panamericana de la Salud (OPS), OMS, 2002.

Messer, Ellen, and Kathryn May. *Back Rooms: Voices from the Illegal Abortion Era.* Buffalo: Prometheus Books, 1988.

Millones, Luis, and Mary Louise Pratt. *Amor brujo: Imagen y cultura del amor en los Andes.* Lima: Instituto de Estudios Peruanos, 1989.

Minna Stern, Alexandra. *Eugenic Nation: The Faults and Frontiers of Better Breeding in Modern America.* Berkeley and Los Angeles: University of California Press, 2005.

Molyneux, Maxine. *Women's Movements in International Perspective: Latin America and Beyond.* New York: Palgrave, 2001.

Monasterios P., Elizabeth, ed. *No pudieron con nostotras: El desafío del feminismo autónomo de Mujeres Creando.* La Paz: Plural Editores, 2006.

Morgan, Jennifer. *Laboring Women: Reproduction and Gender in New World Slavery.* Philadelphia: University of Pennsylvania Press, 2004.

Morgan, Lynn M. "Imagining the Unborn in the Ecuadoran Andes." *Feminist Studies* 23, no. 2 (Summer 1997): 322–350.

Morgan, Lynn M., and Meredith W. Michaels, eds. *Fetal Subjects, Feminist Positions.* Philadelphia: University of Pennsylvania Press, 1999.

Morgan, Lynn M., and Elizabeth F. S. Roberts. "Reproductive Governance in Latin America." *Anthropology & Medicine* 19, no. 2 (August 2012): 241–254.

Mungiu, Cristian, dir. *4 Months, 3 Weeks, and 2 Days.* BAC Films, 2007. DVD, 113 minutes.

Murray, David A. B. *Flaming Souls: Homosexuality, Homophobia, and Social Change in Barbados.* Toronto: University of Toronto Press, 2012.

Nash, June. *I Spent my Life in the Mines: The Story of Juan Rojas, Bolivian Tin Miner.* New York: Columbia University Press, 1992.

———. *We Eat the Mines and the Mines Eat Us: Dependency and Exploitation in Bolivian Tin Mines,* with a new preface by the author. New York: Columbia University Press, 1993.

Necochea López, Raúl. *A History of Family Planning in Twentieth-Century Peru.* Chapel Hill: University of North Carolina Press, 2014.

Nelson, Erica. "Birth Rights: Bolivia's Politics of Race, Region, and Motherhood, 1964–2005." PhD diss., University of Wisconsin-Madison, 2009.

Nina Huarcacho, Filomena. *Detrás del cristal con que se mira: Mujeres del Altiplano, órdenes normativos e interlegalidad.* La Paz: Editora Presencia, 2009.

Olsen, William C. and Carolyn Sargent, eds. *African Medical Pluralism.* Bloomington: Indiana University Press, 2017.

O'Phelan Godoy, Scarlett, Fanni Muñoz Cabrejo, Gabriel Ramón Joffré, and Mónica Ricketts Sánchez-Moreno, eds. *Familia y vida cotidiana en América Latina: Siglos XVIII–XX.* Lima: Pontífica Universidad Católica del Perú, 2003.

Organización Mundial de la Salud (OMS). *Estrategia de la OMS sobre medicina tradicional 2002–2005.* Geneva: OMS, 2002.

Otovo, Okezi. *Progressive Mothers, Better Babies: Race, Public Health, and the State in Brazil.* Austin: University of Texas Press, 2016.

Pacino, Nicole. "Creating Madres Campesinas: Revolutionary Motherhood and the Gendered Politics of Nation Building in 1950s Bolivia." *Journal of Women's History* 27, no. 1 (Spring 2015): 62–87.

———. "Prescription for a Nation: Public Health in Post-Revolutionary Bolivia, 1952–1964." PhD diss., University of California, Santa Barbara, 2013.

Padilla, Mark. *Caribbean Pleasure Industry: Tourism, Sexuality, and AIDS in the Dominican Republic.* Chicago: University of Chicago Press, 2007.

Palmer, Steven. *From Popular Medicine to Medical Populism: Doctors, Healers, and Public Power in Costa Rica, 1800–1940*. Durham: Duke University Press, 2003.

Paredes, Julieta, and Comunidad Mujeres Creando Comunidad. *Hilando fino: Desde el feminismo comunitario*. La Paz: Comunidad Mujeres Creando Comunidad, 2010.

Paredes, Julieta, and María Galindo. *Machos, varones, y maricones: Manual para conocer tu sexualidad por ti mismo*. La Paz: Ediciones Mujeres Creando, 2000.

———. *Sexo, sexualidad, y placer: Manual para conocer tu sexualidad por ti misma*. La Paz: Ediciones Mujeres Creando, 1998.

Passerini, Luisa. *Autobiography of a Generation: Italy, 1968*. Translated by Lisa Erdberg. Middletown, CT: Wesleyan University Press, 1996.

Patai, Daphne. "Ethical Problems of Personal Narratives, or, Who Should Eat the Last Piece of Cake?" *International Journal of Oral History* 8 (February 1987): 7–27.

Paxman, John M., Alberto Rizo, Laura Brown, and Janie Benson. "The Clandestine Epidemic: The Practice of Unsafe Abortion in Latin America." *Studies in Family Planning* 24, no. 4 (July–August 1993): 205–226.

Pedro, Joana María. "A experiência com contraceptivos no Brasil: Uma questão de geração." *Revista Brasileira de História* 23, no. 45 (2003): 239–260.

Perks, Robert, and Alistar Thomson, eds. *The Oral History Reader*, 2nd ed. New York: Routledge, 2006.

Petchesky, Rosalind P. *Abortion and Woman's Choice: The State, Sexuality, and Reproductive Freedom*. Lebanon, NH: Northeastern University Press, 1984.

———. "Fetal Images: The Power of Visual Culture in the Politics of Reproduction," *Feminist Studies* 13, no. 2 (Summer 1987): 263–292.

Peterman, Jean. *Telling Their Stories: Puerto Rican Women and Abortion*. Boulder, CO: Westview Press, 1996.

Pieper Mooney, Jadwiga E. *The Politics of Motherhood: Maternity and Women's Rights in Twentieth-Century Chile*. Pittsburgh: University of Pittsburgh Press, 2009.

Platt, Tristan. "El feto agresivo: Parto, formación de la persona y mito-historia en los Andes." *Estudios Atacameños* no. 22 (2002): 127–155.

Poole, Deborah. *Vision, Race, and Modernity: A Visual Economy of the Andean Image World*. Princeton: Princeton University Press, 1997.

Portelli, Alessandro. *The Battle of Valle Giulia: Oral History and the Art of Dialogue*. Madison: University of Wisconsin Press, 1997.

———. *The Death of Luigi Trastulli and Other Stories: Form and Meaning in Oral History*. Albany: State University of New York Press, 1991.

———. *They Say in Harlan County: An Oral History*. New York: Oxford University Press, 2011.

Porter, Elizabeth. *Feminist Perspectives on Ethics*. New York: Longmans, 1999.

Povinelli, Elizabeth A. *The Empire of Love: Toward a Theory of Intimacy, Genealogy, and Carnality*. Durham: Duke University Press, 2006.

Putnam, Lara. *The Company They Kept: Migrants and the Politics of Gender in Caribbean Costa Rica, 1870–1960*. Chapel Hill: University of North Carolina Press, 2002.

Rance, Susanna. *Planificación familiar: Se abre el debate*. La Paz: Secretaría Técnica del Consejo Nacional de Población and the Ministerio de Planeamiento y Coordinación, 1990.

———, coord. *Abriendo el paquete envuelto: Violencias y derechos en la ciudad de El Alto*. La Paz: Centro de Promoción de la Mujer Gregoria Apaza and Solidaridad Internacional Bolivia, 2009.

Rance, Susanna, and Sandra Vallenas, coord. *Memoria de la reunion sobre embarazo no deseado y aborto en Bolivia y Perú*. La Paz: Population Council, 1999.

Reagan, Leslie J. *When Abortion Was a Crime: Women, Medicine, and Law in the United States*. Berkeley and Los Angeles: University of California Press, 1997.

Riddle, John M. *Eve's Herbs: A History of Contraception and Abortion in the West*. Cambridge: Harvard University Press, 1997.

Rivera Cusicanqui, Silvia. "Construcción de imágenes de indios y mujeres en la iconografía post-52: El miserabilismo en el Álbum de la Revolución (1954)." In *Discursos sobre (a) pobreza: América Latina y/e países luso-africanos*, edited by Martín Leinhard, 171–208. Madrid: Iberoamericana, 1996.

———. "The Notion of 'Rights' and the Paradoxes of Postcolonial Modernity: Indigenous Peoples and Women in Bolivia." Translated by Molly Geidel. *Qui Parle* 18, no. 2 (Spring/Summer 2010): 29–54.

———. *Oprimidos pero no vencidos: Luchas del campesinado aymara y qhechwa de Bolivia, 1900–1980*, con prefacio de la autora. La Paz: Hisbol and the Confederación Sindical Unica de Trabajadores Campesinos de Bolivia (CSUTCB), 2003.

Rivera Cusicanqui, Silvia, ed. *Ser mujer indígena, chola o birlocha en la Bolivia postcolonial de los años 90*. La Paz: Ministerio de Desarrollo Humano, Subsecretaría Nacional de Asuntos Étnicos, de Género y Generacionales, Subsecretaría de Asuntos de Género, 1996.

Roberts, Elizabeth F. S. *God's Laboratory: Assisted Reproduction in the Andes*. Berkeley and Los Angeles: University of California Press, 2012.

Rodríguez, Julia. *Civilizing Argentina: Science, Medicine, and the Modern State*. Chapel Hill: University of North Carolina Press, 2006.

Roosta, Manigeh, coord. *Salud materna en contextos de interculturalidad: Estudio de los pueblos Aymara, Ayoreode, Chiquitano, Guaraní, Quechua, y Yuqui*. La Paz: Plural Editores, 2013.

Rousseau, Stéphanie. "Indigenous and Feminist Movements at the Constituent Assembly in Bolivia: Locating the Representation of Indigenous Women." *Latin American Research Review* 46, no. 2 (2011): 5–28.

Rubel, Arthur. *Susto: A Folk Illness*. Berkeley: University of California Press, 1984.

Sanford, Victoria. *Buried Secrets: Truth and Human Rights in Guatemala*. New York: Palgrave MacMillan, 2003.

Scheper-Hughes, Nancy. *Death without Weeping: The Violence of Everyday Life in Brazil*. Berkeley and Los Angeles: University of California Press, 1993.

Schiebinger, Londa. *Plants and Empire: Colonial Bioprospecting in the Atlantic World*. Cambridge: Harvard University Press, 2004.

Schoen, Johanna. *Choice and Coercion: Birth Control, Sterilization, and Abortion in Public Health and Welfare*. Chapel Hill: University of North Carolina Press, 2005.

Schuler, Sidney Ruth, María Eugenia Choque, and Susanna Rance. "Misinformation, Mistrust, and Mistreatment: Family Planning among Bolivian Market Women." *Studies in Family Planning* 25, no. 4 (July–August 1994): 211–221.

Sedgh, Gilda, Susheela Singh, Iqbal H. Shah, Elisabeth Åhman, Stanley K. Henshaw, and Akinrinola Bankole. "Induced Abortion: Incidence and Trends Worldwide from 1995 to 2008." *The Lancet* 379 (January 2012): 625–632.

Sen, Gita, Adrienne Germain, and Lincoln C. Chen, eds. *Population Policies Reconsidered: Health, Empowerment, and Rights*. Boston: Harvard Center for Population and Development Studies, 1994.

Sheftel, Anna, and Stacey Zembrzycki, eds. *Oral History Off the Record: Toward an Ethnography of Practice*. New York: Palgrave Macmillan, 2013.

———. "Who's Afraid of Oral History?: Fifty Years of Debates and Anxiety about Ethics." *Oral History Review* 43, no. 2 (2016): 228–366.

Shepard, Bonnie. "The 'Double Discourse' on Sexual and Reproductive Rights in Latin America: The Chasm between Public Policy and Private Actions." *Health and Human Rights* 4, no. 2 (2000): 111–143.

Shore, Cris, and Susan Wright. *Anthropology of Policy: Critical Perspectives on Governance and Power*. London: Routledge, 1997.

Sikkink, Lynn. *New Cures, Old Medicines: Women and the Commercialization of Traditional Medicine in Bolivia*. Belmont, CA: Wadsworth, 2010.

Silliman, Jael, Marlene Gerber Fried, Loretta Ross, and Elena R. Gutiérrez, eds. *Undivided Rights: Women of Color Organize for Reproductive Justice*. Cambridge: South End Press, 2004.

Silverblatt, Irene. *Moon, Sun, and Witches: Gender Ideologies and Class in Inca and Colonial Peru*. Princeton, NJ: Princeton University Press, 1987.

Singer, Merrill, and Pamela I. Erickson, eds. *A Companion to Medical Anthropology*. Oxford: Wiley-Blackwell, 2011.

Singh, Susheela, and Deirdre Wulf. "The Likelihood of Induced Abortion among Women Hospitalized for Abortion Complications in Four Latin American Countries." *International Family Planning Perspectives* 19, no. 4 (December 1993): 134–141.

Sistren with Honor Ford-Smith. *Lionheart Gal: Life Stories of Jamaican Women.* London: The Women's Press, 1986.

Sivak, Martín. *El dictador elegido: Biografía no autorizada de Hugo Banzer Suárez.* La Paz: Plural Editores, 2001.

Smith, Andrea. "Beyond Pro-Choice versus Pro-Life: Women of Color and Reproductive Justice." *NWSA Journal* 17, no. 1 (Spring 2005): 119–140.

Sociedad Boliviana de Salud Pública. *Salud Pública en Bolivia: Historia y Perspectivas.* La Paz: Sociedad Boliviana de Salud Pública, 1989.

Soledad Zárate, María. *Dar a luz en Chile, Siglo XIX: De la 'ciencia de hembra' a la ciencia obstétrica.* Santiago: Centro de Investigaciones Barros Arana and the University of Alberto Hurtado, 2007.

Solinger, Rickie. *Beggars and Choosers: How the Politics of Choice Shapes Adoption, Abortion, and Welfare in the United States.* New York: Hill and Wang, 2001.

Spivak, Gayatri Chakravorty. "Can the Subaltern Speak?" In *Marxism and the Interpretation of Cultures,* edited by Cary Nelson and Lawrence Grossberg, 271–316. Urbana: University of Illinois Press, 1988.

Stephenson, Marcia. "Forging an Indigenous Counterpublic Sphere: The Taller de Historia Oral Andina in Bolivia." *Latin American Research Review* 37, no. 2 (2002): 99–118.

———. *Gender and Modernity in Andean Bolivia.* Austin: University of Texas Press, 1999.

Stoler, Ann. *Carnal Knowledge and Imperial Power: Race and the Intimate in Colonial Rule.* Los Angeles: University of California Press, 2002.

———. *Race and the Education of Desire: Foucault's History of Sexuality and the Colonial Order of Things.* Durham: Duke University Press, 1999.

Strobele-Gregor, Juliana, Bert Hoffman, and Andrew Holmes. "From Indio to Mestizo . . . to Indio: New Indianist Movements in Bolivia." *Latin American Perspectives* 21, no. 2 (Spring, 1994): 106–123.

Sujatha, V., and Leena Abraham, eds. *Medical Pluralism in Contemporary India.* Hyderabad: Orient Blackswan, 2012.

Talpade Mohanty, Chandra, Ann Russo, and Lourdes Torres, eds. *Third World Women and the Politics of Feminism.* Bloomington: Indiana University Press, 1991.

Tapias, Maria. "'Always Ready and Always Clean'? Competing Discourses of Breast-Feeding, Infant Illness and the Politics of Mother-Blame in Bolivia." *Body and Society* 12, no. 2 (June 2006): 83–108.

------. *Embodied Protests: Emotions and Women's Health in Bolivia*. Chicago: University of Illinois Press, 2015.

Thompson, Paul. *The Voice of the Past: Oral History*, 3rd ed. New York: Oxford University Press, 2000.

Thomsen, Carly. "The Politics of Narrative, Narrative as Politic: Rethinking Reproductive Justice Frameworks through the South Dakota Abortion Story." *Feminist Formulations* 27, no. 2 (Summer 2015): 1–26.

Thomson, Sinclair, Rossana Barragán, Xavier Albó, Seemin Qayum, and Mark Goodale, eds. *The Bolivia Reader: History, Culture, Politics*. Durham: Duke University Press, 2018.

Thornton, Russell. *Studying Native America: Problems and Prospects*. Madison: University of Wisconsin Press, 1998.

Ticona Alejo, Esteban. "Algunas experiencias metodológicas en Historia Oral." *Boletín de Historia Oral* 1 (November 1986): 1–10.

Tinsman, Heidi. *Partners in Conflict: The Politics of Gender, Sexuality, and Labor in the Chilean Agrarian Reform, 1950–1973*. Durham: Duke University Press, 2002.

United Nations Development Programme (UNDP). *Human Development Report 2011, Sustainability and Equity: A Better Future for All*. New York: Palgrave Mac-Millan, 2011.

Van Vleet, Krista E. *Performing Kinship: Narrative, Gender, and the Intimacies of Power in the Andes*. Austin: University of Texas Press, 2008.

Velasco, Julio César. *La crisis mundial vista desde Bolivia: Lecturas económica y política (2008–2011)*. La Paz: Fundación Konrad Adenauer, 2011.

Vidaurre Andrade, Gonzálo Mario. *El negocio de la muerte: Comercio informal de medicamentos en Bolivia*. La Paz: UPS Publicidad, 2018.

Viel, Benjamin V. "Latin America." In *International Handbook on Abortion*, edited by Paul Sachdev, 317–332. Westport, CT: Greenwood Press, 1988.

Wade, Peter. *Race and Sex in Latin America*. New York: Pluto Press, 2009.

Wadsworth, Ana Cecilia, and Ineke Dibbits. *Agitadores de buen gusto: Historia del sindicato culinarias (1935–1958)*. La Paz: TAHIPAMU, 1989.

Wainer, Jo. *Lost: Illegal Abortion Stories*. Victoria, Australia: Melbourne University Press, 2006.

Wallach Scott, Joan. "The Evidence of Experience." In *Feminist Approaches to Theory and Methodology: An Interdisciplinary Reader*, edited by Sharlene Hesse-Biber, Christina Gilmartin, and Robin Lydenberg, 79–99. New York: Oxford University Press, 1999.

------. *Gender and the Politics of History*, rev. ed. New York: Columbia University Press, 1999.

Waylen, Georgina. "Informal Institutions, Institutional Change, and Gender Equality." *Political Research Quarterly* 67, no. 1 (March 2014): 212–223.

Weismantel, Mary. *Cholas and Pishtacos: Stories of Race and Sex in the Andes.* Chicago: University of Chicago Press, 2001.

———. "Making Kin: Kinship Theory and Zumbagua Adoptions." *American Ethnologist* 22, no. 4 (1995): 685–709.

White, Luise. *The Comforts of Home: Prostitution in Colonial Nairobi.* Chicago: University of Chicago Press, 1990.

WHO. *Reproductive Health Indicators: Guidelines for Their Generation, Interpretation and Analysis for Global Monitoring.* Geneva: WHO, 2006.

———. *Unsafe Abortion: Global and Regional Estimates of the Incidence of Unsafe Abortion and Associated Mortality in 2008.* Geneva: WHO, 2011.

WHO Unit on Traditional Medicine. *Legal Status of Traditional Medicine and Complementary/Alternative Medicine.* Geneva: WHO, 2001.

Yashar, Deborah. *Contesting Citizenship in Latin America: The Rise of Indigenous Movements and the Postliberal Challenge.* New York: Cambridge University Press, 2005.

Yow, Valerie. "Ethics and Interpersonal Relationships in Oral History Research." *The Oral History Review* 22, no. 1 (Summer 1995): 51–66.

Yow, Valerie Raleigh. *Recording Oral History: A Guide for the Humanities and Social Sciences,* 3rd ed. Lanham, MD: Rowman & Littlefield, 2015.

Zelmer, Jennifer. "Abort the System." *NACLA* (January 9, 2017). https://nacla.org/news/2018/01/09/abort-system.

Zulawski, Ann. *Unequal Cures: Public Health and Political Change in Bolivia, 1900–1950.* Durham: Duke University Press, 2007.

Index

4 Months, 3 Weeks, and 2 Days, 212, 317n86
28th of September Campaign for the De-Criminalization of Abortion in Latin America and the Caribbean, 69–71, 75, 290n140

abandonment (men of women), 93, 99, 118, 125–126, 129, 174, 183, 209, 245
abortion: access to, 4, 11, 61, 70, 73, 130, 235–237; complications resulting from, 2, 81–82, 84, 149, 159–160, 183, 201, 205, 209–210, 222; cost of, 158, 204, 206, 214–215; doctors' responses to women's requests of, 2–3, 129–130; forced experiences of, 139, 142–143; in indigenous communities, 23, 104–106; international concern with, 7, 11, 62, 68, 218, 243; knowledge of, 131; legal (*aborto impune*), 60–61, 70, 73–74, 220, 229–232, 293n164; methods of, 22, 69, 157–160, 185, 200, 209, 241; press coverage of, 32–33, 222, 225; providers of, 12, 31–33, 157–160, 161, 185–186, 200, 204, 210–215, 241–242; rates of, 51, 78–86; regulation of, 2, 4, 36, 85, 184, 188, 199, 206, 212, 235–237, 242; self-induced, 2, 22, 130, 157–158, 161, 216–218, 243, 316n70; treatment following, 4, 11, 35, 66–69, 74, 149, 185, 200–203, 241, 243; women's experiences with, 134–139, 160–167, 209–218

abortion, attitudes toward: and ambivalence, 35–36, 39, 102, 126–127, 245–247; as attack on family values, 91, 101–102; demographic arguments against, 91, 100, 245; double discourse on, 35, 77–79, 233, 245–246; and fear, 113, 127–128, 130, 303n29; and guilt, 113, 128, 141, 143; as immoral, 50–51, 95, 127, 131; in indigenous communities, 23, 104–106; and "loss of values," 102–104, 245; as a public health problem, 39, 67, 246; and regret, 142; and relief, 143; religious opposition to, 91, 93–96, 99, 127, 131, 141, 245; as a right, 75, 107, 114, 146, 204; in schools, 96–97, 99–100; and shame, 113, 246; and stigma, 22, 33, 35, 62, 79, 96, 100, 111, 113, 144, 184, 211, 221, 251; tolerated in some circumstances, 78–79, 90, 110–111, 143–144, 232–233, 246
abortion, policies on: efforts to decriminalize, 69–73; initiatives concerning, 56–57, 66–70; and judicial authorizations, 61, 70, 229–230; and legal prohibition, 31, 36–38, 85, 144, 185, 211, 215, 218, 221, 233, 311n82; and policing, 73, 85, 211, 219–232, 318n6; Program for the Treatment of Hemorrhages in the First Half of Pregnancy (HPME), 68–69, 201
abstinence, 89, 92, 178. *See also* fertility regulation; rhythm method

About the Author

Natalie L. Kimball is an assistant professor of history at the College of Staten Island, City University of New York.